The Ethics of Anger

The Ethics of Anger

Edited by
Court D. Lewis and Gregory L. Bock

LEXINGTON BOOKS
Lanham • Boulder • New York • London

Published by Lexington Books
An imprint of The Rowman & Littlefield Publishing Group, Inc.
4501 Forbes Boulevard, Suite 200, Lanham, Maryland 20706
www.rowman.com

6 Tinworth Street, London SE11 5AL, United Kingdom

British Library Cataloguing in Publication Information Available

Library of Congress Cataloging-in-Publication Data

Names: Lewis, Court D., editor. | Bock, Gregory L., editor.
Title: The ethics of anger / edited by Court D. Lewis and Gregory L. Bock.
Description: Lanham : Lexington Books, [2020] | Includes bibliographical references and index. | Summary: "This book provides a variety of diverse perspectives related to the ethics of anger, some more analytical in nature, others focused on practical issues, some in defense of anger, and others arguing against its necessity. This book is an essential resource for scholars who want to reflect critically on the place of anger in contemporary life"—Provided by publisher.
Identifiers: LCCN 2020039369 (print) | LCCN 2020039370 (ebook) | ISBN 9781793615176 (cloth) | ISBN 9781793615183 (epub) | ISBN 9781793615190 (pbk)
Subjects: LCSH: Anger.
Classification: LCC BJ1535.A6 E84 2020 (print) | LCC BJ1535.A6 (ebook) | DDC 179/.8—dc23
LC record available at https://lccn.loc.gov/2020039369
LC ebook record available at https://lccn.loc.gov/2020039370

∞™ The paper used in this publication meets the minimum requirements of American National Standard for Information Sciences—Permanence of Paper for Printed Library Materials, ANSI/NISO Z39.48-1992.

Dedication

The editors would like to dedicate this book to Jeffrie G. Murphy for his substantial and insightful work on ethics, forgiveness, and the moral emotions. May your wisdom be shared for many years to come.

Contents

Introduction

Court D. Lewis and Gregory L. Bock

Anger was not the original focus of our research. For the past several years, we primarily focused on issues relating to forgiveness; but the more we wrote and presented on forgiveness, the more our discussions shifted toward anger. On the one hand, the shift toward anger is natural, anger is often argued to be the most appropriate response to wrongdoing, as wrongdoing is argued to be the necessary precursor to forgiveness. So, for some, anger is a necessary condition of forgiveness. The desire to discuss anger, however, seemed rooted in something deeper than mere philosophical interest in the necessary conditions of forgiveness. There was an anxiety that implied an existential concern over the nature and abundance of anger that pervades contemporary life.

Our lives are full of anger. From the moment we awake to the time(s) we find solitude, anger is a constant threat. News and entertainment stories constantly detail angry leaders and citizens, inept and selfish politicians only concerned with personal gain, and corporate leaders fleecing the poor while receiving millions in tax subsidies and from manipulating loopholes. As teachers, we face an increasing militant student population, supported by equally militant parents, who disregard facts and data, promote sexist and racist propaganda (unintentionally, but sometimes intentionally), and use their power and influence—sometimes via their parents—to defund public colleges, seek litigation against professors who challenge their worldview, and, in some cases, successfully demand the resignation of teachers. Those involved in crafting legislation that determines healthcare and medical coverage lack a basic understanding of biology and science and routinely prevent the most vulnerable from enjoying a basic level of health security. The electorate seems to prefer entertainment personalities over experts, voting against their own best interests, and, when engaged in debates, fail to grasp basic concepts of critical thinking and logic. Each time we travel in our cars, go shopping, and go to school, we risk being killed by others who have no regard for human life. Innocent people are killed by racist vigilantes and militant police officers simply because their skin is the "wrong" color or they were in the "wrong" place. The truth, even though it is currently popular to suggest none exists, is many people have a sense that the world is on the verge of collapse; and in the face of the dusk of a new "Dark Age," people are upset, anxious, frustrated, and angry.

In the face of such challenges, anger often festers within, waiting for some event to allow its release. As detailed in Jonathan Glover's excellent moral history of the twentieth-century *Humanity*, humans have an uncanny ability to internalize frustration and anger until such suppressed anger is released, often in a euphoric act of "going berserk." If not allowed to release, such anger can cause anxiety and depression, along with a whole host of physical ailments. Of course, philosophers are stereotyped as being immune to such emotional responses. Supposedly, all we do is ponder the conceptual features of concepts, and, after careful consideration of the implications and arguments relating to a phenomenon, we calmly offer sound conclusions for how to proceed. This stereotype, however, ignores the fact that we are also humans, with the same feelings of frustration and anger that others experience, sometimes more so, because we have dedicated our lives to studying wrongdoing and preventing injustice. We too experience times when we desire to lash out at the ignorance, frustrations, and injustices in the world. Yet, our training teaches us to do more than go berserk. Our training teaches us to reflect, question, and look for alternatives for how to properly understand and utilize emotions and attitudes such as anger. The authors in this volume have engaged in this reflection and agreed to share their insights with the broader world through the volume you are now reading.

As editors, our goal was to assemble a collection of chapters that would provide a variety of diverse perspectives, some more analytical in nature, others focused on practical issues, some in defense of anger, and others arguing against its necessity. The following is a brief summary of the chapters contained in the book.

Part One is titled "The Human Experience of Anger" and features two prominent authors of forgiveness, Charles L. Griswold and Everett V. Worthington. Griswold's "The Nature and Ethics of Vengeful Anger" discusses the nature and ethics of vengeful anger, focusing in particular on individual vengefulness, asking the question, "Is it ethical to feel such a sentiment or emotion?" He begins by reflecting on whether the sentiment or emotion of anger is *ever* justified, whether it is ever worth our endorsement and, if so, under what conditions. Griswold, then, explores the relation between self-esteem and anger, examining the descriptive and definitional issues on the one hand and the normative ones on the other. Next, he examines arguments presented by Aristotle (in the *Nicomachean Ethics* and the *Rhetoric*) and by Seneca (in *De Ira*), and, after articulating several of the key issues involved in the debate about the praiseworthiness of vengeful anger, he presents several conditions that must be met if vengeful anger is to be appropriate. He concludes by suggesting that the taking of revenge may be appropriate if certain conditions are met, but that it is not justified simply because the emotion from which it springs is justified (if indeed it is justified), which leads to the surprising distinction between the merits of the emotion of vengeful anger and those of the action(s) that may follow from it.

Worthington's chapter "The Psychology of Anger: 'Implicit and Explicit Choices for Ethical Experiences, Expressions, and Control of Anger'" uses moral psychology and virtue ethics to put forth a psychology of anger that draws on modern cognitive psychology in order to argue for an ethics of anger that focuses on the implicit aspect of the contexts, experiences, expressions, consequences, and repair of anger instead of its explicit rational aspects often found in ethics. Worthington provides a psychologist's reflection on the vexing issues surrounding the ethics of anger. His major conclusions are several, including: (1) most of anger is due to implicit cognition; (2) although people hold others responsible for failure to control or limit their angry expression, much of anger is not controllable; (3) therefore, to act ethically when primary or secondary anger is likely, one should take steps early to control situations that are indeed controllable and to build virtuous character strengths that will allow one to control responses; and (4) one needs a set of coping responses that can help limit the expression of anger and return the person to emotional equanimity.

Part Two of our collection examines anger as a moral response, and begins with Krista Thomason's "The Moral Necessity of Anger." In the chapter, Thomason argues that feelings of anger are more central to our moral emotional lives than skeptics realize and that they cannot be removed without altering other valuable moral commitments. Stated differently, anger is not just rational and reasonable, but is also a morally necessary response to wrongdoing. To defend her thesis, Thomason examines what is sometimes called the constitutive view (that feelings of anger are constitutive of the proper moral response to offense, ill treatment, or injustice) and defends it against two objections: (1) there appear to be examples of people who adequately respond to wrongdoing and yet seem not to feel anger; and (2) given anger's clear potential for damage, it would be better for moral agents to respond to wrongdoing without anger.

In "Understanding Joseph Butler's Sermons on Resentment and Forgiveness," Gregory L. Bock explores Bishop Butler's famous eighteenth-century sermons on anger and forgiveness in order to illuminate the Christian perspective on anger. As Bock notes, there is disagreement about how to interpret Butler's understanding of forgiveness and its connection to resentment, and he considers three prominent interpretations: (1) that Butler defines forgiveness as the forswearing of resentment; (2) that Butler defines forgiveness as the forswearing of retaliation; and (3) that Butler intends only a loose connection between forgiveness and resentment. Bock, then, evaluates each interpretation and argues that the best way to understand Butler's understanding of the relationship between forgiveness and anger is that forgiveness requires only the forswearing of *excessive* resentment.

Chapter 5's "Anger as an Unnecessary Response" presents an argument from Court D. Lewis, who argues that anger (especially anger-as-resentment) is an unnecessary moral response to wrongdoing. Inspired by recent literature that counters the traditional Western approach (often inspired by Bishop Joseph Butler) that maintains the necessity of anger, Lewis develops an argument for how requiring anger creates a level-confusion that diminishes (instead of protecting) the self-respect of individuals. What is more, Lewis examines the Eastern religions of Buddhism, Jainism, Confucianism, and Daoism in order to provide both theological and practical reasons for why a life free from anger not only is possible, but also neither condones wrongdoing nor fails to take seriously the moral order.

Colin Lewis's "Moral Anger in Classical Confucianism" continues to challenge the traditional Western conception of anger by presenting an examination of Confucian philosophical thought on anger. Noticing a lack of substantive engagement with classical Chinese thought, Lewis sets out to complete two general projects: one interpretive, one applied. The interpretive project examines the manner in which classical Confucian thought regards anger as having both destructive and constructive aspects, how these aspects are unavoidable human experiences, and how they can (and should) be regulated or recruited by ritualized social forms. It is through adherence to ritual prescriptions that problematic anger is alleviated while moral anger is effectively expressed, achieving prosocial ends without producing undue harm. This understanding and analysis of anger from a Confucian perspective gives rise to an applied project that considers how even contemporary, non-Confucians can ritualize and deploy anger for positive moral and political ends, such as reconciliation, etiquette, and protests.

In chapter 7's "Is Anger Ever Required? Ārya Śāntideva on Anger and Its Antidotes," Will Barnes closes Part Two with an examination of Buddhism. Utilizing work from the eighth-century Buddhist teacher Madhyāmika Ārya Śāntideva, Barnes discusses Śāntideva's argument that because patience and moral vigor acknowledge wrongdoing, empower those disempowered by wrongdoing, and motivate us to address it more effectively than anger, while anger may at times have instrumental value, it is never morally required. Barnes shows that by reflecting on the fact that wrongdoing is caused by conditions rather than spontaneous autonomous choice, any indignation that assumes "this *could/should* not have happened" exhibits an ignorance of causation in its attributions of responsibility. By understanding Śāntideva's position, we realize the complex impersonal causes and conditions of wrongdoing and so have no cause to be angry.

Part Three examines the practical responses to anger and begins with Paula Smithka's "Stoking Anger and Weaponizing Untruth: How Mind Viruses Undermine Social Justice." Smithka builds on Richard Dawkins's concept of memes as cultural informational units transmitted from mind to mind, combining it with Jeffrey Gold and Niall Shanks' notion of mind viruses to show how conformity memes generate "dogmatism-inducing viruses" that propagate intolerance and anger. When individuals use media outlets to weaponize propaganda and untruth they create "viruses" that stoke anger and resentment in those who "contract" them, which promotes intolerance for difference of views (political, social, religious) or people (immigrants, other races or ethnicities, etc.). Smithka, then, discusses how mind viruses foster linguistically violent behavior and physical violence, arguing that a vaccine is needed to guard against the mind viruses that undermine social justice in the form of racism, sexism, and the other negative "-isms." Such a vaccine requires multiple components in addition to an educational component: it has to include fighting against post-truth tactics, remembering the humanism that is the foundation of liberal democracy, and on the larger social/political scale, politicians must uphold the values of mutual tolerance and forbearance that serve as the "soft guardrails" of American democracy.

Next, Jennifer Kling's "Rage against the Machine: The Virtues of Anger in Response to Oppression" shows how to cope with the anger that fills our lives. As Kling notes, she finds herself angry almost all of the time, as oppression (of various kinds) is endemic to our sociopolitical world. In response to the growing philosophical literature that argues against anger as a necessary, virtuous, or important response to wrongdoing, Kling contends that maintaining an anti-anger position is mistaken in regard to the sociopolitical realm, arguing that anger is both an important, and a virtuous, response to the presence of oppression, that is, to the presence of widespread injustices that disproportionately negatively affect certain social groups, and their members, within and across societies. Anger, when in response to oppression, has the potential to be, not a vice, but a virtue. She maintains that when deployed properly, anger toward oppression can both galvanize political change and enable its wielder(s) to live a flourishing life in the midst of oppression. Of course, like any virtue, anger can go wrong. Deployed poorly, it can have many of the negative effects described by Nussbaum and others. But, in the ideal case, anger in response to oppression not only helps propel the fight for justice, but also promotes mental, emotional, and social flourishing for those who must live their lives in an oppressive society.

In chapter 10's "Feminism and Anger," Danielle Poe considers the anger and sources of anger that occur between white women and women of other races. With the hope that the lessons presented in the chapter will also apply to other important relationships of privilege, including class, sexual orientation, gender-identity, religion, and disability, Poe argues that anger is a source of empowerment, a fuel that provides motivation and energy to fight for just treatment and recognition. Anger is a force for change, and, when expressions of anger are heard and listened to, they build solidarity to fight against the ways in which racism permeates popular culture, the legal system, education, housing, and finances. In addition to these injustices, privilege, micro-aggressions, and ignorance are all features of systemic racism, and fighting such a system is exhausting work. Poe maintains that anger provides the energy to continue fighting such a monumental struggle.

Next, Zachary Hoskins's "Anger and Punishment" examines the relevance of anger to various normative questions about whether and how we punish. The bulk of the chapter focuses on the anger-based critique of retributivist theories of punishment, which maintains that retributivist theories are essentially rationalizations of retributive emotions, especially anger, and that anger is an unsavory basis for making decisions about whether and how to punish; thus retributivist theories are not well supported. Hoskins examines several prominent versions of this line of objection and considers possible retributivist responses. He contends that anger-based objections to retributivism are less devastating than their proponents sometimes suggest.

Finally, chapter 12's "Avoiding the Dark Side" presents an examination of anger in popular culture. Lewis and Bock examine *Star Wars*' Anakin Skywalker and his journey through the dark side of the Force. Next, they compare Skywalker's journey to several other prominent characters from popular culture, including *Star Trek*'s Spock and Worf, and Marvel Comics' Logan/Wolverine and Bruce Banner/Hulk. Finally, they examine metal music as a counterargument to the ubiquitous presentation of anger as something dark and best to be avoided. Lewis and Bock show that popular culture presents a variety of perspectives on anger and that research shows how engaging in popular culture that promotes anger is actually a way of coping with and diffusing feelings of anger that result from the world we inhabit.

As the editors, we hope you will find the chapters contained within this collection insightful and helpful for both new research and your own personal understanding of anger's role in the moral life. We attempted to offer a variety of perspectives, and, when possible, create a sort of philosophical dialogue between chapters. What is more, we also hope that the companion to this collection, *Righteous Indignation: Christian Philosophical and Theological Perspectives on Anger* (Fortress Press, 2020), will spur further dialogue and understanding of the role of anger in the moral life.

Part I

THE HUMAN EXPERIENCE OF ANGER

Chapter 1

The Nature and Ethics of Vengeful Anger

Charles L. Griswold

> For this is your truth: you are too *pure* for the filth of the words:
>
> revenge, punishment, reward, retribution.
> Friedrich Nietzsche, *Thus Spoke Zarathustra*[1]

Vengeful anger is the stuff of countless works of literature and art both great and small. Homer's *Iliad*, one of the founding works of Western literature, begins with a particular word for anger (*mênis*) and is in some sense about anger and its epic consequences.[2] Myriad representations of vengefulness also pervade contemporary film, as we see in movies such as Quentin Tarantino's *Kill Bill* series and in numerous Westerns. It is remarkable how often we encounter the phenomenon in life as well. Reading the news reports of Bernard Madoff's thievery, for example, one is struck by the character and intensity of the anger among those he wronged. Elie Wiesel, whose life savings—along with the resources of his philanthropic foundation—were devastated by Madoff's fraud, is quoted as stating that the punishment he wishes for Madoff is that he spend at least five years in a solitary cell that is furnished with a screen on which pictures of his victims are shown one after the other, day and night, while a voice forces his attention to the injury he did to each individual. He is also reported as saying that he cannot forgive Madoff. The judicial sentence imposed on Madoff—150 years of incarceration—might itself express a form of retributive anger.[3] We are also familiar with the phenomenon and its consequences in relatively petty and unimportant situations—academic politics, for example—as well as in graver contexts, such as broken partnerships where the welfare of children and the division of property are at stake. Famously and lamentably, fury is writ large in war and violent conflict. Such examples capture something of the emotion that I shall be discussing here and suggest that vengeful anger broadly conceived is as universal as any emotion is capable of being. It would certainly be hard to find an adult who is not well acquainted with it from personal experience.

Our intuitions about the virtues and vices of vengeful anger are conflicted. Vengefulness is felt to be vindicating on the one hand and vindictive on the other. A long tradition holds that vengeful anger is not an emotion that a virtuous person would feel, in part because pleasure in the pain of another is one of its elements.[4] That vengeful anger and possibly the taking of revenge are accompanied by pleasure is well established, though there is room for debate about what the pleasure is pleasure in, an issue to which I shall return. Others have argued along consequentialist lines that the desire for revenge is destructive of justice and so is a discreditable motive from which to act. It easily grows into blood feuds, vigilantism, and an unprincipled license to violence. The famous propensity of such anger to consume the soul of its owner and to grow out of all proportion to its causes also supports the intuition that we are better off without it. Vengeful anger does not seem to answer well or at all to the demands of impartiality, proportionality, or norms of fairness. In this light, it is not surprising that the proleptically and comprehensively forgiving attitude of the Amish has been widely praised; their almost heroic stilling of vengeful anger and certainly of revenge in response to the cold-blooded murder of a number of their children several years ago commands admiration.[5]

On the other hand, we readily sympathize with, say, the fury of Madoff's victims. Indeed, we are tempted to judge that a failure to feel that fury signals some defect of character—something like a failure in one's ability to stand up for oneself, a failure of self-esteem. Aristotle seems to be expressing just this intuition when, in the *Nicomachean Ethics*, he characterizes as "slavish" (*andrapodôdes*)—a socially loaded term, to be sure—the disposition not to react with anger when one is treated contemptuously and as of no account (literally, as "bespattered with mud," *propêlakizomenon*; 1126a7–8).[6] From his standpoint, the reaction of the Amish to the murder of their children very likely qualifies as "slavish." The reaction of the Amish did generate critical commentary. Your children are murdered; ought you not experience anger in consequence?[7] Then there are consequentialist arguments, as well, that can be adduced in favor of vengeful anger, as suggested by Bishop Joseph Butler.[8] And, of course, in some cultures, the failure to feel anger in response to being wronged and especially the failure to express and act on it are heavily penalized.[9]

Is it ethical to feel such a sentiment or emotion? This is one question I would like to pursue here. I propose to reflect on whether this sentiment or emotion is *ever* justified, by which I shall mean, such as a virtuous person would feel or such as it is virtuous to feel.[10] I am asking not whether it is *always* justified (clearly, it is not) but whether the emotion is ever worth our endorsement and, if so, under what conditions. Of course, the answer is tied to an understanding of the character of this particular emotion, and that is the second question on which I shall focus. As the description of the emotion must precede reflection on its justifiability, I begin with the descriptive or phenomenological issue in section one.

In section two, I explore the relation between self-esteem and anger, since this serves as a bridge between the descriptive and definitional issues on the one hand and the normative ones on the other. I further develop the debate about the virtues and vices of vengeful anger in section three by examining, briefly and selectively, arguments presented by Aristotle (in the *Nicomachean Ethics* and the *Rhetoric*) and by Seneca (in *De Ira*). My goal in this section of the chapter is to articulate several of the key issues involved in the debate about the praiseworthiness of vengeful anger, and the discussion of passages in Aristotle and Seneca is constrained by that purpose. In section four, I set out conditions that must be met if vengeful anger is to be appropriate and sketch some of the broader considerations that, I believe, would need to be worked out to ground a view about the virtues and vices of vengeful anger. To that end, I develop a distinction (already discussed in section three) among three senses of "fittingness" and say a bit more about their interconnection as well as their relation to an ethics of vengefulness. I do not attempt to work out these considerations in detail here, let alone which systematic moral theory would best accommodate my arguments about the ethics of vengeful anger. By way of conclusion (section five), I suggest that the taking of revenge may be appropriate if certain conditions are met, but that it is not justified simply because the emotion from which it springs is justified (if indeed it is justified). As I briefly discuss, this leaves us with a surprising distinction, and possibly divergence, between the merits of the emotion of vengeful anger and those of the action that may (and perhaps normally does) follow from it.

My theme is individual, rather than group, vengefulness. On the present view, individual vengefulness has three characteristics: first, it is what one might call private vengeance (in which revenge is to be taken by oneself); second, it involves the desire for personal revenge in response to wrongs done to oneself rather than to someone else (my primary focus is not indignation or sympathetic resentment); and third, it is directed at a person or persons. The form of vengeful anger on which I focus here assumes all three of these characteristics. For the sake of brevity, I shall speak simply of vengeful (or moral or retributive) anger but will mean, unless otherwise noted, personal vengeful anger in the sense just sketched. Consequently, I am talking about the desire to *take revenge*, not the desire to *avenge* wrongs. I am not exploring the relation between personal revenge and judicial punishment, let alone setting out a theory of punishment. A separate essay would be required to explore issues of collective anger and vengeance. Further, I am not primarily asking about the social utility of norms that sanction the taking of revenge (utility relative to the goal of deterrence, the equalization of power, etc.).[11] There are many shades or shapes of anger; I am not claiming that the well-known phenomenon I am isolating and evaluating here is the essence or paradigm case of anger and am not committed to any view about anger as a "natural kind."

As to the definition of "emotion," for present purposes I am accepting that offered by Peter Goldie, who writes:

> An emotion, I have argued, is a relatively complex state, involving past and present episodes of thoughts, feelings, and bodily changes, dynamically related in a narrative of part of a person's life, together with dispositions to experience further emotional episodes, and to act out of the emotion and to express that emotion. Your expression of emotion and the actions which spring from the emotion, whilst not part of the emotion itself, are none the less part of the narrative which runs through—and beyond—the emotion, mutually affecting and resonating in that emotion, and in further emotions, moods, and traits, and in further actions.[12] (2002, 144)

This sense of "emotion" informs my reflections here on vengeful anger. I shall be assuming that vengeful anger is also a feeling, that is, that it possesses an affective quality for its owner; the feeling in question may be "hot" or "cold" (these labels are themselves slippery). But, as it is in some way about something in the world, it is also an emotion. I am not going to distinguish here between "emotion" and "sentiment" (I will generally avoid the word "passion" when speaking in my own voice, though in its eighteenth-century usage—for example, in Adam Smith—it seems synonymous with emotion and sentiment).[13] I will speak of vengeful anger, vengefulness, and the desire for revenge, meaning the same by all these phrases.

There are numerous empirical issues involved here, and I am aware of the dangers of armchair psychology passed off as considered convictions, intuitions, and such.[14] While I cite some of the relevant psychological literature and no doubt make assumptions of an empirical nature, this chapter does not attempt to assess systematically the relation between empirical and philosophical analyses of the topic.

SECTION ONE: THE PHENOMENOLOGY OF VENGEFUL ANGER

Anger is a highly complex, polymorphous phenomenon. Our language reflects some but not all of its forms: we speak of wrath, indignation, fury, ill temper, ill humor, bitterness, irritation, irascibility, resentment, exasperation, pouting, annoyance, and, of course, vengefulness (which can be "hot" or "cold").[15] These terms are not synonymous or stable in their meanings. Some of these terms are more behavioral or descriptive; others are more physiological (such as talk of ill humor or of something making your blood boil). We predicate anger of nonhuman animals, as well as of infants and young children. Moreover, the meanings of anger-terms vary over time.[16]

By way of isolating the particular shape of anger whose merits I want to assess here, let me start with the relation of hatred and vengeful anger (abbreviated "v-anger" in the rest of the chapter): I may hate without being angry and vice versa. For example, I may hate National Socialism or the fact of a significant disparity of economic wealth between peoples or the effects of global warming on my favorite glaciers in Switzerland, but in themselves these are not instances of vengeful anger. In one of its modulations, hatred seems less personal than v-anger, in that it can arise on account of things that do not affect me personally (or even on account of anybody I know personally) and may be directed at entities that lack intentions or at least that are not responsible for their actions.[17] Further, I could describe myself as hating X without ever actually feeling hatred or anger. The phrase "moral hatred" brings hatred closer to v-anger, though again I can certainly ascribe it to myself, even feel it, without its being vengeful. Finally, as Aristotle remarks (*Rhetoric* 2.4, 1382a12–13), hatred need not be accompanied by pain, whereas, in some sense, the emotion of v-anger is thus accompanied (though it is also, as already noted, pleasurable).

Personal vengeful anger responds to perceived harm done to oneself. There are, of course, many ways in which this harm can be expressed, among them physical harm, harm to those near and dear, and harm to one's property. Further, this harm must also be perceived as a moral wrong. Soldiers in combat are out to harm one another but could in principle see the enemy's attempt to harm them not so much as morally wrong as what soldiers qua soldiers just do. And so it would be possible to respond to being harmed by another—harm one thinks is bad and to be evaded—angrily but not vengefully. V-anger, at least in the form that is the topic of this chapter, is elicited by the perception that the harm is somehow wrong morally and hence is bad in a way that goes beyond its painfulness.[18]

Consequently, the anger felt in response to one's desire being frustrated is not necessarily v-anger. Aristotle remarks in the *Rhetoric* that people "become angry whenever they are distressed; for the person who is distressed desires something" (2.2, 1379a11–12).[19] But even if the cause of the frustration consists in someone blocking one's desire (say, in the example just mentioned, one's desire to continue to live), much depends on how or why the blocking is undertaken.

Let me pause for a moment. I have spoken of "perceived" harm or wrong, leaving open the possibility that one's perception is mistaken. One typically experiences personal v-anger in consequence of what one perceives to be a wrong done to oneself, not in response to what one perceives to be a good done to oneself, however painful. I do not want to take revenge on the dentist who quite rightly and expertly performed a root canal, excruciating and hateful though that experience may have been. Further, if a wrong is done to me but I do not know of it, I do not react with v-anger.

As a consequence, vengeful anger has a cognitive component. No doubt it is also accompanied by a state of bodily excitement or perturbation of some sort. As Aristotle notes in *De Anima* (403a29–403b1), the natural philosopher will describe anger as the boiling of the blood around the heart—a description to be updated but one whose spirit is surely correct. But a necessary condition of v-anger is the perception of wrong, and this may be described, for present purposes, in terms of belief, judgment, recognition, or—in some sense of this ill-defined term—cognition. That cognition is typically described or describable discursively; indeed, a remarkable feature of v-anger is the extent to which it *is* described discursively by its owners, sometimes generating narratives that reach epic length.

Vengeful anger is, then, *moral* anger in the sense I have sketched. Consequently, it takes itself to be *justified*, and quite consciously so; narratives of v-anger are replete with such justification, fueled by and fueling it. Such anger perceives itself as defended by reasons of a noncausal sort. The emotion is thus intrinsically evaluative and highly moralized. V-anger is experienced as righteous.

Part of what makes the relevant harm a *wrong* is that it is *intentionally* inflicted or at least that the offender bears responsibility for the wrong; this too is essential to explaining the reactive sentiment that is vengeful anger.[20] V-anger is properly directed at an agent capable of intention and of responsibility for its actions. Though you angrily curse the cement step on which you stub your toe, or angrily hit the dog that bites you, or angrily rebuke the person who accidentally steps on your foot in a crowded bus, none of these responses expresses v-anger. We no more wish to take revenge for an unintentional wrong than for an intentional right that inflicts pain. This point may seem obvious, but as we will see, Seneca argues against the propriety of anger in part on grounds that wrong is never intentionally inflicted.

As my use of the Strawsonian phrase "reactive sentiment" indicates, vengeful anger also has the characteristic just mentioned; it is reactive, a response to wrong.[21] However, a sentiment might be fitting or appropriate to something taken to be in the world but might not respond to—in the sense of address itself to—that feature in such a way as to seek to affect it. Or to be more precise, a sentiment may or may not seek to affect the agent responsible for that feature. While not all instances of reactive sentiment may have this agent-affecting aim, v-anger does, and revenge is its chosen means to that goal. As should be clear by now, v-anger is other-directed; it has an intentional structure, as it is "about" some value; it targets some agent; and, if it is acted upon, results are deliberately aimed for. There can be no unintentional revenge, for the very meaning of the idea is closely tied to the aim of the angry person.[22]

And, because it is reactive in its particular way (seeking revenge in response to a wrong), this emotion also motivates. One can well understand why, in the *Rhetoric* (2.2, 1378a30–32), Aristotle associates anger so closely with desire (this association is, I add, another reason that anger is not simply a feeling). This is an emotion that prompts its owner to *do* something, and it is typically accompanied by deliberation or, more sinisterly, plotting; hence, Bishop Butler characterizes it as "deliberate" (1896, 139). In this sense too, v-anger is cognitive; it undertakes means-end reasoning, inter alia, and that requires intention on the part of the angry person. Revenge, then, is plotted so as to inflict harm in response to wrong received.[23]

Vengeful anger therefore possesses an interesting combination of retrospectivity, to borrow a thought from a relevant passage in Anscombe (1969, 20),[24] as well as prospectivity—indeed, one is tempted to say, the latter because of the former. This again distinguishes v-anger from hatred, as the latter may not be retrospective and perhaps, on occasion, may not be prospective either. V-anger is tied to agency diachronically understood, a point to which I shall return in the next section when discussing its connection to self-esteem.

The target of the emotion and, thus, of the revenge is not so much the wrong action or even intention but its author or owner—the wrongdoer, in other words.[25] I note in passing that this aspect helps to explain why forgiveness "works" on the victim's emotion of v-anger by moderating or alleviating it, if forgiveness is understood as a response to changes in the offender's attitudes or dispositions (changes signaled by, inter alia, contrition). Both v-anger and forgiveness are deeply interpersonal and bilateral and in that sense social; to that extent, they mirror each other. Correspondingly, the notion of v-anger directed against oneself is difficult to make sense of (the mirror notion of self-forgiveness is similarly complex). Further, both are tied to *memory*. One can no more forgive by forgetting than one can be vengeful by forgetting; both vengefulness and forgiving insist that the offender remember. Indeed, the thirster for revenge not only is energetically committed to remembering but has a much-lamented tendency to hang on to the memory in all its vividness.

Unlike ordinary perceptions, vengeful anger tends not only to linger beyond—often far beyond—the wrong to which it responds but also to augment its intensity.[26] Adam Smith wrote, citing Malebranche, that the passions "all justify themselves, and seem reasonable and proportioned to their objects, as long as we continue to feel them." Smith also remarks in the same paragraph that often "every thing appears magnified and misrepresented by self-love," as when the "violent emotions" (of which v-anger is surely an example) consume us (1982, III.4.3).[27] Ordinary language reflects this aspect of v-anger, as when we speak of enflamed anger consuming everything in its path. Consequently, the object of this emotion is not simply "payback" but payback and then some; it is not just about "getting even" but about getting more than even. Of course, one could certainly get even without counting that as revenge, as when one evens the score in a tennis match.

The currency in which this abundant payback is supposed to be transmitted is, let us underline, pain or suffering. Vengeful anger aims to inflict pain for pain, or suffering for suffering, or death for death.[28] There is no question but that it involves wishing ill for another.

Next, I must make explicit what is perhaps already clear, namely, that vengeful anger typically understands itself to be *retributive* (I am not denying that there may exist other retributive emotions). By this I mean, first, that it is focused on what is taken to be the wrongdoer's desert. In response to a question about why the offender should be made to suffer, the revenge-taker will frequently say something like, "Because he [or she] *deserves* it." This is different from a consequentialist rationale (though, of course, one could seek retribution for consequentialist reasons instead or as well), and that seems to me to be important. The primary purpose of personal v-anger is not deterrence, or the achievement of social utility, or some other such goal. The air of moral purity and even sanctity that can surround vengefulness and revenge-taking derives from their seemingly high-minded devotion to retributivist moral principle.[29]

However, vengefulness may not be retributively "pure" in that, as I shall also argue, it may aim at consequences of a sort. For example, it may seek to force the offender to acknowledge some moral principle (hence, revenge is sometimes referred to as "teaching the wrongdoer a lesson," though if revenge is not to reduce to retaliation or deterrence, this will have to be construed in a manner that does not absolve the wrongdoer of responsibility for having failed to learn the lesson already), or it may seek to restore the victim's self-esteem or both. The very notion that "payback" is to be repayment (with interest!) suggests that something more than desert alone is at stake here or at least that desert is being understood in an unusually complex way (not that the notion is straightforward in any case!). Payback seems conceptually and perhaps also, at a deep level, psychologically intrinsic to v-anger (there does not seem to be nonretributive agent-directed personal moral anger).[30]

There is one further crucial aspect of this remarkable emotion that should be mentioned. As other commentators have noted, vengeful anger would have its target—the wrongdoer—understand the payback not just as painful but as intended by that wrongdoer's victim as payback. This has been referred to as "double intentionality."[31] In what one might call the paradigm case, the returned harm loses much of its point if the intended recipient does not know not just that it is a harm (as would be the case if, say, you stole something whose absence its owner—the offender—never discovered), but that it is meant by this particular victim to be payback for this particular wrong. This observation highlights the fact that the exchange is highly personal: it involves a kind of reciprocity at its core and so mutual awareness on the part of both parties in the manner indicated. In that sense, it is fundamentally *interpersonal.*

Consequently, one is robbed of one's revenge if, say, the wrongdoer is indifferent to the harm the vengeful victim inflicts on him, or is dead, or never knows who inflicted the harm, or does not know why the harm was inflicted. Vengefulness is also not fulfilled and, indeed, may be usurped if the wrongdoer is punished by a third party (including by a court of law) instead of by the victim.

It seems to follow that vengeful anger has a communicative purpose that is intrinsic to it. As the wrongdoer is to understand who is taking the revenge and on account of what, he is also to be made to understand that his deed is (held to be) wrong. This message too seems implicit in the structure of v-anger: what you did to me was wrong, I protest it, and you must recognize that.[32] Indeed, is not the chosen method of protest—inflicting pain of some sort—meant at least in part to compel the wrongdoer to recognize and acknowledge all this? If the answer is affirmative, as I take it to be, we have reason to differentiate between the victim's vengeful wish to inflict pain and that of a sadist or cruel person.

How vengefulness is understood by both parties is therefore essential to its meaning and achievement. The victim is not seeking just to inflict harm or just to see the offender suffer; whatever pleasure may accompany vengefulness need (and ought) not lie just in the suffering or pain of another (else revenge would collapse into sadism or cruelty and lose whatever moral character it may possess). To be sure, wrong must have taken place (or at least be believed to have taken place), so what one might call an "objective" dimension must be present and perceived to be so; but also, both parties to the exchange must understand each other's state of mind in a suitable way—what one might call a "subjective" dimension must be present as well.

Vengefulness cannot be the same, then, as the desire for retaliation, though both have a tit-for-tat structure and are part of the same family of notions. I can retaliate on behalf of someone else—call it third-party retaliation—and could do so without experiencing any particular emotion. Further, I can also retaliate without caring a whit about your recognizing who the retaliator is or why retaliation has occurred. Retaliation does not require my being present to witness your suffering as a result of the retaliation. I can retaliate without thinking that what you did to me is wrong; it may simply have caused me pain.[33]

Let us take this a step further. I have noted that the desire for revenge seeks, inter alia, what is commonly referred to as "getting even." In some sense, the aim seems to be to balance the scales or to reverse or correct the inequality brought about by the wrongdoing. Reciprocity of a sort seems to be fundamental here. Some elemental sense of fairness is at work—an intuition that revenge would be fair insofar as it restores things to how they were before or at least creates the equivalent thereof. Now, given what I have also just said about the other aims of v-anger—including that of forcing the wrongdoer to recognize the source and purpose of the revenge—it appears that there's a connection between rebalancing (getting even) and the wrongdoer's painful recognition of his misdeeds. I have also said that v-anger is retributive in holding that the wrongdoer deserves the given punishment and in wanting to punish the wrongdoer. And I have pointed to a communicative dimension of v-anger as well.

It is difficult to bring these features together into a coherent account, and one possible conclusion is simply that vengeful anger is not itself coherent.[34] Let us see if we can avoid that conclusion by reflecting further on the various aspects of the phenomenology. Now, one temptation is to hold that the rebalancing consists in creating equal amounts of pain on both sides. On this view, vengefulness seeks to rebalance by reestablishing a semblance of the previous balance, but in a peculiar way—by creating an analogous parity of condition between the parties involved. You took my eye, and now you shall lose yours, so we are once again even—though my sight is not thereby restored. Hence there seems to be something tragic in revenge as a response to loss, in that the simulacrum of the earlier balance is rarely more than that. People frequently seek to dissuade revenge-takers for precisely this sort of reason; taking the offender's eye won't give you yours back, won't make it not be the case that yours was taken.

What of the natural desire to take two eyes for one, in spite of *Lex Talionis*? And what of the importance of forcing the wrongdoer into awareness of the cause and rationale of the revenge? The account of rebalancing just sketched not only fails to take into consideration the wrongdoer's consciousness and interpretation of his pain or the victim's wish both to be and to be known as the instrument of revenge but also ignores the fact that vengefulness often seeks to inflict *more* pain than was received. So, reestablishing balance or equality of condition cannot be the whole story, even granting that the status quo ante cannot literally be regained in many cases (I cannot get my eye back by depriving you of yours).

Perhaps the core idea is, instead, something more like this: vengeful anger seeks to restore equality of regard, not of pain or condition, and it sometimes uses means—say, the taking of an eye (or two) for an eye—that *compel* recognition of that equality. Perhaps what vengefulness hopes to regain is a kind of parity, with suffering employed in part because of its capacity to symbolize and communicate equality and in part to compel the wrongdoer to acknowledge that parity.

Now, in some cultural contexts especially, vengefulness may seek to command regard or recognition by a third party—one's peers, say—of the equality of the two parties primarily concerned. Aristotle perceptively, but perhaps too narrowly, defined anger (*orgê*) this way: "Let anger be [defined as] desire, accompanied by [mental and physical] distress, for conspicuous retaliation because of a conspicuous slight [*oligôria*] that was directed, without justification, against oneself or those near to one" (*Rhetoric* 2.1, 1378a30–32; the word translated here by "retaliation" may also be translated as "vengeance" or "revenge"). A "slight" presumably diminishes or belittles one (a connotation implicit in the word Aristotle here uses), at least in the eyes of others. One's standing—or, as one might say in some contexts, one's honor or the esteem in which one is held—is diminished. V-anger might then be understood as seeking to restore that standing in the eyes of third parties by forcibly asserting that one is not to be treated as inferior (hence Aristotle's *NE* use of the term "slavish," earlier mentioned—as though not to feel the appropriate anger confirms one's lowered standing). Empirical studies evidently support Aristotle's definition.[35] So natural is this thought that Elster states: "I believe the phenomenon of honor to be the key to understanding revenge. Asserting one's honor, like enjoying other people's envy of one's assets, is an aspect of a deep-rooted urge to show oneself to be superior to others" (Elster 1992, 176). This would, then, seem to be key to the emotion that typically prompts revenge.

If social standing as determined by a third party is the core issue, however, then forcing the wrongdoer to understand and admit his wrongdoing seems beside the point. The more important object would be to show the third party, rather than the offender, that one is not "slavish." By contrast, it also seems possible to want revenge even though no third party is aware of the transaction or even though social standing is not at issue. Interpreting personal vengefulness in terms of its social usefulness, then, seems not to get to the core of the emotion.

And yet there is some truth to the notion that vengeful anger may counter the perception of lowered standing, as seen from the vantage point of the victim. That is, it initially seems plausible that vengefulness is somehow meant to reassure *the victim* of his or her equal standing and worthiness of equal regard, in that way restoring the earlier balance. Aristotle's definition would limit the cause of v-anger to one or another form of belittling (he mentions three in the chapter of the *Rhetoric* from which I just quoted: contempt, spite, and arrogant insult [*hubris*]); and if what we have in mind here is something like a sense of one's own proper worth in one's own eyes, we arrive at the question of the connection between self-esteem and v-anger. Let us see if further sense may be given to the idea of restoring equality of regard.

SECTION TWO: SELF-ESTEEM AND VENGEFULNESS

Let me reformulate one key thought implicit in Aristotle's account of anger. V-anger is the emotion one feels in response to an affront that both belittles or dishonors or disrespects one in some way and communicates that one is not and ought not to be accorded due regard or esteem. I said earlier that v-anger assumes that the wrongdoer acts willingly and intentionally, as well as wrongly. Now, one could imagine responding just as one would to a wrong done to another person: with indignation, even calm reasoned indignation and a demand for justice, or with studied indifference, depending on the circumstances (including the kind of wrong done, as well as the status of the wrongdoer). One could also imagine retaliating for, say, purposes of deterrence. But reacting with *v-anger* signals that one takes the wrong *personally* in some sense that goes beyond simply being the target of the wrong.

One intuitive way to make sense of that is as follows: vengeful anger expresses its owner's suspicion or, perhaps, anxiety about the possibility that he or she deserves the affront, that the negative judgment about oneself implicit in the wrongdoing is true. Someone comments publicly on the inferior status of your scholarly work, and you respond not by laughing it off or by calm refutation but with v-anger; does this not suggest that perhaps you are in fact worried that the accusation may carry a kernel of truth? If it never crossed your mind to imagine that the affront might somehow be true of you, why should you respond specifically with *vengeful* anger, as I have defined it? Responding with v-anger suggests that your self-esteem is called into question.[36]

There exists clinical literature pointing to interesting ways in which fantasies of revenge can help restore a sense of agency, empowerment, and control over one's life.[37] That a wrong might have this effect of requiring restoration of self-esteem is perfectly understandable, of course, but implies that vengefulness is rooted in weakened self-esteem.[38] Insofar as it is, the term "resentment"—though more narrowly defined here than in Butler (where it comes to what I am calling v-anger, irrespective of the angry person's level of self-esteem)—seems to capture its meaning. And, insofar as resentment is combined with a feeling of powerlessness, *ressentiment*—the French for "resentment," which Nietzsche endowed with this special sense—seems to be the right term.[39] Vengeful resentment may have transient value for its owner, as I have just indicated.

Vengefulness as a response to feeling belittled does make some initial sense of revenge as "getting even" or "payback," for what is to be restored—or so the victim believes—is the victim's own self-regard. V-anger might be thought of as restoring the victim's internal sense of equilibrium by providing "proof" to oneself—in the form of one's power to inflict harm on the offender—that the implicit or even explicit charge contained in the wrongdoing is false.[40] A sort of internal rebalancing is achieved that feels like restoration, like an equalizing. Specifically, vengefulness and perhaps the taking of revenge might feel, to one whose self-esteem is in question, like a restoration of a strong sense of self, a sense of one's own agency. This might also feel like a "reversal" of the state of affairs brought about by the wrong that one has suffered. Moreover, understanding v-anger as an effort to restore self-esteem sheds light on the "and then some" character of the "repayment," especially in cases of (what is felt to be) grave injury, for the nature of the task, self-reassurance, naturally seems to call for reiteration and reinforcement. Let me briefly expand on this point.

Vengeful anger is a structurally flawed strategy if the goal is the restoration of lowered self-esteem. Inflicting pain on those who have wrongly harmed you can never really address the causes of a weak sense of self, for those very probably preexisted the event in question. Lowering another person to a level beneath you does not actually raise you in the decisive sense, though it may have the instrumental and passing value of showing you that you have the ability to lower the offender (and may permit you to rank yourself above the offender, without, however, actually making you more estimable). Further, if your self-esteem hinges on forcing the wrongdoer to acknowledge that you ought not to be treated thus, then your sense of self depends in part on the esteem extracted from another. In the nature of the case, such esteem is always going to be contingent, variable, temporary, and suspect in any reassurance it offers. The strategy is unsuccessful, and perhaps that helps to explain the "and then some" character of the "payback" so often associated with v-anger: the disproportion of the returned harm that v-anger often generates expresses the lack of suitability of means (revenge-taking) to the end (restoration of self-esteem). As there is no proportional "getting even" that will work, one is forced to ever greater measures. It would certainly be difficult to formulate a defense of the ethical value of v-anger if v-anger expresses and seeks to counter lowered self-esteem, especially if proper self-esteem is conceived of as an appropriate disposition to be cultivated, rather than thought of simply in terms of its instrumental psychological utility (with regard to, say, restoring a sense of agency).

Putting ethical considerations aside for a bit longer, though, and staying within a phenomenological frame, let us ask: Must vengeful anger stem from or at least be accompanied by lowered self-esteem? The answer strikes me as negative. I can feel v-anger precisely because my self-esteem is *not* harmed. My conviction that I ought not be treated in a certain way may be affectively expressed as protest, as objection, as standing up for myself—all premised on the firm conviction that I am worth defending, worth my own defense. You may treat me in a way that is demeaning and humiliating or belittling; it does not follow that I am demeaned or humiliated or belittled if I do not regard myself as such. I am interested here in describing and evaluating a form of v-anger that does not stem from and is not a response to low self-esteem.

Yet this leads to another puzzle: if one has been wronged and one's self-regard has not thereby been damaged, would not the appropriate response to a wrong to oneself be a bloodless, affect-less rectification of the wrong? The victim would, it seems, respond impersonally, as though the injustice had been done to someone else. Indeed, why not respond in the manner Nietzsche praises in the passage quoted at the start of this chapter—by rising above any thought of revenge? What warrant for personal v-anger could remain if self-esteem were *not* at stake?

In order to pursue this normative question and, more broadly, the ethics of vengeful anger, let me turn to the debate between Aristotle and Seneca on the virtues and vices of anger.

SECTION THREE: ARISTOTLE AND SENECA

> [L]et us cultivate our humanity. Let us not bring fear or danger upon any one. Let us look down on damages and wrongs, insults and carping criticisms. Let us bear with greatness of mind our short-lived troubles. As they say, we have only to look back, only to turn round—quick now, here comes death!
>
> Seneca, *De Ira* 3.43.5 (2003)[41]

My purpose in this section is not, as already noted, to offer a scholarly assessment of the debate between Aristotelians and Stoics about the nature of the emotions or of Aristotle's and Seneca's views as such. Rather, I shall pick out several of their arguments as a way of furthering, within the confines of this brief discussion, the normative question about the place of v-anger in the good life. In the relevant passages of the *Rhetoric* and the *Nicomachean Ethics*, Aristotle's focus seems pretty clearly to be on the angry desire for revenge. Seneca's subject in *De Ira* certainly includes v-anger and arguably is principally v-anger; indeed, he says that his definition is not far from those of some unnamed others, and Aristotle appears to be among them (1.3.3; see the editors' n. 8, p. 20, in the edition of *De Ira* [2003] that I am using). His analysis at 1.2–3 focuses on vengefulness and distinguishes it from such things as the "anger" of a wild animal or that of a child who falls down and is in pain. I am not claiming, however, that both of their analyses isolate every feature of v-anger in precisely the way that I have. I do believe that what they say about anger sufficiently overlaps with the phenomenology I've offered to permit use of their views to illuminate fundamental features of the debate about the ethics of anger. Further, as will soon become clear, I am not endorsing either of their positions. Let me turn, then, to a brief examination of several relevant aspects of their views.

A. Aristotle

In Book II of the *NE*, Aristotle writes:

> By feelings [*pathê*] I mean appetite, anger [*orgê*], fear, confidence, envy, joy, love, hate, longing, jealousy, pity, and in general whatever implies pleasure or pain. By capacities I mean what we have when we are said to be capable of these feelings—capable of being angry, for instance, or of being afraid or of feeling pity. By states [*hexeis*] I mean what we have when we are well or badly off in relation to feelings. If, for instance, our feeling is too intense or slack, we are badly off in relation to anger, but if it is intermediate, we are well off; the same is true in the other cases. (1105b21–28)

Aristotle argues that virtues are "states." That there is such a thing as being well or badly off with respect to anger is established in Book IV, when Aristotle discusses the virtue of "mildness" (*praotês*), which he declares to be the mean concerned with anger. Aristotle terms the excess of anger "irascibility," and although the defect of anger is nameless, its possessor, as already noted, is termed "slavish" (1125b26–29, 1126a8). Aristotle remarks, "The person who is angry at the right things and toward the right people, and also in the right way, at the right time, and for the right length of time, is praised." Such a person is "mild" and thus "undisturbed (*atarochos*), not led by feeling, but irritated wherever reason prescribes, and for the length of time it prescribes" (for both quotations, see 1125b31–1126a1). So Aristotle seems to think that the virtuous person will feel anger as appropriate. Anger is part of the emotional makeup of the virtuous person. Why does Aristotle think this?

It cannot be because *every* emotion has a "mean"; the description of envy in the *Rhetoric* 2.10 (where it is defined as "a certain kind of distress at apparent success on the part of one's peers in attaining the good things that have been mentioned, not that a person may get anything for himself but because of those who have it"; 1387b23–25) does not make it sound like the sort of thing one could have toward the right thing at the right time and so forth. This inference is validated by *Rhetoric* 1386b16–1387a5 and especially 1388a35–36 ("envy is bad [*phaulon*] and characteristic of the bad [*phauloi*]"). Indeed, at *NE* II.6, Aristotle tells us that "not every action or feeling admits of the mean," and he cites envy inter alia (1107a8–11). For such feelings are inherently base (*phaulon*; 1107a13); presumably one is to extirpate them from one's soul. Why is not vengeful anger, an emotion reputed to be ugly and dangerous, inherently base and also to be extirpated?

Aristotle's answer is surprisingly hard to flesh out.[42] Certainly, the definitions of anger in the *NE* and the *Rhetoric* make it sound as though the emotion can be *fitting* in multiple senses. To begin with, it might be fitting or appropriate to the fact of an affront, to the magnitude of the affront, to the fact that it was an intentional affront, and so forth.[43] Now, one could perhaps construct a case that envy, too, is "fitting" in this sense, even while holding with Aristotle that one ought not feel envy. Fittingness in this first sense may be a necessary condition of ethical praiseworthiness but cannot be a sufficient condition.

Aristotle's biting comment about the deficiency of anger takes us further. He says:

> The deficiency—a sort of inirascibility [*aorgêsia*] or whatever it is—is blamed. For people who are not angered by the right things, or in the right way, or at the right times, or toward the right people, all seem to be foolish. For such a person seems to be insensible and to feel no pain, and since he is not angered, he does not seem to be the sort to defend himself. Such willingness to accept insults to oneself and to overlook insults to one's family and friends is slavish. (*NE* 1126a3–8)

This passage suggests a mix of rationales favoring v-anger as commendable (under the right circumstances and so on). One is consequentialist, having to do with the requirements of self-defense. But another, suggested as much by the tone of the passage as by the term "slavish," holds an appeal to honor as well as to the requirements of pride and to self-esteem. It "is blamed"—the relevant public blames you—if you do not stand up for yourself and yours. You come across as submissive, as deserving humiliation, as not just unable but—far worse—as unwilling to protest affronts. By contrast, anger signals to others that you protest. The context is ineluctably social, and the judgment Aristotle articulates is that of a moral—indeed, moralizing—community.

As the readers of Aristotle's report about how a failure to feel anger appropriately will be interpreted, we are meant to buy in. The way the account is phrased implicitly invites a connection between our self-regard and how others regard us.[44] This may turn out to be a matter of relative social position; more subtly, it may also evince the view that our nature is fundamentally "political" (in Aristotle's sense). But that sort of approach does not give us a particularly impressive ethical justification for v-anger, and in any case it appeals to considerations that are secondary on the analysis I am offering (since it has to do with social status).

There seem to be two other sorts of fittingness at work here, however. One has to do with what is fitting if one is to be a noble person rather than a base (*phaulos*) or slavish person. This sense of the fitting is relative to a picture of the ideal person or life. The other has to do with what is fitting to us as composite (made of body and soul, matter and form), dependent, and vulnerable creatures. Let me say something about these second and third senses of the fitting.

Aristotle's most detailed picture of the noble person is that of the *megalopsuchos*, offered almost immediately before his discussion of virtuous anger. In the *Posterior Analytics* (97b14–26) Aristotle cites *megalopsuchia* as an example of an equivocal term. It may mean, he says, either the sort of thing that Alcibiades, Achilles, and Ajax had in common, that is, an "intolerance of insults"; or the sort of thing that Lysander and Socrates had in common, an indifference to good and bad fortune, indifference (*apatheia*) instead of "not brooking dishonour."[45] Clearly, Aristotle lauds the first meaning and Seneca the second.

Since the *megalopsuchos* is "worthy of the greatest things, he is the best person [*aristos*]" (*NE* 1123b26–27). One might argue that he's best because he possesses all the virtues (1124a1–2; there it is clear that the *megalopsuchos* does have all the virtues), but that is unhelpful since we are trying to understand why there should be a virtuous state with respect to the feeling of anger. Aristotle does not explicitly say that the magnanimous man (for Aristotle, this character does seem to be male, hence my gendered expression) will experience such anger and does say that he is not prone to remember evils (1125a4–5), though he will speak evil of his enemies when it is a matter of their *hubris* (which Irwin translates as "wanton aggression"; 1125a8–9). The magnanimous man does have "hatreds" (1124b26)—presumably of persons who have dishonored him—which surely includes retributive anger. And, since he has all the virtues, he must also have that of "mildness." The idea seems to be that this noble character will in general not react to wrongs with anger, except when the wrongs are great and are delivered by those worthy of his vengefulness. His opinion of himself is (justifiably, by his lights) extremely high. In not needing the approval of others in any routine way, he is self-sufficient and will "determine his life" (1124b31–1125a1; his friends may help, however). The alternative, Aristotle says, "would be slavish" (*doulikon*; 1125a1). So, self-sufficiency seems to be one mark of noble character but also a kind of self-possession, a self-respect grounded in the perception—which he lives up to without inner conflict—that he is "worthy" or honorable. The *megalopsuchos* is in those ways proud of himself.[46]

At the same time—and arguably this is at odds with his self-sufficiency—he is also concerned not just with being honorable but with being honored, though only by the greatest honors (*NE* 1123b20–24; 1124a4–12). That is supposed to be another mark of his greatness. While there is much to say about this complicated sketch of the noble soul, it initially seems that when the magnanimous man does rise to anger, it is not because his self-esteem is damaged. Otherwise, magnanimity would be corrupted by low self-esteem, which Aristotle assigns to the vice of pusillanimity (1125a17–27). Magnanimous anger is not the self-doubting resentment I discussed in section two, and it is certainly not *ressentiment.* Presumably the magnanimous man's appreciation of and desire for honor demands that, when it is denied to him, he react with anger and that those dishonoring him know of his displeasure. It does seem to matter to him that they do know—why else does he care whether or not they honor him (and that he knows that they know that he both knows of and appreciates the honor)? Why else would it not suffice that he alone honors himself appropriately? The communicative or signaling function of anger seems crucial here.

At this deep level, he is not self-sufficient but dependent. By implying that the magnanimous man will respond angrily when it is fitting to do so, Aristotle makes it clear that his paragon of ethical virtue is vulnerable: the magnanimous man can be wronged and angered if great honors are inappropriately withheld. Deserved social regard (offered by those of exceptional virtue) is a chief object of concern for him. The corresponding vulnerability is consistent with Aristotle's view that ethical virtue can be frayed and, in extreme cases (such as that of Priam), badly frayed (*NE* 1101a6–13; note the use of *megalopsuchos* at 1100b32–33).

Why the magnanimous man should be vulnerable in regard to honor remains unclear. Aristotle does not say enough to help us understand exactly why or how the magnanimous man is dependent in this regard (is it an epistemic question, for example, such that he cannot know he is honorable unless honored by the right people?). He does not explain why being honored *matters* to the magnanimous man, and this corresponds to his silence about why feeling the right degree of anger is a virtue. Suppose that other great souls fail to honor you, a great soul: so what? Why not just brush it off? Why does not the great man's magnanimity flow into the second sense of *megalopsuchia* that Aristotle mentions in the *Posterior Analytics* (97b14–26), the one that Lysander and Socrates are credited with?

The opacity of Aristotle's analysis on this issue opens up space for the suggestion that the magnanimous man embodies an unstable combination of self-sufficiency and dependence. It is not that the two *must* form an unstable combination but that, because *honor* matters so greatly to the *megalopsuchos*, the demands of self-sufficiency and of dependence seem destined to collide. Another conception of *megalopsuchia* is required, a Stoic critic might maintain, in order to avoid just this collision.

But perhaps it is possible to help Aristotle out by examining another thought that seems to underlie his picture of virtuous anger, though it is largely unarticulated in the description of the magnanimous man. The thought concerns the importance of assessing what is fitting to us as composite (made of body and soul, matter and form), dependent, and vulnerable creatures. This is the third sense of "fittingness" mentioned earlier, and it stands out by way of contrast when Aristotle sketches the life of theoretical virtue in Book X. The paradigm of theoretical virtue is god, and on Aristotle's account, that noncomposite being lacks emotions to habituate and therefore has no need for the moral virtues. (Aristotle refers in different places to "god" as well as "the gods," but that does not affect the point I am making here.) As a reactive emotion, v-anger concedes that we are vulnerable to other intentional agents and thus that we exist in some sort of community with them, but the divine shares none of these traits (*NE* 1178b10–19). For Aristotle the emotions are in some sense somatic, as we saw with reference to *De Anima* 403a29–403b1, and this may be another reason why Aristotle takes it as a given that we humans cannot be without anger. By contrast, as noncomposite, as pure mind, god has no body. Aristotle's god feels no v-anger and hence cannot stand in a praiseworthy relation with respect to it; god has no interest in honor and is truly "self-sufficient" (see *NE* 1177a27 and context; also 1177b21–22). Insofar as we achieve the godlike life, then, our understanding of which—if any—moral virtues and emotions are appropriate to the noble soul is bound to change profoundly. Aristotle's case for virtuous anger is offered in the context of reflection on what is fitting to embodied, nongodly, political (in his sense) agents.

This line of thought about a third sense of fittingness points to what D'Arms and Jacobson helpfully term "anthropocentric constraints on human value." These come to light through a cluster of reflections on what sorts of emotions and virtues are appropriate to creatures like us, and their weight can be assessed in part by asking what of ourselves we would have to give up if we changed the constraints.[47] The considerations in question concern what D'Arms and Jacobson call "suitable standards of fittingness for humans" (ibid., 118). These determine what I am calling the third sense of fittingness. The second sense of fittingness I sketched has to do with the virtues that are intrinsic to a picture of the ideal person—in the Aristotelian case, a picture of (limited) self-sufficiency and high honor. In combination with Aristotle's view that anger is fitting in the first sense mentioned (as tracking features of the world), we have the core of his defense of the idea that anger can be ethically praiseworthy.

By way of sharpening the issues at stake, let me turn briefly to Seneca.

B. Seneca

De Ira is a sort of grab-bag of arguments about and against anger. There is no question about the main thesis: anger should be extirpated from the virtuous soul. My present purpose is narrow: I simply aim to articulate elements of Seneca's disagreement with Aristotle that help focus my discussion about the ethics of vengeful anger.

The first argument is that anger misinterprets the *import* of the (moral) facts about the world to which it takes itself to be responding, and hence it is a species of cognitive error, an example of bad reasoning. As I read Seneca, his point is neither that there does not exist such a thing as wrongful or unjust treatment of a person nor that v-anger necessarily errs in taking itself as responding to injustice. Rather, the idea is that, as the victim, I should not take myself to be harmed thereby and that furthermore I have positive reasons—regard for my own psychic health, for example—not to interpret the wrong as harming me. Consequently, I should not feel angry. I can grant that you did me wrong and insist on the appropriate punishment (1.15.1); yet, at the same time, I may refuse to see myself as having been harmed, degraded, demeaned, or diminished.[48] The ancestor of this view is undoubtedly Socrates's proud proclamation—delivered, interestingly, to the jurors in the *Apology* (41d1–2)—that no harm can come to a good man. Not surprisingly, Socrates also said that he is not angry with his accusers as they find him guilty (*Apol.* 35e1–36a1), even though what they are doing is unjust (*Apol.* 39b1–6).

Seneca's emphasis on the possibility of choice about whether or not to feel anger (once one is past the pre-anger phase, the initial stirrings caused by the "impression" of the wrong; 2.1–4) helps him to create some space for cognitive readjustment: I was wronged but need not internalize it and need not take myself as harmed. The assumption seems to be that if I had been harmed, then anger *might* be fitting, but as I am not harmed (since I am a Socratic or Stoic), then it is irrational to respond angrily. The important conclusion from this line of reasoning is that anger may be fitting in my first sense of the term but still not warranted or appropriate. Seneca's position is analogous to one that holds that a joke is funny but not morally appropriate to laugh at.[49]

To turn to a second argument: in response to the question "Is it virtuous to be angry at wickedness?" Seneca insists on a negative answer (2.6–10). He notes in support of his answer that people do not do wrong knowingly and thus are not responsible for their wrongdoing. Hence, something like excuse or pardon is the appropriate response: "To avoid anger with individuals, you must forgive the whole group, you must pardon the human race" (2.10.2). It makes no sense to be (vengefully) angry with a child or with nature, and you are able not to be so: "But being human is more of an excuse, and a juster excuse, than being a child" (2.10.2). Instead of responding with anger, look upon the wrongdoers "with the kindly gaze of a doctor viewing the sick" (2.10.7). If Seneca is right about this, then v-anger does look to be based on a mistake. By contrast, I held, with Aristotle, that v-anger assumes that the wrongdoer is responsible for his or her action. Obviously, to settle the matter would require an entirely different discussion. For present purposes, I will stipulate that our commonsense notion that wrongdoers are at least sometimes responsible for their deeds is correct. At least sometimes, they are not to be understood as though they were children, or natural events, or ill. This does not prevent us from recognizing that Seneca's views about comprehensive excusability go hand in hand with his quite moving appeals to our common fallibility (3.26.4: "All of us are *bad*"; cf. 1.14.2, 3) and humanity (3.43.5).

And this brings me to a third argument of *De Ira*. As the sentences I have quoted suggest, Seneca has a picture of the noble soul to set against Aristotle's. The difference between the two turns on the competing interpretations of *megalopsuchia* or high-mindedness already mentioned. Why is it nobler to rise above all insults and belittlement and expressions of dishonor or disrespect than to respond with anger as the occasion demands? A cluster of considerations directs Seneca to his interpretation of high-mindedness. For example, he says that anger is a sign of a mind aware of its own weakness (1.20.3), that is, lacking self-esteem; but "a mighty mind with its true self-awareness will not avenge, since it has not noticed the wrong done to it" (3.5.7; I take Seneca to mean that a "mighty mind" does not feel harmed). To subscribe to some such view requires that our virtue be invulnerable to external pressure, that it be the case that we are not harmed unless we think ourselves so, and, of course, that it is psychologically possible to prevent ourselves from becoming angry. Seneca insists that we can indeed be rid of anger completely (2.12, 13): "Anything that the mind commands itself it can do" (2.12.4).[50] The highest end is happiness understood as tranquility (see 1.21.4), and it is in our power to achieve it. Tranquility and, hence, proper self-care are incompatible with any degree of anger (3.4.4), as anger is toxic to its possessor—especially given the Stoic theory of emotion.[51] And, with this, the Aristotelian link—Seneca would say, the unstable link—between self-sufficiency and dependence through sensibility to honor is severed.

The debate between these positions is obviously multilayered and complex, and, in the debate about the merits of v-anger, a great deal will hinge on one's conception of the ideal human type, as the disagreement about the desirable sense of *megalopsuchia* shows. That is one upshot of this discussion. In the next section, I shall offer a list of conditions that a defense of v-anger would have to satisfy. Doing so will lead me back to consideration of our third sense of fittingness.

SECTION FOUR: THE CONDITIONS OF ETHICAL VENGEFUL ANGER

It seems to me that a number of considerations must be brought to bear on the question of whether it is ever virtuous to feel vengeful anger as I have described that emotion. Whether and how to assign differing weights to these considerations would require a separate essay. However that is worked out, the particular features of v-anger should be preserved in its vindication. It would not be persuasive to vindicate it simply by arguing for the merits of a sense of justice or of righteous indignation. That is too impersonal for present purposes and is a defense of related but distinct dispositions. Vengefulness is, I have argued, personal and requires that the agent (the victim) intentionally wish to inflict harm on the wrongdoer in return for wrong and also that the wrongdoer be able to identify the agent and his or her reason for wanting revenge.

First, for vengeful anger to be justifiable, it must correctly represent its target. Since v-anger is a response to wrong, the wrong must in fact be just that, and must in fact have been enacted by the person against whom the anger is directed. In those ways, the anger must be fitting in our first sense of the term: the beliefs that it implies or assumes must be true.[52] Further, it must be proportionate or exhibit what Adam Smith calls "propriety" (*TMS* I.i.3.6). No doubt a separate essay could be written about how proportionality is to be assessed, but we do recognize the notion of over- (and less frequently, under-) reaction. I have also stipulated that the offender is, in some sense, responsible for his or her wrongdoing and that justifiable v-anger assumes that the offender acted intentionally (in whatever sense accompanies responsibility) and is capable of understanding that he or she committed a wrong, specifically against this victim.

Second, it would make no sense to desire vengeance against an offender who is contrite and has expressed contrition, taken responsibility, made amends, and taken every other conciliatory and emendatory step one could reasonably wish for.[53] This, in turn, means that one ought not be resistant to forgiveness, or become hard-hearted, or succumb to the ongoing pleasures of fury. V-anger should be forsworn and hence be forswearable, so to speak, when faced with the appropriate forgiveness or excuse conditions.

Third, I suggest that vengeful anger that stems from and is meant to compensate for low self-esteem is not an emotion the virtuous person would endorse. To begin with, raising one's self-esteem by wishing to inflict pain on the wrongdoer is an unsuccessful strategy, as already mentioned. It is true that I can get angry because of my poor self-esteem but refrain from acting on it in recognition of the fact that such anger is self-defeating in practice. But the sort of abiding low self-esteem that is one source of v-anger is itself a sign of a deficiency of character (whether because one actually deserves higher self-esteem or because in fact one deserves low esteem). I do not see how a defense of v-anger can be successful if it hinges on defending low self-esteem. And while v-anger can be instrumentally useful for increasing one's deserved self-esteem, that vindication is not of the sort sought here. So a justification of v-anger has somehow to be compatible with and perhaps the expression of warranted self-esteem.

Fourth, however one is to understand the pleasures of vengefulness, they must not collapse into enjoying cruelty or sadism. In the best case, the pleasure of vengefulness seems to come to pleasure both in what is right and in righting a wrong.

Fifth, vengeful anger must be such (in its intensity and duration) as not to damage its owner ethically (by making him or her incapable of other virtues). This is necessary in order to answer Seneca's point about the toxicity of anger to its owner.[54] V-anger that met the conditions just enumerated would seem largely immune to the toxicity he describes. It seems to me that v-anger can, in principle, meet these conditions.

Satisfying the conditions just mentioned would help ensure that vengeful anger is (on the relevant occasion) not unjustifiable. But a further step is needed if it is to be positively commendable.[55] As noted at the end of section three, an upshot of the present inquiry is the suggestion that one cannot resolve the problem of the praiseworthiness of v-anger without also working out which ideal of the good life is to be affirmed and so without working out the second sense of fittingness, as well as the first.

Obviously, I cannot undertake that project here, but as prolegomenon to that effort, I mention two points pertinent to the Aristotle-Seneca debate about archetypes of praiseworthy character that lead back to the third sense of fittingness. The first point is that Aristotle's paragon of ethical virtue is a social or political being in a way that Seneca's is not. Seneca insists on one's being a part of the community of human beings, as his concluding sentences (quoted at the start of section three) indicate, and his vision is cosmopolitan rather than political. Aristotle has something much more local in mind, it seems: this virtuous person's standing in and ties to this or that community. The relations of honor are not cosmopolitan. From a noncosmopolitan perspective, sensitivity to this or that belittlement by this or that person is harder to brush off. V-anger is fundamentally social in character: it expresses and assumes one's connectedness to other particular agents. For Aristotle, we care about these individuals but not about all individuals as such; for Seneca, we care about humanity but about no individual (much) more than another. The second point is that while Aristotle is certainly assuming that the virtuous person is self-directed, in the sense of governed by reason in view of the noble (*to kalon*), his paradigm of the virtuous agent is not autonomous in the way that Seneca's is, as is particularly evident in Seneca's notion that one can be wronged but not harmed if the agent judges him- or herself unharmed. Perhaps another rough and ready way to put the point is that Aristotle assumes (I once again bracket *NE* X) that we are embodied and affective rational animals and hence that our character is not immune to the corresponding pressures. On Seneca's picture, that inference need not follow, if only we follow our reason implicitly.

Can we follow our reason in that way? This brings us to the third sense of fittingness mentioned earlier—fittingness to our situation as human beings. Both Aristotle's and Seneca's competing versions of the ideal of high-mindedness are revisionist (imagine what it would mean to take seriously Aristotle's *megalopsuchos* as your role model). One way to assess which revisionist scheme is preferable is to ask what would have to be given up in order to achieve the ideal in question. As already noted, D'Arms and Jacobson have furnished us with a helpful distinction between "wide" and "deep" concerns, and it should be brought to bear here.[56] That adopting Seneca's view about anger would require wide and deep changes to ordinary human psychology does not seem terribly controversial. Even Seneca seems aware of that, as when he offers the provocative view, already quoted, to the effect that if your father is murdered and your mother raped, you ought not respond with anger. What would have to be true of you in order that you *not* react with anger to such wrongs? What changes in yourself would you have to make in order to become a Senecan Stoic with respect to anger? If any emotion satisfies the "deep-concerns" criterion, it is vengeful anger. To be sure, that is an empirical point, and another upshot of this discussion is that the question of the ethics of vengeful anger cannot be settled absent reliance on empirical propositions of that sort.

The defense of vengeful anger also seems to satisfy the "wide concerns" criterion, as D'Arms and Jacobson's comments about anger suggest.[57] Aristotle does not require us to eliminate anger, and that alone may make his view seem more congenial because it is responsive to wide and deep concerns. While in the *Nicomachean Ethics* he is remarkably silent about such concerns when discussing anger, in *Politics* 7.7 there is a suggestive passage about the connection between "spiritedness"—itself generative of anger—and love as well as friendship. Aristotle writes: "For as to what some assert should be present in guardians, to be affectionate toward familiar persons but savage toward those who are unknown, it is spiritedness [*thumos*] that creates affectionateness; for this is the capacity of soul by which we feel affection.

An indication of this is that spiritedness is more aroused against intimates and friends than against unknown persons when it considers itself slighted [*oligôreisthai*]" (1327b38–1328a3) (1985, 208).[58] As Fisher suggests, anger seems to be a necessary consequence of others *mattering* to us profoundly; if that is true, then its elimination would require tearing out the emotions of love and friendship, as well—a very high cost to pay.[59] The combination of these deep and wide concerns, if buttressed by the empirical data, helps explain why the appropriate response to the relevant sort of wrong to oneself ought not be a bloodless, affect-less avenging or simply a calm turn to judicial redress.

But this third sense of fittingness is not sufficient, only necessary for the justification of vengeful anger. For there may be emotions or dispositions that are undesirable and yet may also, for all we know, satisfy the wide- and-deep-concerns criteria. Indeed, *un*warranted v-anger (anger that does not fulfill the requirements of the first sense of fittingness, say) may be fitting in this sense. The concerns, that is, must be the right ones. And this suggests that what is needed in order to build the ethical case for v-anger is the conjunction of all three senses of fittingness I have mentioned. That is a further upshot of this chapter. Let me offer a few more words, then, about the connection between the second and third senses of fittingness (i.e., about fit relative to a moral ideal that is not outside the bounds of the wide- and-deep-concerns criteria). Much more remains to be said, to be sure, about the conceptual relations among the three senses of fittingness I have sketched.

Aristotle's candidate for the ethical paradigm—the *megalopsuchos*—suffers from its own difficulties relevant to the present discussion. I refer not just to the lack of argumentative support with regard to the place of anger in the virtuous life but also to the unstable combination of self-sufficiency and dependence on the appropriate honors granted by (suitably qualified) others. It is, at the end of the day, difficult to tell whether the *megalopsuchos* responds with anger to what he regards as the unjustified denial of honor because his self-esteem is *not* called into question or because it *is* called into question along with his social standing.

If vengeful anger is to have a defensible place in the emotional repertoire of the virtuous person, we shall have to accept not only the importance of respecting wide and deep concerns but also some sort of dependence of self on other that often is more particularized, less cosmopolitan, than anything Seneca would allow, or, at least, "thicker" in its human and moral ties. The picture of the ideal life will in that respect be more Aristotelian than Stoic. However, the instability I have ascribed to Aristotle's picture would need to be overcome and thus the role of self-esteem stabilized. This would require, I suggest, jettisoning the central importance that Aristotle's magnanimous man places on being honored for noteworthy achievements and deeds. Reliance on being honored ties one's sense of self-worth too tightly to public perception of one's worth. What is needed is a certain dependence on the moral regard of others who matter, one that does *not* call into question self-esteem and yet is not only admirable but also consistent with the wide- and-deep-concerns criteria. The task would be to explain the possibility of v-anger, and thus of being harmed, among people of solid self-esteem who are dependent as well as ethically admirable.[60] It seems to be a part of that picture that the offender be granted the standing to be worthy, so to speak, of one's v-anger; this comes to a kind of esteem of or respect for the offender.[61] Some such view about the offender belonging to the same moral community does not fit well with either the Aristotelian or the Stoic picture, albeit for different reasons in each case, though of the two, the Aristotelian is the more congenial. In sum, one would need to make sense of the idea of responsive agency, of the ability to direct one's life on the basis of a firm sense of who one is, while having—and exhibiting—dependency on others (e.g., by desiring their esteem).

That is obviously a large task, and I shall move to conclude this much more limited effort by attempting to be a bit more precise about how this task might unfold in the present case. Vengeful anger's insistence that the offender be made to know both the reason for and the agent of the revenge testifies to our interdependence, to our character as social beings, and to the fact that others *matter* to us. How is that dependency compatible with strong self-esteem and lack of concern about social standing? This is one of the deepest issues raised by this analysis, and I do not pretend to have resolved it here. The challenge is to explain how the wrong can be taken personally such that the victim may wish to be the instrument of revenge and wish that the offender know who is taking revenge and why, without the victim's self-esteem or concern for social standing or honor being at stake. At the same time, v-anger does not simply consist in the wish that justice be done (by someone). Perhaps an example will help move the discussion forward.

Imagine the case of a betrayal by a partner you had thought of as committed to you (and vice versa) for life. Given the large amount of time, the effort, trust, intimacy, and importance with which you have endowed the relationship (perhaps expressed through the allocation not just of love but of economic resources as well), the betrayal certainly matters greatly to you and likely elicits your v-anger, but not necessarily because of any weak self-esteem on your part. You do not react angrily because some great honor has been denied you or because your self-esteem or sense of social standing is damaged. Rather, something essential of who you are, your identity over time, is contained in this long-term relationship, and its brutal disruption through betrayal is a harm to you. V-anger acknowledges the importance of the relationship by wanting to force—through the imposition of pain and suffering—the other to acknowledge and respect you, as well as the role each of you has played in the other's life. It is also the expression of self-respect, not an attempt to maintain one's standing to claim it, let alone to maintain social standing. Something analogous could be said in cases in which one is assaulted by a complete stranger, for relations of mutual respect as fellow citizens or as fellow human beings are also profound and "thick" in their own ways.[62]

The list of human attachments that are enmeshed with our identities is long. To extirpate vengeful anger surely violates the wide- as well as the deep-concerns criteria, as it suggests that we would have to transform our identities such that others do not matter to us very much (which is the implication of what Seneca is saying). It would also violate what I would argue is a defensible, non-Senecan ethical ideal built on stable self-esteem but committed to ethical excellence in our relations—affectively felt and expressed as appropriate—to others and to ourselves. Fittingness in our second sense should, it seems, be regulated by fittingness in the third sense (I leave open the possibility that, in turn, the third should in some way be conditioned by the second). All this suggests, just as many have said, that the Stoic ideal—and with it, the condemnation of anger—is not acceptable. At the same time, as I have argued, the unstable role of self-esteem in Aristotle's ethical version of the *megalopsuchos* requires revision of Aristotle's view, even though that view has the merit of preserving a place for anger in the virtuous life.

SECTION FIVE: TAKING REVENGE

> Two vices are opposed to vengeance: one by way of excess, namely, the sin of cruelty or brutality, which exceeds the measure in punishing: while the other is a vice by way of deficiency and consists in being remiss in punishing. . . . But the virtue of vengeance consists in observing the due measure of vengeance with regard to all the circumstances.
>
> St. Thomas Aquinas, *Summa Theologica*[63]

The justifiability of taking revenge does not follow simply from the justifiability of vengeful anger. Let us limit ourselves here to cases in which the wrong would normally be subject to the state's authority, while acknowledging that there exists a spectrum of vengeful actions that do not normally fall under jurisprudential or police purview (as when one takes revenge in an interpersonal context by withholding love). To take personal revenge in the sorts of cases at issue here is to take the law into one's own hands. If that is to be done justifiably, a number of considerations must be brought to bear. To begin with, if justified revenge-taking expresses v-anger, such that its merits reflect those of the anger from which it springs, then the latter, too, must be justifiable in the ways already described. Further, taking personal revenge is justifiable only if considerations that to considerable extent parallel those mentioned in section four with respect to v-anger are satisfied: the alleged wrong must really be such, the target of revenge must in fact be the offender, the revenge must be proportional to the offense, the offender must deserve punishment, and the revenge must not be the instrument of sadism or cruelty.[64] And one would have to carefully consider the psychological costs to oneself quite possibly involved in actually making another human being suffer or in taking a human life (this roughly parallels the fifth condition enumerated toward the start of section four).

However, taking revenge is also answerable to a host of other considerations that are not pertinent when evaluating the merits of vengeful anger. One certainly has to justify not deferring to the given judicial system. If the system is working reasonably well and fairly, what could warrant one's taking revenge as one sees fit? That question must be answered impartially before revenge is taken. If it is the case that the system is corrupt or simply does not exist, then one first has to assess the feasibility of alternate routes of action, such as taking steps to get a judicial system up and running. I would argue that those routes would have to be shown to be out of reach or not timely given the circumstances to justify one's taking revenge. One also has to satisfy legitimate demands for impartiality and proportionality across cases, so that the law one has taken into one's own hands preserves relevant features of *law*. Such considerations are motivated not only by the demands of fairness but also by the famous problem of spiraling tit-for-tat violence that revenge-taking can instigate. And, of course, one has to assess the physical dangers to oneself involved in taking revenge. I venture the suggestion that in view of the problems of social coordination (to which a judicial system should respond), the chaos that results when people take the law into their own hands, and the other considerations just mentioned, the case against taking revenge is overwhelming even if defeasible, though much depends on the empirical circumstances at the relevant time.

In sum, the virtuous person will feel vengeful anger as appropriate but will take revenge only after careful deliberation and in view of the additional considerations and conditions just sketched. This leaves us with what I referred to at the start of this chapter as a surprising distinction—in some cases, collision—between justifications for vengefulness and justifications for taking revenge. For if my vengeful anger is justified, then it seems that the wrongdoer deserves to be punished at my hands (and to know that that is the case and why)—this is his or her just desert that only my acting can provide—and yet good reasons of a different order may proscribe my acting, such that the offender must be deprived of this just desert. When reason forbids the revenge to which I am entitled, regret and even angry disappointment may well follow. The potential here for tragic moral conflict is undeniable.[65]

NOTES

1. I am grateful to Julia Annas, Jeffrey Blustein, Richard Carrington, Roger Crisp, Remy Debes, Zina Giannopoulou, Peter Goldie, Trudy Govier, Stephen Griswold, Jeffrey Henderson, P. J. Ivanhoe, Simon Keller, Erin Kelly, David Konstan, Annice Kra, Josh Landy, Mitchell Miller (to whom I am especially indebted for discussion about my last paragraph, as well as some of the phrasing thereof), David Roochnik, Amelie Rorty, Steve Scully, Jeffrey Seidman, Nick Smith, Daniel Star, and John Tomasi for discussion about and comments on this essay. I also thank Kelsie Krueger for her work in assembling secondary sources and David Jennings for his careful proofreading. Drafts of this essay were presented at the American Philosophical Association (2009 Eastern Division Meeting), as part of an invited panel on "Transitional Justice, Reconciliation, Identity, and Memory," and at Boston College (as an A. J. Fitzgibbons Lecture), Brown University, Davidson College, the University of Memphis, the University of New Hampshire, and Vassar College. I am indebted to these various audiences for their questions and comments. I gratefully acknowledge fellowships from the American Council of Learned Societies and the Boston University Humanities Foundation that supported my research during the 2009–10 academic year, and a Fellowship Research Grant from the Earhart Foundation that supported my work during the summer of 2010. I dedicate this essay to the late Peter Goldie with deep gratitude for his friendship. This essay was first published in Nomos LIII: Passions and Emotions, ed. J. E. Fleming (New York: New York University Press, 2013): 77–124, and is reprinted here with the kind permission of New York University Press (for purposes of this reprint, bibliographical information in footnote 13 and several minor stylistic changes were introduced; in addition, NYU Press' editorial conventions were replaced by those of Lexington Books, and the epigraph to section one was replaced with a reference in footnote 15). I thank Valerie Williams, Getty Lustila, and Femke Hermse for their help in preparing an earlier reprint of this piece (in *Recht und Emotion II: Sphären der Verletzlichkeit*, ed. H. Landweer and F. Bernhardt (Freiburg: Karl Alber, 2017), pp. 145–95), and Cansu Hepcaglayan for help in preparing this reprint.

Friedrich Nietzsche, *Thus Spoke Zarathustra* (1976, 206). Excerpt from *The Portable Nietzsche* by Friedrich Nietzsche, translated and edited by Walter Kaufmann, copyright © 1954, 1968. Copyright renewed 1982 by Penguin Random House LLC. Used by permission of Viking Books, an imprint of Penguin Publishing Group, a division of Penguin Random House LLC. All rights reserved.

2. The *mênis* referred to at the start of the *Iliad* is, of course, that of Achilles. Homer's vocabulary for "anger" is complex, and "mênis" (also translatable as "wrath") is but one term that he uses. There may be several types or shapes of anger described in the *Iliad*. For discussion, see Konstan (2006, 48–56).

3. I am relying on the reports published by CNN, February 27, 2009, http://www.cnn.com/2009/CRIME/02/27/wiesel.madoff/index.html, and by the *New York Times*, February 26, 2009, http://www.nytimes.com/2009/02/27/business/27madoff.html (the latter states that Wiesel and his wife "lost their life savings" as a result of Madoff). On the judicial sentence imposed on Madoff, see the *New York Times* report of June 29, 2009, http://www.nytimes.com/2009/06/30/business/30madoff.html?pagewanted=1&ref=bernardlmadoff. That report contains quotations from other of Madoff's victims.

4. For example, C. S. Lewis (1967) remarks: "The least indulgence of the passion for revenge is very deadly sin. Christian charity counsels us to make every effort for the conversion of such a man: to prefer his conversion, at the peril of our own lives, perhaps of our own souls, to his punishment; to prefer it infinitely" (109). See also Govier (2002, 11–13); and in a historical vein, Frank (1990, 269–281).

5. For an account of the events referred to, see Kraybill et al. (2007). For a popular case (billed as a "National Bestseller") against anger, see Hanh (2002).

6. I am using Irwin's (1999) translation throughout: *Aristotle: Nicomachean Ethics* (hereinafter *NE*), 2nd ed.

7. On criticisms of the Amish's response to the murder of their children, see Kraybill et al. (2007, 57).

8. See *The Works of Joseph Butler, D.C. L.* (1896); vol. II, Sermon VIII ("Upon Resentment"), 136–149, and Sermon IX ("Upon Forgiveness of Injuries") (150–167). My citations and quotations from Butler are from this edition of these sermons. The consequentialist argument just referred to is to be found in "Upon Resentment," 139–143 (the idea is basically that God gave us that emotion for the purpose of the prevention or remedy of injury). I note that Butler uses the term "resentment" as synonymous with "deliberate anger" (e.g., 140), the meaning of which overlaps closely with what I am calling vengeful anger. A similar appeal to the utility of anger or resentment is found in Shaftesbury's *An Inquiry Concerning Virtue or Merit*, in *Characteristicks of Men, Manners, Opinions, Times* (2001), 2: 83–85. However, Shaftesbury also offers stringent criticisms of anger in those pages. I offer commentary on Butler's two sermons, and some discussion of resentment more generally, in my *Forgiveness: A Philosophical Exploration* (2007). The present chapter builds on—and, I hope, complements—*Forgiveness.*

9. On cultural norms favoring or even requiring revenge, see Elster (1992, 163–165).

10. For an analogous effort, see Kristjánsson (2002). However, he grounds his views about the morality of these emotions in what he calls "a sophisticated form of utilitarianism" (5). For an argument in defense of envy, see D'Arms and Jacobson (2006, 119–125). See also Murphy's instructive "Two Cheers for Vindictiveness," ch. 2 of his *Getting Even: Forgiveness and its Limits* (2003, 17–26).

11. My focus is thus substantially different from that of Barton (1999), *Getting Even: Revenge as a Form of Justice*. He writes: "The central claim [of his book] is that victim justice, to be worthy of that name, requires the substantial empowerment of victims by law, giving them the legal right to become involved in the relevant legal processes, some of which may culminate in impositions of punishment on their

wrongdoers." He is out to vindicate "revenge's undeservedly poor image" (see xiv for both quotations), whereas I am primarily out to consider the ethical merits of vengeful anger.

12. This definition seems broad enough to handle the case of someone who undertakes vengeful plotting over time, only sometimes experiencing the "hot'" emotion. For further discussion of the cognitive nature of the emotions, see Debes (2009, 1–27). I shall not be talking about vengeful anger as a "mood," both because that seems out of keeping with common parlance and so as to sidestep the complicated question as to the relation between moods and emotions (about which see Goldie 2002, 143–151).

13. Some theorists distinguish between sentiments and emotions. For example, see Ben-Ze'ev (2000, 83), as well as Prinz (2013, 10)—he there glosses sentiments as "dispositions to feel emotions."

14. Prinz (2004) remarks "Intuitions derive from reflecting on our concepts (hence 'conceptual analysis'), and concepts may contain information that is false or misleading" (29). After enumerating other dangers, he continues: "These concerns threaten traditional philosophical methods quite broadly. Anyone who hopes to make progress by reflection alone should be wary. Reflection may reveal more about the person reflecting than about the phenomenon on which she is reflecting. If one wants to explain something other than one's own personal beliefs, one should exploit more objective methods" (ibid.). I have perhaps not exploited those methods sufficiently but have nonetheless tried to cultivate the requisite wariness.

15. For a striking expression of this famous and complex passion, see Euripides' *Medea* lines 1354–1360, in *Euripides I* (1975, 105).

16. See Braund and Most (2003), Kaster (2005), Harris (2001), Knuuttila (2004), and especially Konstan (2006), chapter 2 (on anger).

17. Ben-Ze'ev (2000) notes: "Hate may be characterized as involving a global negative attitude toward someone considered to possess fundamentally evil traits. . . . Anger is similar to hate and disgust in involving a negative evaluation, but it is the evaluation of a specific action rather than a global attitude" (380). He also remarks: "Hate is a long-term attitude whose generation is frequently not triggered by a personal offense. Hate requires an evaluation of the object as possessing inherently dangerous traits; the object of anger is guilty of merely instrumental negative actions" (381). At *Rhetoric* 2.4 (1382a2–7), Aristotle too notes that anger is directed at individuals, whereas hatred may also be concerned with classes thereof (say, all thieves). He adds that anger but not hatred is curable in time and that, while anger wants revenge, hatred aims for the extirpation of its object.

18. My approach differs from that of Uniacke (2000), who claims that, unlike vengeance, "revenge can be taken for an injury that is not an offence nor regarded as such by the person taking revenge. We can believe ourselves to have been injured, and resent the injury, without regarding ourselves as wronged." Her examples include resenting "someone's beating me in what I accept was fair competition." Further: "The emotion that gives rise to the desire for revenge is resentment: bitter feelings about an injury sustained. The emotion appropriate to vengeance is moral indignation: anger excited by perceived meanness, injustice, wickedness, or misconduct"

(62-63). That seems implausible. We might jokingly call beating our tennis partner next time around "revenge," but, if it were really such or if the effort really were accompanied by resentment, we would judge it (and the accompanying emotion) inappropriate precisely because no moral wrong is being responded to. So I am also disagreeing with Wallace (1995), who urges that we distinguish "between vindictive and non-vindictive revenge. Shylock exemplifies the pursuit of the former, our squash victor achieves the latter. It must be stressed that in both cases it is correct to talk of revenge; it is neither flowery nor metaphorical to suggest that the squash player gains his revenge" (372). This leads Wallace to such counterintuitive statements as: "Revenge can be sought without malice and without endangering friendship" (373). (I am grateful to Roger Crisp for discussion of the possibility of nonmoralized vengeful anger.)

19. I am using Kennedy's translation of Aristotle's *Rhetoric* (1991) throughout.

20. The relation between intention and responsibility (not to mention the related idea of "taking responsibility") is, of course, complex. There may be a spectrum of cases in which one has warranted v-anger at someone who has not intentionally done wrong but is responsible (or culpable) for the wrong.

21. See P. F. Strawson (1980). Strawson speaks of "*reactive* attitudes and feelings" (6) rather than sentiments, but in the present instance this seems to be a semantic point, especially given his concluding comment: "It is a pity that talk of the moral sentiments has fallen out of favour" (24). Strawson also refers to reactive attitudes such as resentment and forgiveness as "essentially reactions to the quality of others' wills towards us, as manifested in their behaviour: to their good or ill will or indifference or lack of concern. Thus resentment, or what I have called resentment, is a reaction to injury or indifference" (14). This is in line with my argument.

22. In this I am in agreement with Stainton (2006). He there adds to the condition that an agent taking revenge must intend to do so and have reasons, that the "agent must also have the concept REVENGE" (15).

23. What Prinz says of Aristotle's theory of the emotions generally fits v-anger nicely: "Emotions are, thus, felt, action-directed, cognitive states of the body." *Gut Reactions*, 11. In characterizing Aristotle's theory, Prinz notes that it is a hybrid—a behavioral, a cognitive, as well as a feeling theory. Ibid., 10–11. This much seems to be consistent with the characterization of "emotion" by Goldie quoted at the start of this chapter.

24. Anscombe (1969) there notes: "I will call revenge and gratitude and remorse and pity backward-looking motives, and contrast them with motive-in-general," for they give "something that *has happened* (or is at present happening) . . . as the ground of an action or abstention that is good or bad for the person (it may be oneself, as with remorse) at whom it is aimed." Further on, she remarks: "I call a motive forward-looking if it is an intention" (21). Anscombe refers in these pages to revenge, not vengeful anger, but her point applies to both.

25. I agree with Prinz's (2004) observation that anger tends to focus on the person who, say, uttered the offensive words, rather than on the words: "Insults instigate anger, but anger latches onto the insulter" (227).

26. On the debate about whether emotions are perceptions, see Prinz (2004), chapter 10. He there concludes that "emotion is a form of perception" (240).

27. I am using Adam Smith (1982), *The Theory of Moral Sentiments* (hereinafter *TMS*), ed. Raphael and Macfie throughout. Interestingly, the famous *Lex Talionis* (*Exodus* 21:24) may be interpreted as an effort to *restrain* the otherwise spiraling ambitions of revenge-taking, as is suggested by Frijda (1994, 264).

28. As Aristotle notes in *De Anima*, 403a30–31.

29. Does the legitimacy of vengeful anger therefore depend on a retributivist theory of punishment? The answer may well be affirmative, though the line from a theory of the moral emotions to the theory of punishment is not direct and, in any event, is not my topic here.

30. Of course, not all retribution is revenge or vengeful; judicially administered punishment might be thought of as retributive in some sense but not necessarily as revenge or vengeful. Retribution may thus be impersonal, whereas revenge is personal, as Nozick (1981) argues in *Philosophical Explanations* (367).

31. I refer to the fine article by Bar-Elli and Heyd, "Can Revenge Be Just or Otherwise Justified?" (1986, 71–72). As they put it: "Furthermore, for the act of revenge to be fully successful, it must be understood by its recipient as intentional. This feature of 'double intentionality' is very significant for the understanding of the nature of revenge. It highlights the *personal* dimension which is its most important, though theoretically disturbing, trait" (71). Several of the points I am making in this paragraph are elegantly stated by Adam Smith (*TMS* II.i.1.6): "If the person who had done us some great injury, who had murdered our father or our brother, for example, should soon afterward die of a fever, or even be brought to the scaffold upon account of some other crime, though it might sooth our hatred, it would not fully gratify our resentment. Resentment would prompt us to desire, not only that he should be punished, but that he should be punished by our means, and upon account of that particular injury which he had done to us. Resentment cannot be fully gratified, unless the offender is not only made to grieve in his turn, but to grieve for that particular wrong which we have suffered from him. For a brilliant argument to the effect that Smith is ambivalent about the emotion of resentment (vacillating between a view tied to an ethic of honor and retaliation and one tied to an ethic of equal dignity and mutual accountability), see Darwall (2010, 106–123). I am indebted to Darwall's discussion of Smith and of resentment in that article as well as in his (2006) *The Second-Person Standpoint: Morality, Respect, and Accountability* (see especially pages 67–68 and 80–86 of *The Second-Person Standpoint* on resentment, indignation, and retaliation).

32. Nozick (1981) too sees revenge (and in a different way, retribution, which is his main focus in this respect) as having a communicative function (370). P. J. Ivanhoe has suggested to me that perhaps the communicative character of revenge should be stated more broadly: it informs others that it is wrong to treat *anybody* in the way that I was treated and so is a protest registered on behalf of other victims (even potential ones). Moreover, revenge can also publicly mark the offender as untrustworthy. I have not foregrounded these possible functions of revenge-taking because I am avoiding reference to social utility as the basis for explaining and defending

v-anger. A more Socratic line would emphasize that punishment aims to *cure* the wrongdoer (see *Gorgias* 478e2–4, 480a6–b5).

33. Nozick (1981) notes: "Revenge involves a particular emotional tone, pleasure in the suffering of another, while retribution either need involve no emotional tone, or involves another one, namely, pleasure at justice being done. Therefore, the thirster after revenge often will want to experience (see, be present at) the situation in which the revengee is suffering, whereas with retribution there is no special point in witnessing its infliction" (367). I add that interpreters tend to assume that the pleasures of imagining and plotting revenge carry over to the act of taking revenge itself; but different hedonic, as well as moral, valences may attach to each.

34. Indeed, Bar-Elli and Heyd (1986) conclude that "the metaphors of balancing, restoration, and equality are misleading when used in this context [of revenge]. They are already hard enough to apply on the 'material' level of penal justice. However, they seem totally paradoxical when extended to the 'mental' level of personal attitudes, which are not controllable by penal intervention and are partly a matter of the individual's free choice" (84).

35. See Haidt (2003, 856). With respect to Aristotle's point in the *Rhetoric* 2.2 (1378b1–2) that anger is accompanied by the (pleasurable) expectation of revenge, Haidt remarks: "More recent studies confirm that anger generally involves a motivation to attack, humiliate, or otherwise get back at the person who is perceived as acting unfairly or immorally . . . . The fact that anger often involves a motivation for revenge has been noted in a great many cultures" (ibid., 856).

36. Uniacke (2000) comments: "While the desire for revenge seems principally grounded in notions of self-esteem and reputation, there are significant exceptions" (66). The sorts of exceptions she cites, however, are about (in my terminology) retaliation or even, as she notes, a desire to make sense of a tragedy that has befallen a loved one by "blaming someone, however unreasonably" (ibid., 67). Hampton (1988) usefully distinguishes an action that has the effect of diminishing one's value and rank from one that has "*revealed* a rank that is lower" than one had thought (50). In describing the resentment a victim feels in response to wrongdoing, she credits it with the "fear" that one's worth can be lowered or has been revealed to be lower than one thought (ibid., 57). Hence resentment is "a personally defensive protest," meaning among things that it is "a defense against the action's attack on one's self-esteem" (ibid., 56, phrase in the second quotation italicized in the original). Hampton also notes: "Resentment is nonetheless an emotion which betrays weakness. Resenters mount a defense against a challenge to their value and rank to which they are in danger of succumbing" (ibid., 148). As I understand the argument, this protest or defense is retributive in character (e.g., see ibid., 142–143). In the terms I am adopting, Hampton roots resentment, that is, vengeful anger, at least in part in low (or lowered) self-esteem and thus brings it close to Nietzschean *ressentiment*, as Murphy implies (ibid., 93).

37. See Horowitz (2007, 25), Frijda (1994, 276–277), and Averill (1982, 173–174). As Averill notes, the relationship between low self-esteem and anger is complex, since "persons with very low self-esteem may perceive a threat as justified (e.g., as congruent with their own self-image)" and *not* respond with anger (ibid.,

174). He there continues: "At the other extreme, persons with high self-esteem are less likely than others to perceive as threatening minor slights or rebuffs." Lazarus (1991) writes that anger has several "*primary appraisal* components," the third of which is introduced as follows: "The basic motive to preserve or enhance self-esteem against assault, which is one *type of ego-involvement*, must also be activated for anger to occur" (222). The close tie between vengeful anger and self-esteem is also drawn by Fisher (2002): "The excitations of anger mark out the places where self-worth or honor has been transgressed"; and "A measure of self-esteem, or of endangered self-regard, is defended with the energies of anger that locate and announce that injustice has been felt and must be revenged" (176-177). See also Fisher (ibid.) 184–194.

38. I agree with the definition of self-esteem in Deigh (1983): "So while we would have said, loosely speaking, that self-esteem came from one's having a good opinion of oneself, we may now say more strictly that it comes from a good opinion of oneself as the author of one's actions, more generally, one's life. Accordingly, this opinion comprises a favorable regard for one's aims and ideals in life and a favorable assessment of one's suitability for pursuing them" (229). I am not here concerned with the interesting problem of the relation between self-esteem and self-respect, about which see Darwall (1977, 48) and Sachs (1981).

39. See Nietzsche (1998), First Treatise, Section 10, p. 19: "The slave revolt in morality begins when *ressentiment* itself becomes creative and gives birth to values: the *ressentiment* of beings denied the true reaction, that of the deed, who recover their losses only through an imaginary revenge. Whereas all noble morality grows out of a triumphant yes–saying to oneself, from the outset slave morality says 'no' to an 'outside', to a 'different', to a 'not-self': and *this* 'no' is its creative deed." Nietzsche's "noble human being" (ibid., 21) bears an interesting family resemblance to Aristotle's *megalopsuchos*, though the latter does permit himself vengeful anger (but not *ressentiment*). There can be no hitting of the Aristotelian mean with respect to *ressentiment*, and I will not be making the case that *ressentiment* could be justifiable.

40. Once again, consider Frijda (1994), who comments on the propensity to cruelty, including that associated with revenge: "Need for proof of power or self-efficacy at this level has a ring of need for proof of a sense of self—again, as the counterpoint of being a victim." "The Lex Talionis," 281.

41. *De Ira*, in *Seneca: Moral and Political Essays*, edited and translated by J. M. Cooper and J. F. Procopé (Cambridge: Cambridge University Press, 2003), p. 116. © Cambridge University Press 1995. Reproduced with permission of The Licensor through PLSclear. I am using this edition and translation of *De Ira* throughout and have incorporated the page references directly into the text. I am not drawing here on any other of Seneca's writings.

42. Kraut (2002) notes: "Unfortunately, he [Aristotle] finds it so obvious that anger should sometimes be felt and expressed that he does not argue against a hypothetical opponent who advocates its elimination. The latter view was adopted by the Stoics; see esp. Seneca, *De Ira*" (334 n. 23).

43. D'Arms and Jacobson remark in "Anthropocentric Constraints on Human Value": "Reasons of fit are those reasons that speak directly to what one takes the emotion to be concerned with, as opposed to reasons that speak to the advisability or

propriety of having that emotion. So reasons of fit for fear are roughly those that speak to whether or not something is a *threat*" (2006, 108). This seems tolerably close to the first conception of "the fitting" I am sketching here.

44. Konstan (2006) comments: "Anger for Aristotle, then, is anything but a reflex to pain or harm, even when the cause is intentional. Aristotle envisages a world in which self-esteem depends on social interaction: the moment someone's negative opinion of your worth is actualized publicly in the form of a slight, you have lost credit, and the only recourse is a compensatory act that restores your social position. Anger is precisely the desire to adjust the record in this way" (74–75).

45. See Aristotle (1995), I:161.

46. For some helpful discussion of pride, self-respect, and self-esteem with reference to the *megalopsuchos*, see Kristjánsson (2002, 95–97, 104–108). With regard to the relation between gender and (the acceptability of) v-anger, an issue that has much to do with the perceived "standing" to be angry, see Frye (1983, 84–94), Spelman (1989, 263–273), and Lorde (1984, 124–133).

47. D'Arms and Jacobson (2006) helpfully distinguish between two sorts of considerations bearing on the question of the cost of a revisionist moral view. The first has to do with our "deep concerns," ones that "are firmly entrenched in their possessors, such that it would be either impossible or extremely costly to excise them." The second has to do with our "wide concerns." These "play a broad psychological role in the mental economy of their possessor. When the object of a concern prompts a variety of evaluative attitudes, not just a single emotion or desire; when desire for it (or aversion to it) arises in many different situations; when it is implicated in the ability to get or avoid many other things people care about; when its pursuit or avoidance grounds disparate actions and plans; when, in short, it is firmly enmeshed in our web of psychological responses, this is evidence of the width of a concern" (116). As an example of a wide concern they cite anger, and in disagreement with the "stoic and Christian foes of anger" they note: "Yet anger is not just a passion for vengeance. It also manifests concern for social regulation, which focuses on personal slights and social transgressions" (ibid., 117). They immediately concede that one could have concern for respectful treatment independently of anger, however, which is a bit confusing (and provides Seneca with an opening). The more general claim is "that psychological facts constrain the tenability of norms of fittingness. . . . Rationalists can point to a sublime Socratic ideal of a person so self-sufficient in his virtue that he does [*sic*] care about honor, wealth, or even life; or to an impartial observer whose only concern is to maximize net happiness. If nothing matters but the state of one's soul, and no harm can befall the virtuous person, then there is truly nothing to fear" (ibid., 118). They also remark: "But why should the fact that the stoic has been able to describe a logically possible human being who can embrace these consequences be thought to show that they are suitable standards of fittingness for humans?" (ibid.). I am in sympathy with both these more general points, as will become clearer in section four.

48. Seneca takes this all the way at 1.12.1: "'Tell me then, is the good man not angry if he sees his father slain and his mother ravished?' No, he will not be angry. He will punish and protect." Consider also 1.12.5: "Anger for one's friends is the

mark of a weak mind, not a devoted one." So we are not to rise to indignant anger or sympathetic resentment, either. This seems quite close to the conclusion drawn by the Amish (though no doubt they do so on somewhat different grounds).

49. He thus would not seem to succumb to what D'Arms and Jacobson call the "moralistic fallacy." See D'Arms and Jacobson (2000, 66); they there use the example of the joke. They remark: "Put most simply, to commit the moralistic fallacy is to infer, from the claim that it would be wrong or vicious to feel an emotion, that it is therefore unfitting. We shall contend, to the contrary, that an emotion can be fitting despite being wrong (or inexpedient) to feel" (ibid., 68–69). Their definition here of "fitting" as a match-up between emotion and features in the world it takes itself to be responding to (ibid., 72) captures my first sense of "fitting."

50. For an interesting discussion of the Epicurean condemnation of anger, see Annas (1993, 194–200). Her remarks on 218–219 about the importance of the conception of our final end to the assessment of the propriety of anger mesh perfectly with my argument.

51. As Seneca indicates in *De Ira* 2.3.4, the emotion of anger (as distinct from the "impression" that sets it going) has already enlisted (faulty) reason on its side. So, once we are angry, reason cannot stand *against* the anger; it is already working on behalf of the anger (e.g., by rationalizing revenge-taking or exaggerating the harm done to the victim). And that underlines the danger of anger—its toxicity—and the impossibility of moderating it to the point that it expresses moral excellence. (My thanks to Julia Annas for pressing this point on me.) The mitigated defense of anger I am working toward in this chapter would require rejecting this Stoic theory of the emotions.

52. This may be contested on the grounds that it suffices for the agent to have good reasons for believing that his or her v-anger tracks what is in fact the case (so that the agent's course of action is subjectively right, even if it is objectively wrong). While this is too large an issue to be further explored here, my broadly Aristotelian approach (for Aristotle, the virtues depend on *phronesis*, and reason or judgment tracks truth; for example, *NE* 1140b5, 21) avoids the counterintuitive result that it would be virtuous to feel v-anger that is mistakenly directed at the innocent, for example. A full assessment of the matter would have to take into account whether or not the mistake is culpable. (I am grateful to Daniel Star for pressing me to confront this point.)

53. The steps I would argue for are to be found in my *Forgiveness*, chapter 2.

54. One question to be addressed in working out this point is whether a "unity of the virtues" thesis is being assumed.

55. For a similar point, see Taylor (1975, 397–402). My list is compatible with—and to some extent overlaps with—hers (see 394–397). As she rightly notes: "Justifying one's anger on any particular occasion is, then, a complicated procedure" (397).

56. See note 47.

57. See the passages cited in note 47 from D'Arms and Jacobson, "Anthropocentric Constraints on Human Value." I read their comments about anger as applying to vengefulness.

58. Aristotle continues at 1328a8–12: "But it is not right to say that they are harsh toward those who are unknown. One ought not to be of this sort toward anyone, nor are magnanimous persons [*megalopsuchoi*] savage in their nature, except toward those behaving unjustly. And, further, they will feel this rather toward their intimates, as was said earlier, if they consider themselves treated unjustly" (ibid.).

59. I refer to Fisher's gloss on these *Politics* passages: "Aristotle's seemingly odd claim can be restated as an argument that the sudden anger we feel driving us to retaliate also informs us of two things: first, that we have been held in contempt; second, that the person who has slighted us matters to us. The flaring up of anger informs us about how much we care for this person's regard, and how injured we are by any sign of contempt on his or her part" (2002, 192).

60. One of the greatest modern reflections on the problem of reconciling interdependence, anger, and strong self-esteem is to be found in Rousseau's *Emile* (the epigraph to which is taken from *De Ira*). The present chapter will be developed further in conjunction with a study of Rousseau and Adam Smith.

61. Correspondingly, one would have to grant that the offense does not dehumanize the offender or make him or her into a "moral monster." Aristotle's view seems to be that many offenders are simply not worth one's anger—they do not have the standing to warrant it. And while Seneca emphasizes our common humanity, in comparing the offender to a natural event, child, or illness—with the result that the wrongdoer is not worthy of one's anger—his view risks dehumanizing the offender. By contrast, the view I am pointing to holds that the wrongs to which v-anger responds are the work of agents who *qua* agents have the standing to be addressed by this emotion, as it were. That helps to explain why equality of regard (and therefore the offender's regard of the victim) matters. The idea of second-personal address is worked out systematically in Darwall's *The Second-Person Standpoint* (2006).

62. V-anger holds the wrongdoer accountable and thus is also mobilized for the sake of that other, as it seeks to get him or her to see what it means both for you to have been wronged and that you are not to be wronged. In holding the offender accountable, one stands in for his or her better self (this is not incompatible with desert, even when the offender deserves death). This thread of the justification for v-anger preserves its communicative function and might be all the more relevant if the other has mattered greatly to you.

63. Aquinas (1922), 2:69 (Q. 108 Art. 2, reply to Objection 3).

64. This list overlaps to some extent with that of French (2001), who posits four conditions for defensible revenge-taking (115). But French's analysis is not only focused on revenge-taking rather than on the emotion of vengefulness; on his view, revenge may justly be taken on behalf of another (hence he speaks throughout of avenging; see, for example, ibid., 172).

65. This is not to say, however, that the virtuous person's v-anger is therefore turned into Nietzschean *ressentiment* (such that v-anger is *repressed*) when revenge ought not be taken. Self-command and repression, the reasoned decision not to act on a sentiment and the inability to act on it, are quite different things. The view being sketched here would have to be joined to an appropriate conception of agency such

that *not* acting on warranted v-anger does not compromise agency. John Tomasi suggests to me that a conception of political agency (which reflects one's status as citizen) might help to resolve the tension here.

REFERENCE LIST

Annas, Julia. 1993. *The Morality of Happiness*. Oxford: Oxford University Press.

Anscombe, G. E. M. 1969. *Intention*. Ithaca: Cornell University Press.

Aquinas, Thomas. 1922. *Summa Theologica*. Translated by Fathers of the English Dominican Province. New York: Benziger Brothers.

Aristotle. 1985. *Aristotle: The Politics*. Translated by C. Lord. Chicago: University of Chicago Press.

———. 1991. *On Rhetoric: A Theory of Civic Discourse*. Translated with Introduction, Notes, and Appendices by G. A. Kennedy. Oxford: Oxford University Press.

———. 1995. "Posterior Analytics." In *Vol. I of The Complete Works of Aristotle (Revised Oxford Translation)*, edited and translated by Jonathan Barnes. Princeton, NJ: Princeton University Press.

———. 1999. *Aristotle: Nicomachean Ethics*, 2nd edition. Translated by Terence Irwin. Indianapolis: Hackett.

Averill, J. R. 1982. *Anger and Aggression: An Essay on Emotion*. New York: Springer-Verlag.

Bar-Elli, Gilead, and David Heyd. 1986. "Can Revenge Be Just or Otherwise Justified?" *Theoria* 52, no. 1–2: 58–86.

Barton, Charles K. B. 1999. *Getting Even: Revenge as a Form of Justice*. Chicago: Open Court.

Ben-Ze'ev, Aaron. 2000. *The Subtlety of Emotions*. Cambridge, MA: MIT Press.

Braund, Susanna, and Glenn W. Most, eds. 2003. *Ancient Anger: Perspectives from Homer to Galen*. Cambridge: Cambridge University Press.

Butler, Joseph. 1896. *The Works of Joseph Butler, D.C. L.*, 2 vols. Edited by William E. Gladstone. Oxford: Clarendon Press.

D'Arms, Justin, and Daniel Jacobson. 2000. "The Moralistic Fallacy: On the 'Appropriateness' of Emotions." *Philosophy and Phenomenological Research* 61, no. 1: 65–90.

———. 2006. "Anthropocentric Constraints on Human Value." *Oxford Studies in Metaethics* 1: 99–126.

Darwall, Stephen. 1977. "Two Kinds of Respect." *Ethics* 88, no. 1: 36–49.

———. 2006. *The Second-Person Standpoint: Morality, Respect, and Accountability*. Cambridge, MA: Harvard University Press.

———. 2010. "Smith's Ambivalence about Honour." *Adam Smith Review* 5: 106–123.

Debes, Remy. 2009. "Neither Here nor There: The Cognitive Nature of Emotion." *Philosophical Studies* 146: 1–27.

Deigh, John. 1983. "Shame and Self-Esteem: A Critique." *Ethics* 93: 225–245.

Elster, Jon. 1992. "Norms of Revenge." In *Ethics and Personality: Essays on Moral Psychology*, edited by John Deigh, 155–178. Chicago: University of Chicago Press.

Euripides. 1975. *Medea*, in *Euripides I*. Translated by R. Warner, with an Introduction to the volume by R. Lattimore. In *The Complete Greek Tragedies*, edited by David Grene and R. Lattimore. Chicago: University of Chicago Press.

Fisher, Philip. 2002. *The Vehement Passions*. Princeton: Princeton University Press.

Frank, Daniel H. 1990. "Anger as a Vice: A Maimonidean Critique of Aristotle's Ethics." *History of Philosophy Quarterly* 7: 269–281.

French, Peter. 2001. *The Virtues of Vengeance*. Lawrence: University Press of Kansas.

Frijda, Nico H. 1994. "The Lex Talionis: On Vengeance." In *Emotions: Essays on Emotion Theory*, edited by Stephanie H. M. van Goozen, Nanne E. van de Poll, and Joseph A. Sergeant, 263–289. Hillsdale, NJ: Lawrence Erlbaum.

Frye, Marilyn. 1983. "A Note on Anger." In *The Politics of Reality: Essays in Feminist Theory*, 84–94. Freedom, CA: Crossing Press.

Goldie, Peter. 2002. *The Emotions: A Philosophical Exploration*. Oxford: Oxford University Press.

Govier, Trudy. 2002. *Forgiveness and Revenge*. London: Routledge.

Griswold, Charles L. 2007. *Forgiveness: A Philosophical Exploration*. Cambridge: Cambridge University Press.

Haidt, Jonathan. 2003. "The Moral Emotions." In *Handbook of Affective Sciences*, edited by R. J. Davidson, K. R. Scherer, and H. H. Goldsmith, 852–870. Oxford: Oxford University Press.

Hanh, Thich Hanh. 2002. *Anger: Wisdom for Cooling the Flames*. New York: Riverhead Books.

Harris, William V. 2001. *Restraining Rage: The Ideology of Anger Control in Classical Antiquity*. Cambridge, MA: Harvard University Press.

Horowitz, Mardi J. 2007. "Understanding and Ameliorating Revenge Fantasies in Psychotherapy." *The American Journal of Psychiatry* 164, no. 1: 24–27.

Kaster, Robert A. 2005. *Emotion, Restraint, and Community in Ancient Rome*. Oxford: Oxford University Press.

Knuuttila, Simo. 2004. *Emotions in Ancient and Medieval Philosophy*. Oxford: Oxford University Press.

Konstan, David. 2006. *The Emotions of the Ancient Greeks*. Toronto: University of Toronto Press.

Kraut, Richard. 2002. *Aristotle: Political Philosophy*. Oxford: Oxford University Press.

Kraybill, Donald B., Steven M. Nolt, and David L. Weaver-Zercher. 2007. *Amish Grace: How Forgiveness Transcended Tragedy*. San Francisco: John Wiley.

Kristjánsson, Kristján. 2002. *Justifying Emotions: Pride and Jealousy*. New York: Routledge.

Lazarus, Richard S. 1991. *Emotion and Adaptation*. Oxford: Oxford University Press.

Lewis, C. S. 1967. *The Problem of Pain*. New York: Macmillan.

Lorde, Audre. 1984. "The Uses of Anger: Women Responding to Racism." In *Sister Outsider: Essays and Speeches*, 124–133. New York: Crossing Press.

Murphy, Jeffrie. 2003. *Getting Even: Forgiveness and Its Limits*. Oxford: Oxford University Press.

Murphy, Jeffrie G., and Jean Hampton. 1988. *Forgiveness and Mercy*. Cambridge: Cambridge University Press.

Nietzsche, Friedrich. 1976. "On the Virtuous." In *Part II of Thus Spoke Zarathustra*, In *The Portable Nietzsche*, edited and translated by Walter Kaufmann. New York: Penguin.

———. 1998. *On the Genealogy of Morality*. Translated by Maudemarie Clark and Alan J. Swensen. Indianapolis: Hackett.

Nozick, Robert. 1981. *Philosophical Explanations*. Cambridge, MA: Harvard University Press.

Prinz, Jesse J. 2004. *Gut Reactions: A Perceptual Theory of Emotion*. Oxford: Oxford University Press.

———. 2013. "Constructive Sentimentalism: Legal and Political Implications." In *Nomos* 53, *Passions and Emotions*, edited by J. E. Fleming, 3–18. New York: New York University Press.

Sachs, David. 1981. "How to Distinguish Self-Respect from Self-Esteem." *Philosophy and Public Affairs* 10, no. 4: 346–360.

Seneca. 2003. *Seneca: Moral and Political Essays*. Edited and translated by J. M. Cooper and J. F. Procopé. Cambridge: Cambridge University Press.

Shaftesbury, Anthony Ashley Cooper. 2001. "An Inquiry Concerning Virtue or Merit." In *Characteristicks of Men, Manners, Opinions, Times*. Introduction by D. Den Uyl. Indianapolis: Liberty Fund.

Smith, Adam. 1982. *The Theory of Moral Sentiments*. Edited by D. D. Raphael and A. L. Macfie. Indianapolis: Liberty Press.

Spelman, E. V. 1989. "Anger and Insubordination." In *Women, Knowledge, and Reality: Explorations in Feminist Philosophy*, edited by Ann Garry and Marilyn Pearsall, 263–273. Boston: Unwin Hyman.

Stainton, Robert J. 2006. "Revenge." *Critica* 38: 3–20.

Strawson, P. F. 1980. "Freedom and Resentment." In *Freedom and Resentment and Other Essays*, 1–25. New York: Methuen.

Taylor, Gabriele. 1975. "Justifying the Emotions." *Mind* 84, no. 335: 390–402.

Uniacke, Suzanne. 2000. "Why Is Revenge Wrong?" *Journal of Value Inquiry* 34, no. 1: 61–69.

Wallace, Gerry. 1995. "Wild Justice." *Philosophy* 70, no. 3: 363–375.

Chapter 2

The Psychology of Anger

Implicit and Explicit Choices for Ethical Experiences, Expressions, and Control of Anger

Everett L. Worthington, Jr.

When we think of the ethics of anger, we often conjure a theological or philosophical, explicit, slow-reasoning decision-making to guide people in their individual acts, social differences, and societal conflicts. If people do not follow the ethical norms, we would expect that punishments, sanctions, and external social judgments follow. Sometimes ethical prescriptions seem more practical than moral. We might think, do not go to bed angry. Or we might advise, do not lose your temper or you will blow the sale. To control anger, we might say, change your thinking, and you will eliminate your anger. Or turn your anger toward (1) ethically rooting out evil like Batman or (2) when triggered, smashing it, like Hulk, or (3) using anger and fighting for largely personal reasons, like Wolverine, or (4) rising above it like Superman (Smith 2018).

In fact, I began in my original draft of this chapter by summarizing—generally from the viewpoint of a talented amateur (though many might contest the "talented" part)—theologies (mostly Christian) and philosophies of anger. I considered differences between theologically conservative views (which emphasized God's wrath and retributive justice more than God's compassion) from theologically progressive views, which emphasized God's compassion and restorative justice). I looked at theologies of human anger as sinful (generally more conservative theologies) versus those that treated anger as natural and thus easier objects of grace and mercy.

In philosophies, I contrasted deontological approaches of Immanuel Kant with consequentialist approaches of Jeremy Bentham and John Stuart Mill. I looked at the French Enlightenment that emphasized bringing emotions under rational, reasonable control in contrast to the British Enlightenment approach of David Hume, in which sentiments played a larger role. Generally, even though I am neither a theologian nor a philosopher, I reasoned that neither are most people, yet it is these remnants of amateur theology and philosophy that inform and serve as the intellectual backdrop for people's understanding of anger. In the end, I have opted to begin with touching on two philosophical approaches that are more relevant to the psychology of anger, and then concentrate on the psychology—the new synthesis in moral psychology and virtue ethics.

In putting forth a psychology of anger, I draw on modern cognitive psychology. I contend that the implicit aspect of the contexts, experiences, expressions, consequences, and repair of anger is usually stronger than explicit rational ethics. I summarize a psychological understanding of anger that emphasizes the implicit. I argue that despite a largely intuitive control over anger, an ethics of anger is still possible.

THE NEW SYNTHESIS IN MORAL PSYCHOLOGY

My approach has much in common with the "new synthesis" in moral psychology. At the root of this approach is the psychological understanding of cognitive psychology emphasizing the implicit over the explicit in guiding most (but clearly not all) human behavior—especially the immediate human behavior we respond to in most daily living outside of deliberate reflective principle-driven contemplation. This understanding has percolated since Kahneman and Tversky's (1979) work in the 1970s, but has been popularized widely in the past decade due to *Switch* by Chip and Dan Heath (2010), *Thinking, Fast and Slow* by Daniel Kahneman (2011), *The Righteous Mind* by Jonathan Haidt (2012), and *The Social Animal* by David Brooks (2012). Thus, drawing on (and extending to anger) the science behind these sources, I argue that much of the implicit experience of anger is not subject to conscious control. Yet, we are not helpless to control anger. Rather, this understanding of anger merely directs our conscious control to different areas than seeking to bolster willpower. We can expect ethical anger experience, expression, and control by managing situations we think will provoke anger, building a virtuous character to foster preemptive internal control, and coping with inevitable times when we cannot prevent unwanted anger.

Crudely put, some have despaired that over 2,500 years of philosophical and theological debate and rational inquiry, broadly applied, have failed to definitively identify what we *should* do morally. Thus, even in the face of Hume's law—that one cannot derive the *ought* from the *is*—the advocates of the new synthesis have sought to use empirical methods to seek to identify what people should do morally. Psychology is a science, especially when bolstered by cognitive neuroscience, and has traditionally thought to be aimed at describing what Aristotle called *efficient* causes. Those discover how behavior is caused. Science does not, indeed cannot, determine *final* causes (i.e., teleological end-points), which are why we behave as we do (Bahr 2016). Ethics and morals, however, have been about deciding what is good—what we *should* do. A variety of approaches to ethics have been advocated. These include attempts to find absolute moral goods—what theologies claim and what philosophers like Kant called deontological ethics. From Jeremy Bentham onward to John Stuart Mill and others, consequentialist approaches to ethics have sought to identify what is good by what produces the best consequences for the most people.

What the New Moral Synthesis Tries to Do

Often advocates of the new moral synthesis try to describe the synthesis as involving mostly a culture-sensitive combination that mostly emphasizes empirical description of a phenomenon with the sense of good being taken as (a) what helps people survive or (b) what makes people of the culture or subculture thrive or makes them happy. Evolution has typically served as the most common basis of the new moral synthesis, but Darwinian emphasis on survival (i.e., biological evolution) has been supplanted with a joint emphasis (i.e., evolutionary psychology) on survival and flourishing (see Christakis 2019; Wilson 2019). Still, not all positive psychologists have embraced a secular evolutionary psychology. Some have blended a deontological approach drawn from Christian theology (i.e., Thomas's virtue ethics or more Protestant-influenced theology) or secular philosophy (such as Aristotelian philosophy) with the evolutionary psychology.

Critique of the New Scientific Moral Synthesis Theories

In *Science and the Good*, James Davison Hunter and Paul Nedelisky (2019) have analyzed and critiqued the approach to morality embodied in the new synthesis. The new morality, as discussed by Hunter and Nedelisky (2019), involves a combination of concepts imported from evolution (i.e., how emotions, specifically anger, came to be and what adaptive functions they serve), utilitarian philosophy, and positive psychology. The critique is sophisticated. We might oversimplify it by saying that largely the new moral synthesis rejects Hume's law (which is not wise to do) and argues that people can, and should, behave in accordance with what evolutionary survival pressure, utilitarian consequences, and positive psychology's technology of application suggest. Instead of accepting an evolutionary-utilitarian-technological set of values, Hunter and Nedelisky advocate public discourse.

VIRTUE THEORIES

Virtue ethics seeks to define the good in terms of what people of virtuous or good character choose to do. Virtuous character is seen as being built through a process by which one identifies a virtue to pursue. Then the person seeks to practice the virtue perfectly until it becomes a habit of the heart. Then, the virtue must be put under strain through facing trials, temptations, tests, and suffering, all of which can prove the virtue if one perseveres. This will lead to ultimate satisfaction or contentment. Happiness might be experienced, but it is fleeting and not the proper lasting source of ultimate satisfaction.

Virtue theory suggests that people have the capacity to order their behavior toward virtue or vice. The particular virtues that are valued might be those that are individually or interpersonally oriented, and virtue theory within positive psychology often advocates *eudaimonic* virtues, which are thought to be acts that are good for oneself and others. This appropriation of *eudaimonia* from the Greek does change the meaning, because in Aristotelian and other Greek philosophical thinking, *eudaimonia* suggested that a strong male leader would act honorably and would thus enrich the *polis* through his honorable and virtuous acts. In the positive psychology use of the term, however, one engages in virtues that not only bless the self (like self-control, wisdom, conscientiousness), but also bless others (like forgiveness, gratitude, compassion, altruism, love, and justice).

Virtue theory does not presuppose that people automatically pursue virtue, but rather it advocates ordering behaviors into virtue hierarchies in which both individuals and their communities (including increasingly larger communities that could extend to all of humankind or all of the natural order). Virtue theory is philosophical or religious, and yet it is supported by psychological science in which findings show that such pursuits typically have more positive than negative consequences for most people (utilitarian justification) or are prescribed by one or more religions (deontological justification), or supported by a new scientific moral synthesis justification.

A PAUSE FOR REFLECTION

Centuries of theological and philosophical reflection have not resulted in universal agreement on an ethic of anger. I personally am unwilling to accept the new moral synthesis, which arrives at this same conclusion and advocates accepting the *is* of evolution and *ought* of utilitarianism combined with a technology of positive psychology supplying the *how-to*. Nor am I willing to jump wholeheartedly aboard any theological or philosophical bandwagon.

To disclose ahead of time, I lean toward a theology that is deontologically informed. That is, I do believe there are absolutes, though they might not be epistemologically available to human perception. My theology is more influenced by N. T. Wright than toward either a theology of wrath or of complete accepting grace. Rather, like Thomas (who drew on Aristotle), I would like to find that Golden Mean, though I think it floats around according to situations and to what aspects of people's internal life they are attending to at the moment. The remainder of this chapter is my lurching after an understanding of ethics of anger that will fit with my beliefs, values, and practices. My approach is governed by my professional commitments as a psychologist. Therefore, I turn to seeking a psychological understanding of anger.

A PSYCHOLOGICAL UNDERSTANDING OF ANGER

The Experience of Anger

Anger, as Experienced, Is an Embodied Emotion.

Typically, the way we often treat anger—or most emotions in general—is that the brain creates both the experience and expression of anger. Psychologists now typically see that understanding as impoverished. Emotions are not just in the brain and spreading out into the body for their expression. Rather, emotions are fundamentally embodied responses consisting of brain, biochemical, neurological, chemical-hormonal, central nervous system, and peripheral nervous system, implicit cognition, and explicit rational reasoning processes, integrated into an embodied experience. The experiences might be a *feeling* (i.e., working memory's label for the moment-by-moment embodied experience), an *emotion* (i.e., a transitory related experience, but more lasting than a feeling), or a stable *affective experience* that averages out moods (disregarding momentary feelings and emotions that depart from the average mood).

Is Anger a Moral Emotion?

Shame and guilt are often treated as self-conscious moral emotions because they are experienced when a person does something that he or she considers morally wrong (Tangney and Fischer 1995). Is anger also a moral emotion? At first blush, it might seem so. Anger occurs when we feel that someone or something has wronged us. When we are hurt or offended or treated unjustly, we feel wronged. When we are outraged by an egregious wrong done to others, we might feel righteous anger aimed at righting the wrong. Those seem to be anger in a moral context.

But less clear is the anger we feel sometimes when we are frustrated by a jar lid that won't unscrew. The lid did not do anything to intentionally hurt, offend, or frustrate us. So, is this a moral emotion? There are also times when we feel "hangry" from being hungry and primed to respond to frustrations in anger. Again, that is not an agent's intentional harm inflicted upon us. In fact, this type of anger—nonhuman-instigated anger—occurs frequently in life. Thus, some anger might be morally tinged. Others, not so much.

Generally, anger is an emotion and the action tendency associated with it is to remove blocks to one's pleasure. There are a number of motives that derive from that action tendency—these include exerting goal-directed force to remove blocks to pleasure and thus accomplish one's goals, acting aggressively, harboring resentment and grudges, restoring one's impugned honor, and doing any of these along a continuum from lashing out in impulsive responding to cold, calculating response.

Primary and Secondary Anger

At extremes of anger (i.e., rage), our behavior is often discontinuous from how we react when anger is low to mild to moderate. Emotion-focused therapy (Pascual-Leone et al. 2013) suggests that unadulterated anger is a primary reaction. But when anger is elaborated unconsciously, it becomes secondary.

Our limbic system—the inner brain structures that are most involved in anger experience and expression—is highly engaged in reacting to anger initially. It takes a few seconds to modulate reactive anger into a deliberate response. It is adaptive for animals, including people, sometimes to respond instantly to anger-provoking stimuli. Thus, the body has evolved direct systems to get the reactions into gear—emotions, motivations, and actions—without waiting around for the slow progression of neurohormones such as adrenaline and cortisol to make their way into the bloodstream, around the circulatory system to the brain, and out from the brain to the muscles. The vagal nerve in the parasympathetic nervous system (PSNS) winds like a vagabond throughout the body, calming sympathetic nervous system (SNS) responses one by one. Under normal living conditions, the SNS is kept quiescent by a "vagal brake," which is PSNS dampening of SNS responses. With a fear- or anger-provoking stimulus, a direct pathway to the amygdala is activated, projecting directly to disengage the PSNS. The vagal brake is released, and the SNS immediately (within hundredths of a second) fires up multiple responses—increased heartrate, messages to the muscles to contract, and so on. The release of the vagal brake also triggers adrenaline and cortisol to be discharged from the adrenal gland, and that results in a later (~45 seconds) surge of arousing neurochemicals. Other pathways, such as gut responses in which the proprioceptive nervous system sends messages from gut to cortex signaling the cortex to respond to threat, operate with just a few seconds latency. Thus we can see that neuropsychology has shed light on many controversies about which classic account of emotion is "correct." There is an immediate pre-appraisal physiological response, a response after a few seconds that involves appraisal (but can occur either implicitly or explicitly), and a response from 45 seconds (extending out to years later) involving appraisal and tends more often to be explicit *extremes of anger (i.e., rage).*

At emotional extremes, with anger, we often see violence, aggression, lack of prosocial control, saying things we regret, and lack of hope to persevere. In addition, we find that unforgiveness is secondary and can manifest as revenge motives or avoidance motives. In high anger or rage, we see an unfocused ranting and raging rather than a focus on the situation at hand. We see perseverating focus on venting anger. Secondary anger often involves cortical elaboration that takes longer than a minute to build up by incorporating many associations, conscious and intuitive cognition, memories, and practiced patterns of behaving when very angry. Not surprisingly, secondary anger is complex. It can grow uncontrollable as memories and associations feed the emotional experience. With much more to process than in simple angry reactions, it also is not surprising that it can be hard to control.

At Moderate and Lower Levels of Anger

If anger is moderate, even if it is secondary to the initial angry reaction, it is less driven by associations, memories, and unconscious dynamics. Thus, we find that conscious anger-control strategies are used more often, with more deliberation, and with more success than in strong secondary anger. Instead of focus on the anger, we can focus on more adaptive coping strategies.

Phineas Gage and Anger

A classic case in psychology is Phineas Gage (Damasio 1994). Gage was a pillar of the community, a foreman in charge of clearing a path for a railroad. Rocks were blasted out of the way. That procedure first involved drilling a hole for the blasting powder. Blasting powder was inserted, and a rag was placed in the hole. The foreman used a long tamping iron to press down the rags and powder. The rags prevented a spark from the iron on rock from igniting the powder.

One day, Gage forgot the rag, and the spark from the tamping iron on stone caused the powder to explode. It drove the tamping iron through Gage's cheek and out the top of his skull. Amazingly, he not only survived, but was conscious. He sat up, dazed, with a giant hole through his head. The crew transported him to the physician, who cleaned the wound by passing a cloth through the skull. Although Gage survived, his moral life was never the same. He made bad, risky decisions, got in trouble, and ended up working in a traveling circus as a novelty, passing objects through his head.

Physiologist Hannah Damasio got the skull, which was on display at Harvard, and used it to create a computer model of which of Gage's brain structures must have been damaged. Her husband, Antonio Damasio, studied emotion. He found modern patients who had damage to the same structures as did Gage. They had similar symptoms. At first, Damasio thought he had uncovered a center of morality in the brain. Later, he found a different story. The damaged structures in the brain simply passed neural information from gut to brain. When a risky decision is about to be made, the gut tenses. That information is transmitted to the cortex. An uninjured person evaluates the input from the various structures in brain and body. The prefrontal cortex is primarily responsible for decision-making and executive functioning. Information from the senses and the context is the slate on which the other information is projected. Other information includes past memories and associations. But it also involves quickly changing neural patterns of electrical activity from structures like the amygdala (which is usually involved in reacting to stimuli that are scary or anger-provoking) and neurotransmitter balances. There are many inputs from the body including input from the gut—that is, gut feelings—from the large muscles (describing gross body movement, such as clenching the fists, holding the breath, and the like), and from the subtle muscles (like narrowing the eyes, staring hard, or clenching the jaw). The neocortex integrates the information from all over the body and arrives at an interpretation: I'm feeling angry (for primary reaction), or I'm feeling vengeful (from secondary anger elaborated into more complex motives). In short, emotion is more about what happens in the entire body—small and large muscle groups—than what happens solely in the situational context or the rational brain centers. Emotion is an embodied experience. Note that rational thought, which is slow, joins the primary emotional experience late in the process. Rationality is usually involved with secondary emotion and is part of the elaboration that gives secondary anger its nuance into resentment, bitterness, anger, rage, and so on.

Damasio's (1994) understanding of the experience of anger supports the idea that much of cognition is implicit rather than explicit. Neuronal firing is not limited to rational thought. In fact, most reactive primary anger does not even include rationality.

Anger Experience Is Different from Anger Expression

Anger Experience

People can experience anger and yet no one knows. However, when people express anger, that expression is public behavior, regardless of whether anyone actually observes the expression. It is the expression of anger, not its experience, that others observe. However, we have some sense of self-awareness, and we can, and often do, monitor our internal experience of anger. Thus, we can feel self-condemnation for experiencing anger, or pride in our Oscar-worthy control of its expression. We can judge our own experience of anger, so its morality is not merely a social phenomenon.

A commonsense implication of this is that anger experience is far different from anger expression. Anger experience might occur with almost no (gross) muscle involvement. The person might simply stare hard at a hated person or adopt a poker face to hide anger. Anger expression, on the other hand, involves the entire body. The facial muscles and the gross body muscles contract and move when one slams a fist in the palm, strikes the wall, or smacks a stubborn jar lid on the table to loosen it. All of the additional input from one's own body yields a different experience from simple anger experience.

Anger Expression

Lightning flashes and thunder rolls, and a person in a large apartment complex steps onto the balcony and shouts: "I'm mad as hell and I'm not going to take it anymore." More thunder. Others join in. "I'm mad as hell and I'm not going to take it anymore." As the storm gains intensity, so do the voices. News anchor Howard Beale, in the 1975 film classic film *Network*, finds that the desires of the mob are as unpredictable and effectual as the thunder. Beale becomes the symbolic spokesperson for the masses. He eventually realizes that the system will eventually have its way. In the end, he finds that it is merely better network ratings that matter. This is a morality parable. It suggests that anger *expression* rarely changes anything. But, in unbridled anger expression, we can lose our own personal voice.

Emotional expressions are varied. They can result in actions that are goal-directed, personal, interpersonal, mere venting, and aggressive. Emotional expressions of anger have consequences—intended, collateral, and perhaps delayed unintended consequences, which are rarely implicitly or explicitly considered in acting on angry emotions and motivations.

Once anger is expressed, it will have consequences. It will shape the person's self-perception (Bem 1967). It also will affect social perceptions. Thus, if anger expression is harmful to others, people might seek to repair the social damage by making amends, asking for forgiveness, and vowing not to transgress by losing one's temper again.

Anger Theories

Catharsis Hypothesis

An early exploration into anger was Freud's *catharsis hypothesis.* This hypothesis treated anger merely as a natural phenomenon that responded to internal impulses and drives, which were a result of early childhood experiences modified by learned defense mechanisms. Learning was not necessarily under conscious control. In Freud's theory, catharsis reduced pent-up emotional energy, making the person less at the beck and call of those nasty unconscious motives. Research over the past century has thoroughly discredited the catharsis theory of anger.

Criticisms of catharsis theory peaked in the early 1970s. Albert Bandura (1973) called for a moratorium on catharsis theory. He did not suggest that individuals do not utilize catharsis. Rather, he argued that catharsis was ineffective at reducing anger. Geen and Quanty (1977) argued that cathartic venting did not reduce, but increased, aggression. These findings have been supported (e.g., Bushman et al. 1999). Geen and Quanty (1977) noted that physiological arousal could be reduced by venting anger, but only when people express their anger directly to the person who angered them, without fear of retaliation. In addition, venting indirectly against a substitute target (i.e., displaced aggression) did not reduce arousal. Finally, Berkowitz (1989) reformulated the hypothesis more generally, suggesting that any negative affect can (but does not necessarily) lead to aggression. Expressing anger intensifies its experience and expression (for a review, see Anderson et al. 2010). One reason is that when people believe that anger is cathartic, they have a justification for the expression of anger (Bushman et al. 2001; Bushman and Whitaker 2010).

Frustration-Aggression Hypothesis

Dollard et al. (1939) put forth the *frustration-aggression* hypothesis—when frustration is experienced, aggression is more likely to follow it. They identified two conditions that must be met for *frustration* to occur: (1) the person must be expected to perform a certain act, and (2) the act is prevented from happening. Dollard et al. (1939) defined *aggression* as a "sequence of behavior, the goal-response to which is the injury of the person toward whom it is directed" (9). Aggression has been often studied. Recently, Dewall et al. defined aggression as "any behavior intended to harm another person who does not want to be harmed" (Dewall et al. 2011, 449). Thus, there are three critical factors comprising aggression. First, aggression is a behavior, not merely a thought, feeling, or intention. Second, aggression is a behavior intended to harm another person. If, for example, a person asked her friend to recall painful memories because she wants to help, then the pain is not aggression. Third, aggression is pain inflicted on someone who does not want to be harmed. In general, the frustration-aggression hypothesis has spotty supportive evidence.

Anger Is Natural but Not Necessarily Moral

Anger is a natural emotion, which does not make it moral. Being natural, it is virtually universally experienced at times. How we respond to anger is not dictated by the emotion itself. Rather, the situation, our history, our practiced habits, and our strategic and tactical objectives all play into how we respond.

CONTROL OF ANGER

Blame and Responsibility: Can We Control Our Anger?

Anger Self-regulation

People are judged in part, by their self-regulation. Thus, when people see someone exert obvious self-control to squelch or redirect the expression of anger to prosocial ends, or at least not to direct it to socially harmful ends, then social approval is likely. However, it is not always the case that control of anger is morally praised. Consider a person who believes his or her honor has been violated. Observers might judge that person harshly for not responding—especially in an honor culture (Nisbett and Cohen 1996). Or, consider a person considered to be a protector of someone harmed who cannot defend himself or herself (i.e., in child abuse). Observers might judge the "protector" for not showing anger.

What Is and Isn't under Conscious Control?

Observers do not normally consider feelings, emotions, and affective states to be under full conscious control. However, they are considered to be experiences for which people are responsible. There are several reasons why people hold others responsible for their emotional expression. People are expected to at least try to:

- exert conscious control over feelings or emotional states in the moment;
- change their baseline emotional experiences so that negative emotions will not be expressed as often or as dramatically in the future;
- choose, to some extent, their environments such that loss of control of their behavioral responses when angry are not as likely;
- practice calming coping strategies (i.e., meditation, mindfulness, compassion, self-compassion, preparation-for-childbirth breathing patterns, etc.);
- try to repair interpersonal (and intrapersonal) damage done (physically, emotionally, morally, spiritually, etc.) when unwanted emotions injure oneself or others;
- try to establish group, community, and societal norms that minimize damage done within the group and to some degree damage done to out-group members and groups.

Because feelings, emotions, and affect are subject to moral acts of prevention, amelioration, or repair, observers can make attributions of morality that surround the experience and especially the expression of anger. They also can speak of what is ethical regarding one's anger. Thus, even though observers might believe that people cannot fully control their experience and expression of anger, the observers might judge people morally and ethically on how well they are perceived to try to control unwanted and unwarranted expression of emotion. One way of controlling such expression, of course, is to control one's experience of anger. Regardless of whether that avenue is adopted, one is judged by the control of anger expression in light of group norms and expectations.

Anger Experiences and Expressions Are Not Usually Conscious and Rational

Psychology is attuned to the implicit situations and personal variables that might affect whether, how, when, where, and why people experience and express anger. The situational context includes (1) what humans have latent from evolutionary history; (2) norms of the group, subculture, and culture; and (3) situational cues that activate unconscious (implicit) schema.

Personal characteristics might be activated or made salient by the situational cues. These could include memories of personal historical events; traits or dispositions; attachment experiences as a child, adolescent, or adult; one's hierarchy of values; one's valued moral foundations; and decision-making schemas.

Using Anger Ethically

People are not merely objects of ethical judgments. They can act ethically. Therefore, one can use anger ethically. Anger removes blocks to pleasure. Some blocks to pleasure can be unjust. The injustices can be due to personal attacks or offenses. The injustices can be due to unjust social and societal structures (i.e., prejudices, discrimination, social injustice, war). Righteous anger can motivate a fight against injustice. A good example is the Civil War, which ended up leading to the abolishment of slavery in the United States. Another is *Brown versus Board of Education*. Another is Bryan Stevenson's (2014) Equal Justice Initiative, which seeks to prevent unjust capital punishment. The danger is that anger provokes much self-justification and rationalization, so often, when we think we are experiencing righteous anger, we are in fact justifying our own biased pursuit of personal motives.

Rational, Conscious Self-Control Efforts—Willpower

Self-control of Anger Experiences and Expressions by Rational Application of Positive Psychological Interventions

There are numerous methods of anger control—most importantly, control of the expression of anger action tendencies that are not prosocial. These include positive psychological interventions like mindfulness, cultivation of self-compassion, and the pursuit of the virtues of self-control and patience.

Self-control of Anger Experiences and Expressions through Implicit Personality Control

We know that, as humans, we fail to control our experience or expression of anger at times. Thus, part of the ethics of anger involves how one deals with and attempts to repair (or exacerbate) such ethical failures. Besides employing effortful willpower-directed self-control, we can seek to develop our personalities to make virtuous responses more likely than vicious responses. We might do this for many motivations. First, we might do so because we are following a deontological moral code—whether secular or religious. Second, we might do so for consequentialist reasons—because we wish to make unpleasant consequences or unpleasant emotions less likely, or to behave in ways that will provoke more positive and less negative social responses from others. Third, we might do so as an outworking of virtue theory. That is, we believe that forming a virtuous character will lead to more probable self-controlled behavior. In the following section, we examine some of the personality or character virtues that might be developed.

Role of Cognition—as We Understand It Today

What makes this more difficult than it might sound at first blush, however, is the role of cognition, as psychologists understand it today. Enlightenment thinking tended to view rational thought as the answer to self-control. Modern cognitive psychology, however, has given lie to that assumption. Kahneman (2011) summarized and popularized this understanding of modern cognitive psychology, which suggests that most thinking is what he called System 1 thinking. It is fast, intuitive, unconscious, automatic, and often driven by relational forces of which people simply are not aware. It is biased, based on heuristics that favor quick rule-of-thumb decisions that are right most of the time but cut rational corners. Kahneman suggested that approximately 90 percent of mental activity is System 1 thinking. Rational thought, called System 2 thinking, is slow, deliberate, systematic, practiced, logical, and rule-driven. Often it is impressed into service by intuitive, irrational System 1 desires. So, what seems like rational decision-making to the one making a decision is, about half of the time, driven by System 1 motives—that is, rationalizations. The reasons actually follow the decision rather than precede it. Thus, when people are angry, a churning sea of System 1 motives, emotions, and self-justifying desires is sweeping people along a pathway toward non-prosocial anger expression. Thus, exerting willful cognitive control over such impulses is difficult. Willpower is limited in its effectiveness (Baumeister and Tierney 2011)—much more limited than we believe.

How Then Should We Control Anger?

Often control of anger experiences and expressions must rely not on controlling anger in the moment, but rather on setting up internal and external conditions that prevent anger from occurring in the first place. This highlights the strategies of (1) self-monitoring and (2) situational management of potentially anger-provoking situations (i.e., avoiding provocations; limiting contact with someone who is aggravating, selecting jobs, mates, and acquaintances who are not provoking; development of virtues; finding common ground instead of differences on which to center interactions). Second, it can involve building virtuous character. Third, it can involve cultivating a repertoire of rehearsed coping strategies that can be called upon in the moment of emotional anger. I will discuss each of these below.

SITUATION MANAGEMENT

In this section, I highlight the first of three ways of managing anger—identifying some strategies of situational management of potentially anger-provoking situations. This predominately involves a priori changes in the environment to make provocation less likely.

Avoiding Provocations

Some level of self-monitoring is needed to discern situations that are likely to provoke a person. Then, the person must have the requisite motivation, skill, and opportunity to avoid situations that are likely to be provocative. A man might discern that his boss triggers him, and he has come dangerously close to exploding several times. Even if he has the motivation to avoid the boss and the skill to cut interactions off without making the boss think he is being disrespected, the man might simply not be able to avoid meetings that always result in confrontations with the boss. Nevertheless, some provocations can be minimized, though not eliminated, by limiting contact with someone who is aggravating.

Selecting Jobs, Mates, and Acquaintances That Are Not Provocative

We make many choices in life that send us down a road that has more or fewer potholes. For example, as a clinical psychologist, I control my workday to some extent. I could move toward seeing patients, testifying in court, and consulting with businesses in internal conflict. Each of those choices would place me often in the midst of conflict. But I could also choose to teach, do research, and write books. Each of those choices structures my day in ways that make potential conflicts less likely. We all make similar choices in mate selection, though we rarely create a calculus of conflict avoidance–approach when we fall in love. We make similar choices in the people who are our acquaintances, and we do have much more control over the number and type of interactions with acquaintances.

Finding Common Ground instead of Differences on Which to Center Interactions

Moral Foundations on Which People Agree

Haidt (2012) identifies six moral foundations: fairness/cheating, care/harm, freedom/oppression, authority/subversion, loyalty/betrayal, and sanctity/degradation. Each person values each moral foundation more or less, and people can be oriented in each case either to promote or to police the value. For example, some people who highly value fairness/cheating are disposed to promoting fairness; others are more oriented toward preventing and punishing cheating. Most people agree on the value of fairness/cheating and care/harm with (in the United States) much agreement on freedom/oppression. According to much research by Haidt (2012) and others there is less agreement on the value of authority/subversion, loyalty/betrayal, and sanctity/degradation. Haidt claims that research shows that political conservatives place much more value on those three than do political progressives.

Finding Interests behind Positions

Thus, one strategy for finding some common ground is to emphasize the moral foundations on which people agree rather than those about which they disagree. Fisher et al. (2011) have developed a method of resolving differences in ways that yield win-win solutions more often (than other methods of negotiation). They advocate focusing on the interests underneath positions rather than on the incompatible positions that people stake out. Thus, focusing on the moral foundations on which people agree at least forms a platform to jump from in seeking to resolve differences.

CULTIVATING VIRTUES

Whereas managing situations is usually done in the moderate to near term as people see potential provocative situations unfolding, the second method of controlling anger is to build personal and community virtues, which is a long-game strategy. We cannot wait until a potential provocation is about to occur to modify our character. Rather, we must pursue virtue well ahead of potential anger-provoking situations.

In this section, I draw widely from ethical and moral sources, namely, virtue ethics to determine the final causes and from positive psychology (including modern cognitive, social, personality, developmental, and neuropsychology) to determine efficient causes. My synthesis is thus a combination of what is empirical from the new scientific moral synthesis (but not adhering quite rigorously to the new moral synthesis emphases on evolutionary psychology and consequentialist, especially utilitarian, ethics) and having "mere" Christian deontological boundaries. Those boundaries are informed by classical and Christian virtue theory. For examples, see the book of *James* in Christian Scriptures, theologians like Wright's (2010) *Virtue Reborn*, and Christian psychologists like McMinn's (2017) *The Science of Virtue: Why Positive Psychology Matters to the Church.* Yet, we live within a postmodern cultural situation, and that historical placement inevitably has affected my philosophy.

Virtue is aimed not at happiness, which I hold to be more fleeting than might be a suitable ethical goal, but at virtue of character for individuals and for a society characterized by actions from a people of virtue. What this ethics arrives at is prescriptive norms, conventions, laws and punishments, sanctions, and interpersonal social judgments. While laws, punishments, and some conventions are explicit, most of these ethical prescriptions and proscriptions are implicit. Being implicit (rather than explicit) does not absolve people of responsibility and accountability. It just puts practical boundaries on what can and cannot be done.

In my consideration of virtues below, many seem as though they reside in the individual, which derives from the Greco-Roman tradition. Yet the new synthesis suggests that virtues cannot exist without some community. Brooks's (2012) *The Social Animal* is an excellent and persuasive case regarding how individual qualities derive from relationships. As I discuss virtues below, be aware that I might seem to locate them as individual, yet I believe that they are derived from communities.

Classical Virtues

Since Plato's *Republic* Book IV, Cicero, Augustine, and Thomas, four virtues were recognized as cardinal (or hinge) virtues: prudence, temperance, fortitude, and justice. Prudence is the ability to discern the appropriate course of action in a given situation at the appropriate time. It involves practical wisdom (*phronesis*) and more generic wisdom (*sophia*). Temperance is self-control to indulge oneself in moderation. Fortitude (also courage) is the strength and endurance to confront fear and intimidation. Justice is social or societal fairness and acting rightly.

Christian Virtues

From 1 Corinthians 13's concluding verse, Christians identified three additional cardinal virtues. This include faith, hope, and love (1 Cor 13:13a)—the theological virtues. As Paul argued, "The greatest of these is love" because faith and hope will someday pass away when people meet God face to face (2 Cor 5:6–8), but love will abide (1 Cor 13:13b).

Faith

According to Christian Scripture, "Now faith is confidence in what we hope for and assurance about what we do not see" (Heb 11:1). Faith, therefore, is the strength of conviction that empowers faithful behavior that is directed toward the object of faith.

Hope

Hope is the motivation to persevere. It has two elements that make it up according to Snyder's hope theory (Snyder 1994). It involves a sense of agency to be able to bring about desired goals (called willpower). Hope also involves knowing various ways, or pathways, to bring about desired goals (called way-power). According to Snyder, hope will disappear if either agency or pathways is insufficient for one's desired goals to seem attainable. We might call this *maturing hope* because in younger people—up to the young-old (in their sixties)—still pursue goals, and even when goals seem hopelessly out of reach, people still search for pathways and attempt to elevate their sense of agency. However, from Christian theology (Kapic 2017; Marcel 1962), it is argued that we might not always be able to obtain our desired goals—at least on earth. Thus, one must also cultivate the motivation to persevere when one's desired goals seem unlikely or impossible to attain. We might call this wait-power (Worthington 2005) or *mature hope* because this is most frequent in older people.

Love

Love is being willing to value and not devalue a person. Many theories of love exist, but perhaps the best known psychological theory is Sternberg's (1985) triangular theory of love. Sternberg argues that love has three components: passion, intimacy, and commitment. On each dimension, people can be high or low in magnitude, yielding eight types of love. *Consummate love* is being high in all three components. The virtue of love is that it binds people together for their mutual benefit, though psychological and relational forces can poison the love and make the emotional bond toxic. Christian views of love locate love within a person. Thus people have a capacity to love one or more objects of their affection. This might be called their disposition of love. But they might also have a particular attitude (involving the affective, behavioral, and cognitive components) toward particular people, and not as a personality trait.

Relational Virtues

Community Identification

People identify with their primary group. Putnam (2020) calls *bonding social capital* investment in people with whom one has a shared group identity. This is contrasted with *bridging social capital*, which is investing in cross-group connections, or *linking social capital*, which is investing in links across levels (i.e., from local groups to government). Bonding with groups is a virtue, though each social capital has its own costs.

Authority/Subversion

People yearn to be free, and yet they also function well in hierarchies. Thus, respect for authority—as long as it is not too great or too small—is a virtue in the Aristotelian Golden Mean tradition. Haidt (2012) calls authority/subversion one of six moral foundations. He posits that people seek to honor authority and other people seek to prevent people from subverting authority. Thus, two different foci of this virtue exist.

Loyalty/Betrayal

Similar to authority, loyalty/betrayal describes two ways people embrace this moral foundation—either acting out of loyalty or seeking to root out and eliminate betrayal (Haidt 2012).

Self-sacrifice

Good relationships are often built on the willingness to sacrifice for someone who is valued (Van Lange et al. 1997). Sacrifice for a loved one or a group signals the value of the loved one or group, and thus increases group bonds—bonding social capital.

Humility

Personal virtues like humility might be cultivated. Humility can make easy offense less likely. Humility is thought to have four necessary and sufficient conditions (Worthington and Allison 2017). One must have (1) accurate awareness of one's strengths and weaknesses; (2) willingness to be teachable to correct weaknesses; (3) modest self-presentation; and (4) other-orientation to lift others up and not put them down. This necessarily will result in ego quietness (as an alternative fourth quality). Worthington and Allison take other orientation to be central to the definition, which is one reason I placed humility within community virtues.

In humility, emotions springing from anger, like contempt (see Gottman 1993), are to be eschewed as incompatible with the other-orientation of humility. Polarization is to be examined, and (we hope) reduced because polarization elevates one's own group over others, contradicting modest self-presentation. Humility, rather than contempt for others who hold different beliefs and values, might lead to acts like forgiving, practicing convicted civility in discourse with out-group members (see Mouw 2010), and even loving one's enemies (see Arthur Brooks 2019).

Forgiveness

Anger is embedded within a web of interpersonal interactions, especially those in which wrongs occur. Personal virtues like forgiveness might be cultivated to aid repair of anger-inducing harms, hurts, injustices, and offenses. Thus, forgiveness of the one whom one perceived as the offender is important in reducing lingering or future anger.

Compassion

Personal virtues like compassion also are not possible unless there is a valued community. One needs people to feel compassionate toward. Compassion is sympathy plus wanting to aid a needy other person.

Generosity

Personal virtues like generosity also require a relationship with someone who is needy to whom one can be generous.

Gratitude

Personal virtues like gratitude require a benefactor to whom one can feel and perhaps show gratitude.

Altruism

Altruism is likewise a relational virtue. Altruism is the unselfish regard for the other. Others are needed for altruism to occur.

Personal Virtues with Community Benefits (*Eudaimonic* Virtues)

Wisdom

Personal virtues like wisdom allow people within the community to draw on the wise person and make better, more beneficial decisions that affect the entire community.

Self-Compassion and Self-Forgiveness

Personal virtues like self-compassion (Neff 2011) and self-forgiveness (Worthington 2013) can repair damage to one's own psyche that might produce self-condemnation and lead to defensive lashing out at others. Often a dominant experience is one's experience of self-condemnation, with accompanying guilt, shame, remorse, regret, and contrition. Many methods are available to deal with such experiences and remove or reduce self-condemnation. These involve responsible efforts to seek to restore one's relationship with the sacred, seek to make amends, and seek to repair psychological or moral injury to oneself (see Griffin et al. 2015). They also involve self-forgiveness, and the related but different experience of self-acceptance. In addition, people make commitments to live into the future without repeating moral mistakes. But there are other ways to reduce one's sense of injustice—such as seeking to restore justice by making amends, self-punishment, compensation, letting oneself off of the moral hook, seeking absolution from the one harmed or from an authority such as a priest (Woodyatt et al. 2017).

Individual Efforts to Cultivate Virtues

One way to cultivate virtue is to read self-help material (and I include listening to podcasts, and seeking web-based material, and the like; https://www.ted.com/talks/ryan_martin_why_we_get_mad_and_why_it_s_healthy). Such sources are legion. Consider UC Berkeley's Greater Good website (https://greatergood.berkeley.edu/). It has helpful articles, directions to other resources, and discussions. More systematic ways to promote virtues involve do-it-yourself (DIY) workbooks (e.g., see http://www.evworthington-forgiveness.com/diy-workbooks), apps (www.calm.com), and self-help websites (https://selfhelpforlife.com/11-benefits-of-gratitude-practice-daily/). These more systematic approaches are more engaging because they encourage people not to listen or read passively, but to use their own examples and work through exercises that help change experiences.

Group-Based Efforts to Provide the Soil in Which Virtues Grow

People benefit from groups for many reasons. Yalom (1985) has summarized the curative group factors and he has shown that all sorts of groups can help people with tasks like managing their anger. This includes group psychotherapy, but also psychoeducational groups, social groups, 12-Step groups, Bible study groups, book clubs, and virtually any group of people that meets together and shares ideas from their own lives and might bring in additional expertise to bear on a problem like how to control anger.

Community-Based Efforts to Support the Thriving of Virtues

Learning communities have become a good way to support virtue development. This includes a variety of sources. For example, TED Talks, the Nantucket Project, and Chautauqua Institution, which have seasons in which people come together for a short-term community, share, and learn. Other communities exist for the long term. These include religious colleges, parochial schools, classical schools, and even the home school movement.

(Relatively) Permanent Moral Communities like Faith Communities

Faith communities also provide a long-term group of people with whom one can develop accountability and grow toward a more virtuous character. They have many positive characteristics. They usually divide into small groups, gaining the benefits of groups (Yalom 1985). They provide religious education across the life span. They use congregational activities such as corporate worship, outreach to the community, and activities to strengthen the bonding capital within the group. They also allow for group meetings that provide opportunities for people to practice virtues. Because faith communities are made up of imperfect humans in leadership, peer, and subordinate roles, there are ample opportunities for power politics and offenses to occur, providing a real-life laboratory for practice of virtues like anger management, forgiveness, and humility. Other communities, such as L'Arche Internationale and L'Arche USA, might have some similar dynamics because they are moral communities even if not explicitly faith-based communities.

College-based or Public-Health-Based Larger Community Campaigns

Public leadership, like community leaders, politicians, and even organizational leaders can instigate public campaigns that seek to promote better control of anger. These campaigns can be undertaken in any large collective, like a college, a workplace, a community, or a city. Campaigns might be aimed at better public health, public mental health, or civility. But the methods are aimed more at influencing a large group of people to change their behavior than at influencing small identified groups or individuals to change. Both prevention of problems and promotion of well-being are targets of public campaigns. Because the targets are diffused across a large population, intervention is aimed more at assessment, policy for the organization, and efforts to persuade or encourage adherence to policy recommendations.

Developing a Repertoire of Practices Coping Strategies to Use When Provoked

We have examined two ways of controlling anger: managing situations and developing a virtuous character. Both are essentially preventive methods. However, events happen that provoke anger despite our best efforts to limit the provocations or avoid them altogether. We need responses after the fact to ameliorate anger and to prevent primary anger experiences and expressions from becoming secondary anger involving rage, unforgiving emotions (i.e., resentment, bitterness, hostility, hatred, and trait anger), and toxic internally directed anger that might yield self-condemnation, shame, and chronic guilt. This involves developing a repertoire of coping strategies to use when one is provoked.

Methods of Anger Control When Anger Threatens Harmful Expression

We now consider methods of anger control—most importantly control of the expression of anger action tendencies that are not prosocial. These include positive psychological interventions like mindfulness, cultivation of self-compassion, and the pursuit of the virtues of self-control, patience, and especially forgiveness. In addition, personal virtues like states of humility might be cultivated to make easy offense less likely.

It might sound like managing anger is a matter of imposing rational willful control over unruly emotions. This is a cultural expectation that arose from the aftermath of the French Enlightenment—rather than the British Enlightenment, which saw a more dominant role for one's sentiments.

Positive Distraction

Focusing on a task that requires attention might help. Focusing on other emotions (like, I love my child) might also help.

Positive Religious Coping

Stressors produce appraisals of the threat that the stressor makes to a person's well-being. Appraisal (often at the implicit, intuitive, unconscious level) leads to stress reactions that have physiological, emotional, motivational, cognitive, and behavioral components. The person then seeks to manage stress reactions through problem-solving coping, emotion-focused coping, and meaning-focused coping. Problem-solving coping attempts to resolve the stressor, change the appraisal, and manage the stress reactions. Emotion-focused coping seeks to control one's emotional reactions, which can be helpful when emotional arousal is so high that problem-solving and meaning-focused coping methods are impaired. Meaning-focused coping seeks to understand the framework around the stress.

Pargament and others (Pargament et al. 2000) have identified religious coping methods. Anger is a reaction to a stressor, so people might employ positive or negative religious coping methods to resolve the situation and manage anger. Positive religious coping includes having a collaborative style with God (i.e., accepting that God and people both have responsibilities), making benevolent reappraisals of the stressor, and seeking spiritual support from God, clergy, or members of one's religious group. These coping methods help people find meaning, experience a sense of control, feel close to God, and achieve a positive life transformation. Carver et al. (1989) used four items to assess religious coping. These involved trusting God, praying, finding comfort in religion, and seeking God's help.

Negative Religious Coping

Negative religious coping usually leads to spiritual struggle. It includes questioning, distance or conflict from God and others one identifies with religion, and perceiving God negatively.

Emotion-focused Coping

Most of those coping methods are problem-solving or meaning-making methods. People can also use emotion-focused methods, appealing to God to take away the anger or direct it in a righteous direction.

Physiological Interventions like Deep Slow Breathing

Anger is accompanied by SNS arousal. Thus, any way to reduce SNS arousal is likely to modulate anger. When people take deep slow breaths, the out-breath lowers the heart rate and can activate PSNS calming. By using deep slow breathing, one is using an emotion-focused coping method.

Attentional Changes like Mindfulness

Mindfulness exists in many forms, but one of the most used is to attend to the here and now. That might involve focusing on the body and scanning for tension, then releasing it. That might also involve attending to the external environment, and if angry thoughts invade consciousness, just let those pass on by. By diverting attention to positive events in the body or environment, anger is reduced. Mindfulness, of course, can be practiced for its own sake. However, one might employ mindfulness to reduce one's angry arousal or derail anger expression, using it like an emotion-focused coping method.

Attitudes toward the Self like Self-Compassion

People often extend compassion to needy others. If we see a person overwhelmed by anger, we might feel sorry for the person and even want to help. Neff (2011) has suggested that people can extend the same compassion to the self that one might extend to others. Self-compassion might therefore see ourselves as angry and seek to treat ourselves with self-compassion. By being compassionate toward ourselves, we employ an emotion-focused coping strategy—one that was not noted by Pargament et al. (2000).

Attitudes toward Others like Empathy, Tolerance, Compassion, or Even Love

One might seek to practice non-angry stances toward a provocative person or situation. Thus, by empathizing with the provocative person, we might be able not only to reduce our anger but also to solve the problem of how to deal with the person. Thus, this can be both an emotion-focused and a problem-solving coping strategy. Adopting a stance of tolerance, compassion, or even love toward the other can also change not only our emotions but also our acts, transforming not only our emotional life but the provocative situation as well.

Exhibiting Self-Control and Patience

Patience is waiting peacefully under conditions of provocation. By cultivating patience, we give the situation time to resolve and, in the midst of it, we calm our angry arousal. This lowers anger experience and makes it less likely that we express ourselves in negative angry behavior. Self-control or self-regulation, when applied to anger, involves strategies that prevent outbursts of anger expression. Self-control strategies may be categorized into those that attempt to manage the situation (i.e., stimulus control strategies like avoiding a provocative person) and those that use behavioral programming (i.e., those that reward oneself for desired behavior, like treating oneself to ice cream because one did not blow up at the *idiot* relative who said outlandish, troll-ish things at Thanksgiving dinner).

Forgiving

One reason why people get angry in the moment is because they have unresolved hurts and offenses about which they carry simmering resentment. It takes little to trigger an eruption when bitterness is a bubbling cauldron in the unconscious. Forgiving grudges can reduce the likelihood that a small provocation triggers an explosion. For resources, see www.EvWorthington-forgiveness.com, and for summaries of interventions, see Wade et al. (2014) and Wade and Tittler (2020). One might use forgiveness also as situation control, pre-emptively forgiving one who almost always triggers an angry interaction. Thinking to oneself, in the face of an outlandish statement *I've already realized he is going to say terrible things, and I've already forgiven that*, can allow the person to disengage and allow the moment to pass.

State of Humility

Humility is a virtue that can be cultivated as a character strength (Worthington and Allison 2018). But one can also use humility as a helpful state. If we anticipate that an interaction is likely with an ego-challenging person, we can get our minds focused before entering the interaction. We can remind ourselves of our strengths and weaknesses and also realize that we indeed want to be teachable to correct the weaknesses. We can remind ourselves to present ourselves modestly. We also can seek to be other-oriented, getting into the frame of reference of the provocative person and empathizing, then seeking to look out for the needs of the other instead of being preoccupied with defending our own ego.

CONCLUSION

Anger raises many ethical questions. Many of these center around our findings that anger control is often not under rational, reasoned System 2 cognitive control. To the extent that emotions are not under conscious control, how then can one be blamed for losing one's temper? How does one control anger when most of the experience of anger and the expression of anger are not subject to conscious control?

In this chapter, I have provided a psychologist's reflection on the vexing issues surrounding the ethics of anger. My major conclusions are several. First, most of anger is due to implicit cognition. Second, although people hold others responsible for failure to control or limit their angry expression, much of anger is not controllable. Third, therefore, to act ethically when primary or secondary anger is likely, one should take steps early to control situations that are indeed controllable and to build virtuous character strengths that will allow one to control responses. Finally, one needs a set of coping responses that can help limit the expression of anger and return the person to emotional equanimity.

REFERENCE LIST

Anderson, Craig A., Akiko Shibuya, Nobuko Ihori, Edward L. Swing, Brad J. Bushman, Akira Sakamoto, Hannah R. Rothstein, and Muniba Saleem. 2010. "Violent Video Game Effects on Aggression, Empathy, and Prosocial Behavior in Eastern and Western Countries: A Meta-Analytic Review." *Psychological Bulletin* 136, no. 2: 151–173. https://doi.org/10.1037/a0018251.

Barr, Stephen M. 2016. *The Believing Scientist: Essays on Science and Religion.* Grand Rapids, MI: William B. Eerdmans Publishing Company.

Baumeister, Roy F., and John Tierney. 2011. *Willpower: Rediscovering the Greatest Human Strength.* New York: Penguin Books.

Bem, D. J. 1967. "Self-Perception: An Alternative Interpretation of Cognitive Dissonance Phenomena." *Psychological Review* 74, no. 3: 183–200. https://doi.org/10.1037/h0024835.

Berkowitz, L. 1989. "Frustration-Aggression Hypothesis: Examination and Reformulation." *Psychological Bulletin* 106, no. 1: 59–73. https://doi.org/10.1037/0033-2909.106.1.59.

Brooks, Arthur C. 2019. *Love Your Enemies: How Decent People Can Save America from the Culture of Contempt.* New York: HarperCollins.

Brooks, David. 2012. *The Social Animal: The Hidden Sources of Love, Character, and Achievement.* New York: Random House.

Brooks, David. 2015. *The Road to Character.* New York: Random House.

Bushman, Brad J., and Jodi L. Whitaker. 2010. "Like a Magnet: Catharsis Beliefs Attract Angry People to Violent Video Games." *Psychological Science* 21, no. 6: 790–792. https://doi.org/10.1177/0956797610369494.

Bushman, Brad J., Roy Baumeister, and Collen M. Phillips. 2001. "Do People Aggress to Improve Their Mood? Catharsis Beliefs, Affect Regulation Opportunity, and Aggressive Responding." *Journal of Personality and Social Psychology* 81, no. 1: 17–32. https://doi.org/10.1037//0022-3514.81.1.17.

Carver, Charles, Michael Scheier, and Jagdish K. Weintraub. 1989. "Assessing Coping Strategies: A Theoretically Based Approach." *Journal of Personality and Social Psychology* 56, no. 2: 267–283. https://doi.org/10.1037//0022-3514.56.2.267.

Christakis, Nicholas A. 2019. *Blueprint: The Evolutionary Origins of a Good Society*. New York: The Hachette Book Group.

Damasio, Antonio R. 1994. *Descartes' Error: Emotion, Rationality and the Human Brain*. New York: Putnam.

Dollard, John, Leonard W. Doob, Neal E. Miller, O. H. Mowrer, and Robert R. Sears. 1939. *Frustration and Aggression*. New Haven, CT: Yale University Press.

Fisher, Roger, William L. Ury, and Bruce Patton. 2011. *Getting to Yes: Negotiating Agreement without Giving In*, 3rd ed. New York: Penguin Books.

Gottman, John M. 1993. "A Theory of Marital Dissolution and Stability." *Journal of Family Psychology* 7, no. 1: 57–75. https://doi.org/10.1037/0893-3200.7.1.57.

Griffin, Brandon J., Everett L. Worthington, Jr., Caroline R. Lavelock, Chelsea L. Greer, Yin Lin, Don E. Davis, and Joshua N. Hook. 2015. "Efficacy of a Self-Forgiveness Workbook: A Randomized Controlled Trial with Interpersonal Offenders." *Journal of Counseling Psychology* 62, no. 2: 124–136. https://doi.org/10.1037/cou0000060.

Haidt, Jonathan. 2012. *The Righteous Mind: Why Good People are Divided by Politics and Religion.* New York: Pantheon Books.

Heath, Chip, and Dan Heath. 2010. *Switch: How to Change Things When Change Is Hard*. New York: Broadway Books.

Hunter, James Davison, and Paul Nedelisky. 2019. *Science and the Good: The Tragic Quest for the Foundations of Morality*. New Haven, CT: Yale University Press.

Kahneman, Daniel. 2011. *Thinking, Fast and Slow*. New York: Farrar, Straus, Giroux.

Kahneman, Daniel, and Amos Tversky. 1979. "Prospect Theory: An Analysis of Decision under Risk." *Econometrica* 47, no. 2: 263–291. https://doi.org/10.2307/1914185.

Kapic, Kelly M. 2017. *Embodied Hope: A Theological Meditation on Pain and Suffering*. Downers Grove, IL: IVP Academic.

Lazarus, Richard S., and Susan Folkman. 1984. *Stress, Appraisal, and Coping*. New York: Springer.

LeDoux, Joseph. 1996. *The Emotional Brain: The Mysterious Underpinnings of Emotional Life*. New York: Simon & Schuster.

Marcel, Gabriel. 1962. *Homo Viator: An Introduction to the Metaphysic of Hope*. New York: Harper & Row.

McMinn, Mark R. 2017. *The Science of Virtue: Why Positive Psychology Matters to the Church*. Grand Rapids, MI: Brazos Press.

Mouw, Richard J. 2010. *Uncommon Decency: Christian Civility in an Uncivil World*, rev ed. Downers Grove, IL: InterVarsity Press.

Neff, Kristin. 2011. *Self-Compassion: The Proven Power of Being Kind to Yourself*. New York: HarperCollins.

Nisbett, Richard E., and Dov Cohen. 1996. *Culture of Honor: The Psychology of Violence in the South.* Boulder, CO: Westview Press.

Pargament, Kenneth I., Harold Koenig, and Lisa M. Perez. 2000. "The Many Methods of Religious Coping: Development and Initial Validation of the RCOPE." *Journal of Clinical Psychology* 56, no. 4 (April): 519–543. https://doi.org/10.1002/(SICI)1097-4679(200004)56:4<519::AID-JCLP6>3.0.CO;2-1.

Park, Crystal L. 2007. "Religiousness/Spirituality and Health: A Meaning Systems Perspective." *Journal of Behavioral Medicine* 30, no. 4 (September): 319–328. https://doi.org/10.1007/s10865-007-0111-x.

Pascual-Leone, Antonio, Phoenix Gilles, Terence Singh, and Cristina A. Andreescu. 2013. "Problem Anger in Psychotherapy: An Emotion-Focused Perspective on Hate, Rage, and Rejecting Anger." *Journal of Contemporary Psychotherapy* 43, no. 2: 83–92. https://doi.org/10.1007/s10879-012-9214-8.

Putnam, Robert D. 2020. *The Upswing: How America Came together a Century Ago and How We Can Do It Again.* New York: Simon & Schuster.

Smith, Travis. 2018. *Superhero Ethics: 10 Comic Book Heroes; 10 Ways to Save the World; Which One Do We Need Most Now?* West Conshohocken, PA: Templeton Press.

Snyder, C. R. 1994. *The Psychology of Hope*. New York: The Free Press.

Sternberg, Robert J. 1986. "A Triangular Theory of Love." *Psychological Review* 93, no. 2: 119–135. https://doi.org/10.1037/0033-295X.93.2.119.

Stevenson, Bryan. 2014. *Just Mercy: A Story of Justice and Redemption.* New York: Spiegel & Grau.

Tangney, June Price, and Kurt W. Fischer, eds. 1995. *Self-Conscious Emotions.* New York: Guilford Press.

Van Lange, Paul, Caryl E. Rusbult, Stephen M. Drigotas, Ximena B. Arriaga, Betty S. Witcher, and Chante L. Cox. 1997. "Willingness to Sacrifice in Close Relationships." *Journal of Personality and Social Psychology* 72, no. 6 (June): 1373–1395. https://doi.org/10.1037/0022-3514.72.6.1373.

Wade, Nathaniel G., and Meredith V. Tittler. 2020. "Psychological Interventions to Promote Forgiveness of Others: Review of Empirical Evidence." In *Handbook of Forgiveness*, 2nd ed., edited by Everett L. Worthington, Jr., and Nathaniel G. Wade, 255–265. New York: Routledge.

Wade, Nathaniel G., William T. Hoyt, Julia E. M. Kidwell, Everett L. Worthington, Jr. 2014. "Meta-Analysis of Psychotherapeutic Interventions to Promote Forgiveness." *Journal of Consulting and Clinical Psychology* 82, no. 1 (February): 154–170. https://doi.org/10.1037/10035268.

Wilson, David S. 2019. *This View of Life: Completing the Darwinian Revolution.* New York: Pantheon Books.

Woodyatt, Lydia, Everett L. Worthington, Jr., Michael Wenzel, and Brandon J. Griffin, eds. 2017. *Handbook of the Psychology of Self-Forgiveness.* Cham, Switzerland: Springer Nature.

Worthington, Everett L., Jr. 2005. *Hope-Focused Marriage Counseling: A Guide to Brief Therapy, rev. ed. with a New Introduction.* Downers Grove, IL: InterVarsity Press.

Worthington, Everett L., Jr. 2013. *Moving Forward: Six Steps to Forgiving Yourself and Breaking Free from the Past.* Colorado Springs, CO: WaterBrook/Multnomah.

Worthington, Everett L., Jr., and Scott T. Allison. 2018. *Heroic Humility: What the Science of Humility Can Say to People Raised on Self-Focus.* Washington, DC: American Psychological Association.

Wright, N. T. 2006. *Evil and the Justice of God.* Downers Grove, IL: InterVarsity Press.

Wright, T. 2010. *Virtue Reborn.* London: SBKT.

Yalom, Irvin D. 1985. *The Theory and Practice of Group Psychotherapy.* New York: Basic Books.

Zahnd, Brian. 2017. *Sinners in the Hands of a Loving God.* Colorado Springs, CO: WaterBrook Press.

Part II

MORAL RESPONSES

Chapter 3

The Moral Necessity of Anger

Krista K. Thomason

Philosophers have long been divided on the moral status of anger. On one side are the skeptics who think that anger is damaging, dangerous, or irrational. Seneca, for example, describes anger as "raging with an inhuman desire to inflict pain" (2010, 14). More recently, Nussbaum has argued that anger is either irrational or narcissistic (2016, 24–29). It is, as she puts it "always normatively problematic" (2016, 5). On the other side, there are the optimists who think that anger can be morally valuable and even morally necessary. Aristotle argues that the right kind of anger is a virtue and that "people who do not get angry in the circumstances one should are thought to be foolish" (2002, 152/1126a5). Solomon argues that anger is both "rational and reasonable" when it is a response to a serious offense (2007, 25). As Bailey puts it, "Anger is the emotion of injustice" (2018, 93).

My aim in this chapter is to defend a strong version of the optimist's claim. Anger is not just rational and reasonable, but also a morally necessary response to wrongdoing. The version of the argument that I will defend is sometimes called the constitutive view.[1] That is, feelings of anger are constitutive of the proper moral response to the offense, ill-treatment, or injustice.[2] The constitutive view has been the target of at least two objections. First, there appear to be examples of people who adequately respond to wrongdoing and yet seem not to feel anger. Second, given anger's clear potential for damage, it would be better for moral agents to respond to wrongdoing without anger. In order to defend the moral necessity of anger, I argue against both of these objections. First, I will explain the constitutive view and the objections against it in more detail.

THE CONSTITUTIVE VIEW

Several philosophers have defended a version of the constitutive view of moral emotions. The constitutive view is inspired by P. F. Strawson's arguments about resentment and its connection to our practices of holding people responsible (1963/2003). Roughly, on this view, emotions are at least partially constitutive of some feature of moral psychology (e.g., judgments, responses, values, practices, or commitments). Constitutivists are not univocal in their explanations. For example, Wallace argues that feelings of resentment are constitutive of holding others to moral expectations (1994, 20–24). Murphy argues that resentment is constitutive of one's sense of moral self-respect (2003, 19–20). In spite of these differences, constitutive views share the same basic strategy. The aim is to explain the role that emotions have in our moral psychology by showing how emotions (at least partially) constitute some psychological features of moral agency.

In spite of their differences, constitutive views are vulnerable to the same type of objection. The objection goes this way: the constitutive view is false because it cannot show that emotions are necessarily constitutive of moral judgments or responses. That is, we can think of cases in which moral agents have the moral judgment or response in question without also feeling the corresponding emotion. If these cases are legitimate, then the emotion is not really constitutive after all.

This objection is particularly salient when we consider negative emotions that seem to have significant potential for damage or harm. Take shame as an example. Many philosophers have argued that shame is a valuable moral emotion because it shows that we care about living up to ideals that we value (Rawls 1971/2003; Taylor 1985; Mason 2010; Deonna et al. 2012). On views like these, shame is constitutive of the painful realization that we have fallen short of the ideals to which we aspire. Skeptics point out how damaging shame can be: feelings of shame often drive people to self-destructive behavior, including self-harm and suicide (Isenberg 1949; Kekes 1988; Manion 2002; Nussbaum 2004). Surely, the skeptics will claim, we do not necessarily need feelings of shame in order to care about living up to our ideals. In fact, getting over shame seems to be psychologically healthier. If it is both possible and desirable to train ourselves out of damaging emotions, we ought to do so.

This same skeptical argument is used against anger. Constitutivists have argued that anger partially constitutes the recognition of an expression of ill will or wrongdoing (Strawson 1963/2003; Murphy and Hampton 1988; Wallace 1994; Murphy 2003; Darwall 2006). If someone does me a wrong or expresses ill will toward me and I do not react with anger, constitutivists will argue that, absent some other explanation, I have failed to perceive this treatment as wrong or undeserved. Similar to shame, skeptics will argue that it is possible for an agent to recognize ill-treatment without feeling anger (Watson 1993; Pettigrove 2012; Nussbaum 2016). Moreover, given anger's potential for damage or harm, it would be desirable for everyone to feel less anger or to get over such feelings as much as possible.

There are two claims that comprise the skeptical position: what I will call the necessity claim and the desirability claim. The first denies that feelings of anger are necessary in order to properly respond to wrongdoing. The second asserts that, given anger's downsides, it is morally desirable that we try to feel less of it or get over it as much as is possible. I will argue against both of these claims.

THE NECESSITY CLAIM

Skeptics usually deploy two strategies to argue that anger is not morally necessary in order to respond to wrongdoing. One is to argue that it is conceptually possible to separate feelings of anger from judgments of wrongdoing.[3] The other is to appeal to moral exemplars who seem to have gotten over their anger.

To illustrate the first strategy, Pettigrove and Tanaka introduce the distinction between anger being warranted and anger being necessary (2014, 273). To claim that anger is warranted as a response to ill-treatment is merely to claim that it would be intelligible or perhaps even permissible for the victim to feel anger when she is mistreated. Arguing that anger is warranted is a weaker claim than that it is necessary. Pettigrove and Tanaka argue that this weaker claim is more plausible because we can see both from philosophical literature and from everyday experience examples of people who are able to make moral judgments and yet do not feel anger (2014, 276–277). If these examples are plausible, then it appears as though the stronger version of the constitutive view is false.

The strategy of divorcing feelings of anger from responses to wrongdoing raises an important question for the constitutive view. What precisely does it mean to say that anger is a necessary part of our responses to wrongdoing? Philosophers who ascribe to the constitutive view provide different answers to this question. Here I will rely on a version of the account that I have defended elsewhere (Thomason 2018). On this version of the constitutive view, a liability to anger is constitutive of our capacity to recognize, judge, or appreciate intentional wrongdoing or ill-treatment.[4] There are several parts of this account to clarify. First, I and other philosophers who defend this view will speak in terms of *liability* to anger.[5] Advocates of the constitutive view accept that our emotions are not under our direct control and that they sometimes surprise us. They can arise in situations when we do not expect them, and they can fail to show up when we assume they will. We may, for example, suffer a serious betrayal at the hands of a loved one and, to our own shock or confusion, not feel anger (Thomason 2018, 147–148). It therefore makes more sense to talk about a liability to anger being a necessary part of recognizing wrongdoing. Having a liability to an emotion means that we are disposed to feel it in some set of specified circumstances because of values or commitments that we hold. The fact that we might not feel anger at a particular moment does not pose an objection to this version of the constitutive view.

Additionally, it is important to understand what is meant by a recognition or response to wrongdoing on this view. Crucially, recognizing a wrong is not a simply matter of assenting to a proposition. This way of thinking is to misunderstand the complex nature of judging or responding to wrongdoing. As Solomon argues, "Anger is not just a judgment of offense, but a network of interlocking judgments concerning one's status and relationship with the offending party, the gravity and mitigating circumstances of the offense, and the urgency of revenge" (1988, 186). On the constitutive view, the network that Solomon describes comprises the liability to an emotion. Holding some set of values, beliefs, desires, and commitments is to be susceptible to emotions that are relevant to them. A liability to an emotion is not merely the belief that such an emotion would be warranted. The constitutivist will deny that we can easily separate our beliefs about wrongdoing from our emotional responses to it. To use Rawls's example, to love another person is to be liable to joy in her presence and sorrow in her absence, and my love for her is present in these emotions (Rawls 1971/2003, 426). If I am liable to neither this joy nor sorrow, the constitutive view will claim that I do not actually love her. In the case of anger, if I am not liable to anger when someone wrongs me, then I fail to recognize or appreciate the wrong. There is no such thing as a bare, dispassionate, merely propositional judgment that someone wronged me (Solomon 1988, 187). This is not to claim that judgment must be explosive or expressive, or that our anger must be obvious and overt (Solomon 1988, 188). The constitutive view will, however, insist that judging something as wrongdoing or ill-treatment must involve a liability to feelings of anger. Again, not feeling a particular emotion at a particular moment does not affect the liability to that emotion. The focus of the constitutive view is not on emotions as episodes. Instead, its focus is the role that emotions play in our network of judgments, commitments, and values.

The version of the constitutive view that I and others defend also classifies anger as a reactive attitude. Reactive attitudes arise within the context of what Strawson called the participant stance (1963/2003, 79). The participant stance is so named because it presupposes our participation in relations with others (1963/2003, 76–79). Within the participant stance, we see others as responsible moral agents to whom we owe some basic form of goodwill and from whom we can expect basic goodwill (1963/2003, 76). It is because of this mindset or commitment that we are liable to feelings of anger when another person shows us disregard. Strawson contrasts the participant stance with the objective stance (1963/2003, 79). Taking an objective stance toward another person is to see that person "as an object of social policy" or someone to be "managed or cured or handled or trained" (ibid.). The objective stance does not presume that another person is a responsible agent capable of acting autonomously and intentionally or capable of showing us proper regard and disregard. We would not be liable to anger toward, suppose, a rude automaton who was built to hurl insults at passersby.[6] When constitutivists claim that anger is a necessary part of recognizing and responding to wrongdoing, we assume that the wrongdoing is intentional and that it originates from a responsible fellow moral agent. We are liable to anger because we see our fellow agents as responsible persons rather than mere causes of events, automatons, or objects of social policy. To summarize, the constitutivist will argue that a liability to anger is a necessary part of recognizing a wrong done by a fellow moral agent.

Skeptics will argue that we have examples of people who can recognize wrongdoing without anger. The first question to raise is whether they react to wrongdoing without feeling anger or without being liable to anger. The constitutivists can accept that people do not always respond to wrongdoing by experiencing the emotion of anger. Again, our emotions are not perfectly under the control of our will, so we do not feel them on command. What constitutivists will deny is that a person can properly recognize wrongdoing without being liable to anger—that such a person literally never feels anger or has never felt anger in other cases. The skeptical case made here needs to be filled out in more detail. One possible interpretation is that we can imagine someone who can assent to the proposition "This action is wrong" without feeling anger. This version of the objection mistakes the complex act of judging or recognizing for simply assenting to a proposition (Solomon 1988, 186). What it means to judge, recognize, or appreciate wrongdoing is complex and cannot be reduced to one proposition or belief. Another possible interpretation is that we are able to imagine the conceptual possibility of someone who does not feel anger and can still judge wrongdoing. It is difficult to know what precisely this conceptual imagining amounts to. Suppose we try to construct a similar case: imagine a parent who takes care of his children, plays with them, participates in their lives, wishes them well, is pained by their suffering, and overjoyed by their happiness and yet also, let us suppose, does not actually feel love for them. A case like this seems to distinguish acts of love and care, loving relations, and parental commitments from something like a raw emotional feel. The constitutivist will argue that this move is possible only in the most abstract sense. The mere conceptual possibility of such a person poses no risk to the constitutive view because the necessity claim is not merely a conceptual claim. It is a claim about moral relations as they exist in the world for creatures like us.

The reply from the skeptic helps us segue into the second strategy. Skeptics often appeal to cases of moral exemplars who appear to have gotten over or transformed their feelings of anger. These exemplars, they will argue, show that judging wrongdoing without anger is not a mere conceptual possibility. Indeed, these cases show that creatures like us can recognize wrongdoing without the liability to anger. The two most common exemplars are Martin Luther King, Jr. and Mahatma Gandhi (Watson 1993, 147–148; Nussbaum 2016, 218–225). Nussbaum's discussion of King and Gandhi is thorough and helps illustrate how they function as exemplars for getting over anger. Nussbaum argues that both King and Gandhi see anger as inherently tied to an immature and destructive wish for retaliation (2016, 221). King and Gandhi argue that feelings of anger ought to be "channeled" or "purified" through self-discipline and the reorientation of one's attitude toward the objects of one's anger (2016, 221–222). This process will create a new outlook in which one "carefully separates the deed from the doer, criticizing and repudiating the bad deed, but not imputing unalterable evil to people" (2016, 222). According to Nussbaum, King and Gandhi replace their anger with healthier emotions such as grief and love (2016, 225). This replacement allows them to respond appropriately to wrongdoing without the dangers and errors of anger. Additionally, Pettigrove and Tanaka appeal to Śāntideva's writings on anger to show that the Bodhisattva likewise makes moral judgments and yet feels no anger (2014, 272–273). On their reading, Śāntideva recommends weeding anger out of our lives as much as possible in part because anger presupposes a mistaken view about the importance of our own perspectives (2014, 273). Nevertheless, the Bodhisattva (or the person who aspires to be one) can still make moral judgments. Despite never feeling anger, "they adopt the right sort of stance to the wrongdoing they identify, seeking to avoid such moral failings in themselves and their actions and opposing them in others" (2014, 276).

I think we should we wary of the appeal to moral exemplars. First, the fact that King and Gandhi are two of the most cited examples of people who have gotten over anger might demonstrate that they are more anomalous than they appear. If skeptics think that getting over anger is readily psychologically available to us, it seems we should have more than two examples of people who have achieved it. King also studied the nonviolent philosophy of Gandhi, which suggests the commitments they share may be unique to them (Thomason 2018, 167). Pettigrove and Tanaka resist this move by arguing that the criticisms about anger are far more widespread. They point out that warnings against anger appear not just in Śāntideva, but also in many other Buddhist texts, Eastern traditions, Stoicism, early Christian and Jewish philosophers, and the sentimentalist tradition from the eighteenth century (2014, 274–275). Of course, the fact that a view is widely shared does not show that it is correct; the view that anger is central to our moral lives is also widespread. Rather, Pettigrove and Tanaka's point is that we cannot dismiss views like Śāntideva's (or King's and Gandhi's) as anomalous. Although this conclusion is surely right, much more work needs to be done to determine the details of these criticisms of anger. While I cannot examine all these accounts of anger here, I will focus on King and Śāntideva and try to show that their positions on anger are less straightforward than Nussbaum, Pettigrove, and Tanaka present them.

Beginning with King, his views on anger are clearly complex. When he describes the mindset of nonviolence, he says it is "nonaggressive physically, but strongly aggressive spiritually" (1986, 7, 12, 18). Likewise, King insists that while the nonviolent resister is physically passive, "his mind and his emotions are always active, constantly seeking to persuade his opponent he is wrong" (1986, 18). He encourages Black Americans to remain "maladjusted" to the injustices of segregation and discrimination (1986, 14). He also repeatedly emphasizes that nonviolence should not be mistaken for or built on cowardice (1986, 7, 12, 17). Given these remarks, King's views on anger are not unequivocally negative. It is difficult to know how to interpret his claim that we ought to be emotionally active and spiritually aggressive without an appeal to something like anger. More specifically, philosophers have argued that King's arguments presuppose a fitting or virtuous anger (Cogley 2014; Bell 2009). It is abundantly clear that King rejects violence and hatred as permissible responses to injustice (1986, 7–8, 12–13, 17–20). Yet rejecting violence and hatred does not require rejecting anger. Other interpreters of King might object to the characterization of spiritual and emotional activity as anger, but my point here is merely to show that King's views about anger are not so straightforward. He might reject anger or he might only reject excessive anger, hatred, and violence (Thomason 2018, 166).

Śāntideva's views about anger are likewise complicated. First, it should be noted that, contrary to popular conceptions of Buddhist philosophy, there is no single view about anger in Buddhism. For example, McRae argues that Tantric Buddhism advocates transforming, rather than eliminating, one's anger (2015, 472–473). With regard to Śāntideva, there is controversy in the literature about the extent to which his text is meant to be a program for cultivating virtue. For example, Garfield argues that Śāntideva's text is, like much of Buddhist ethics, an attempt to solve the existential problem of suffering. On Garfield's view, Śāntideva tries to solve that problem by "by developing an understanding of our place in the complex web of interdependence (*pratītyasamutpāda*) that is our world" (2011, 338). To interpret this project as a set of recommendations for moral self-improvement is to shoehorn Śāntideva's views into the framework of Western virtue ethics (Garfield 2011, 335). Even if we set aside concerns like these, understanding Śāntideva's position on anger is still not straightforward. Bommarito, for instance, argues that there is a tension in Śāntideva's criticism of anger and his purpose in describing the way to the enlightened mind (*bodhicitta*). On Bommarito's view, Śāntideva argues against anger because anger assumes that other people are anything more than the sum of conditions and causes (2011, 364–365). According to this interpretation, Śāntideva seems to suggest that being angry with people for the wrongs they do would be equivalent to being angry with a storm that damages our house. As Bommarito points out, however, the advice that Śāntideva provides is directed toward people who are presumed to have at least some kind of agency—otherwise they would be incapable of aspiring to *bodhicitta* (2011, 368–370). This tension may lead us to ask whether Śāntideva really thinks that anger is as irrational or misguided as interpreters claim. Of course, Śāntideva may still reject anger for other reasons. My point is that the details of interpretation may show that the rejections of anger from philosophers like King and Śāntideva are not what they seem.

For the sake of the argument, let us suppose that King and Śāntideva do reject anger. According to skeptics of the constitutive view, this conclusion would mean that they make moral judgments without feeling angry. Presupposed in this argument is the view that they make *the same* moral judgments that those of us who are disposed to anger will make. I think we should resist this assumption. Both King and Śāntideva have substantive moral and metaphysical commitments that lead to their rejection of anger. These commitments reveal particular views about themselves, others, and the universe that are in tension with the presuppositions of the constitutive view.

Let us start with King. King argues that the philosophy of nonviolence involves seeing the forces of justice and evil at work in the world. He writes, "There is something in the universe that unfolds for justice," and the nonviolent resisters have felt "that as we struggled we had cosmic companionship" (1986, 13–14). The job of the nonviolent resister is to prevent further evil from entering the world—she must "cut off the chain of hate . . . by projecting an ethic of love into the world" (1986, 19). Seeing people as fighters for either justice or evil is also supported by King's commitment to the interconnectedness of humanity. He writes, "All humanity is a single process . . . If you harm me, you harm yourself" (1986, 20). As a result, the target of the spiritual aggression of nonviolence is not the individual who does wrong, but the evil of the universe. He writes that "the attack is directed against the forces of evil rather than against persons who happen to be doing the evil" (1986, 8, 18). King is clear throughout his writings that accepting the philosophy of nonviolence is a difficult task in part because he recognizes a powerful temptation to give in to hatred, bitterness, or violence (1986, 8, 10).

Śāntideva is committed to overcoming the centrality of the self as part of the development of the enlightened mind (*bodhicitta*) (Bommarito 2011, 364–366; Garfield 2011, 343–344). That is, weeding anger out of one's life is possible when we come to the full realization and appreciation that the self and its attachments and aversions are illusory. This requires weakening the boundaries between self and others (Garfield 2011, 340–341), seeing the actions of others as no different from the conditions or causes in the world (Bommarito 2011, 360–362), and seeing oneself and others as ephemeral and impermanent (Bommarito 2011, 365–366; Garfield 2011, 341–342, 347–348). Śāntideva's path to *bodhicitta* is meant to engender an "insight into the nature of reality so deep that it transforms our way of seeing ourselves and others" (Garfield 2011, 334).

The ethical outlooks of King and Śāntideva contain commitments (to greater and lesser degrees) to what I will call depersonalization. They both encourage us to see people as caught up in forces of the universe and to deemphasize the extent to which people are agents in the harm or suffering they cause. Additionally, they ask us to see ourselves as fundamentally connected to others, including those who wrong us. They also argue that we should see ourselves as less agential than we think. For King, we are part of the forces of justice and light, and we are bound to use the force of love in the face of wrongdoing. For Śāntideva, we are interconnected, interdependent, and ephemeral. Arguments like these pose no challenge to the constitutive view. The constitutive view accepts the Strawsonian claim that anger is a reactive attitude, which arises from within the participant stance (1963/2003, 79). Being in this stance requires that we see other people as autonomous agents who are not mere causal events or caught up in forces outside of them. It is precisely this perception that King and Śāntideva ask us to deemphasize. King and Śāntideva are committed to moral worldviews that do not presuppose the kind of moral agency that Strawson does. Indeed, they advocate for a moral point of view that transforms our traditional way of understanding ourselves and each other. King and Śāntideva recognize that it is natural for us to be angry, given the commitments that we hold. What they ask is that we give up or change those commitments and, in doing so, we will stop being angry. The constitutive view can agree that if we alter or give up the participant stance, then we may no longer feel anger toward wrongdoers. But this is just to say that if we transform our views about ourselves, others, and the nature of wrongdoing, then we will feel different emotions. Characterized this way, skeptics can no longer claim that King and Śāntideva are making the same moral judgments as the rest of us. They understand agency and wrongdoing differently, which is why they do not respond to ill-treatment with anger.

Moral exemplars like King and Śāntideva do not pose counterexamples to the constitutive view. If anything, they show that if we alter our values, beliefs, and commitments, our emotional lives will likewise be altered.

The skeptic can argue that we should do what figures like King and Śāntideva ask. They might say that we would be morally better off rethinking our relations to others and our conceptions of ourselves so that we were less prone to anger. Notice that this is a new argument: the claim is no longer that we can make the same moral judgments without feelings of anger. It is now that we should alter our moral outlooks so that we can get rid of anger. This is the desirability claim, to which I will now turn.

THE DESIRABILITY CLAIM

Recall that the desirability claim states that we would be better off getting over our feelings of anger. There are two versions of this claim. The first version argues that because anger is damaging, harmful, or dangerous, we ought to do our best to feel it as little as possible. Notice that this argument does not outright reject the constitutive view. It simply emphasizes the downsides of anger. The second version also argues that anger is dangerous or harmful, but adds that we ought to follow the example of people like King and Śāntideva. We should, in other words, rethink the values and commitments that make us liable to anger because a world without anger would be a better world. I respond to each of these versions of the desirability claim in turn.

We must examine more closely the claim that anger is harmful or damaging. One way to understand this claim is that some kinds of anger can be harmful. The constitutive view can accept this claim. Of course, anger can sometimes be excessive. For example, people can be rightly criticized for being too angry about a relatively minor offense. Additionally, we might think that it is bad to have a short temper, to stay angry for too long, or to be angry too often. None of these criticisms are of anger per se, but rather how people manage or relate to their anger. We might make the same criticisms about other emotions, including positive ones—we might say that someone is being too forgiving or too sympathetic. Also, some of these criticisms are not about our emotions, but about a lack of perspective or proportionality (Thomason 2015, 252–253). The person who is too angry at a small slight could be criticized for being unfair or unreasonable. We might say that such a person lacks perspective or fails to have good judgment about what sorts of wrongs are worth getting upset about. We are able to make all of these criticisms without claiming that there is something wrong with the person's anger *qua* anger. The constitutivist need not argue that every episode of anger is good and valuable. She is committed to the claim that a liability to anger is valuable because it partially constitutes the recognition of wrongdoing. Defending anger in this way does not entail that anger can never go wrong or can never be criticized. The constitutivist holds that, in spite of its potential dangers, anger is a valuable part of our emotional lives and that should not wish to be rid of it.

I take it those who advocate for the desirability claim mean something more than just that anger can sometimes be excessive. A stronger argument is that there is something inherently wrong with anger. One version of this argument is that anger is basically confused or irrational. For example, Pettigrove and Tanaka (inspired by Śāntideva) argue that we become angry when our desires are thwarted, but many of our desires are confused or not worth our investment (2014, 277–279). In this way, anger is more often than not an inappropriate or confused emotion. They further appeal to empirical evidence that anger negatively influences our other judgments. Some psychological studies purport to show that angry people are more likely to attribute negative traits to people who are unlike them, to rely on stereotypes when making judgments, and to see themselves as less biased (2014, 279–280). Studies like these support Pettigrove and Tanaka's claim that "anger is systematically misleading" (2014, 281). Nussbaum also suggests that anger is inherently irrational. On Nussbaum's view, at the heart of anger is a wish for payback for the harm done (2016, 15). The payback "is seen as somehow assuaging the pain or making good the damage" caused by the original wrong (2016, 24). Yet according to Nussbaum, such a belief is irrational. To imagine that by paying back the offender in kind, our own pain will thereby be alleviated is "magical thinking" (ibid.). Alternatively, anger is a response to a perceived diminution in status (2016, 25). An offender's wrong is an act of down-ranking, and so payback is a way to restore balance by bringing the offender low (2016, 26). Nussbaum argues that this way of understanding anger is likewise irrational because it is fundamentally narcissistic (2016, 29). Wrongdoing is not about comparatively high or low status, but rather about injustice (ibid.).

There are several points in these arguments that should be separated. The first thing to note is that the conclusion about anger's irrationality will depend a great deal on the specifics of the accounts of anger. Pettigrove, Tanaka, and Nussbaum argue that the payback wish is central to anger (2014, 277–278; 2016, 15). On these grounds, they then suggest that payback is irrational or confused. One might dispute that the payback wish is part of the internal logic of anger. We might, for example, think of anger as a challenge or a protest against the offender's behavior.[7] On a view like this, anger accuses rather than punishes. Even though the wish for payback might be a common experience when people are angry, it may nevertheless not be an essential part of anger. It could instead be a kind of common coping mechanism (Thomason 2017, 6). It may be quick and easy psychologically to move from recognizing that a person has wronged me to wanting to see that person hurt in return. There could be any number of reasons why this move occurs: perhaps the offender has made me feel powerless and hurting that person alleviates those feelings. Maybe the payback wish is a desire to bring about a reciprocal appreciation from the offender. If I hurt the offender as she has hurt me, she will realize what it was like to be of the receiving end of ill will (Thomason 2017, 6). We need not settle on one explanation here. The point is merely to show that it is an open question whether the wish for payback is essential to feelings of anger. If it is not, then we cannot conclude that since the payback wish is irrational, anger itself is irrational. We can pose the same questions about Pettigrove and Tanaka's claims that anger is about a thwarted desire (2014, 277–279) or Nussbaum's claims that anger is about down-ranking (2016, 26–27). If anger turns out to be neither of these things, then whatever conclusions we draw about anger from these accounts will not figure into anger's rationality.

My main aim in this chapter is to defend the constitutive view's claim that anger is a morally necessary response, so building and defending my own account of anger would require more work than I can accomplish here. Also, I wish to be pluralist to a certain extent because constitutive views are not univocal in their characterizations of anger. Nonetheless, we should have some sense of what anger is in order to respond to arguments about its irrationality. Let me briefly sketch an account that draws on the work of other versions of the constitutive view.[8]

The constitutivist will claim that anger is part of the recognition that another person has treated me with disrespect or ill will. Feeling anger is not a matter of merely believing that this is the case or making a judgment that an event of a certain kind has occurred (Solomon 1988, 185–186). Anger is an emotional protest or resistance to an offense or expression of ill will. It arises in response to ill will because of the way one understands oneself, the offender, and the relationship between the two. The reason I am liable to anger when someone treats me with ill will is because I see myself as a moral agent and I see that person as a moral agent (Strawson 1963/2003, 76–79). As Hieronymi puts it, the victim's anger "affirms both [the offense's] wrongfulness and the moral significance of both herself and the offender" (2001, 530). It is only because we recognize an expression of ill will as coming from a fellow moral agent that we protest it. I would not be angry at a tree for falling on my car during a storm, but I would be angry at my neighbor for cutting her tree down so that it falls on my car. The reason we protest such treatment is because we see ourselves as existing in a relationship of mutual expectation and obligation. As a fellow moral agent, I see myself as deserving a basic form of regard from my fellows and as owing them the same basic regard.[9] When another shows me disregard,

I protest this treatment and feelings of anger are partially constitute that protest.

Given this sort of definition, advocates of the constitutive view will argue that there is nothing irrational about anger. It is not irrational because protesting the display of ill will from another moral agent is not irrational. Since we see ourselves and others as standing in relations of mutual regard, when that mutual regard is violated, we will resist it. Anger is not, contra Pettigrove and Tanaka, about our thwarted desires. It is not merely the case that I desire to be treated as a moral agent, but rather that I expect to be and that the offender is obligated to treat me as such. Contra Nussbaum, anger is also not about status. Anger at the offender is not about righting an imbalance or even bringing her low. It is a protest against her ill will or disrespect.

Skeptics of the constitutive view can at this point dispute at least two of the above claims. The first is the claim that we must be liable to anger in order to see ourselves and others as moral agents, and they will point to moral exemplars to make this case. Since I argued against moral exemplars earlier, I will move on to the second claim. Skeptics might instead argue that there is a better, more enlightened way of responding to wrongdoing than with anger. In other words, even if anger is not confused or irrational, we would still be better off if we were to train ourselves out of it. Those of who defend the constitutive view can admit that anger is sometimes damaging and hurtful. An angry person is usually not a good friend, coworker, or spouse. Angry people can be overly judgmental and unfairly expect more of others than they expect of themselves. As Nussbaum puts it, "The world has been propelled to a large extent by rage and retribution, but let us create something better, in ourselves and in political culture" (2016, 247). Nussbaum makes two points here: (a) anger's downsides give us sufficient reason to want it out of our lives and (b) that we would be better off or more virtuous if we decided to see ourselves, others, and the world in such a way that would make anger less central.

Are anger's downsides enough to outweigh its value? We must be careful here that we are not motivated to reject anger on the wrong kinds of reasons.[10] Often injunctions against anger originate from its deleterious effects to the person who becomes consumed by it. Of course, we can be rightly wary of being consumed by an emotion without being wary of the emotion itself. Think, for example, of the warning "Love is blind." No one treats this caution against love's tendency to make us overlook the flaws of our beloved as a reason to get over love altogether. The trouble, according to the skeptics, is that even run-of-the-mill anger can have negative effects. As Pettigrove and Tanaka argue, empirical psychology studies appear to provide evidence for "spillover anger." When we are angry, we tend to be more judgmental and more assured of our own righteousness (2014, 279–280). At the same time, as Cherry argues, the mistakes that people attribute to anger can also be attributed to our anger evaluations (2018, 57–58). That is, we tend to judge people who express anger harsher than we should, we tend to be unsympathetic toward them, and we often do not take the time to try to understand why they are angry (2018, 52–56). It may be the case, then, that the assumptions we make about anger's downsides are not as clear-eyed as we imagine.

Even if it is true that normal amounts of anger can have downsides, we must ask whether they amount to sufficient reason for getting over anger. There is a tendency to treat anger (and negative emotions in general) as a psychological problem. Anger "eats away at my peace of mind—I lose sleep, snap at my friends, become less effective at my work, and so on" (Murphy 1988, 23). That is, we ought to get over anger as a matter of good mental health, achieving better productivity, having a more positive outlook, or just being overall happier. Perhaps it is true that the person who never feels anger is generally a healthier and more positive person, but on the constitutive view, she would not thereby be morally better than the rest of us. Suppose that she gotten over her anger because, by reading many articles about analytic metaphysics, she has become convinced that all people, including herself, are simply collections of atoms. She no longer sees herself as an agent and she no longer sees others as agents. This view provides her with deep feelings of serenity and happiness because she no longer feels the weight of responsibility. Her new outlook leads her to be patient and compassionate with all of her fellow creatures. Constitutivists will object that no matter how happy or compassionate this person is, this would not count as moral improvement. Once she has given up Strawson's participant stance and no longer sees anyone as an agent, she had abdicated a foundational moral commitment. Even if one is not a constitutivist, one must ask whether the change she makes is a morally better one. Should we morally prefer an outlook that gives up on the concept of agency provided it leads to peace of mind and compassion with our fellow creatures? On what grounds do we assign so high a value to positive attitudes?

My suspicion is that most skeptics do not seek to reconfigure our moral commitments so radically. They simply think that anger is not necessary and, since it is also undesirable, we should train ourselves out of it. This innocuous-sounding view, I suggest, is closer to its radical counterpart than it seems. If the constitutivist can show that anger is neither irrational nor inherently dangerous, the anger skeptic may still claim that it is better or more virtuous to respond to wrongdoing with patience or compassion. The reasons to which they will appeal to support this claim, however, often require the person feeling anger to downplay either her own agency or the wrongdoer's agency.

Suppose I am deeply betrayed by a loved one. She had no excuse, no sympathetic reasons, and did not act out of ignorance. Those who argue for the desirability claim might see my anger as warranted, but will nevertheless say that it would be better for me not to be angry. What reasons will support this claim? Skeptics might implore me to have compassion for the wrongdoer because she is merely human and humans make mistakes. This reason presents the wrongdoing as a kind of error and suggests that human foibles are inevitable or simply to be expected. To characterize wrongs as stemming from human error is an attempt to defang the seriousness of the wrong—to make it seem more innocent than it is. This sort of reason invites me to see the wrongdoer as acting less intentionally, which is to treat her betrayal as not really expressive of her agency. Likewise, appeals to my loved one's difficult circumstances (supposing she had them) aim to convince me that her bad behavior is the result not of her own doing, but rather the product of her conditions. Suppose instead someone reminds me that I too might be capable of such a betrayal: "There but for the grace of God go I." These kinds of appeals aim to undermine my own reasons to be hurt by or to object to the betrayal. I ought to go easy on my betrayer because it is merely a matter of luck that I am not in her shoes. Again, this encourages me to see both her actions and my actions as the result of luck and not of agency. Reasons like "You should be the bigger person" ask me to see compassion and patience as an expression of maturity or higher virtue. Here they assume without justification that compassion is more mature than anger. They also paint a picture of the offender as immature or childlike. "Be the bigger person" invites me to see myself as superior to rather than equal to my betrayer. Also, these appeals do not address the reason I am angry in the first place.[11] The fact that patience would make me the bigger person does not give me a reason not to be hurt by my love one's betrayal; it only gives me reason to be (allegedly) more mature.

Once we rule out the idea that anger is inherently vicious, irrational, or damaging, we need some further reason to prefer positive attitudes to it, especially if we grant that anger can be fair and justified. The reasons that advocates of the desirability claim usually give in support of compassion and patience rely on a more moderate version of the radical revisionist moral outlook than it first appears. The reasons given in favor of positive responses to wrongdoing usually require me to orient myself away from the participant stance or deemphasize its importance. Those who argue in favor of compassion and against anger may not argue that we should give up on the concept of agency altogether, but the reasons they give for responding to wrongdoing with positive attitudes often attempt to minimize the role of agency in wrongdoing.

Still, one might think there is no denying that patience and compassion are good and anger is bad. Compassion causes us to alleviate suffering, to help us be realistic about our own flaws, and to be forgiving. Anger causes us to want to hurt others, wrecks relationships, and makes us feel as though we are righteous and justified in punishing. Skeptics about anger mistakenly believe that its presence is incompatible with the presence of patience and compassion. As Hieronymi points it, not only do we get angry at those we love, we love them while we are angry with them (2001, 539). Parents know all too well how anger and patience can exist together, especially when they are punishing their children for bad behavior. The constitutivist will go further: it is not merely that anger is compatible with compassion, but that we cannot separate our positive and negative emotions so neatly. Philosophers have often argued that anger is an expression of valuing or caring about something.[12] As Callard puts it, "Anger, fear, sadness, disappointment, jealousy—these are signs of caring" (2018, 127). It is *because* I care about my relationship with my loved one that I am angry at her betrayal. Feelings of compassion and feelings of anger can both be expressions of valuing one and the same person. Imagine a father who feels both compassion and anger at his teenage son who makes stupid choices because he seeks acceptance and belonging. The father sympathizes with his son's needs and yet is angry because he wants his son to realize that acceptance doesn't have to come at the cost of prudence. These kinds of complex emotional states are not mysterious, and they show that anger and positive attitudes are not necessarily in competition with each other. In fact, sometimes they arise from the same source. The constitutive view can agree that compassion and patience are good attitudes to have. Yet it will deny that these attitudes are always better than anger.

We are liable to feelings of anger because we occupy the participant stance with our fellow moral agents. When others show us disregard, ill-treatment, and disrespect, we get angry because we value ourselves and our moral relations. Getting over anger would require us to give up the participant stance or to no longer see ourselves and others as responsible moral agents in relations of mutual regard. Skeptics of the constitutive view believe that we can get rid of anger and leave the rest of our moral psychology untouched or perhaps even better off. I have argued here that getting over anger would require a more radical transformation than the skeptics are willing to accept.

NOTES

1. The term "constitutive" comes from Watson (1993, 120). Versions of this view can be found in Strawson (1963/2003), Rawls (1971/2003), Murphy and Hampton (1988), Murphy (2003), Gibbard (1990), Wallace (1994), Roberts (2003), Hieronymi (2004), Smith (2005), Darwall (2006), Bell (2013), and Thomason (2018).

2. In keeping with Strawson (1963/2003), philosophers who defend this view often use the term "resentment" rather than "anger." I think there is no difference between

the two, so I will use them interchangeably. As I will make clear, I define anger is a way that is consistent with the definitions of resentment that one finds in the literature.

3. Solomon (1988) has a thorough discussion of objections like this.

4. My version of the constitutive view draws most directly on Strawson (1963/2003), Rawls (1971/2003), Murphy and Hampton (1988), Murphy (2003), and Solomon (1988).

5. The term comes from Rawls (1971/2003, 428).

6. Some might object here that we do get angry at inanimate objects. For example, I might yell obscenities and bang on my steering wheel when my car won't start. Philosophers who advocate for the view I defend here usually distinguish anger and frustration (Wallace 1994, 21; Solomon 2007, 18). I am frustrated when my car won't start, when it rains on my picnic, or when the bus is late, but I am angry at people. It is of course possible that we could be angry in cases where we anthropomorphize objects or events, or when we focus on the intentions of the people who might have made the objects or cause the events ("What kind of idiot wrote these directions?" I might think as I struggle to assemble the bookcase).

7. Hieronymi characterizes resentment in this way (2001, 546–549).

8. Strawson (1963/2003), Murphy and Hampton (1988), Murphy (2003), Solomon (1988, 2007), Wallace (1994), and Hieronymi (2001).

9. This is what Hieronymi calls "mutual regard" (2004, 124).

10. Murphy (1988, 22–23) and Hieronymi (2001, 530–531) discuss this point regarding reasons to forgive.

11. Callard makes this point (2018, 128).

12. Solomon (2007), Bommartio (2017), and Callard (2018).

REFERENCE LIST

Aristotle. 2002. *Nicomachean Ethics*. Translated by Christopher Rowe. New York: Oxford University Press.

Bailey, Alison. 2018. "Anger, Silence, and Epistemic Injustice." *Royal Institute of Philosophy Supplement* 84: 93–115.

Bell, Macalester. 2009. "Anger, Virtue, and Oppression." In *Feminist Ethics and Social and Political Philosophy: Theorizing the Non-Ideal*, edited by Lisa Tessman, 165–183. New York: Springer.

———. 2013. *Hard Feelings: The Moral Psychology of Contempt*. New York: Oxford University Press.

Bommarito, Nicolas. 2011. "Bile and Bodhisattvas: Śāntideva on Justified Anger." *Journal of Buddhist Studies* 18: 356–381.

———. 2017. "Virtuous and Vicious Anger." *Journal of Ethics and Social Philosophy* 11, no. 3: 1–27.

Callard, Agnes. 2018. "The Reason to be Angry Forever." In *The Moral Psychology of Anger*, edited by Myisha Cherry and Owen Flanagan, 123–137. Lanham, MD: Rowman & Littlefield.

Cherry, Myisha. 2018. "The Errors and Limitations of our 'Anger-Evaluating' Ways." In *The Moral Psychology of Anger*, edited by Myisha Cherry and Owen Flanagan, 49–65. Lanham, MD: Rowman & Littlefield.

Cogley, Zac. 2014. "A Study of Virtuous and Vicious Anger." In *Virtues and Their Vices*, edited by Kevin Timpe and Craig A. Boyd, 199–224. New York: Oxford University Press.

Darwall, Stephen. 2006. *The Second-Person Standpoint*. Cambridge, MA: Harvard University Press.

Deonna, Julien, Raffaele Rodogno, and Fabrice Teroni. 2012. *In Defense of Shame: The Faces of an Emotion*. New York: Oxford University Press.

Garfield, Jay. 2011. "What Is It Like to be a Bodhisattva? Moral Phenomenology in Śāntideva's Bodhicaryāvatāra." *Journal of the International Association of Buddhist Studies* 33: 333–357.

Gibbard, Allan. 1990. *Wise Choices, Apt Feelings*. Cambridge, MA: Harvard University Press.

Hieronymi, Pamela. 2001. "Articulating an Uncompromising Forgiveness" *Philosophy and Phenomenological Research* 62, no. 3: 529–555.

———. 2004. "The Force and Fairness of Blame." *Philosophical Perspectives* 18: 115–148.

Isenberg, Arnold. 1949. "Natural Pride and Natural Shame." *Philosophy and Phenomenological Research* 10, no. 1: 1–24.

Kekes, John. 1988. "Shame and Moral Progress" *Midwest Studies in Philosophy* 13: 282–296.

King Jr., Martin Luther. 1986. *A Testament of Hope: The Essential Speeches and Writings of Martin Luther King, Jr.* Edited by James M. Washington. New York: HarperCollins.

Manion, Jennifer. 2002. "The Moral Relevance of Shame." *American Philosophical Quarterly* 39, no. 1: 73–90.

Mason, Michelle. 2010. "On Shamelessness." *Philosophical Papers* 39, no. 3: 401–425.

McRae, Emily. 2015. "Metabolizing Anger: A Tantric Buddhis Solution to the Problem of Moral Anger." *Philosophy East and West* 65, no. 2: 466–484.

Murphy, Jeffrie, and Jean Hampton. 1988. *Forgiveness and Mercy*. New York: Cambridge University Press.

———. 2003. *Getting Even: Forgiveness and Its Limits*. New York: Oxford University Press.

Nussbaum, Martha. 2004. *Hiding from Humanity: Disgust, Shame, and the Law*. Princeton, NJ: Princeton University Press.

———. 2016. *Anger and Forgiveness: Revenge, Generosity, Justice*. New York: Oxford University Press.

Pettigrove, Glen. 2012. "Meakness and 'Moral' Anger." *Ethics* 122, no. 2: 341–370.

Pettigrove, Glen, and Koji Tanaka. 2014. "Anger and Moral Judgment." *Australasian Journal of Philosophy* 92, no. 2: 269–286.

Rawls, John. 1971/2003. *A Theory of Justice*. Cambridge, MA: Harvard University Press.

Roberts, Robert C. 2003. *Emotions: An Essay in Aid of Moral Psychology*. New York: Cambridge University Press.

Seneca, Lucias Anneas. 2010. "On Anger." In *Seneca: Anger, Mercy, Revenge*, translated by Robert Kaster and Martha Nussbaum, 14–129. Chicago, IL: University of Chicago Press.

Smith, Angela. 2005. "Responsibility for Attitudes: Activity and Passivity in Mental Life." *Ethics* 115, no. 2: 236–271.

Solomon, Robert. 1988. "On Emotions as Judgments." *American Philosophical Quarterly* 25, no. 2: 183–191.

———. 2007. *True to Our Feelings: What Our Emotions are Really Trying to Tell Us*. New York: Oxford University Press.

Strawson, P. F. 1963/2003. "Freedom and Resentment." In *Free Will*, edited by Gary Watson, 72–93. New York: Oxford University Press.

Taylor, Gabriele. 1985. *Pride, Shame, and Guilt*. New York: Oxford University Press.

Thomason, Krista K. 2015. "Forgiveness of Fairness?" *Philosophical Papers* 44, no. 2: 233–260.

———. 2017. "Review of Anger and Forgiveness: Resentment, Generosity, and Justice." *Essays in Philosophy* 18, no. 1: 1–8.

———. 2018. *Naked: The Dark Side of Shame and Moral Life*. New York: Oxford University Press.

Wallace, R. Jay. 1994. *Responsibility and the Moral Sentiments*. Cambridge, MA: Harvard University Press.

Watson, Gary. 1993. "Responsibility and the Limits of Evil: Variations on a Strawsonian Theme." In *Perspectives on Moral Responsibility*, edited by John Martin Fischer and Mark Ravizza, 119–148. Ithaca, NY: Cornell University Press.

Chapter 4

Understanding Joseph Butler's Sermons on Resentment and Forgiveness

Gregory L. Bock

When it comes to the place of anger and forgiveness in Christian ethics, Bishop Butler's eighteenth-century sermons on the topic are essential reading. In fact, in the philosophical literature on forgiveness, his sermons play an important reference point for any scholar, religious or not. Consider the admiration that Jeffrie Murphy shows to Butler. He writes, "One of the most insightful discussions of forgiveness ever penned is to be found in Bishop Joseph Butler's 1726 sermon 'Upon Forgiveness of Injuries' and its companion sermon 'Upon Resentment.' These sermons are long and carefully reasoned philosophical essays on the character of forgiveness, and they must have greatly tried the patience of his congregation" (Murphy 2012, 52). Despite their influence, however, what Butler thinks about the relationship between anger and forgiveness in the sermons is subject to dispute. In this chapter, I consider three different interpretations: (1) that Butler defines forgiveness as the forswearing of resentment (Murphy), (2) that Butler defines forgiveness as the forswearing of retaliation (Paul Newberry), and (3) that Butler intends only a loose connection between forgiveness and resentment (Shelby Weitzel). I evaluate each interpretation and argue that Butler defines forgiveness as the forswearing of *excessive* resentment.

BUTLER'S TWO SERMONS

In this section, I summarize Butler's two sermons with the intention of being neutral with regard to interpretive difficulties and controversies, which I address later. Sermon 8 is entitled "Upon Resentment," and Sermon 9 is entitled "Upon Forgiveness of Injuries." Butler's guiding question in Sermon

8 is why God created in us the capacity for anger, given the fact that he is perfectly good and commands us to love our enemies. Butler asks, "Why had man implanted in him a principle, which appears the direct contrary to benevolence?" (8.1).

Butler acknowledges that some think that our enemies are the natural and appropriate objects of our wrath; however, he says that this is contrary to Christian teaching, and just because a passion occurs naturally does not mean that it manifests in the way God intends. The divinely endowed passion might be abused or even neglected. Therefore, he says, "It will be needful to trace this up to its original, that we may see, what it is in itself, as placed in our nature by its Author; from which it will plainly appear, for what ends it was placed there. And when we know what the passion is in itself, and the ends of it, we shall easily see, what are the abuses of it, in which malice and revenge consist" (8.3).[1] In other words, he intends to sift through all of the abuses of resentment in order to find the original emotion in its divinely ordained state.

Butler distinguishes two kinds of resentment. First, there is the "hasty and sudden" kind. This kind is automatic and common to animals and infants as a matter of instinct for the sake of protection, and he compares it to the reflex action of the blinking of the eye when a foreign object gets too close. The second kind is called "settled and deliberate." We experience this kind when we hear of an injustice committed against others or when we experience a wrong committed against ourselves. The former concerns the prevention of harm to oneself. The latter concerns the prevention of moral injury.

What are the abuses of resentment? Butler identifies two abuses of the "hasty and sudden" kind: passion and peevishness. Both of these are, he says, "the same principle" or kind (8.10). He describes passion as a sudden outburst; peevishness, on the other hand, is a persistent but slow manifestation of the same feeling "upon every thing which comes in its way" (8.10). Of the "settled and deliberate" kind of resentment, there are several types of abuse:

(1) falsely thinking a wrong has occurred,
(2) exaggerating the wrong that has occurred,
(3) thinking someone has morally wronged us when it was unintentional,
(4) responding disproportionately, and
(5) harming someone on the basis of resentment (retaliation) (8.11).

These abuses have in common one's being dominated by resentment.

Butler also examines the positive aspects of resentment, calling it God's helpful "instrument of death" (8.13) and a "generous movement of mind"; it is, in other words, a blessing bestowed by God in the face of the reality of sin (8.17), for punishment exists for the sake of peace. Resentment is a proof of the existence of the moral law and its relevance to one's behavior. It also promotes a proper response to wrongs committed because it mandates punishment and limits the amount of compassion we naturally have for offenders. Also, it restrains would-be wrongdoers from acting out in the future because of their fear of punishment and of falling subject to the public's resentment. He also comments that it is not cool-mindedness, but hot indignation, that pursues justice for the wrongdoer (8.14).

Sermon 9 is about forgiveness, but what is striking about it, especially after the carefulness Butler brings to his analysis of resentment in Sermon 8, is the very little he seems to say about forgiveness per se, instead choosing to discuss benevolence and further exploring resentment and revenge. About resentment, he says, "Mankind naturally feel some emotion of mind against injury and injustice . . . Let this be called anger, indignation, resentment, or by whatever name anyone shall choose" (9.2). In this, he collapses the many into one, saying there is but one negative emotion that is called by different names. He says that this emotion is sufficiently restrained in most people, at least when hearing about wrongs committed against others. It becomes excessive, however, when it comes to wrongs committed by others against the self (9.2). This leads to retaliation and revenge. He states the thesis of the sermon as follows: "I will shew the absolute unlawfulness of [revenge]; the obligations we are under to [love our enemies]; and then proceed to some reflections, which may have a more direct and immediate tendency to beget in us a right temper of mind towards those who have offended us" (9.3).

First, he offers reasons for thinking that revenge is wrong. In the first case, he offers a *reductio ad absurdum*, saying, "Let us begin with the supposition . . . that we were allowed to 'render evil for evil.'" What would happen? Resentment begets resentment, and retaliation begets retaliation. He says, "There would be no bounds, nor any end," and "It is of the very nature of this vice to propagate itself" and "lay waste the world" (9.5).

Also, the passion of resentment has as its goal the pain and misery of others. Butler says, "No other principle, or passion, hath for its end the misery of our fellow creatures" (9.10). So, it should be used only "in order to produce some greater good" only as it is necessary to address moral injury and not to produce more.

Turning his attention to forgiveness, Butler writes, "To that love of our enemies, which is commanded; this supposes the general obligation to benevolence or good-will towards mankind: and this being supposed, that precept is no more than to forgive injuries; that is, to keep clear of those abuses before-mentioned" (9.12). The abuses he refers to here are the five abuses of the "settled and deliberate" kind of resentment listed previously. Instead of more deeply analyzing the concept of forgiveness here, he discusses the relationship between resentment and benevolence, focusing on their mutual compatibility. He says, "Resentment is not inconsistent with good-will" (9.13).

Although they may "lessen" one another, they can coexist. To support this claim, he gives a parenting example in which parents can both love and resent their children. He also explains that the command to love our enemies does not require us to feel especially affectionate about them; it only requires us to have the same level of love for enemies as we would have toward strangers.

How much resentment is too much? Butler says that if we are wronged by others, the resentment we have toward them should rise to no greater level than we have when we hear of a stranger being wronged (9.19). Butler says, "We may therefore love our enemy, and yet have resentment against him for his injurious behaviour towards us" (9.13). As long as we are able to continue to love those who wrong us, then the level of anger we experience is still within the bounds.

Butler concludes his sermon with some reflections he hopes will help his readers manage their resentment. First, he thinks that the feeling of resentment diminishes one's capacity to properly appraise the situation. Second, most legitimate moral injuries spring from character flaws in wrongdoers that we also find in ourselves, so we ought to be as forgiving of others as we are of ourselves. Third, quoting Matthew 6: "If ye forgive men their trespasses, your heavenly Father will likewise forgive you," Butler says that we should consider that we will stand before God someday, so we should show the same forgiveness to others that we hope God shows us.

MURPHY: FORGIVENESS AS FORSWEARING RESENTMENT

Although nowhere in the sermons does Butler explicitly state a clear and unambiguous definition of forgiveness, Jeffrie Murphy attributes the following one to Butler: forgiveness is the overcoming of resentment (Murphy and Hampton 1988, 20). Murphy correctly believes the purpose of both sermons is to explain how the divinely bestowed emotion of resentment is compatible with a Christian ethics of love. He says, "What is not consistent with a gospel of love is being dominated by the passion of resentment or acting unjustly on the basis of that passion; and thus Butler sees forgiveness as a virtue that functions to check resentment and keep it within proper bounds" (Murphy and Hampton 1988, 22).[2] Murphy notes that this definition needs elaboration because there are instances of overcoming resentment that would not qualify as forgiveness on Butler's account. Murphy provides two examples. First, he considers the example of simple forgetting. Forgetting about one's resentment is, in a sense, "overcoming resentment," but it is not the same as forgiveness because forgetting does not involve the will in ways that forgiveness clearly does. Second, he considers the example of therapeutic forgiveness, when one forgives simply for one's own well-being and not for the sake of the other because it is better to do so than hang onto the negative emotions. He calls this selfish, and forgiveness cannot be selfish. So, he attributes the following expanded definition to Butler: *forgiveness is the forswearing of resentment on moral grounds* (Murphy and Hampton 1988, 24).

The interpretation of Butler's concept of forgiveness as having moral grounds is correct because in his sermon on forgiveness, he emphasizes the diminishing effect that resentment has on benevolence and states that loving our enemies involves forgiving them. He says, "When this resentment entirely destroys our natural benevolence toward [the one who wronged us], it is excessive, and becomes malice or revenge. The command to prevent its having this effect, i.e. to forgive injuries, is the same as to love our enemies; because that love is always supposed, unless destroyed by resentment" (9.13). For Butler then, forgiveness is understood as benevolent, as interpersonal and not simply psychological.

Evidence that Butler has a morally thick interpretation of forgiveness in mind may also be drawn from his analogy to divine forgiveness at the end of sermon. He encourages his readers to pursue forgiveness because one day they will stand before God and answer for their lack of forgiveness. Citing Matthew 18:35, Butler says that God is forgiving but warns that if we have not demonstrated a "forgiving spirit towards others," we cannot expect "hope for pardon of our own sins; as ever we hope for peace of mind in our dying moments, or for the divine mercy at that day when we shall most stand in need of it" (9.28). There is no reason to think that divine forgiveness is simply therapeutic or forgetting on God's part or just God overcoming his bad feelings toward us for his own sake. God's forgiveness is about us, his love for us, and his pardoning of our sins. Insofar as human-to-human forgiveness is modeled on divine forgiveness, it must also be other-centered.

However, Murphy's definition suffers from one flaw, which his critics point out.[3] Butler nowhere says that all resentment needs to be overcome; in fact, the point of his sermons is, in part, to show that resentment is divinely ordained. Shelby Weitzel, one of Murphy's critics, says, "When Butler says the precepts 'forbid only the excess and abuse of resentment,' he means they forbid only abuses of resentment as opposed to forbidding all resentment" (Weitzel 2007, 242). Strangely, Murphy agrees. He says, "What is not consistent with a gospel of love is being dominated by the passion of resentment or acting unjustly on the basis of that passion; and thus Butler sees forgiveness as a virtue that functions to check resentment and keep it *within proper bounds*" (Murphy and Hampton 1988, 22).[4] In addition, Murphy more recently writes, "Butler essentially wants to apply Aristotle's idea of the mean to the passion of resentment—developing an account of the circumstances that justify it and the degree to which it is legitimate to feel and be guided by it" (Murphy 2012,

12). So, Murphy understands Butler on the relationship between forgiveness and resentment, but for some reason, this is not reflected in the definition of forgiveness he ascribes to Butler. Murphy's lack of precision here has perpetuated an ongoing misunderstanding among readers of Butler and scholars of forgiveness.

NEWBERRY: FORGIVENESS AS FORSWEARING RETALIATION

Paul A. Newberry argues against Murphy's interpretation, saying, "Forgiveness is not the foreswearing of resentment but the overcoming or foreswearing of abusive or excessive resentment. In other words, forgiveness is the checking of revenge, or forbearance" (Newberry 2001, 233). Newberry sees that Butler means only to proscribe excessive resentment, but Newberry believes incorrectly that this refers only to acts of revenge—abuses of action, not emotion. He claims that both Butler and Murphy presuppose a different theory of emotions. Murphy's approach is informed by a cognitive theory of emotions while Butler's is informed by a feeling theory of emotions. Newberry explains that this is the reason Murphy misreads Butler.

According to Newberry, a cognitive theory of emotions defines emotions in terms of their cognitive elements, such as beliefs, so particular emotions are constituted, at least in part, by particular beliefs. Moreover, on a cognitive account, people have a certain degree of freedom and responsibility in regard to one's emotions and can be praised or blamed for having them. Newberry mentions, for example, Robert Solomon's view that we exercise direct control over our emotions. Interpreting Butler through a lens of a cognitive theory of emotions will lead to a moral theory of forgiveness that emphasizes the responsibility one has in reducing feelings of anger, which is an element of Murphy's interpretation.

Newberry defines a feeling theory of emotions as one that states that "emotions . . . are involuntary and thereby outside our control because we are passive recipients of feelings" (Newberry 2001, 239). Newberry traces the feeling theory of emotions to Descartes, who says, "The most that the will can do while this disturbance is at its full strength is not to yield to its effects and to inhibit many of the movements to which it disposes the body. For example, if anger causes the hand to rise to strike a blow, the will can usually restrain it; if fear moves the legs in flight, the will can stop them; and similarly in other cases."[5] Interpreting Butler through the lens of such a theory will lead one to the opinion that Butler's forgiveness is not about overcoming feelings but overcoming the tendency to act negatively in response to them—in revenge.[6]

Newberry describes Butler's theory of emotions as a feeling theory, but nowhere does Butler explicitly state this, as Newberry admits. Newberry's attribution of such a theory to Butler is based solely on the claim that Butler does not condemn feeling resentment—only acting in revenge, but is this correct?

Newberry's case seems to focus entirely on the fifth type of abuse (retaliation) described by Butler in Sermon 8. Butler writes that this abuse is "when pain or harm of any kind is inflicted merely in consequence of, and to gratify, that resentment, though naturally raised" (8.11). However, Butler mentions four other types of abuse, too: misplaced resentment, exaggerated resentment, mistaken ascription of mal-intent, and disproportionate resentment (8.11). So, there are five abuses, but Newberry acknowledges only one of them. The most charitable explanation for this move, in my opinion, is that he is applying the "feeling theory interpretation" to this section, as well.[7] In other words, if Newberry is right and Butler is operating with a feeling theory of emotion, then the first four "abuses" are not abuses of emotions per se but epistemic errors that causally determine emotions. On the other hand, if Butler is operating with a cognitive theory of emotion, then these abuses are, in fact, abuses of emotions, in which case Butler would be enjoining his readers to forswear both retaliatory actions and excessively resentful emotions.[8]

Other reasons to believe that Butler considers feelings themselves to be a matter of moral concern include the following. First, in Sermon 9, Butler describes how the telos of the emotion of resentment is "the misery of our fellow-creatures" (9.10). Second, it is this emotion that opposes benevolence, and when the emotion grows too strong, it "becomes malice or revenge." Newberry could reply by saying this is the threshold at which point resentment becomes a moral problem, but there are two points to raise in response: (1) whether "become" in this sentence means that this "too strong emotion" is a sufficient condition for malice and revenge or simply a necessary condition[9] and (2) whether Butler uses "malice" to refer only to actions and not also to emotions.[10] Third, in Sermon 9 as he wraps up his main arguments, Butler says that his point in the sermon has been to convince his readers that their obligation is in regard to both a "temper of mind and course of behaviour" (9:21);[11] in other words, he means to address the overcoming of both certain actions *and* certain emotions. Finally, Butler says later in Sermon 12 that benevolence toward one's neighbor, like love for God, involves the affections, not just actions. Butler says, "The precept [to love thy neighbor] may be understood as requiring only, that we have the same kind of affection to our fellow-creatures, as to ourselves . . . so we should cultivate the affection of good-will to our neighbor" (12.7). If benevolence is an affective neighborly disposition that resentment disturbs, then it makes sense that Butler would call for the overcoming of the emotion of resentment in order to love one's neighbor properly.

WEITZEL: FORGIVENESS UNDEFINED

Shelby Weitzel thinks that both Newberry and Murphy misinterpret Butler because they tie the concepts of forgiveness and resentment too closely together. On their views, Weitzel says, "Resentment is a response to wrongdoing, and forgiveness is a response to resentment" (Weitzel 2007, 242). She claims, however, that this is not Butler's view. She writes, "Rather than define forgiveness as the process whereby one overcomes one's hurt and resentment, Butler thinks that excessive hurt and resentment impede one's ability to forgive. We know that if one is able to forgive, then one is not feeling excessive resentment, since forgiveness and excessive resentment are incompatible" (Weitzel 2007, 251). She thinks that Murphy and Newberry make overcoming resentment a sufficient condition for forgiveness when Butler believes it is only a necessary one (Weitzel 2007, 243).

She says that Butler does not define forgiveness and just assumes that his readers understand what it means. She writes, "Butler's overall approach to ethics includes the notion that one need not examine moral terms in order to know what they mean . . . it seems strange to attribute to Butler the idea that forgiveness is merely 'keeping clear of abuses of resentment,' as this is not at all intuitive" (Weitzel 2007, 245).[12]

She argues that Butler's concept of forgiveness has more to do with benevolence than resentment. To make her point, she draws a parallel to Butler's discussion of self-love and benevolence in Sermon 1, explaining how Sermon 1 shares a common structure with Sermons 8 and 9. In Sermon 1, Butler shows how self-love and benevolence are compatible, that benevolence is not the absence of self-love. She writes, "Benevolence—what it is, why we act on it, and what is good about it—in no way depends upon self-love. It shortchanges the concept of benevolence to define it as merely the avoiding of abuses or excesses of self-love" (Weitzel 2007, 247). In the same way, she argues, the concept of forgiveness is not dependent on the concept of resentment. Butler is simply concerned to show that forgiveness is compatible with resentment, just not excessive resentment, just as benevolence is not compatible with excessive self-love.

However, this seems mistaken. Butler is not interested in showing that forgiveness is compatible with resentment but that benevolence is. Nowhere does he claim that forgiveness is compatible with resentment but that goodwill is (9.13). In other words, a better comparison would be the connection between benevolence and self-love (Sermon 1) and between benevolence and resentment (Sermon 9). Both self-love and resentment are compatible with benevolence, and neither depends on benevolence for its definition. However, it is difficult to imagine forgiveness without any conceptual connection to resentment, for what purpose does forgiveness serve except to respond in some way to wrongdoing? As Charles Griswold says, "If one felt *no* resentment in response to someone's injurious action against oneself, it would make no sense to forgive them for their deed" (Griswold 2007, 40). Butler believes that forgiveness is the mitigation of resentment so that goodwill toward others may resume. He says, "The command to prevent its having this effect, i.e. to forgive injuries [or to prevent resentment from destroying benevolence], is the same as to love our enemies" (9.13). To say that forgiveness is the same as loving our enemies is not to say that love and forgiveness are conceptually identical but to say that forgiveness is what love does (or how it manifests) when resentment arises. So, the definition of forgiveness is conceptually linked to resentment.

Of course, there is more to love or benevolence than just forgiveness, and Butler captures this well in his other sermons on loving one's neighbors. Weitzel is correct that it is excessive resentment, not resentment per se, that is incompatible with benevolence, but she seems to confuse forgiveness with benevolence. Forgiveness is what benevolence does when confronted with wrongdoing.[13]

CONCLUSION

In short, forgiveness is conceptually linked to resentment, contra Weitzel. Butler understands forgiveness to be the forswearing of excessive resentment. Excessive resentment gets in the way of loving our neighbors, and forgiveness is the proper response to resentment, enabling us to love better. Forgiveness is about overcoming the abuses of resentment, which include both emotions and actions, contra Newberry, because Butler includes both in his list of abuses (8.11). Murphy's interpretation is mostly correct. Butler defines forgiveness as the forswearing of resentment on moral grounds, but for some reason, Murphy's definition does not capture what Murphy himself understands about Butler's theory of forgiveness, that forgiveness is the overcoming of *excessive* resentment, not all resentment.[14] Butler's purpose is to show that benevolence is compatible with our divinely ordained capacity for resentment as long as forgiveness keeps the abuses in check.

NOTES

1. All references to Butler's sermons are to the sermon and section number in Butler (2017).

2. In his introduction to Butler's sermons, David McNaughton argues that Butler should make a distinction between resentment and indignation in order to provide a clearer account of the difference between acceptable and unacceptable resentment, for on Butler's account, the difference between acceptable and unacceptable resentment is just a matter of degree, not of kind. In 9.2, Butler identifies only one negative emotion, which he calls by different names. Butler says we feel a stronger emotion when a wrong is committed against us than when it is committed against others. He says, "Therefore the precepts in the text . . . must be understood to forbid only the excess and abuse of this natural feeling, in cases of personal and private injury." McNaughton claims that Butler would be helped if he reserved the term "resentment" for the excessive emotion, which appears only with personal moral injuries and "indignation" for the justified emotion felt in response to injuries to others. McNaughton's point, however, is not a matter of interpretation but a critique, so it must be left for another time. See Butler (2017, xxviii–xxxi).

3. Newberry and Weitzel are both critical of Murphy on this point. See below.

4. Italics mine.

5. As quoted in Newberry (2001, 239).

6. Newberry doesn't defend a feeling theory of emotion; in fact, he indicates some dissatisfaction with Butler's approach, interpreted as such (Newberry 2001, 242). Newberry's aim is simply to show that Murphy, and other like-minded interpreters, get Butler wrong.

7. The trouble with this move is that it derives an interpretive principle (feeling theory of emotion) by being selective with the evidence (considering only the fifth abuse in the list) then applies the principle to discount the rest of the evidence. This does not follow the principles of sound inductive reasoning.

8. David McNaughton holds this view but argues that Butler only means to proscribe the emotion of resentment, not indignation. See endnote 2.

9. Shelby Weitzel makes a similar observation. She says, "Newberry has construed what was a necessary condition for forgiveness as a sufficient one" (Weitzel 2007, 243).

10. Newberry raises this possibility for "malice" only to dismiss it (Newberry 2001, 237).

11. See also 9.3.

12. Weitzel correctly believes that Newberry's "theory of emotion" critique is irrelevant to the proper interpretation of Butler. She says, "Whether or not the emotion is directly or indirectly under one's control, what is relevant is that both Butler and Murphy do conclude that one is morally responsible for how one feels about wrongdoers" (Weitzel 2007, 250).

13. Weitzel remarks that Murphy and Newberry's definition seems strange, that the object of forgiveness is the wrongdoer, not one's resentment. However, this point can be accommodated under an understanding that resentment is directed outward. As Murphy explains, forgiveness is not simply therapeutic. It is other directed, but it relates to an affective disposition occurring in the one who was wronged. See Murphy and Hampton (1988, 22–23).

14. See endnote 4.

REFERENCE LIST

Butler, Joseph. 2017. *Joseph Butler: Fifteen Sermons Preached at the Rolls Chapel and Other Writings on Ethics*. Edited by David McNaughton. New York: Oxford University Press.

Griswold, Charles L. 2007. *Forgiveness: A Philosophical Exploration*. New York: Cambridge University Press.

Murphy, Jeffrie G. 2012. *Punishment and the Moral Emotions: Essays in Law, Morality, and Religion*. New York: Oxford University Press.

Murphy, Jeffrie G., and Jean Hampton. 1988. *Forgiveness and Mercy*. New York: Cambridge University Press.

Newberry, Paul A. 2001. "Joseph Butler on Forgiveness: A Presupposed Theory of Emotion." *Journal of the History of Ideas* 62, no. 2 (April): 233–244.

Weitzel, Shelby. 2007. "On the Relationship Between Forgiveness and Resentment in the Sermons of Joseph Butler." *History of Philosophy Quarterly* 23, no. 3 (July): 237–253.

Chapter 5

Anger as an Unnecessary Response

Court D. Lewis

Contemporary accounts of forgiveness often assume or praise the need for some sort of anger, often as resentment, in securing the self-respect of individuals who are victims of wrongdoing.[1] Nevertheless, there is a growing set of literature that maintains anger is an unnecessary response to wrongdoing.[2] Such an idea, however, is nothing new. Eastern religions, for the most part, eliminate the need for anger, and though they are slowly being recognized in the literature, there remains a divide between both approaches.[3] There are several theological and historical reasons for this divide. For one, Western accounts of forgiveness often rely explicitly or implicitly on Abrahamic traditions that see God as angry for justice and promote an understanding of humans as rational autonomous, individualistic beings who deserve blame and punishment after committing wrongdoings. (Christianity, with its teachings on unconditional love, sometimes serves as an outlier, but it too has long theological and mainstream traditions that promote resentment and—sometimes eternal—punishment for wrongdoings.) On the other hand, Eastern religions often eliminate or limit the role of an individualistic self, while at the same time retaining notions of justice and negating the conceptual framework that necessitates anger.

The following pages develop the critique of anger as a necessary response to wrongdoing. I begin by developing what might be called the "typical Western response to wrongdoing" that sees anger as a necessary response to preserve self-respect. I limit my discussion of anger to resentment, as a rational form of anger that responds to wrongdoing as a means to protect the self-respect of individuals and to illustrate a commitment to the moral order. Since resentment is framed as a rational response to a wrongdoing that occurs within the moral order, resentment will occur only toward other moral agents. Any "resentment" toward objects is at best mistaken and at worst irrational.

I close section one by contrasting the necessity of resentment with recent work by Kathryn Norlock, Margaret Holmgren, and Martha Nussbaum, who provide arguments against such a necessity. Next, I develop the argument that anger is an unnecessary response to wrongdoing, and requiring resentment commits a level confusion that actually diminishes the self-respect of individuals. Though anger is sometimes discussed as a strategy to educate, promote justice, and/or prevent cynicism and despair, I hope to show that it is best to eliminate anger from our moral repertoire.[4] To help show how eliminating anger is possible, I discuss several practical examples and four Eastern religions (Buddhism, Jainism, Confucianism, and Daoism) to illustrate why and how such an elimination neither condones wrongdoing nor fails to take seriously the moral order. In fact, they, along with the conceptual arguments developed in the chapter, show anger to be unnecessary.

ANGER AND SELF-RESPECT

The typical argument for why anger is necessary after wrongdoing goes something like the following. Intentional wrongdoing sends a message to victims—it tells victims that they are of less (or have no) moral worth, and, as a result, they can be treated in disrespectful ways. Anger, on the other hand, is a message victims send to wrongdoers, letting them know that their actions are inappropriate. Anger shows that victims recognize their own moral worth, recognize they have been wronged, and that they do not condone such wrongdoing. Wrongdoers, then, should at a minimum recognize the same and commit to proper future behavior. Because anger involves the recognition of moral worth and non-condonation of wrongdoing, it serves victims as a means of illustrating self-respect. It shows that victims take themselves seriously as moral agents and serves as a way of ensuring proper treatment. This section examines the arguments for why anger is thought to be necessary in the face of wrongdoing.

Aristotle provides one of the earliest accounts of anger in his *Nicomachean Ethics*. Charles Griswold explains Aristotle's virtuous anger as "to be angry 'at the right things and toward the right people, and also in the right way, at the right time, and for the right length of time, is praised' (1125b31-32)" (2007, 6). From this description, anger is framed as a rational and measured response to some wrongdoing, and since such a description differs from the typical connotations of irrational anger, Aristotle refers to it as mildness or calmness (*praotês*) (ibid.). Such a virtue, for Aristotle, runs the risk of being a vice. Again, as Griswold explains, "[mildness] errs more 'in the direction of deficiency, since the mild person is ready to pardon (*sugnômê*), not eager to exact a penalty' (1126a1-3). Being too mild and pardoning is 'slavish', for a person fails to defend himself and his own" (ibid., 6–7). From this account, we gain the idea that there are at least two types of anger—one rational (a virtue) and the other irrational (a vice)—and that virtuous anger (mildness) becomes a vice when it ceases to be properly measured and/or fails to protect the person's self-respect.

Most discussions of anger incorporate in some way the notion of virtuous anger, though they often use different terms. Antti Kauppinen refers to it as "mature anger" and suggests that it occurs as a result of "violating a normative expectation, . . . a standard to which we hold others (or ourselves)" (2018, 32). Jeffrey Blustein calls it "moral protest" and maintains it serves to promote one's own sense of self-worth, when wrongdoing calls it into question—it serves to remind others of a person's self-worth (2014, 58). Jean Hampton calls it "indignation" and says, "Indignation is the emotional protest against immoral treatment whose object is the defense of the value which this action violated . . . Indignant people see their moral cause as competing with the wrongdoer's immoral cause, and they aim to defeat it" (1988, 59). Martha Nussbaum calls it "Transition Anger" and describes it as "well-grounded anger" (anger resulting from a wrongful act that was intentionally inflicted and caused serious damage) that, instead of containing a sense of payback, contains the emotion: "How outrageous! Something must be done about this" (2016, 35). Finally, Jeffrie Murphy tends to call it "resentment," "suggesting that the primary value defended by the passion of resentment is *self-respect*, that proper self-respect is essentially tied to the passion of resentment, and that a person who does not resent moral injustices done to him . . . is almost necessarily a person lacking in self-respect" (1988). Due to my own work on forgiveness, I also tend to discuss rational anger in terms of resentment. As argued in *Repentance and the Right to Forgiveness*, "Victims must accurately recognize and appraise their moral worth," and in order to protect themselves from victimization, the appropriate response to wrongdoing is resentment—as a means of asserting one's self-respect (Lewis 2018, 37). These authors illustrate that it is appropriate to talk of a type of anger that is fundamentally rational and tied to protecting/asserting the self-respect of victims. To help simplify the discussion and because of my previous work on resentment, I will treat "resentment" as synonyms with the types of rational anger previously mentioned.

Let me say a little more about resentment. If properly understood, resentment offers the strongest case for why anger is both appropriate and necessary after wrongdoing. David Shoemaker describes resentment as a "cognitively sharpened" form of anger, one that involves a moral agent being wronged and the recognition that "You wronged me!" (2018, 69). The claim "You wronged me!" sends a message to oneself (the victim) of recognizing one's moral worth and the moral infraction, and it sends a message to the wrongdoer, letting her or him know that a wrong has been committed and that he or she should respond appropriately. Similarly, Murphy maintains that resentment defends the values of self-respect, self-defense, and respect for the moral order by requiring allegiance to a moral order and motivating action to defend the proper treatment of humans by one another (2003, 19–20). To borrow the language and schema of Bennett Helm, when wronged, a victim's anger has three "objects": (1) the target, who is the wrongdoer; (2) the formal object, which is the evaluation of the wrongdoer; and (3) the focus, which is "the background intentional object of that emotion that has import to the subject and whose relation to the target normally explains the evaluation of the target in terms of the formal object implicit in the emotion" (2017, 36–37, 69). When understood in this way, resentment is a valuable tool in maintaining moral order. Resentment protects the self-respect/-worth of victims, demands wrongdoers show proper respect, and promotes a process of accountability that serves the basis for a strong moral order.

Of course, resentment is not without its shortcomings. As Murphy notes, resentment that devolves into a *ressentiment*, a term popularized by Friedrich Nietzsche meaning "spiteful and malicious envy," should be avoided, for once resentment becomes *ressentiment*, it loses its rational moral standing (Murphy 2012, 26). Instead of focusing on justice and repairing moral relationships, *ressentiment* seeks a type of vengeance dedicated to seeing the wrongdoer suffer more than her or his moral worth deserves. Recently, several other authors have raised issues with requiring anger as a defense of self-respect/-worth. Kathryn Norlock was one of the early critics of requiring self-respect after wrongdoing. As she notes in *Forgiveness from a Feminist Perspective*, requiring a robust self-respect and autonomy undermines forgiveness by creating a binary between genuine vs. fake forgiveness. This binary is then used to preclude certain types of forgiveness often performed by women, such as "conflict-avoiding forgiveness," and so demeans agents who engage in this type of forgiveness, and thereby, limits the richness of appropriate moral interactions. As she says, "One example of such a binary approach is Jean Hampton's argument that a hypothetical woman who 'forgives' a boorish visiting father-in-law to preserve family peace is not engaging 'in genuine 'forgiveness' . . . [because] to drop that judgment and the anger feeling it engenders' is instead 'condonation'" (Norlock 2009, 18–19). Norlock suggests dropping the requirement of resentment, in order to protect a more diverse set of moral actions relating to wrongdoing and forgiveness.

Margaret Holmgren's conception of forgiveness has changed over the years, but in *Forgiveness and Retribution: Responding to Wrongdoing*, she reconceptualizes the relationship between resentment and self-respect. Influenced by Buddhist teachings, she argues that moral agents should develop dispositional attitudes of unconditional forgiveness. She says, "An attitude of genuine forgiveness toward an unrepentant offender is fully compatible with the victim's self-respect, whereas an attitude of resentment is not," and that "if she [the victim] truly respects herself, she will be secure in these judgments and will not feel threatened by the wrongdoer's confused attitude" (Holmgren 2012, 67). Furthermore, she says, "If we truly recognize and respect our own worth, we will feel no need to spend our lives proving to others that we have it. This crucial part of our identity is *not* socially construed" (ibid., 71). Once we recognize our own worth, "We will have no further need to vindicate ourselves, either by adopting an attitude of resentment or by amassing a public record of achievement" (ibid.). Instead of anger and resentment, we should extend attitudes of respect, compassion, and goodwill.

Finally, Martha Nussbaum argues that all anger that contains a payback desire is irrational and normatively problematic. As mentioned previously, the only appropriate anger is Transition Anger that rationally motivates individuals to oppose injustice. So far, I have developed resentment as a type of Transition Anger, but I believe Nussbaum would (justifiably) worry that resentment too often contains a payback desire. For Nussbaum, Transition Anger most often flourishes in the parent-child relationship, a relationship in which resentment is rare. What is more, Nussbaum suggests that resentment is not necessarily a moral response because we can resent a just state of affairs—for example, a particular college justifiably rejects my child's application. Even when the rejection is fair, I can still perceive the rejection as unjust and resent the decision (Nussbaum 2016, 262). Shoemaker would say this type of anger is blame, not resentment, but I will refrain from discussing this tension until the next section. Nevertheless, if Nussbaum is correct, then not only would rational resentment be rare, but as the school-rejection example implies, it appears to rest on mere perceptions of wrongdoing, which raises doubt about the whole rational nature of resentment. In other words, Nussbaum calls into question resentment as a rational means of protecting self-respect, because it is all-too-human to overestimate our self-worth and perceive interactions as unjust, or to overestimate a slight wrong as something monumental. If correct, then resentment threatens to be as irrational as the motives that often ground vengeance.[5]

Nussbaum challenges readers to reconsider the necessary grounds for resentment and to recognize that anger (for wrongs and/or perceived wrongs) often only serves to diminish the self, especially when we factor in social pressures. To quote at length:

> But anger does nothing to solve such a person's real problems, and it positively impedes progress, for a number of reasons. First, it diverts one's thoughts from the real problem to something in the past that cannot be changed. It makes one think that progress will have been made if the betrayer suffers, when, in

> reality, this does nothing to solve the real problem. It eats up the personality and makes the person quite unpleasant to be with. It impedes useful introspection. It becomes its own project, displacing or forestalling other useful projects, and importantly, it almost always makes the relationship with the other person worse. There was something likable about the person, and even if marriage is no longer possible or desirable, some other form of connection might still be, and might contribute to happiness. Or it might not. But the whole question cannot be considered if angry thoughts and wishes fill up the mental landscape. Far from being required in order to shore up one's own self-respect, anger actually impedes the assertion of self-respect in worth-while actions and meaningful life. (Nussbaum 2016, 125)

When resentment resembles Transition Anger, then it might be well-grounded in protecting the self, others, and the moral order, but such instances will be rare, according to Nussbaum. So, instead of focusing on past wrongs, we are better-served creating a new self by focusing on "singing lessons, or going to the gym, or, more generally, focusing on areas of competence and self-esteem, and making new friends (a task that is not assisted by a persistent focus on anger and blame)," in order to throw "off the dead weight of the past" (ibid., 126).

Accounts from Norlock, Holmgren, and Nussbaum raise doubts about the value and necessity of resentment, as a rational means of ensuring self-respect after wrongdoing. For some, such doubts might be enough to conclude that anger is unnecessary, but I worry that such a hasty conclusion would just lead to further semantic bickering. What we need is an argument (or set of arguments) for a well-grounded way of life that shows how living without anger is not only possible but also desirable.

ANGER AS UNNECESSARY (AND INAPPROPRIATE) RESPONSE

The previous pages presented resentment as a rational form of anger necessary for protecting self-respect and the moral order. The final few paragraphs raised three objections to requiring resentment. This section will formalize these objections into an argument that shows why anger is unnecessary and that requiring resentment commits a level confusion that actually threatens to undermine the self-respect and moral worth of victims after wrongdoing.

Let me begin by suggesting that determining the role of anger in wrongdoing rests on how we understand the nature of resenting objects and states of affairs. To resent is to recognize a wrong, so resentment is fundamentally a moral concept. Even in Nussbaum's case of resenting the just denial of my child's admittance into a specific college when there is no actual wrong, it is the perception of a wrong that motivates a feeling of resentment. Because resentment is a moral response to a wrong, physical objects cannot justifiably be the target of one's resentment. Wrongdoing occurs only when one moral agent violates or fails to carry out what is required in relation to another moral agent, and inanimate physical objects lack the capacities required to be moral agents. Of course, similar to Nussbaum's college denial case, we often use "resent" in relation to physical objects. I "resent" my cell phone for not working, I "resent" the self-checkout machines for being too slow, and I "resent" the red light that refuses to change. However, when we use "resent" in such cases what we have done is confuse that target of resentment. When my cell phone does not work, the real target of resentment is the programmer/designer who made an object that does not live up to my unrealistic expectations. If we carefully examine the cases in which we "resent" an object, we should find that the object serves as a substitute for the real target of our anger. To reiterate, there is no actual wrong occurring in these situations, unless there is an evil programmer/designer intent on making my life difficult, but the important thing to notice is how easy it is to confuse the target of anger, whether it be well-grounded or merely perceived wrongdoing.

It seems uncontroversial to claim that it is improper to resent physical objects, even if it occurs regularly in natural language. Now for the controversial claim: I suggest that past states of affairs (i.e., historical events) be understood in the same way as we understand physical objects, and if I am correct, then resentment (and by implication, all anger) after wrongdoing becomes unnecessary. Let me be clear, I am not making some deep metaphysical claim about the nature of historical events. What I am suggesting is that, like physical objects, historical events are artifacts that exist as items for analysis and evaluation. What is interesting about human perception is that events of the present instantaneously become historical events. In fact, if we are precise, what we perceive as the present is several nanoseconds in the past of what is actually occurring—it takes the brain those nanoseconds to interpret our engagement with the environment. Therefore, by the time we register a wrongdoing, let us say someone unjustly slapping your face, the state of affairs in which you were wronged is a historical event, and though it is not tangible like a physical object, the target of your anger is a memory that (like physical objects) lacks the capacity for committing wrongs. It is merely the memory of wrongdoing (an object for analysis and evaluation), and, as such, fails to be a proper target of resentment.

To move forward, however, we must address the proper way to understand the relationship between wrongdoer and wrong. First, we can understand the wrongdoer as being separate from the wrong. This approach appears often in the forgiveness literature and suggests that the wrongdoer is an individual who makes decisions, some right, others wrong, but is to be understood as importantly differently from her or his actions. The common phrase is "hate the sin, love the sinner," or, to use Helm's terminology, the wrongdoer is the target of resentment, while the formal object (evaluation) and focus (importance to oneself) relate to the wrongdoer's act. Utilizing this approach separates the ever-present wrongdoer from her or his historical acts. If it is improper to resent an object, then we should not feel resentment for the wrong, since it exists only in the past. Resentment would be proper only at the moment of the transgression, but due to the nature of human perception, our recognizing a wrong is always a matter of reflecting on a past event. Therefore, as soon as the wrong occurs, it is in the past, the wrongdoer and victim are no longer identical with whom they were at the time of the wrong, and so, resentment becomes inappropriate. Therefore, to justify resentment, separating wrongdoer and wrong is not the approach one should pursue.

The second option is to keep wrongdoer and wrong together, and the best way to justify this approach is to maintain that the wrong is part of the wrongdoer's character. A character-based approach allows victims to continually interpret the wrongdoer in relation to the wrong in the present, because part of what it means to be the wrongdoer is to be the perpetrator of the wrong. When interpreted this way, the necessity of anger becomes a practical issue of what is the best response to wrongdoing: that is, what produces the most flourishing, what promotes justice, and so on. As illustrated in the previous sections, there are several arguments for why anger is necessary or unnecessary, and regardless of your "faith" in the power of reason to speak to interlocutors, most people accept arguments only when arguments match their common intuitions about an issue. So, regardless of the strength of Nussbaum's and Norlock's respective arguments, if you have a strong intuition that morality needs "teeth," you will accept the arguments that promote the need for anger. In order to avoid devolving into semantic hairsplitting and tests of logical acumen, both of which would be unhelpful, let me suggest a way to reinterpret the intuition that morality needs the teeth of anger, such that anger becomes unnecessary.

Holmgren provides a nice illustration of someone whose view on resentment has developed over the years. From stressing the need for resentment, to rejecting it usefulness, Holmgren's most recent approach implies that typical Western accounts engage in what might be called a level confusion over the necessity of resentment. Similar to level confusions that occur in epistemology,[6] the level confusion over the necessity of resentment occurs between a moral agent having self-respect and a moral agent having to prove to others that he or she has self-respect. As cited previously, "If we truly recognize and respect our own worth, we will feel no need to spend our lives proving to others that we have it. This crucial part of our identity is *not* socially construed"

(Holmgren 2012, 71). Our self-respect is a matter of personal introspection and knowledge and does not require external validation to exist. Granted, signs of self-respect will often occur in ways that are socially observed, but because I do not live up to the standards of self-respect held by others does not imply that I do not have self-respect. Recall Norlock's example, of the wife that forgives a boorish father-in-law to preserve family peace, as a means of conflict-avoidance. As presented by Norlock, the wife is confident in her self-respect, and instead of choosing to confront the father-in-law, which would more than likely lead to further conflict, she quietly forgives. Requiring that she prove her self-respect by becoming resentful and making demands of the father-in-law only promotes anger in the father-in-law, anger in the wife, and anger in other familial relationships. In other words, it underestimates the wife's moral maturity in regard to her self-respect and lack of resentment and demands that she prove her self-respect by promoting feelings of resentment and other types of irrational (i.e., payback) anger. What is more, if the wife is comfortable in her own sense of self-respect, requiring a higher-level demonstration of such self-respect implies that the wife is somehow morally flawed—she does not take her moral worth seriously, she condones the father-in-law's behavior, and so on.

Such replies reeks of sexism or some other form of moral elitism, when in reality there are numerous examples of post-wrong actions that seek conflict-avoidance over resentment. The Amish response to the 2006 school shooting that killed several children is probably the most popular example. As detailed in "Anabaptist Forgiveness in Cultural Context: An Amish Example," Donald Kraybill explains how the Amish utilize a forgiving disposition based on Christian teachings that negate the need for resentment (2018). Another example, one that illustrates Nussbaum's recommendation of avoiding anger in the pursuit of creating a new self, appears in the case of Gee, the mother of a young black man murdered with an ice axe by racist thugs. Instead of resenting and becoming consumed with anger, Gee worked to ensure her son's death was a "catalyst for racial harmony, not further bloodshed" (Henderson 2009, 100–101). These replies illustrate that resentment is unnecessary in the aftermath of wrongdoing, and that because one does not feel anger does not imply that one condones wrongdoing or fails to take seriously the moral order.

In addition to these practical examples, we can also look toward well-grounded religious conceptions of the good life. As previously mentioned, the typical Western approach to resentment often traces its conceptual roots to Christianity, specifically the sermons of Bishop Joseph Butler (1662–1752), and though there are mainstream Christian traditions that call for resentment and vengeance, there are also love-centered interpretations of Christianity that promote unconditional love and peace. Love-centered approaches often promote pacifism and nonviolence, framing the main teachings of Jesus as lessons on loving all humans, even enemies. Though there are arguments within Christianity for when anger might be appropriate, the main teaching is to overcome the need for anger via "turning the other cheek" and "forgiving trespasses."[7]

In addition to Christianity, Eastern religions typically frame anger as unnecessary. Since such religions often go unexamined, let me present some key features of four Eastern religions: Buddhism, Jainism, Confucianism, and Daoism. Writings on Buddhism consistently promote the idea of the shared plight of *samsara*, promoting compassion over any retributive or self-centered emotions/responses that only serve to entangle persons in *samsara*. Since Buddhism is more interested in particular experiences over abstract concepts, the best way to see Buddhism's approach to compassion and anger is through an example. In "Forgiving the Unforgiveable," John Thompson tells the story of the Buddha's embrace of a terrorizing murderer named Aṅgulimāla—an epithet that brings attention to his habit of wearing severed fingers as a necklace (2018, 140). As Thompson points out, the three obvious responses to Aṅgulimāla are to run away in fear, seek your own justice as a vigilante, or let the authorities seek justice (ibid., 144–145). All three approaches failed. It was not until the Buddha approached Aṅgulimāla with compassion, absolving him of all guilt, that Aṅgulimāla let go of his past wrongs, began meditating, and eventually became enlightened. At least some of the villagers remained angry, for they attacked Aṅgulimāla during his begging rounds; but the Buddha comforts Aṅgulimāla to feel no hatred, just as he held no hatred toward Aṅgulimāla for trying to kill him. The moral of the story, then, seems best summed up with the words of King Pasenadi—the king of the village. He notes how the "blunt or bladed weapons" of the town failed to tame Aṅgulimāla, and that only the Buddha's compassionate approach was effective. Stated differently, anger and violence are karmic facts of existence that promote a sense of self via cravings, and it is only through letting go of such cravings of the self that we become enlightened.

Bryce Huebner's examination of the teachings of Śāntideva, a revered Buddhist monk and philosopher, supports this interpretation and further illustrates the unnecessary nature of anger. As Huebner notes, anger makes us focus on the other-as-a-separated-self and isolates our own "self," feeding the ego of self-interestedness. Instead of focusing on anger, we should focus on "the information that is encoded in signals of anger," learning to recognize the motives of anger, as alerts to oppression, not as personal attacks; transforming them into motives for compassion (Huebner 2018, 98). By eliminating anger from our moral repertoire, we work toward the liberation of all sentient beings (*bodhicitta*)" (ibid., 89). We do not simply ignore anger, but we diffuse anger by eliminating the need for a self that requires anger for protection. As Śāntideva argues:

> We can act to prevent further suffering (*duḥkha*) by focusing on the factors that produce our anger, uncovering the cause of our suffering, and using this knowledge to break down our habitual patterns of attachment. Doing so requires practicing patience (*kṣānti*) in the face of discomfort, and doing so in ways that retain our access to the morally salient information that seems to be embodied in the experience of socially situated anger. (ibid., 92)

By uncovering the assumptions that necessitate anger, as discussed in the previous section, we become capable of changing the attitudes formed about ourselves, from self-interestedness to compassion, by "imagining ourselves taking on the suffering of another being" (ibid., 96). Stated differently, by diffusing our anger, we uncover the "underlying network of causal forces" that create perceptions of wrongdoing and anger, and, as a result, diffuse the sense of self that grounds delusions of negative emotions (Gyatso 1997, 41).

Jainism developed during the same time as Buddhism, and, as an offshoot of Hinduism, endorses an ascetic lifestyle designed to promote the release of the soul from the body. Conceiving of life as a set of endless cycles of time, Jainism traces its roots to the life of Vardhamana, later called Mahavira (or "great hero"). Mahavira became the twenty-fourth Tirthankara ("crossing builders" who help build a bridge from this life to enlightenment), teaching a life dedicated to *ahimsa* (nonviolence), the renunciation of all possessions, and extreme asceticism. The goal of Jainism is to awaken the knowledge and liberation that is part of the soul by escaping the endless cycle of karmic forces that cause false views of reality (Ludwig 2006, 177). The central false view of reality is of a self that enjoys pleasures and attachments, and, as a result, feels anger and seeks violence when "wronged." For Jains, we are to abandon such a view of self and live a life of nonviolence, always seeking truth, refraining from stealing, and renouncing pleasure and all attachments.

Jainism's concept of *ahimsa* undercuts any foundation on which to ground anger. *Ahimsa* denies the selfish motives that promote anger by framing such motives as a matter of harming other beings. Instead of anger, even after being wronged, we are to show benevolence. We should find joy in the sight of other beings, show compassion toward those who suffer, and display tolerance toward the ill-behaved (ibid., 186). In fact, since discomfort aids in enlightenment, it is unclear if being "wronged" is bad for the victim, for a "wrong" that helps in the liberation of the soul is "beneficial" in achieving release. Such a conceptualization suggests that gratitude might be a more appropriate response to wrongdoing. Regardless, Jainism provides another conceptual framework that illustrates why anger is unnecessary.

Confucianism is arguably more a philosophical system of social ordering than a religion, but since it is typically included as a major world religion, I will treat it as such. Developed by K'ung—"K'ung the master" (i.e., "K'ung Fu-tzu" or the Westernized "Confucius")—in the fifth century BCE, Confucianism provides guidance on how best to structure society through individuals properly discharging the responsibilities as defined by their roles in society. We all have certain roles in society (father/mother, son/daughter, brother/sister, teacher/student, leader/subject, etc.), and by both cultivating proper behavior as a human (Ren) and following the laws that govern social interaction (Li), we contribute to the harmony, prosperity, and peace of society.

Wrongdoing occurs when one fails to do what is required from one's role. For instance, when a father fails to love and care for his son, he ceases to be a father. According to Confucianism, in such a case, the son is asked to look at the ethical quality of his response as a son, not his response as a wronged individual. In other words, the focus is on the relationship, not the individual self. Resentment is not valued in Confucianism because it implies a separation of the individual from the relational aspects that make up the individual. As Man-to TANG argues, Confucianism centers on the term *Shu*, asking us to put ourselves in the "shoes" of the other person, as a means to promote harmony between relationships (Tang 2016, 201–221). Therefore, instead of having feelings of anger/resentment after wrongdoing, we should have feelings of benevolence and compassion, seeking the return to proper relationship and the rectification of the wrongdoer's name—the father begins acting like a father, and, thereby, regains his standing as father.

Daoism is a deeply philosophical system that incorporates several mystical aspects. Developed around the time of Confucianism, Daoism teaches people to remove themselves from the manufactured structures of society and, instead, follow the Dao (i.e., the way) of nature. Based mainly on the teachings of Laozi (Lao-tzu) and Zhuangzi (Chuang Tzu), Daoism is an attempt to harmonize with reality, which requires no action, no rules, just Dao. We are to remove the shackles of human-made conventional thoughts and concepts and live as trees and rivers—in peaceful harmony with the universe. As a result, concepts related to ethics, wrongdoing, anger, self-respect, forgiveness, and so on are merely artificial constructs that disconnect us from universal harmony. Daoism's sole commitment is to promote this harmony. To illustrate, imagine your Self as a sack, and each time you feel resentment after a wrong, you place a potato in your sack. Before long, your sack will not only become heavy and difficult to carry, but it will also become rotten. Conventional wisdom would tell us either not to feel resentment (i.e., anger) at being wronged, or develop attitudes of unconditional forgiveness. In both ways, you avoid the discomfort of carrying the potatoes by not putting them in your "sack." Daoism, however, tells us to get rid of the "sack" (the Self) entirely, because the concept of a Self, and all of its accompanying features, is just another figment that prevents us from achieving Dao.

What we see in each of these accounts are alternatives to the typical Western response of requiring anger to protect self-respect. When these long-standing religious conceptions of how to approach anger and wrongdoing are coupled with the practical examples and theoretical backing of Norlock, Holmgren, and Nussbaum, we are presented with a strong case for why anger is unnecessary. If we consider the wrongdoer as separate from her or his actions, then resentment becomes irrational, losing its moral standing as an appropriate response to wrongdoing. If we identify the wrong as part of the wrongdoer, we gain a conceptual grounding for resentment, which are undercut by the cases and arguments presented in this section. Instead of necessitating resentment, morally mature individuals should strive to be confident in their own self-respect, negating the need for resentment, and any higher-level displays of resentment will become tactical moves, similar to Nussbaum's Transitional Anger, designed to promote social justice. On the other hand, requiring anger undermines the self-respect and moral maturity of individuals who have no need to resent.

CONCLUDING REMARKS

What I have shown is that there are well-established conceptions of the good life that show resentment (i.e., rational anger) is unnecessary in securing self-respect and the non-condonation of wrongdoing. Requiring a display of anger commits a level confusion that implies individuals cannot have self-respect unless they are able to demonstrate such self-respect via resentment. The arguments and examples examined show that individuals can have self-respect without displaying it to others, and, as a result, morally mature individuals who remove resentment from their moral repertoire prove that though anger might be a common response, it is by no means necessary.

NOTES

1. See Griswold (2007), Murphy (2012), Blustein (2014), and Lewis (2018).
2. See Norlock (2009), Holmgren (2012), and Nussbaum (2016).
3. See Lewis (2016), Bock (2018), and Huebner (2018).
4. Thank you to Jennifer Kling, Keith Abney, BB Bieganski, and Kate Schmidt for the valuable comments at the 2019 Annual Meeting of the Concerned Philosophers for Peace.

5. See Lewis (2018, 73–83).
6. See Alston (1980).
7. There are instances in the Bible where Jesus gets angry, but I refrain from engaging in how to interpret such passages because doing so would take us too far afield.

REFERENCE LIST

Alston, William P. 1980. "Level-Confusions in Epistemology." *Midwest Studies in Philosophy* 5, no. 1: 135–150.

Blustein, Jeffrey M. 2014. *Forgiveness and Remembrance: Remembering Wrongdoing in Personal and Public Life*. Oxford: Oxford University Press.

Bock, Gregory L., ed. 2018. *The Philosophy of Forgiveness, Volume III: Forgiveness in World Religions*. Wilmington, DE: Vernon Press.

Cherry, Myisha, and Owen Flanagan, eds. 2018. *The Moral Psychology of Anger*. Lanham, MD: Rowman & Littlefield.

Griswold, Charles. 2007. *Forgiveness: A Philosophical Exploration*. Cambridge: Cambridge University Press.

Gyatso, Tenzin. 1997. *Healing Anger*. Translated by Geshe Thupten Jinpa. New York: Snow Lion.

Hampton, Jean. 1988. "Forgiveness, Resentment, and Hatred." In *Forgiveness and Mercy*, edited by Jeffrie G. Murphy and Jean Hampton, 35–87. Cambridge: Cambridge University Press.

Helm, Bennett W. 2017. *Communities of Respect: Grounding Responsibility, Authority, and Dignity*. Oxford: Oxford University Press.

Henderson, Michael. 2009. *No Enemy to Conquer: Forgiveness in an Unforgiving World*. Waco, TX: Baylor University Press.

Holmgren, Margaret. 2012. *Forgiveness and Retribution: Responding to Wrongdoing*. Cambridge: Cambridge University Press.

Huebner, Bryce. 2018. "Anger and Patience." In *The Moral Psychology of Anger*, edited by Myisha Cherry and Owen Flanagan, 89–104. Lanham, MD: Rowman & Littlefield.

Kraybill, Donald B. 2018. "Anabaptist Forgiveness in Cultural Context: An Amish Example." In *The Philosophy of Forgiveness, Volume III: Forgiveness in World Religions*, edited by Gregory L. Bock, 33–46. Wilmington, DE: Vernon Press.

Lewis, Court, ed. 2016. *The Philosophy of Forgiveness, Volume I: Explorations of Forgiveness: Personal, Relational, and Religious*. Wilmington, DE: Vernon Press.

———. 2018. *Repentance and the Right to Forgiveness*. Lanham, MD: Lexington Books.

Ludwig, Theodore M. 2006. *The Sacred Paths: Understanding the Religions of the World*, 4th ed. Upper Saddle River, NJ: Pearson-Prentice Hall.

Murphy Jeffrie. 1988. "Forgiveness and Resentment." In *Forgiveness and Mercy*, edited by Jeffrie Murphy and Jean Hampton, 14–34. Cambridge: Cambridge University Press.

———. 2003. *Getting Even: Forgiveness and Its Limits*. Oxford: Oxford University Press.

———. 2012. *Punishment and the Moral Emotions*. Oxford: Oxford University Press.

Norlock, Kathryn. 2009. *Forgiveness from a Feminist Perspective*. Lanham, MD: Lexington Books.

Nussbaum, Martha. 2016. *Anger and Forgiveness: Resentment, Generosity, and Justice*. Oxford: Oxford University Press.

Shoemaker, David. 2018. "You Oughta Know: Defending Angry Blame." In *The Moral Psychology of Anger*, edited by Cherry, Myisha and Owen Flanagan, 67–88. Lanham, MD: Rowman & Littlefield.

Tang, Man-to. 2016. "The Double Intentionality of Forgiveness: A Non-Reductive Account of Forgiveness in Ricoeur and Confucius." In *The Philosophy of Forgiveness, Volume I: Explorations of Forgiveness: Personal, Relational, and Religious*, edited by Court Lewis, 201–221. Wilmington, DE: Vernon Press.

Thompson, John M. 2018. "Forgiving the Unforgiveable: The Buddha and Aṅgulimāla." In *The Philosophy of Forgiveness, Volume III: Forgiveness in World Religions*, edited by Gregory L. Bock, 133–150. Wilmington, DE: Vernon Press.

Chapter 6

Moral Anger in Classical Confucianism

Colin Lewis

Philosophical discussions of the moralization of anger have not, to date, substantively engaged classical Chinese thought. This is unfortunate, given the abundance of appeals to moral anger in the classical literature, especially among the Confucians, and the suppression, expression, and functionalization of anger. Accordingly, this chapter engages in two general projects: one interpretive, one applied. The interpretive project examines the manner in which classical Confucian thought regards anger as having both destructive and constructive aspects, how these aspects are unavoidable human experiences, and how they can (and should) be regulated or recruited by ritualized social forms. Specifically, while the early Confucians at times depict anger as a precarious feeling to be assuaged, there are circumstances in which anger is not only understandable, but morally warranted. In this tradition, adherence to ritual prescriptions is a primary means by which problematic anger while moral anger is effectively expressed, achieving prosocial ends without producing undue harm. This understanding and analysis of anger from a Confucian perspective gives rise to an applied project that considers how even contemporary, non-Confucians can ritualize and deploy anger for positive moral and political ends. In particular, I examine how forms of reconciliation, etiquette, and protest can be construed as rituals through which moral anger is effectively channeled.

THE INTERPRETIVE PROJECT

A History of Anger

The flourishing period of classical Confucianism is traditionally dated between the fifth and third centuries BCE, originating with the teachings of

Confucius (Kongzi 孔子 or "Master Kong," 551–479 BCE) and extending through the Warring States Period (~475–221 BCE) of China's history. In many ways, Confucianism's rise and development are reactionary to this era of mass civil war: against a backdrop of bloodshed, corruption, and decay, Confucianism advocated philosophical and political resolutions to the widespread chaos. These resolutions were intended not merely to establish sociopolitical order, but to promote flourishing and harmony throughout the realm. To this end, one of the foci of the Confucian ethical-political project was the aim of establishing communities whose members could harmoniously coexist, a goal that required means for handling potentially disruptive dispositions including sorrow (*ai* 哀), disgust (*wu* 惡) and, most importantly for present purposes, anger (*nu* 怒).[1,2]

It will likely come as no shock that the early Confucians recognized anger's propensity for driving humans to violent and morally problematic actions and outlooks; anger has a destructive aspect. For example, Mengzi (Meng Ke 孟軻, 372–289 BCE) claims that a mark of moral goodness is that one does not "store up" anger against siblings and regards them affectionately (*Mengzi* 5A3, 9.3/47/12).[3] Clinging to the anger, allowing it to build up over time, increases the likelihood of one becoming violent or distant, even with one's kin.[4] Additionally, anger is sometimes regarded as a cause of clouded judgement, and so cannot be a consistently reliable resource for determining best courses of action. Similar to Mengzi, Xunzi (Xun Kuang 荀況, third century BCE) acknowledges that acting on (or in) anger can lead to deleterious consequences. In particular, Xunzi urges rulers that self-restraint is of utmost importance when angered, especially in the application of punishment (e.g., *Xunzi* 24/118/18, 24/119/3), or when hearing from subordinates (*Xunzi* 27/127/18).[5] Thus, even though one feels anger, that anger cannot be allowed to drive one to violence or foolishness; a more calculated, level-headed way of engaging with the world is ideal (e.g., *Xunzi* 31/147/17-18). One should aim to restrain oneself and behave in a manner that is conducive to civility and harmony.[6]

Given such rebukes of anger, it might come as a surprise to find that early Confucians, while emphasizing moral cultivation, political order, and social harmony, are not wholly averse to advocating anger. Contrary to schools of thought that call for strict purgation of disruptive emotions, such as certain strands of Buddhism and Daoism, the Confucians instead look on anger as a basic, natural human disposition; that is, part of being human simply is having and experiencing anger.[7] Consequently, the Confucians do not regard anger as being inherently morally bad. In point of fact, several historical figures that the Confucians depict as moral exemplars are described as faultlessly displaying anger in their moral endeavors. Of particular note are Wen and Wu, the first kings of the Zhou Dynasty, whose culture the early Confucians claim as a recurring source of inspiration. According to Mengzi, Wen, with a display of anger, could provide tranquility for all in the realm, a trait shared by his successor:

> If there was a single villain in the realm, then King Wu was ashamed. This was the courage of King Wu, and with just one show of anger he was able to pacify the people of the realm. (*Mengzi* 1B3, 2.3/8/31)

Xunzi offers similar praise:

> When King Wu of Zhou was stirred to anger
> To the fields of Mu he brought his army.
> The soldiers of [Tyrant] Zhou changed their direction.
> (*Xunzi* 25/120/8-9, Hutton trans., modified, 264)

Kwong-loi Shun suggests that this appeal to anger is akin to moral outrage that manifests by spurring one to action to rectify unjust or immoral circumstances (2015, 314). The invocation of Wu's anger in these passages, then, does not necessarily refer to any sort of blind or bodily rage, nor is it necessarily associated with an intent to harm or do ill to another person. Rather, it is a rectificatory anger aimed at promoting pro-moral and harmonious political ends. In this sense, anger also has a constructive aspect.

Before proceeding further with this analysis, it will help to distinguish anger from a disposition like rage (*fen* 忿). Rage, which the Confucians treat as a disposition unto itself, is typically depicted as sudden and severe, its expression akin to an outburst or a tantrum (*Analects* 12.21/33/1-3). Rage is a moment of being mindlessly incensed. Anger, on the other hand, can endure and even possess intellectual qualities (e.g., the aforementioned aim of moral or political rectification). One feels a burst of rage when being cut off in traffic; one feels a seething anger when one is faced with systematic abuse by a (toxic) friend. In the former case, the feeling is immediate and violent, but tends to pass not long after the incident.[8] In the latter case, however, the feeling can wax and wane, but nonetheless persist indefinitely and be accompanied by thoughts about the nature of the abuse that give rise to a variety of psychological complexes. The two can co-occur and may influence one another, but are nonetheless distinct dispositions.

Returning to the Confucian notion of anger proper: the regard for anger as a response that moral exemplars may rightly have suggested that the Confucians were not mere pacifist pedants,[9] but scholarly advocates for what they perceived as positive social transformation. While stopping far short of advancing a democratic or revolutionary political theory, the appeals to the anger of Wen and Wu imply that the Confucians perceive an imperative to strive for what is morally righteous, and that anger can serve as a legitimate motivating force for one's striving.[10] The relevant passages also imply that even the mere display of anger, if it be truly in the right, is sufficient to at least begin a social project of correction, culminating in harmony.[11] Why, however, ought one to think that anger, which can have destructive and disruptive properties, is conducive to such an ethical-political project? To answer this question, it will help to understand the Confucian treatment of anger as a natural and inalienable feature of human living.

Anger as Natural Response

The classical Confucian account of the origin of anger is an appropriate topic with which to begin this deeper inquiry. As noted earlier, anger is thought by the Confucians to originate as one of the most basic dispositions of the human psyche.[12] Xunzi in particular explicitly suggests that, while proper control over such dispositions is quintessential to flourishing, so too is accommodating and nourishing them (*Xunzi* 17/80/9-15).[13] Consequently, the Confucians regard anger as an inherent feature of the human experience: being human includes not only the capacity to feel anger, but actually experiencing it and living through it.

Giving anger a natural status has interesting implications for how the Confucians deal with this disposition that can be destructive and antisocial. The early Confucians adopt the stance that the human being, in terms of both the corporeal body and vital energies (*qi* 氣), should be kept healthy and intact when possible as part of a more general pursuit of flourishing.[14] This view is plausibly a source of inspiration for Mengzi's remarks about the need for moral cultivation to align (in some manner) with facts about human psychological constitution:

> Is one able, simply by following [its nature], to make the willow tree into cups and bowls? Surely one must forcefully injure and steal from the willow tree and only then can one make cups and bowls. If one must, by forcefully injuring and stealing from the willow tree, make cups and bowls [from it], then must one also forcefully injure and steal from humans in order to make them benevolent and righteous? How swiftly, then, would all the people in the world come to regard benevolence and righteousness as calamities! (*Mengzi* 6A1, 11.1/56/17-19, bracketed text added)

Mengzi claims that any practices or methods adopted as part of the moral cultivation process should respect the integrity of the human being. If moral cultivation were to work violently against the most fundamental human dispositions, then it would inevitably do harm to humans by mutilating them at their core. Anger is among one's natural dispositions, so trying to eliminate anger would be akin to mutilating oneself. Consequently, the feeling of anger should not be eliminated, but accommodated and, at least in a sense, even nourished.[15]

A further upshot of this view is that anger is not inherently associated with moral badness; again, anger can be constructive and conducive to moral progress, as with the campaigns of Wen and Wu. It is important to qualify, though, that anger's place in Confucianism is complex: anger's moral valence is often dependent on things like setting and the manner in which it is exhibited. For the

Confucians, whether anger is conducive or counterproductive to moral aims is a function of context. Specifically, if anger is enacted in the appropriate setting and in the appropriate way, then the overarching moral performance is good; if anger is enacted in either an inappropriate setting or inappropriate manner, then the performance is morally problematic. Consider Confucius's handling of his brash student Zilu (子路): though loyal, Zilu is depicted as prone to aggressive displays, a trait that Zilu considered conducive to directing the military. When Zilu implies that he would be an ideal companion to serve alongside Confucius in commanding an army, however, Confucius subtly admonishes him:

> One who would wrestle a tiger or gallop through a river, who would die without regret: I would not associate with such a person. The one with whom I would associate would serve cautiously, be good at strategy, and complete his tasks. (*Analects* 7.11/15/17-18)

Zilu's fault lies not in his willingness to fight, but in the lack of gravity he affords violent conflict. This implies a lack of restraint analogous to what Xunzi warns against: even in cases where one might be (rightly) angered, to act without restraint or calculation is still to act poorly. It is not necessarily morally wrong to become angry; however, it can be morally wrong to act on that anger without due consideration of other morally salient features, and so the early Confucians do not license completely giving over to anger. Again, feelings of anger are an inevitability of human living, are motivating, and can even be morally appropriate, but anger should never be the *sole* basis of one's actions; moral goodness demands that one act in a way that advances personal and interpersonal flourishing, and anger can stymie this pursuit.

In order to further flesh out the nuances of anger's functionality in the Confucian account, it will help to look at the circumstances in which anger is conducive to psychological and social flourishing. For one, given that it is a basic feature of human experience, humans must be allowed displays of anger as part of maintaining personal tranquility. Xunzi states that "if people are not permitted displays of happiness or anger, then there will be chaos" (*Xunzi* 20/99/25). If anger is "stored up," as Mengzi says, then people become more prone to violent displays; thus, it is not in the interest of either the personal or the relational health of humans to be prevented from showing anger. Accordingly, humans need outlets to express anger without disrupting relationships or the general community.

In addition to the practical necessity of anger, multiple passages list anger as a disposition that moral exemplars both possess and deploy in appropriate scenarios. Xunzi describes this facet of anger in reference to the exemplar kings of old:

> Thus, it was by music that the former kings ornamented their happiness; it was by military campaigns and weaponry that the former kings ornamented their anger, and so the former kings' happiness and anger both were equally achieved. Thus, when they were happy all under heaven was at peace; when angry, the violent and chaotic were made fearful. This was the way of the former kings, and ritual and music are its zenith. (*Xunzi* 20/99/10-12)[16]

Along with the aforementioned passage discussing the exploits of Wen and Wu, the anger of the exemplar kings more generally is treated as a virtue unto itself, as it was deployed to both express righteous attitudes, and quell chaos and ill intent in the realm.

In particular, this feature of anger helps to manifest the additional virtue of "courage" (*yong* 勇) displayed by Wen and Wu. While an account of courage in the Confucian tradition can be provided without referencing anger, it is arguable that anger, or some form of it, is recruited into certain expressions of courage that appear in classical Confucian thought. As Shun explains:

> On the Confucian view, when one is wrongfully injured, the focus of one's attention should be on the ethical quality of one's response rather than on how one's standing is challenged by the offender. One may respond with anger to the ethically problematic quality of the situation . . . But, ideally, there should not be an additional element of the response that is directed to the way one's standing has been challenged because, on the Confucian view, one's standing is a matter of one's own ethical qualities rather than the way one is viewed or treated by others. (2014, 29–30)

Shun's explanation emphasizes a Confucian belief that, ideally, one's emotional and behavioral responses should focus on moving forward in life and not dwelling on how an injury challenges one's own standing. Were one to stew in or store up that anger, then one would risk becoming fixated and mired in the situation. This, in turn, increases the risk of one's otherwise moral anger devolving into base malice that could lead to ignoble action, which would exemplify mere animosity rather than courage. Confucian courage, then, can be understood in part as the harnessing of anger not for petty vengeance, but as a motivator for moral rectification.

The ability of Wen and Wu to pacify the realm in a display of anger is exemplary of such cultivation and is said by Mengzi to mark a morally "great" form of courage (*dayong* 大勇) that is distinct from "petty courage" (*xiaoyong* 小勇). Mere petty courage is concerned with maintaining exterior shows of honor (e.g., responding to insult or steeling one's will), while great courage is oriented toward maintaining and perpetuating moral goodness. Moreover, and as P. J. Ivanhoe notes, "One of the characteristic features of great courage is that those who possess it know that they are in the right and justified in their cause" (2006, 224). Ivanhoe's addition reinforces the idea that great courage links moral righteousness and the aforementioned form of anger that is focused on making good on that attitude. Indeed, such anger, in the service of courage, might even be morally requisite.

It is clear, then, that the early Confucians regard anger as playing an important role in bringing about personal flourishing and positive social transformation. Again, though, it is necessary to emphasize that this moral anger is distinct from petty and problematic cases of anger. Furthermore, moral anger is not merely something that manifests and is to be deployed spontaneously. Rather, the anger is to be felt, directed, and deployed in manners that further the ethical and political projects. This is achieved in large part by the application of ritual forms.[17]

Ritualizing Anger

Before explaining how the Confucians advocate giving anger proper form, it will help to clarify the Confucian notion of ritual. While the character translated as "ritual" (*li* 禮) originally referred to sacrificial practices (e.g., to one's ancestors), by the time it came into use by the Confucians its meaning had broadened to a number of other activities and standards (including ranks, etiquette, and general expectations in relationships).[18] According to the Confucians, these rituals originated from the efforts of ancient, exemplar kings who, in the interest of promoting harmony and flourishing for the population, established and implemented the rituals so as to both provide for social order and help fulfill individual psychosocial needs.[19] The claim is not that these rituals are magical, but that they provide real, meaningful ways of recruiting, coordinating, or working through various human dispositions and interactions. Confucius himself establishes a tie between this concept of ritual and an overarching ethical ideal of *ren* (仁), variously translated as "benevolence" or "humaneness" (e.g., *Analects* 3.3, 12.1). Coupled with the fact that *ren* is depicted as caring for others (*Analects* 12.22), and that such care is plausibly construed as a matter of acknowledging, taking seriously, and responding accordingly to a person's worth,[20] I suggest understanding Confucian rituals as prescriptions governing the practices and standards that embody expressions of respect and related humane attitudes.[21]

Having said this, it may not be immediately clear how anger can be ritualized as part of a prosocial project: Does caring for others not preclude feelings of enmity? Anyone who is or has ever been a parent or teacher is likely to respond to this question with an emphatic "no," as those to whom care is directed can behave in ways that frustrate (and even infuriate) their caregivers. Indeed, the Confucians seem all too aware of this fact, as Mengzi indicates in his explanation for the practice of having a son's moral education be conducted by someone other than his father:

> One [who teaches] must teach what is correct. If what one teaches as correct is not carried out, then one is sure to foster anger. If one fosters anger then, contrarily, one produces animosity. [The student sees this and says,] "He teaches what is correct, yet he himself does not yet follow what is correct." Consequently, this results in mutual animosity between father and son. When father and son have mutual animosity, the result is badness. Those of the past exchanged their sons and taught them, so that between father and son there were no admonitions about goodness; such admonitions cause estrangement, and there is no greater misfortune than estrangement [between father and son]. (Mengzi 4A18, 7.18/39/1-3, bracketed text added)[22]

Mengzi's explanation is interesting because it speaks not only to the inevitability of anger toward a deviant child or student, but also to the *appropriateness* of that anger. If a student, on receiving instruction, goes on to act contrarily to what is correct, then the teacher cannot but be aggrieved. According to the passage, in such cases it is not merely that the student has erred in trying to put what is correct into practice; the student has also acted without respect for the instruction. This sentiment is further clarified in the *Liji* ("Nei Ze 内則" passage 17), in which it is made explicit that rejection of instruction *should* move a parent to anger (although expression of said anger should be private, not public). This is because such rejection is an affront not only to the teacher, but also to the values and prescriptions encoded in the instruction. As such, the teacher's anger reflects not merely indignation, but moral righteousness since, from the Confucian perspective, the teacher has a moral obligation to instill said values and prescriptions in the student.

At the same time, the passage reflects the fact that the Confucians do not license *all* displays of anger, as even a novice is capable of discerning the inappropriateness of showing animosity. The important distinction here is that it is not anger itself that is problematic, but what anger can sometimes incite: estrangement, abuse, injury, and general badness. Hence, Xunzi counsels against a "moment's anger" in favor of restraint (*Xunzi* 4/12/21) but does *not* insist on one's living a life devoid of anger. The key is to provide the aforementioned means of guiding and accommodating anger in a way that does not provoke animosity but is conducive to moral aims. Learners must develop an ability to discern between morally destructive expressions of anger and morally constructive expressions of anger. This is where the turn to ritual occurs.

For Xunzi, and Confucius as well, ritual is key to moral cultivation.[23] According to Xunzi, at birth humans lack the resources for (harmoniously) coping with and responding to a variety of hardships, including emotionally disruptive scenarios, being without sufficient sustenance, and even generally interacting with others. When confronted with such circumstances, humans may deploy (and even tend toward) chaotic or ethically problematic behaviors: attacking others out of grief, stealing from others in desperation, and being generally aloof to the well-being of others. By nature, Xunzi claims, humans are effectively morally incompetent. It is only by learning, practicing, and appreciating ritual that one becomes a fully realized moral person (e.g., *Xunzi* 1/3/10-11). Xunzi illustrates this with the metaphors of shaping and honing, comparing human nature to crooked wood and blunt metal, and claiming that humans must therefore be rectified with instruction in ritual and righteousness (*Xunzi* 23/113/9–10). Ritual helps organize, coordinate, and even prime affective responses to these sorts of scenarios, restructuring a learner's psychological landscape by helping to inculcate responses to, and understandings of, a variety of ethically charged situations.

Of additional interest is ritual's ability to channel and refine dispositions to make them appropriate, tolerable, and comprehensible to oneself and others in various situations. Similar to how mastering a verbal language aids one's analysis of both the world and oneself, ritual facilitates moral development by prescribing norms that are then assimilated into one's sense of moral judgement (*Xunzi* 4/15/13–17).[24] Xunzi's program uses ritual to refine one's sense of judgement in a way that enhances self and social awareness when seeking to fulfill one's dispositional desires, helping to achieve harmony. When deliberating whether or how to act on a disposition, one is subject to the cultivated sense of moral judgement as framed by social ritual. Establishing these norms throughout a community via ritual sets a basis for moral order.

Accordingly, Xunzi claims that it is by ritual that proper limits and form are given to anger (19/92/5). This reflects ritual's general function: providing models for social harmony. Admittedly, Xunzi rarely explicitly connects anger and ritual, but there are several occasions where his language harkens to this connection. For example, Xunzi states that

> When angry, [the noble person] is not excessively harsh . . . [and such a person] is not excessively harsh when angry . . . because adherence to the proper model overcomes any selfishness. (*Xunzi* 2/8/13-15, Hutton trans. modified, 15)

As evinced in several other passages, the models to which Xunzi refers are the rituals (e.g., *Xunzi* 1/3/7-12, 2/8/4, 12/60/10, 17/82/22-17/83/1, 19/92/16-17, 23/114/10-11). This is a common styling for Xunzi, who occasionally relates the function of ritual to other types of standards, such as measurements and blueprints. For example, when speaking of the noble scholar, Xunzi describes such a person as one who dwells within an edifice of ritual (e.g., *Xunzi* 19/95/15, 8/34/20-24), and suggests that rituals also provide guidance as sorts of social "depth markers" (*Xunzi* 17/82/22-17/83/1). The wording depicts ritual as something that enables practitioners to move and work through both the social world and internal psychological struggles, giving helpful direction as well as shape to their thoughts, attitudes, and actions.

It is plausible, then, that Xunzi's general treatment of ritual, with its handling of dispositions, will have implications for anger. Consider Xunzi's remarks on the different ritual prescriptions to which one should adhere for the various dispositions: music for joy, quasi-asceticism for sorrow, and martial and corrective affairs for disgust.[25] All of these prescriptions are established both to allow the expression and full experience of the relevant disposition in a manner that signals one's dispositional state to others, and to allow one to have the experience in a manner that maintains both social and personal harmony. Such prescriptions can also nurture and accommodate anger, as noted in Xunzi's previous connection between anger and how the former kings "ornamented" their anger with the military practices referenced herein, as well as the idea that anger is stirred by a moral violation. It is by means of the ritual forms, then, that the experience and expression of anger is facilitated so as to make it a constructive, pro-moral event, rather than a destructive one.

Unfortunately, neither Xunzi nor any of the other early Confucians detail specific rituals for anger, at least not for those who are in positions unsuitable for commanding armies.[26] Rather, when detailing rituals that concern natural dispositions, Xunzi tends to focus on sorrow, especially in the case of lost loved ones. In an extended example, Xunzi goes into detail about the funeral rites for a deceased parent, discussing how one makes offerings to the deceased that they would have required in life, but only provides items that are well worn or imperfect in some significant way (*Xunzi* 19/95/9-13). The purpose is to simultaneously express reverence for the deceased and the grief of loss while also acknowledging that person's passing and moving on accordingly.[27] It is plausible that similar ritual prescriptions exist for coping with and expressing anger, even if the Confucians do not detail them in depth. Anger, much like sorrow or happiness, is an unavoidable human disposition, and so it is highly unlikely (perhaps impossible) that there would not be a ritual means of handling anger.

What might such rituals look like, though? In addition to the use of reflection and calculation to pause one's anger, I suggest that rituals dealing with the aforementioned virtue of courage (*yong* 勇), especially moral courage, are among those to which the Confucians appeal for handling and expressing anger. Specifically, I submit that it is through courage that anger is mobilized for moral ends. Recall that the ideal target of anger is something like immorality or injustice, suggesting that displays of great (i.e., moral) courage are those directed specifically against such moral badness (e.g., as with Wen and Wu). If this is an accurate understanding of the classical Confucian position,[28] then it provides an additional hint as to what rituals of anger might look like for even a commoner: they are displays of righteousness in the face of moral adversity and, insofar as these rituals channel anger, the anger expressed is specifically *moral* anger; it is prosocial and conducive to justice.

With this Confucian account of moral anger and ritual in hand, I turn to modernity and examine how rituals of the Confucian sort might be used to deploy anger for positive moral and political ends, particularly in terms of identifying and responding to immorality or injustice.

THE APPLIED PROJECT

Accepting Anger's Place

As mentioned previously, the early Confucian texts depict properly deployed, moral anger as having a role in projects of moral and political transformation and rectification. This account fits nicely with some of the contemporary work on anger. Helena Flam (2005, 2015), for example, has written extensively on the importance of "reclaiming" anger as a necessary part of achieving positive social change against an oppressive status quo. Additionally, Dirk Lindebaum and colleagues have argued for a kind of "moral anger" that stands distinct from other forms of anger, depicting this disposition as:

> (i) an aroused emotional state stemming from (ii) a primary appraisal of a moral standard violation that (iii) impacts others more than oneself, and (iv) motivates corrective behaviour intended to improve the social condition, even in the face of significant personal risk. (Lindebaum and Geddes 2015, 6)

Moral anger has two dimensions: one informative and the other energic. Moral anger is informative in the sense that it provides a source of appraisal, particularly with regard to the ethical nature of a scenario; it is energic in the sense that it moves one to act against an ethical breach (Lindebaum and Gabriel 2016, 904–905). Such features of moral anger clearly resonate with the Confucian depictions of kings Wen and Wu, whose actions are part of a broader narrative of rulers who work toward ethical-political rectification when they, infuriated by the maltreatment of their people by an uncaring authority, depose a tyrant and establish a kingdom on benevolent principles. This resonance further suggests that classical Confucian thought on moral anger is of interest even in modernity, particularly when considering *how* such anger can be harnessed through ritual forms to achieve ethical and political transformation that aims at personal flourishing and social harmony.

I suspect that some readers will be wary of such a project: the idea that any social form (ritual or otherwise) could successfully allow one to experience, express, or work through one's anger without disrupting harmony may seem laughable. After all, expressions of anger, even nonviolent ones, can serve as gateways to more problematic attitudes, such as Martha Nussbaum's (2016) "payback" wish, which inclines its holders to exact some sort of vengeance on those who have wronged them. This retributive desire is morally problematic in its demand that, in order for one's anger (inclusive of any moral aims) to be effectively expressed and appeased, one must necessarily do injury to others. If one must do injury to others in order to fully express one's anger, however, then it seems unlikely that the anger's expression can be compatible with the aim of social harmony.

Moreover, there is a live concern that anger can trap its holders in a cycle: when anger results in action that does injury to others, then those others become aggrieved and respond in kind; the circle then perpetuates itself. This is made all the worse by the fact that anger motivates not only individually, but communally, and all those members of a group infected with anger become less receptive to those outside the group. Deborah Cantrell (2019) seizes on this fault to argue against the use of anger as a moral motivator, claiming:

> that anger, at its core, is destructive and unhelpful . . . its goal is to inflict some kind of "payback" on another, which orients responsive action towards the past and not towards change going forward. (5)

The cycle of anger can be regressive for the individual, trapping them in a state of feeling wronged and seeking retribution without offering any real means of moving forward even if such retribution is achieved. While it is right to call out injustice, which does not necessarily require a feeling of anger, it is not helpful to engage with attitudes that only serve to further disintegrate the threads of communality. Hence, anger looks to be incompatible with social harmony.

On the one hand, I am sympathetic to the concern that anger can be misplaced and destructive, even when the avowed sources and directions of the anger are morally oriented. For example, and as Cantrell aptly notes, violent protest, even if the cause is righteous, can alienate possible supporters (ibid.), so one must be wary of anger. On the other hand, this line of thinking seems to minimize the fact that anger does admit of genres,[29] and that developing an ability to discriminate among these genres is part of moral cultivation. Moreover, it is possible that many of the most problematic cases typically referred to as "anger" are, in fact, misidentified instances of what the Confucians would call "rage" (e.g., hurling a brick through a window during a tense demonstration). Distinctions must be drawn between mere frustration, reflexive tantrums, and genuine moral outage. This is a core feature of the overarching Confucian program which, as part of its ethical project, urges learners *not* to become stuck or fixated in their anger, but to move through (or with) it in a manner that is forward-looking and morally productive.

A similar issue surrounds resentment (*yuan* 怨), which, in the Confucian tradition, is a kind of frustration with one's circumstances that is phenomenologically similar to, though not necessarily the same as, anger (Ing 2016, 19; Sung forthcoming).[30] While resentment is generally discouraged by the early

Confucians,[31] likely due to the fact that it can inhibit prosociality by breeding contention between persons, it is not rejected outright. Winnie Sung argues (plausibly) that it is best to understand the Confucian position on resentment as permitting the experience of resentment while rejecting any *clinging* to said resentment, as this can prohibit one from flourishing or from contributing to the flourishing of others.[32] Moreover, resentment is apparently endorsed when it is morally proper. Sung offers the example of Mengzi's critiquing an officer who lacked resentment following his mistreatment by an unrighteous lord, a fault that Sung depicts as a lack of seriousness and that Mengzi refers to as a lack of (self-)respect (*gong* 恭) (*Mengzi* 2A9, 3.9/18/29-30). Mengzi's remarks reflect a general Confucian sentiment that, while ministers should demonstrate loyalty to their superiors, such loyalty cannot consist in mere toadying: when one witnesses or experiences impropriety, one ought to offer remonstration. His remarks also reflect the impression that resentment, at least in this case, provides a litmus test for one's own moral understanding: if one is treated genuinely morally badly, then one *ought* to feel resentment, since the feeling of frustration indicates that something is ethically amiss.[33]

Accordingly, while reducing resentment toward others is a general aim of the Confucian program, resentment is also construed as a feeling appropriate to certain circumstances when deployed righteously and in moderation.[34] Anger, I suggest, has a similar function: generally, it is not ideal to hold anger against other humans, since it can devolve into more malicious attitudes. There are, however, circumstances in which it is both right and reasonable that one develops and expresses moral anger, such as when morality is breached. If this understanding is apt, then anger should be accorded a place as a judgmental disposition, even if it is not the sole or guiding one. The dangers of anger should not be construed as reasons to abandon anger itself; they are simply obstacles of which to be wary during moral cultivation.

Furthermore, Cantrell's suggestion that anger be rejected as a motivator for things like positive social change seems to run up against one of the core points of the Confucian project, namely, that anger is a human disposition that needs to be accommodated. To clarify, Cantrell's point is not that humans should not feel anger, but that humans should not look to anger as a primary motivator for things like social activism given its caustic nature. Nonetheless, I think that Cantrell's strategy of replacing anger-as-motivator with other emotions, namely, "fierce love" (2019, 30),[35] is insufficient to handle the fact that most humans are prone to anger as a primary response to perceived injustice: simply because a different disposition is more prone to eliciting pro-moral results does not mean that anger has been overcome or expelled. Even if one were to adopt a more typically prosocial disposition, one will still need to have a means of structuring and handling anger when it arises. Such is the function of ritual.

Moving Forward with Anger and Ritualized Righteousness

What is left now is the matter of outlining rituals that can both promote sociomoral harmony and satisfy the disposition of moral anger. Recall that there are at least two forms of anger: destructive anger and constructive/moral anger. Destructive anger is, in a sense, untethered: stewing in it, it boils over and one displays morally problematic animus. Such anger is destructive, so it should either be harnessed for constructive ends or, failing that, moved through effectively and peaceably. For anger of this sort, the Confucians recommend engaging specifically in reflection (*si* 思) as part of ritual (e.g., *Xunzi* 22/110/17–18). Reflection involves a number of cognitive and metacognitive capacities, including contemplation, deliberation, reminiscence, and even visualization. Reflection demands that one halt one's action and engage in circumspection that includes the nature of the perceived injury and what sort of response is warranted. Again, and as noted earlier, this response should be forward-looking and should help to move one away from a static focus on injury. In so doing, one's anger is (ideally) quelled at least to the degree that it prevents violence, thus ending the destructive threat.

Moral anger, however, will not be pacified simply by reflection, since one discerns that a genuine moral wrong has been committed. How ought one work with such a disposition? There are, I think, obvious ways of using ritual simply to help negotiate and dispense with anger via participation in an activity that allows one to either move through or convert one's anger into another disposition. Informally, this is sometimes pursued by doing things like vigorous exercise: running, weightlifting, and sparring are all instances where both reflexive and moral anger can be allowed to burn until one attains a calmer mind. This by no means entails that one relinquishes one's sense that moral wrongdoing has occurred and needs to be addressed, but it provides time to focus and transmute anger, and possibly move away from more violent urges. As Xunzi notes, such rituals are not only proper outlets for one's dispositions, but also morally appropriate in their conduciveness to prosocial ends.[36] For grief, one might engage in ritual wailing, fasting, or seclusion among other practices that allow one to live through the disruptive experience. It is probable that anger can be handled in a similar manner: exclamations, vigorous physical displays, and temporarily distancing oneself from others can all help with working through the bodily aspects of experiencing anger.

Perhaps a more formal, ritualized practice that could serve moral anger is the writing, but not sending, of angry, condemnatory letters.[37] Maria Konnikova documents several famous examples of such "hot letters":

> Harry S. Truman once almost informed the treasurer of the United States that "I don't think that the financial advisor of God Himself would be able to

> understand what the financial position of the Government of the United States is, by reading your statement." In 1922, Winston Churchill nearly warned Prime Minister David Lloyd George that when it came to Iraq, "we are paying eight millions a year for the privilege of living on an ungrateful volcano out of which we are in no circumstances to get anything worth having." Mark Twain all but chastised Russians for being too passive when it came to the czar's abuses, writing, "Apparently none of them can bear to think of losing the present hell entirely, they merely want the temperature cooled down a little." (2014)

To clarify, the hot letter is not merely a case of one rapidly penning a note and then crumpling it up and tossing it away (else there would not be treasure troves of unsent missives). One actually sits down to compose a formal letter in which one fully and unequivocally expresses one's thoughts and feelings on the source of moral outrage. In so doing, one becomes creatively, intellectually engaged with one's anger, and possibly facilitates a shift away from rage.

The practice and effects of hot letter writing are comparable to the way in which one uses ritual sacrifices and offerings to the deceased to work through sorrow: just as one knows (intellectually) that the offerings will not actually be used by the deceased, it brings one a sense of fulfillment all the same; similarly, simply writing the letter may be sufficient to express and work through the brunt of one's moral outrage. As one allows the excess of energy generated by one's anger to dissipate, one is left bodily calmer and less distracted by the immediate sensation of the metaphorical fire in one's belly. This allows one to turn one's attention fully to the intellectual aspect of one's moral anger and proceed accordingly.

There are also several ways in which ritual can help to navigate and actively deploy moral anger for the purpose of moral rectification, even for those unable to deploy militaries to pacify (and correct) the unrighteous; that is to say, ritual forms can be applied to harness one's moral anger and more directly address wrongdoing. Both the *Analects* (14.21/39/6-11) and the *Liji* ("*Nei Ze*" passage 18), for example, depict cases of remonstrating with authority figures when one thinks morality has been upended: it is to be done respectfully, even reverentially, but if one encounters wrongdoing, then there is both reason and protocol to make clear one's concerns.[38] In modernity, this might take the form of structured disputation or some sort of reconciliatory practice. Even if such interactions fail to result in immediate transformation, it is still better to express the anger and make the problem known than to sit by and do nothing, which could allow the transgression to persist or for one's own anger to possibly fester and revert to reflexive, destructive anger.

A practice that could benefit from (or coopt) such ritual treatments of anger is the modern Truth and Reconciliation Commission (TRC). TRCs are typically developed and deployed for the purpose of creating historical accounts of, and assisting in the healing process for, those affected by widespread or national atrocities (e.g., Apartheid in South Africa or the Residential Schools Settlement Agreement in Canada), and for promoting reconciliation between involved parties.[39] TRCs offer an opportunity for reparative or restorative justice, as opposed to retributive approaches to justice that may engender further conflict among parties. As such, TRCs are increasingly popular and have been touted as active and effective contributors to both reconciling and unifying society generally, as well as to democratization specifically (e.g., Gibson 2006).

In some ways, TRCs are already ritualized spaces, offering a variety of practices and settings that are made sacred by the prescriptions placed on what is to be shared and how. Citing the description of the Canadian TRCs, Anne-Marie Reynaud reports the following instructions:

> Survivors or intergenerational victims are to speak of their residential school experiences and their impacts, or of reconciliation. They should try to respect the 15-minute time frame. There is available health support for all. The tears witnesses "shed without shame" are healing . . . and not garbage. Therefore, the tissues people use are not to be thrown away but collected and burnt in the sacred fire. She reminded the audience that this room is a witness of sacred sharings . . . and that the TRC is independent from the government. It is necessary, she also said, not to name an aggressor if this person has not been to court or if they are not dead. (2014, 374)

This approach to constructing the space of the TRC employs the sorts of prescriptions that would be considered ritual on the Confucian account: they delineate roles and responsibilities, cover specific practices and rules of decorum, and aim at establishing and preserving respect.

Despite the appeal of TRCs, however, their actual efficacy in helping victims recover from their traumas remains unclear. In particular, while TRCs arguably provide a space in which to work toward reconciliation between victim and victimizer, it is not obvious that these spaces truly or fully accommodate the particular material or emotional needs of those who have been victimized, including their anger. In fact, Archbishop Desmond Tutu, architect of the TRCs in South Africa, effectively condemns the presence of anger in such spaces, claiming that:

> Anything that subverts or undermines this sought-after good [of reconciliation] is to be avoided like the plague. Anger, resentment, lust for revenge, even success through aggressive competitiveness, are corrosive of this good. (1999, 34)

This construal and treatment of victims' anger is problematic for a number of reasons. First, and most obviously, it makes fully speaking truth difficult for victims who carry anger. These victims are prohibited from displaying, understanding, or validating their full range of emotions when restrictions are placed not only on what they are allowed say, but also on how they are allowed to say it. If anger is indeed caustic, as is suggested by scholars like Cantrell, Nussbaum, and Tutu, then it is best to alleviate this burden, rather than suppress it and thereby saddle the victims with additional pressure. Moreover, there is no evidence to date that TRCs effectively purge this feeling anyway (e.g., Flam 2013; Mendeloff 2009; Reynaud 2014). Consequently, even when TRCs are ritualized, it is not clear that they are presently effective rituals, at least insofar as their aim is to assist in healing and anger is indicative of injury.

Second, such construals assume that anger is necessarily divisive and caustic, and such a characterization ignores the fact that anger may vary in genre. Anger does not have to be destructive or divisive; it can, as I have argued throughout this chapter, also be conducive to moral projects.[40] Indeed, in her interviews with survivors who attended the Canadian TRCs, Reynaud notes that, although the events did little to alleviate their anger, none of the victims expressed anything akin to Nussbaum's payback wish (378), and some even refused to relinquish their anger on the grounds that it was part of both their personal healing process and the way forward in terms of eliminating systemic injustices (376). This is more in line with the moral anger that I have attributed to the Confucians: it is an anger that arises in response to moral transgressions and moves one to seek rectification or transformation of those individuals or systems responsible. As such, the moral anger depicted herein need not be construed as retributive or at odds with reparative/restorative justice. On the contrary, its aims are reparative/restorative, as the ethical-political project is pro-, rather than anti-, social.

My suggestion, then, is that TRCs can benefit from maintaining their ritualized atmosphere, but ought to alter the rituals (or provide additional rituals) such that they embrace anger and empower victims, rather than aim to snuff out their fire. This means that the ritual space of the TRC must be carefully constructed such that the ritual forms on offer simultaneously maintain an atmosphere of respect without invalidating the emotions of those offering testimony. For example, in the ritual of deposition it may help to emphasize that not only are speakers' words valued, but that their tone and nonverbal expressions are also valued by those in attendance; this must be so regardless of the nature of the emotion behind the expression, since that emotion is equally part of their testimony, their truth. Consequently, it would be wrong to censure those who express anger, especially since such expressions often reflect the very sort of distress that indicates an obstacle to reconciliation.

More effectively ritualizing TRCs also means being highly sensitive to the particular needs of those who would give testimony. Continuing with the example of the Canadian TRCs, Reynaud notes that the event, held at the Queen Mary Hotel in Montreal, was perceived as deeply problematic due to the Crown's role in perpetuating the target injustice, as well as the irony of sealing a "ritual" box containing written testimonials that had been "boxed-in" for so long (378). Although the event and the ritual were both well intentioned, they overlooked crucial features of the interaction between symbols (the name of the hotel and the sealing of the box) with the nature of the injustice (the government-sanctioned abuse of aboriginal peoples and the invalidation of their anguish). Following the Confucian guidelines, the ritual space should be selected or designed such that the space "fits" the circumstances, including the attitudes of those who have been injured. Additionally, any particular rituals that are incorporated into the TRC should be devised with an awareness of power dynamics; they should aim to maximally empower victims so that they are able to more effectively harness and express their full truths (again, inclusive of emotions like anger) and to avoid diminishing victims or their feelings. Such rituals can assist in harnessing anger and working directly toward its aim of moral rectification.

There are also less institutional ways of ritualizing moral anger that carry their own nuances. The Confucians, for example, tend to disparage the use of overt insults in direct confrontation with wrongdoers, but they do not shy away from expressing strong disapproval of wrongdoing by appeal to historical analogs. In several passages (e.g., *Analects* 3.1, 3.2), Confucius comments on the behaviors of the three great ministerial families in his home state who, in their hubris, carry on as if they carry the authority of not only dukes, but kings. When doing so, he does not engage in mere name-calling, but by identifying specific practices and alluding to how they, culturally or historically, reflect breaches of propriety. In other words, the wrongdoing is set specifically within the context of ritual or, perhaps more accurately, its transgression; it is a subtle "call-out" on wrongdoing. The philosophy behind such an approach is similar to Karen Stohr's (2006) account of the manner in which etiquette functions as the primary vehicle by which moral sentiments and attitudes are expressed. According to Stohr, there is a very real sense in which being a moral person requires one to understand and adopt social conventions as part of the expression and exchange of moral sentiments. This is not to suggest that morality is simply conventionalism: rather, as Stohr points out, "the conventions are the starting point . . . The thought may be what counts, but the vehicle for expressing it is itself part of the thought" (195). These etiquette conventions, then, are integral to proper moral practice and serve an important role in coordinating affect and action.

An approach of effectively calling out breaches of propriety/ritual thus reflects the aforementioned informative aspect of moral anger on two levels. On the one hand, appeal to ritual can enable expression of one's own moral outrage; on the other, it can reflect the thought that there is a sociohistorical explanation for why one is morally outraged and makes this explanation public. This is an interesting tactic for expressing moral anger, as it places the object(s) of anger in an interesting position: if they are to (meaningfully) respond to the challenge, then they must do so by addressing the explanation, which requires a more substantive and intellectual line of thought and communication. Consequently, by utilizing this mode of expression, one can effectively "raise the level of discourse" and possibly come closer to invoking the target moral or social change, as it forces the parties involved to reflect.[41]

A last way in which ritual can accommodate moral anger is simply to strive to embody and express the moral ideal that has been affronted. In so doing, one is able to both respond to the source of the immorality, injustice, or general moral transgression and productively work through the anger felt. Moreover, one is able to actively work toward setting right the situation through one's own agency, as actively being a morally good person requires one to act against immorality or injustice. To achieve this, from the Confucian perspective, requires that one exemplify ritual performance in general. This is because, according to the Confucians, sincere ritual practice simply does embody and express moral righteousness (e.g., *Analects* 15.18/43/11; *Xunzi* 19/93/23-19/94/1, 19/94/8). If moral anger motivates one to work toward moral rectification, then certainly this is the best way to achieve that end while exercising one's anger. In this way, one goes on to perform an analogue of what the exemplar kings themselves did, displaying anger through a courageous righteousness.

Are there modern examples of ritual being used in such a manner? An interesting case is made by David Kertzer that certain funeral rituals in South Africa can be construed as expressions of moral outrage against Apartheid. Detailing one such event, Kertzer writes:

> On April 13 [1985] . . . a mass funeral was held for twenty-seven blacks—many of them youths—killed by police. Most of the victims had been killed when police opened fire on mourners who had gathered for a previous funeral. The sixty thousand participants in the rite . . . "mixed solemnity with politics, mourning with exhortation and clenched fists with the soft swelling of African singing." The coffins were draped in the black, green, and gold colors of the outlawed African National Congress. Emotions ran high. (Kertzer 1988, 171)

This ritual was not merely for the purgation of grief and impotent outrage, nor was it simply to offer condolence or remembrance. The ritual cultivated the moral anger of the people and transformed it into action. As Kertzer goes on to note, the mass funeral allowed the people to not only unify in their anger, but also to demonstrate a shared identity and the possibility of a new national leadership (ibid., 172). In other words, the mass funeral served as more than just an expression of moral anger, but the application of that anger to help launch genuine opposition to their oppressors. This exemplifies the harnessing of moral anger into ritual and then using said ritual for (or toward) the enactment of positive moral change.

To reiterate, the Confucians regard anger as one of the most difficult dispositions that humans possess, and one that can easily be turned to violent, immoral ends. At the same time, being a natural disposition means that anger warrants care and attention and, moreover, can even be coopted in the service of attaining the moral ends toward which the person of noble character aims. As I have shown, one way of achieving moral aims through anger is to make use of ritual prescriptions to both express and work through one's anger, as well as harness that anger for the purpose of positive moral and sociopolitical change.

NOTES

1. It is noteworthy that, for the Confucians, even what are often thought of as positive dispositions (e.g., joy, affection, and happiness) can become disruptive in terms of how they influence or distort judgement, behavior, and relationships. Rather than attempt to cut off such feelings, however, the Confucians argue that it is better to find means of accommodating them, placing the Confucians in interesting opposition to (among others) the Stoics, who begin with similar premises and yet reached different conclusions.

2. There is a concern about cross-cultural (and cross-temporal) identification of emotions. To clarify, I am not assuming that nu is necessarily equivalent to what most readers will construe as anger. Rather, I offer up an interpretation of the Confucian notion of anger, its treatment in the literature, and how both the concept and its enactment bear on contemporary ethical issues. Similar considerations apply to all other emotions/feelings discussed herein.

3. ICS concordance numbers are used where possible for all citations from classical Chinese texts. Conventional passage numbers are also provided for the *Mengzi*. Translations are the author's own unless otherwise indicated.

4. Mengzi's admonitions here, and others like them, are congruent with the valuation of familial relationships that is notably prominent in Confucianism. Early in the *Analects*, for example, filial piety is listed as the root of benevolence (1.2/1/6-7). For concerns about how family can be jeopardized by anger, see *Analects* 12.21/33/1-3.

5. Xunzi additionally idealizes ministers and generals who are unable to be provoked by anger (*Xunzi* 15/71/4).

6. See, for example, *Analects* 12.1/30/17: "Restraining oneself and according with ritual propriety constitutes humaneness." I will elaborate on the role of ritual in moral goodness later in this chapter.

7. Scholars familiar with the work of Mengzi may object that the thinker does not depict anger as being a key feature or "sprout" of human nature. While this may muddy anger's place in Mengzi's philosophy, he still seems to regard anger as a feeling that can and does occur naturally, and so I will not treat him as an outlier among early Confucian thought on the topic.

8. Discussion with Joonho Lee was most helpful in formulating this distinction.

9. For a recent review and critique of scholars advancing such interpretations, see Zhang (2015).

10. Throughout the text I occasionally make mention of "righteous" attitudes, but I opt to depict anger as "moral anger" or "promoral anger" rather than necessarily as righteous anger. I do this to avoid (as much as possible) conflation of moral anger with the concept and disposition of righteousness (yi 義) often referenced in Confucian texts. While I suspect that moral(ized) anger and yi at least can fit together in the classical Confucian context, and perhaps often do, they are not depicted as practically or logically equivalent or entailing one another. As such, I err on the side of caution with my diction. I am appreciative of Andrew Ruble for helping me to explain this point.

11. Consequently, it is arguable that the Confucian notion of harmony, at least as I understand it here, is not a state devoid of what we might think of as disruptive feelings; rather, it involves the appropriate channeling and application of these feelings so that they do not become disruptive or result in disruptive behavior or action. My thanks to Eirik Harris for pressing me on this issue.

12. For example, Xunzi's list of natural dispositions includes liking (*hao* 好), disgust (*wu* 惡), joy (*xi* 喜), anger (*nu* 怒), sorrow (*ai* 哀), and happiness (*le* 樂) (*Xunzi* 22/107/23).

13. Interested scholars may also attend to the "Liyun" chapter of the Liji, which provides an elaboration of the so-called "seven feelings" (qi qing 七情) for later Confucian thought. This list notably includes anger (nu) alongside joy (xi 喜), sadness (ai 哀), fear (ju 懼), love (ai 愛), aversion (wu 惡), and desire (yu 欲).

14. This seems to have been an ancient mode of thought and one that the Confucians often associated with both filial piety (*xiao* 孝) and a more general notion of personal flourishing. See, for example, *Analects* 2.6/3/9.

15. Though not at the expense of moral values or commitments (e.g., *Mengzi* 6A14, 11.14/60/14-19)

16. A similar remark appears in the *Liji* (*"Yueji* 樂記" passage 49).

17. To clarify, I am focusing exclusively on the Confucian appeal to ritual in this project as a way of engaging with anger in a moral manner. This is not to suggest that the Confucians looked at ritual as the only resource by which anger could be coopted for moral ends, though (e.g., Mengzi makes a number of remarks about how humans have promoral core dispositions that can be used to rein in feelings like anger, and Xunzi suggests that a sense of approbation, once tutored, can also help to appropriately guide motivating feelings like anger). My thanks to Gordon Mower for recommending this addition.

18. See, for example, *Xunzi* 10/43/1-3: "In ritual, noble and lowly are ranked, old and young are differentiated, poor and rich, casual and grave, all of these are distinguished . . . Virtue must be accorded position, position must be accorded prosperity, and prosperity must be accorded use."

19. See in particular *Xunzi* Book 19, "On Ritual" (*Lilun* 禮論).

20. I here draw from Sin-yee Chan's (2006) interpretation of the related concept of respect (*jing* 敬) in Confucianism.

21. For first use of this description, see Lewis (2018). For an extended defense of this reading, see Lewis forthcoming.

22. A similar sentiment appears in *Analects* 16.13/47/3-9.

23. Mengzi says relatively little on the topic of ritual education.

24. Bockover (2012), Lewis (forthcoming), Li (2007), and Nam (2014) also employ analogies between language and ritual.

25. *Xunzi* 19/98/3-7, Hutton trans., p. 215.

26. The *Liji*, for example, details directions for coordinating the military with anger (e.g., *Qu Li Shang*, passage 69).

27. Of particular note are Xunzi's remarks on the rites of mourning and sacrifice detailed in *Xunzi* 19/95/17-18 and *Xunzi* 19/97/20-19/98/3.

28. Original text: 用人之勇去其怒.

29. Cantrell notes that James Jasper's (2011) work on emotion includes a "taxonomy" of anger that distinguishes moral anger from destructive, reflexive anger (Cantrell 2019, 11–12). Cantrell ultimately concludes, however, that "anger is caustic and too often brings about change that requires one group to benefit at the intentional expense of another group" (ibid., p. 33) and that it is therefore unsafe as a resource.

30. Michael Ing suggests that resentment is a form of anger; Winnie Sung argues that the two are conceptually distinct.

31. Ing here cites Xunzi: "Those who understand themselves do not resent others. Those who understand their lot in life do not resent *tian* (heaven)" (*Xunzi* 4/13/19; cited in Ing 2016, 20).

32. Sung interprets the Confucians as claiming that, when one is resentful, one objectifies oneself into a passive stance and become fixated, preventing one from realizing genuine benevolence and moral propriety. The early Confucians do criticize fixation and caution learners against becoming "stuck," so to speak, so Sung's interpretation is plausible, though it may not be the primary or exclusive rationale behind the general discomfort with resentment.

33. Ing offers a more specific instance of appropriate resentment, suggesting that it applies in cases where "those close to us take advantage of the vulnerability necessary for entering into meaningful relationships rooted in care" (2016, 24) and citing the appropriateness of resentment toward family who commit serious grievances detailed in *Mengzi* 6B3 (12.3/62/25-12.3/63/8). That is to say, resentment is appropriate when care, in some form, is withheld by those one considers intimately close; it is effectively a response to a special kind of betrayal.

34. Hagop Sarkissian (forthcoming) offers a similar analysis of the role of contempt (wu 惡) in Confucianism. Like resentment, contempt is undesirable due to its propensity for generating antisocial inclinations, but it also serves an important role in detecting and rectifying moral wrongs (e.g., *Analects* 4.3/7/9: "Only one who is humane is [truly] able to love people, is [truly] able to despise people").

35. Cantrell's characterization of "fierce love" is not entirely precise, but suggests that one ties a sense of ferocity (perhaps referring to a particular motive force) not to anger, which is injury-oriented, but to love, which is unity- and dignity-oriented, and is committed to a proposition that "none in humanity rises until all rise" (2019, 26).

36. See again *Xunzi* 19/97/20-19/98/3.

37. My thanks to Joshua de Bonilla for this example.

38. Similarly, one is encouraged to remonstrate with friends in error as well (*Analects* 12.23/33/15). One is also advised, however, to give up the attempt if the friend refuses advice, lest one be dragged down with them.

39. See, for example, the depiction of TRC aims at https://www.justice.gov.za/trc/ and https://www.cbc.ca/news/canada/faqs-truth-and-reconciliation-commission-1.699883.

40. For further argumentation for this point, Paul Muldoon (2008) provides an excellent (and recent) elaboration.

41. Of course, it is possible that this approach could just as easily result in further entrenchment in the problematic position(s) that have given rise to conflict. The Confucians traditionally would have advocated a more comprehensive moral education to ameliorate this sort of worry, but I acknowledge that, in modernity, there may not be available recourse to such a resource. Then again, my argument was never that such means are foolproof, and I suspect that it is preferable to offer *some* means of handling moral anger than no means at all.

REFERENCE LIST

Cantrell, Deborah. 2019. "Love, Anger, and Social Change." *University of Colorado Law Legal Studies Research Paper No. 19-14*.

Flam, Helena. 2013. "The Transnational Movement for Truth, Justice and Reconciliation as an Emotional (rule) Regime?" *Journal of Political Power* 6, no. 3: 363–383.

———. 2015. "Micromobilization and Emotions." In *The Oxford Handbook of Social Movements*, edited by Donatella Della Porta and Mario Diani, 264–276. New York: Oxford University Press.

Flam, Helena, and Debra King, eds. 2005. *Emotions and Social Movements*. New York: Routledge.

Gibson, James L. 2006. "The Contributions of Truth to Reconciliation: Lessons from South Africa." *The Journal of Conflict Resolution* 50, no. 3: 409–432.

Hutton, Eric. 2014. *Xunzi: The Complete Text*. Princeton, NJ: Princeton University Press.

Ing, Michael. 2016. "Born of Resentment: *Yuan* in Early Confucian Thought." *Dao* 15, no. 1: 19–33.

Ivanhoe, P. J. 2006. "Mengzi's Conception of Courage." *Dao* 5, no. 2: 221–234.

Jasper, James M. 2011. "Emotions and Social Movements: Twenty Years of Theory and Research." *Annual Review of Sociology* 37: 285–303.

Kertzer, David I. 1988. *Ritual, Politics, and Power*. New Haven, CT: Yale University Press.

Konnikova, Maria. 2014. "The Lost Art of the Unsent Angry Letter." *The New York Times*, March 22, 2015. https://www.nytimes.com/2014/03/23/opinion/sunday/the-lost-art-of-the-unsent-angry-letter.html.

Lau, D. C. 1995. *A Concordance to the Lunyu*, ICS series. Hong Kong: Commercial Press.

Lau, D. C., and F. Z. Chen, eds. 1992. *A Concordance to the Liji*, ICS series. Hong Kong: Commercial Press.

Lau, D. C., H. C. Wah, and C. F. Ching, eds. 1995. *A Concordance to the Mengzi*, ICS series. Hong Kong: Commercial Press.

———. 1996. *A Concordance to the Xunzi*, ICS series. Hong Kong: Commercial Press.

Lewis, Colin J. 2018. "Ritual Education and Moral Development: A Comparison of Xunzi and Vygotsky." *Dao* 17, no. 1: 81–98.

———. Forthcoming. *Confucian Ritual and Moral Education*. Lexington Books.

Lindebaum, Dirk, and Deanna Geddes. 2016. "The Place and Role of (Moral) Anger in Organizational Behavior Studies." *Journal of Organizational Behavior* 37: 738–757.

Lindebaum, Dirk, and Yiannis Gabriel. 2016. "Anger and Organization Studies: From Social Disorder to Moral Order." *X and Organization Studies* 37, no. 7: 903–918.

Mendeloff, David. 2009. "Trauma and Vengeance: Assessing the Psychological and Emotional Effects of Post-Conflict Justice." *Human Rights Quarterly* 31, no. 3: 592–623.

Muldoon, Paul. 2008. "The Moral Legitimacy of Anger." *European Journal of Social Theory* 11, no. 3: 299–314.

Nussbaum, Martha. 2016. *Anger and Forgiveness: Resentment, Generosity, Justice*. New York: Oxford University Press.

Reynaud, Anne-Marie. 2014. "Dealing with Difficult Emotions: Anger at the Truth and Reconciliation Commission of Canada." *Anthropologica* 56, no. 2: 369–382.

Sarkissian, Hagop. Forthcoming. "Virtuous Contempt (*wu* 惡) in the *Analects*." In *The Oxford Handbook of Chinese Philosophy*, edited by Justin Tiwald. New York: Oxford University Press.

Shun, Kwong-loi. 2014. "Resentment and Forgiveness in Confucian Thought." *Journal of East-West Thought* 4: 13–35.

———. 2015. "On Anger: An Essay on Confucian Moral Psychology." In *Returning to Zhu Xi: Emerging Patterns Within the Supreme Polarity*, edited by David Jones and Jinli He, 299–324. Albany, NY: State University of New York Press.

Stohr, Karen. 2006. "Manners, Morals, and Practical Wisdom." In *Values and Virtues: Aristotelianism in Contemporary Ethics*, edited by Timothy Chappell, 189–211. Oxford: Oxford University Press.

Sung, Winnie. Forthcoming. "The Early Confucian Worry About Yuan (Resentment)." *The Journal of Value Inquiry*. https://doi.org/10.1007/s10790-019-09694-5.

Zhang, Feng. 2015. "Confucian Foreign Policy Traditions in Chinese History." *Chinese Journal of International Politics* 8, no. 2: 197–218.

Chapter 7

Is Anger Ever Required? Ārya Śāntideva on Anger and Its Antidotes

Will Barnes

According to Aristotle, anger has psychological, conative, cognitive, and intentional content, combining the painful view that a moral damage has occurred with the attribution of culpability and a pleasing desire for payback, describing anger as "a desire accompanied by pain for an imagined retribution on account of an imagined slighting inflicted by people who have no legitimate reason to slight oneself or one's own" (*Rhetoric* 1378a31-33).[1] Aristotle advises harnessing the moral efficacy of anger as a response to wrongdoing while abating its destructive consequences through moderation. According to Aristotle, not only are there situations where anger is praiseworthy,[2] if we do not become angry in such situations it is either because we are "ignorant of right and wrong, have a weak disposition, or lack self-respect," indeed, that we are "slavish" (*Nicomachean Ethics* [*NE*] 1126a5-10).

Aristotle's is a common view. It's popular to view anger as an appropriate response to immorality and injustice and to believe that, properly placed, it promotes dignity and empowerment. There is considerable sympathy for the view that justice requires anger, and trends in contemporary ethical, social, and political theory are keen to locate justified anger among the virtues.[3] Support for this position centers on the view that anger has a unique power to acknowledge wrongdoing appropriately, to empower those disempowered by wrongdoing, and empower us to address it. Emily McRae and Martha Nussbaum offer qualified defenses of anger on these lines. To support this view, Nussbaum cites the following case told to her by colleagues at the West Point Philosophy Department:

> Elie Wiesel was a child in one of the Nazi death camps. On the day the Allied forces arrived, the first member of the liberating army he saw [. . .] began to curse, shouting at the top of his voice. As the child Wiesel watched, he went on

> shouting and cursing for a very long time. And the child Wiesel thought now, with that anger, humanity has come back. (Nussbaum 1994, 403)

Before developing her defense of anger, Martha Nussbaum criticizes the popular Aristotelian view. In *Anger and Forgiveness: Resentment, Generosity, Justice*, Nussbaum updates Aristotle's picture of anger to include the pain of a wrongful or inappropriate action against oneself, or people, values, and worldviews close to one's own, and a will-to-retribution prefaced on complex causal thinking and moral evaluation. Nussbaum targets an archaic and erroneous metaphysics within retributive anger, namely, that it presupposes a cosmic telos that can be derailed by wrongdoing and restored by retribution. For example, when a family grieving for a murdered child pursues the death penalty to provide reparation, Nussbaum claims that this makes sense only if we assume wrongdoing can be undone by visiting painful punishment on the wrongdoer. Nussbaum argues that because retributive anger cannot correct the wrong/damage/injustice it perceives or provide the closure it promises, it is irrational and should be relinquished.

Nussbaum also diagnoses a form of anger that seeks retribution through establishing relative superiority in a social hierarchy through violence, diminution, and abasement without demanding justice or contributions to collective well-being. Nussbaum calls for relinquishing this form of retributive anger because it is cruel and morally indifferent and reveals its ubiquity in customary western moral thinking.[4] For example, Nussbaum exposes status retributivism in public shaming, virtue signaling, and other popular expression of righteous anger, as well as in "transactional forgiveness," the state where certain conditions such as shaming, confession, repentance, ostracization, condemnation, or soliciting guilt must be met before forgiveness is granted. In this way, albeit under the guise of reestablishing a moral equilibrium within the subjectivity of the other, through an imposed self-abasement, status anger and transactional forgiveness solicit and satiate retributivism's cruelty and moral indifference. For these reasons, Nussbaum concludes, it too should be relinquished:

> In a sane and not excessively anxious and status focused person, anger's idea of retribution or payback is a brief dream cloud, soon dispelled by saner thoughts of personal and social welfare. (Nussbaum 2018, 30–31)

In the Bodhicaryāvatāra and the Śikṣāsamuccaya eighth-century Madhyamika Buddhist monk Śāntideva also offers a normative critique of status-based retributivism operating within anger (krodha), 5 targeting its inability to restore: "If your wish [for retribution] was fulfilled, what pleasure would there be for you in their suffering?" (Śāntideva 1996, IV v. 88)

Concerning the moral immaturity of status-based retributivism Śāntideva writes: "Like a child that howls a wail of distress when his sandcastle is broken, so my own mind appears to me at the loss of praise and renown" (Śāntideva 1996, I v. 93). The primary focus of Śāntideva's critique, though, is the incoherence and egocentricity of anger based on the assumption of culpable autonomous agency.[5] Concerning egocentricity, according to Śāntideva, because we get more angry when wrongdoing is perceived to target ourselves, our values, or others we identify with, it is prejudiced and egocentric: "If you argue that your dislike of one who speaks ill of you is because he is harming living beings, why then do you feel no anger when he defames others in the same way?" (Śāntideva 1996, IV v. 64). This relatively superficial example highlights the fact that in general particularly retributive anger is somewhat self-interested, relative, and partial. Concerning incoherence, the common mistake in indignant responses, Śāntideva tells us, is to assume that the wrongdoer is outside the material, social, and psychic causal world and decides ex-nihilo to act harmfully for the sake of victimizing the subject of the wrongful act. By reflecting on the fact that wrongdoing is caused by conditions rather than spontaneous autonomous choice, Śāntideva would have us thwart indignation by removing its rationale. Because there are always complex causes for wrongdoing, any indignation that assumes "this *could/should* not have happened" exhibits an ignorance of causation in its attributions of responsibility, and he or she who assumes "this could/should not have happened to *me, my people, values, or worldview*" exhibits an obfuscating egocentrism. If we perceive things as they really are, Śāntideva argues, we would not get angry:

> I feel no anger towards bile and the like, even though they cause intense suffering. Why am I angry with the sentient? (Śāntideva 1996, IV v. 22)
>
> Whatever transgressions and evil deeds of various kinds there are, all arise through the power of conditioning factors. (Śāntideva 1996, IV v. 25)
>
> Some commit offenses out of delusion. Others, deluded, grow angry. Who among them should we say is free from blame, or who should we say is guilty? (Śāntideva 1996, IV v. 67)

Rather than endorsing the view that causality exculpates, Śāntideva is explaining that once we realize the complex impersonal causes and conditions of wrongdoing, we have no cause to be angry. Because wrongdoing is not autonomous, designating a wrongdoer is a misnomer. As Śāntideva puts it, "At what does one get angry?" (Śāntideva 1996, IV, v. 31). Following this realization, we are less determined by reactive emotions and are better equipped to uphold the values eschewed by wrongdoing. That is, once we become conscious of a cause of our actions, our actions no longer fall under the auspices of that cause: "Everybody is subject to the force of prior actions [. . .] But realizing this, I shall make the effort to perform good actions" (Śāntideva 1996, IV vv. 68–69). In this sense, the correct metaphysical perspective constitutes a new causal variable. Under these new conditions, the only appropriate response to wrongdoing is to avoid it.

According to Martha Nussbaum, there is a variety of anger that can acknowledge injustice, empower those disempowered by wrongdoing, motivate us to address it, and promote collective well-being, all without desiring payback. This "Transitional Anger" (Nussbaum 2018, 35) retains the morally valuable aspects of Aristotle's account—the recognition of non-accidental wrongdoing (ibid., 37)—but is purged of retributivism, shifting its focus to reducing the likelihood of its reoccurrence (ibid., 36). Citing Dr. Martin Luther King's provisional endorsement of anger, Nussbaum argues that transitional anger is morally valuable because of its sensitivity to wrongdoing and because it "usefully energizes us towards" (ibid., 39) cultivating and acting toward the restoration or revolutionary establishment of institutions and attitudes that "promote well-being" (ibid.). Indeed, Nussbaum argues, if anger heightens moral sensitivity, energizes us to address wrongdoing, and is non-retributive, it may in fact be morally required.

Although footnoting Śāntideva, Nussbaum provides no analysis of the multiple contributions to the study of anger from the Buddhist tradition.[6] In contrast, in "Metabolizing Anger: A Tantric Buddhist Solution to the Problem of Moral Anger," Emily McRae theorizes a form of morally efficacious anger from Indo-Tibetan Buddhism, specifically two texts preserved in Tibetan by ninth-century Indian Vaibhāṣika-Madhyamika Dharmarakṣita: *The Wheel-Weapon That Strikes at the Enemy's Vital Spot* and *The Poison-Destroying Peacock Mind Training*. Following in the tradition of Wendy Donner (2002), McRae interprets these texts as arguing that accomplished moral agents can recruit the power and energy of anger for beneficent ends. On McRae's account, through the course of practice, one is able to redirect anger toward "one's own ego-clinging and the accompanying inability to fully comprehend the full moral significance of other members of the moral community" (McRae 2015). Unlike "normal anger," metabolized anger is non-compulsive and can be dropped at will; it is oriented toward beneficence, being "grounded in love and compassion" (ibid.), and therefore lacks a desire to harm. Although agreeing that love, compassion, and forgiveness are often more effective methods for achieving these endsMcRae also argues that, on occasions, anger is morally required. In presenting her case, McRae develops Nussbaum's example of the liberating soldier restoring Elie Wiesel's humanity:

> Now, imagine a similar scenario, but, instead of cursing, the soldier started to cry. Would that also restore humanity? [. . .] the expression of sadness does not properly recognize the wrongdoing of the Nazi guards because sadness is about loss, pain, and suffering. It is not sufficiently specific to track suffering [. . .] the typically meek response of showing pity and concern may not fully restore humanity since it does not recognize an important aspect of the survivor's reality, namely that she has survived a grave injustice. (McRae 2015, 471)

According to McRae, anger is justifiable if, and only if, it recognizes wrongdoing and suffering, counteracts it more effectively than alternatives, empowers victims of wrongdoing, and is non-retributive, and because tantric anger achieves all three more successfully than non-angry alternatives it can be morally required. Contrary to compassion, empathy, understanding, grief, or "meekness," McRae argues, "tantric" anger is equipped to provide this restorative effect because it both "recognizes wrongdoing" and the "suffering caused by injustice" and counteracts it more effectively than the alternatives.

Nussbaum and McRae both defend the view that non-retributive anger can be morally required because it has a unique power to acknowledge wrongdoing, empower those disempowered by wrongdoing, and motivate us to address it more effectively than other responses. To refute this view, we will turn to Śāntideva's antidotes to anger; the perfection of patient forbearance (*kṣānti-pāramitā*)[7] and the perfection of vigor (*vīrya-pāramitā*) the foremost among a collection of virtues Śāntideva prescribes instead of, and against, anger. These virtues combine the willingness to suffer (*duṣkhādhivāsanakṣā nti* Śāntideva 1990, vv. 11–21),[8] the commitment to correctly understanding reality (dharmanidhyānakṣānti Śāntideva SS. Vv. 22–32), and the willingness to help others (*parāpakāramarṣanakṣānti* Śāntideva 1990, vv. 33–75)[9] with a cultivated, forward-looking, enthusiasm for virtue prefaced on a fear of others' suffering. Following Śāntideva, the thesis defended here is that because patience and moral vigor acknowledge wrongdoing, empower those disempowered by wrongdoing, and motivate us to address it more effectively than anger, while anger may at times have instrumental value, it is never morally required.

Śāntideva problematizes both the claim that anger is equipped to serve the aforementioned ends and that it is uniquely equipped to do so. Concerning the first, Śāntideva argues that anger's powers of recognition are suspect because it is structurally self-oriented, that it clouds moral judgment, and that it presupposes and reinforces self-regard. Understanding this objection can be aided by returning to Aristotle's definition of anger as combining the painfulness of "an imagined slighting," with the desire for "an imagined retribution."[10] This is why, according to Aristotle, anger has a "pleasantness" (*Rhetoric* 1378a 31–33)[11] as well as being painful; which is to say, anger satisfies and ameliorates. Indeed, the restorative power of anger derives, at least in part, from the desires and pains of the angry. Śāntideva plausibly reduces the ameliorative appeal of anger to its power to reinforce the sense of self. That is, anger is a partial alleviation of the vulnerability and powerlessness experienced due to wrongdoing, and this is necessarily, if not entirely, self-oriented. According to Śāntideva, then, anger is not optimally occupied on the other; therefore, it is not optimally equipped to acknowledge wrongdoing, empower those disempowered by wrongdoing, and motivate us to address it. The concern here is not that self-orientation is inherently ethically problematic, as moral concern for Śāntideva targets suffering wherever it arises, but rather that because moral anger seeks the amelioration of the angry in addition to understanding or addressing the moral problems that compel it, it is not best equipped to understand or address the problems that compel it.[12]

Returning to the definition of anger in the *Rhetoric*, Aristotle uses the term "imagined" twice, implying that anger can arise on the basis of moral understandings that are structurally independent of any objective analysis of the situation. According to Śāntideva, anger's metaphysical underpinnings and intentional structure invariably presuppose and generate a faulty analysis. Nussbaum agrees with Śāntideva about anger's intentional structure: "There is always a thought of an agent, or quasi-agent who has inflicted the damage" (Nussbaum 2018, 45). Sidetracked as it is, by the erroneous reification of a culpable agent, anger fails to take seriously the analysis of the causes and conditions of wrongdoing that problematized the attribution of blame to an actual or abstract agent.[13] It is precisely in the agent-oriented nature of anger that it compromises the possible morality of its justification. Therefore, anger cannot be optimally focused on the restoration, or revolutionary establishment, of institutions and attitudes which promote well-being. Contrary to the view of transitional anger as signaling and/or raising moral awareness and motivating effective action in response to wrongdoing, in misunderstanding its causes, anger obscures both the morally significant features of a situation and the path to addressing wrongdoing.

The centrality of the critique of anger can be further elaborated in reference to the four virtuous emotions (the *brahma-vihāras*) at the heart of Śāntideva's model of ethical cultivation. *Maitrī*/friendliness is being committed to the happiness of others.[14] *Karuṇā*/care is an active commitment to care for all beings.[15] *Muditā*/sympathetic joy is the ability to take delight in the happiness and good qualities of others. *Upekṣā*/impartiality includes the ability to accept what arises without anger and to extend the other three *brahma-vihāras* to all sentient beings equally, without preference, prejudice, or exception. Without the appreciation of the fact that all human behavior is the result of a vast network of causes of conditions (*prajñā*), and the purging of egocentrism, *upekṣā* is impossible. Because anger presupposes and reinforces self-regard, misattributes autonomy, and reifies the culpable, it cannot develop this all-inclusivity. This is why, according to Śāntideva, moral development, anti-egoism, and the elimination of anger work together. This is also why Candrakīrti, a huge influence on Śāntideva and the whole subsequent Buddhist ethical tradition, likens patience to the sun because it shines equally for all, that is, impartially. Anger, by contrast, even when containing moral intent, is necessarily partial.

Śāntideva also problematizes the view that anger is morally efficacious and empowering: consider, for example, the following from the *Bodhicaryāvatāra*: "Anger wells up against one's will" and, "a person does not get angry at will, having decided, 'I shall get angry'" (Śāntideva 1996 IV. v. 24).[16] For Śāntideva, a phenomenology of anger reveals it to oppose, rather than manifest, freedom, and that this should lead us to realize the ubiquity of casual determination in the first and the third person. Which is to say, according to Śāntideva, realizing that "when I am angry, I am not free," we simultaneously realize that we should not condemn the angry, because since they too are not acting freely when angry, they are not acting autonomously. If we take empowerment as the realization of inherent worth and dignity and not in the sense of arousing psycho-psychological energy, it is hard to square the view that anger is empowering in the relevant sense.

In addition to problematizing the claim that anger is uniquely equipped to recognize the morally significant, to empower the agent, and to motivate moral action, Śāntideva offers us alternatives that are more suitable than anger to achieve these ends and to empower those affected by wrongdoing. It is through analysis of the antidotes that we can problematize the claim that anger empowers the victims of wrongdoing more effectively than alternatives, thus supporting the view that anger is never morally required. In the *Śikṣāsamuccaya*, Śāntideva explains that the fear of others' suffering provides "empowerment," in the psycho-physiological energetic sense, sufficient to motivate moral action and should be cultivated for that reason. In the *Bodhicaryāvatāra*, Śāntideva talks about righteous-desire and moral-pride as among six capacities that help one to increase *vīrya*: "The sage has sung that righteous desire is the root of all skillful deeds" (Śāntideva 1996, VII v.32). Also, in the *Bodhicaryāvatāra*, Śāntideva suggests that if it remains firmly tethered to a supervening egoless and nondiscriminatory compassion, pride can have moral efficacy: "Stood in the midst of the hosts of defilements, one should be a thousand times more hotly proud, invincible to the hosts of defilements" (Śāntideva 1996, VII v.60). Śāntideva is clear that this adoption of dangerous mental states is justified if and only if we relinquish reactive emotions, egocentricity, and reification, and have a clear moral purpose. To this end Śāntideva employs the familiar Buddhist distinction between divine and human emotions, where the latter refers to the conventional egocentric reactive emotions, and the former to the qualities of deities imaginatively embodied though tantric practices and visualizations utilized for ethical ends. This is why, Śāntideva writes, "desire for what is good should be created, meditating carefully" (Śāntideva 1996, VII v.53) and that "the root of that is ever meditation upon the resulting consequences" (Śāntideva 1996, VII v.40). And while for pride and desire, Śāntideva distinguishes between non-egocentric and egocentric varieties, he does not say the same about anger.[17]

Returning to our central example, the liberating soldiers' anger reminded Elie Wiesel that a community in which human dignity is recognized persists, thus enabling the self-affirmation of moral worth that had been battered by the banality and brutality of gross wrongdoing. Following Śāntideva's account of the antidotes, we can call into doubt Nussbaum's claim that only anger could restore Wiesel's humanity. Combining *vīrya* with *kṣānti*'s willingness to support others, driven by a "fear of the suffering of others" and "meditation on the benefits of virtue" (Śāntideva 1996, VII.31), we can see how recognizing others in pain would sufficiently trigger a passionate desire to address wrongdoing and the practical commitment to help. It need not have been anger that brought the soldier to liberate Wiesel. It need not have been anger that enabled him to respond appropriately to the barbaric inhumanity of the death camps. Indeed, the soldier seems a paradigm of understanding and fearing the suffering of others, as well as the enthusiastic moral commitment to helping others.

But perhaps we have still not done enough to explain why it need not have been anger which restored Wiesel's humanity. As well as supporting the thesis that patience is better equipped than anger to acknowledge wrongdoing and motivate us to address it, the emphasis on the willingness to grieve, the first of Śāntideva's three-part model of patience, may shed light on why Nussbaum and McRae, who also defend the view that non-retributive anger can be morally required, are wrong to suggest anger is well equipped to empower those disempowered by wrongdoing. In her work with tantric Buddhist anger, McRae deals with Wiesel's case, and argues that grief cannot have similar morally restorative in effects because, in contrast to anger, grief "does not properly recognize the wrongdoing" or convey the "morally relevant information" and because "it is about loss, pain, and suffering," which is not "sufficiently specific to track the suffering caused by injustice." This perspective is shared by Nussbaum when she argues that anger is more cognitively sophisticated and politically useful than grief because it includes complex causal thinking and the attribution of agency, autonomy, and culpability, as well as the orientation toward reparations, be they through the unhelpful and base lust for retribution, or the useful welfare-consequentialism of transitional anger (Nussbaum 2016 47–48).

Following Śāntideva, we can see how McRae's and Nussbaum's claims are problematic. First, to see why anger is not more cognitively sophisticated than grief and communicates less morally relevant information than grief, consider mourning for a murder victim. Grief communicates highly complex morally relevant information: it acknowledges the gravest of wrongdoings, the value of love, and the destruction of a vision of the future, it initiates detailed memories and engenders complex and diverse responses relative to complex and diverse evaluative and explanatory frameworks, it can derail superficial habits of thought, manifest as transformative existential reflection on the precariousness and preciousness of life, and the unity of the violently bereaved. As Śāntideva puts it, "From the shock it [grief] causes, intoxication falls away and there arises compassion" (Śāntideva 1996 VI, v. 21). The intoxication in question is the self-orientations, exclusivity, and narrowmindedness typified by anger. According to Śāntideva, inasmuch as non-retributive anger imputes spontaneous autonomy to agents of wrongdoing, and narrows one's focus while increasing egocentric edification, it is not at all sophisticated, but rather the effect and cause of delusion. This is why Śāntideva focuses on the preciousness and precariousness of human existence in the attempt to cultivate moral enthusiasm, to generate compassion for the wrongdoer, and to cultivate a willingness to grieve, as superior alternatives to the consoling but delusional ameliorations of reactive anger.[18]

To further problematize Nussbaum's claim that anger contains more complex causal thinking than grief, consider anger versus grief in response to the United States' decision to abandon their Kurdish allies to the Turks and ISIS in Northeast Syria. Because grief does not attribute blame to specific autonomous agents it remains open to complex causal analysis. Anger, by contrast, makes sense of events by situating them within a recognizable frame of autonomous subjective agency, absolving us of coming up with broader explanations for events, even drowning out critical modes of questioning. Nussbaum's claim, then, that anger is more sophisticated than grief because of its attribution of agency, autonomy, and culpability is plausible only if one adopts a causal oversimplification, eschewing analysis of complex material, psychic, and social structures, and only if one fails to see that anger forces a misleading focus on autonomous culpable agents, even if it doesn't seek retribution. While it is true that grief may fail to recognize wrongdoing appropriately, to track the suffering caused by injustice, or distinguish between injustice and misfortune, it is surely capable of all three. Due to its specificity, its obscuration of complex analysis, and its intentional narrowness, anger is more likely to be deficient than grief, in all these respects.

Following Śāntideva, not only have we cast doubt over Nussbaum and McRae's contention that grief cannot properly recognize wrongdoing, track the suffering caused by injustice, or convey morally relevant information, the view that anger is more cognitively sophisticated and morally useful than grief has also been problematized. Consider again Elie Wiesel: The grief that arises at Wiesel's situation allows for, if not entails, an appreciation of the highly causally complex geopolitical machinations of National Socialism, the historic plight of the ethnically Jewish, as well as the evaluation and application of dignity and abhorrence at its absence. Grief at the atrocities of Wiesel's situation, born of compassion, empathy, and understanding, is at least as complex as anger in its power to recognize wrongdoing and suffering caused by injustice. And, in its ability to comprehend Wiesel's situation, grief is more causally sophisticated than anger precisely because it functions independently of anger's need to attribute blame, to superimpose causal simplicity, and presuppose explanatory power.

Moreover, even if we grant the problematic claim that non-retributive anger is more psycho-cognitively complex than grief, there is reason to doubt that this is indicative of its superior restorative utility. It is a common view in psychological, sociological, and psychoanalytic schools of thought that anger is closely linked to a refusal to grieve.[19] Nussbaum endorses this view, writing that anger functions "as a way of assuaging or compensating for one's own pain" (24) and stems from "an unwillingness to grieve" or "accept helplessness" (29).[20] Anger often arises because it is psychically easier than, not morally superior to, grief. Unlike anger, grief can acknowledge wrongdoing without targeting a culpable party, without satiating self-regard, without denying interdependence and vulnerability, and with heightened and inclusive other regard. As such, grief is better equipped to empower those disempowered by wrongdoings and motivate us to address it, than anger.

This account of the power of grief also undermines a view implicit in McRae and Nussbaum, and explicit in many popular defenses of anger from P. F. Strawson to social media, namely, that it empowers the angry, because it, and only it, can restore self-regard. Indeed, its ability to empower the victims of injustice drives McRae and Nussbaum's defenses of non-retributive anger. The response from the perspective of *duṣkhādhivāsanakṣānti*, the first of Śāntideva's tripartite alternative, locates a pathological narcissism inherent in anger. When we are angry, there is an unconscious as well as a cognitive internality compelling the causal oversimplification within anger's evaluative content. The desire to blame reifies an autonomous culpable agent and stems from a blow to one's sense of power, agency, and efficacy thwarted by the perceived wrong, and which resolves itself in the assumption of explanatory power and moral superiority. When we are damaged by others we internalize and idealize the source of that humiliation to preserve self-regard, and, much like retaliation, the angry ascriptions of moral superiority and culpability are sufficient psychosocial proof that the damage done has not, after all, compromised self-worth. This is an empowerment anger may provide. However, because the lack of self-regard restored by anger is a symptom of injustice, it appears anger, at least here, is a solution to a symptom of injustice rather to injustice itself. Because low self-esteem caused by sociopolitical injustice is merely ameliorated by anger, taking into account its aforementioned deficiencies, and numerous dangers, it cannot be the optimally effective response to it. To be very clear, this is not to condemn the anger of the oppressed, quite the opposite; as Śāntideva prescribed, correctly analyzing the determining causes of one's own anger renders any condemnation of another's anger incoherent and therefore morally pernicious, especially when those determining causes are so clear. Anger is an inevitable response to oppression, and the solution is to remove oppression. The position I defend here is not to deny the obvious instrumental and therapeutic value of anger, particularly for the oppressed; it is rather, to appreciate that anger is as sign of distress at least as much as it is of insight.[21] Recalling Śāntideva's phenomenology, if anger is not compelled by freedom, it is not empowering in the relevant sense. If we take empowerment as the realization of inherent worth and dignity, precisely as McRae and Nussbaum did in their analysis of Elie Wiesel, even assuming anger's energizing power and contributions to self-regard, it is hard to square the view that reactive anger manifests dignity and moral worth. Concerning communities forced into anger either due to trauma or in the recognition that they will be not noticed otherwise, while feigned anger is sufficient for the latter, genuine anger aimed at immorality and injustice is a response and symptom, rather than a solution to it.[22] The question is not "should I be angry" at oppression and injustice, the questions is "What are the causes of oppression and injustice and how do we change them?", precisely the position undergirding the successful responses to injustice and oppression in the sublime work of Martin Luther King, Mahatma Gandhi, and Nelson Mandela.[23]

Because anger superimposes an erroneous metaphysics of autonomy and culpability, obscures the morally relevant features of a situation, and does not morally empower victims of injustice and immorality, it cannot be the best response to wrongdoing. The optimally moral response to oppression is not to encourage or endorse anger, nor is it to consider one's lack deficient and to cultivate anger; it is to understand and contest the complex psychic, physiological, and sociopolitical causes of injustice, immorality, and oppression. And while anger is an antidote to the feeling of vulnerability, grief is more useful in the project of understanding and contesting the complex sociopolitical causes of oppression, as well as for reforming or working toward the establishment of institutions aimed at collective welfare, precisely because it is radically inclusive, anti-retributive, and non-blaming. While Nussbaum and McRae claim that anger is more useful than grief in empowering those disempowered by wrongdoing and its efficacy in relation to restoration and reparation, in risking excluding the perpetrators of wrongdoing from restorative justice, and its faulty causal analysis of wrongdoing, by contrast, anger is morally inferior to grief.[24]

In the project of relinquishing anger, Śāntideva would have us see the agent, or agency, be it actual or abstract, of wrongdoing, not as an obstacle to be rejected, avoided, denied, or destroyed, but as that which must be included in the restorative response. This includes cultivating the willingness to encounter both anger and that at which it is aimed positively, rather than other responses anger can lead to including the attributions of blame, self-protection and amelioration, and/or the denial of interdependence and vulnerability. To cultivate a willingness to grieve is to become better equipped to achieve the ends to which defenders of anger appeal, without misunderstanding the causality of wrongdoing, presupposing and reinforcing the sense of self, or being distracted by amelioration. Consider some divergent potential objects of anger—a white supremacist, a misogynistic Supreme Court justice, or a President keeping families apart at the Mexican border—Śāntideva would have us see these persons, even if "extremely malignant" as those for whom "all that is skillful should be done" (Śāntideva 1996, VI v. 120). While this may seem extreme, it is rational. In relation to those who are wrong about or hateful of measures conducive to well-being, we should ask whether anger toward them helps. To ensure our actions are committed to the good, and to increase the chances of those with whom we disagree pausing, learning something, or at least not having their predispositions triggered by our ire, we should meet them, if not with love, generosity, and forgiveness, then at least patience, but not continued anger. If transforming unjust conditions is our goal, then the transformation of persons and institutions consciously or unconsciously complicit with the current conditions is also a desideratum. Whether or not we succumb to outrage precisely when others eschew human welfare is a test of our commitment to it.

According to Śāntideva, the task is to move from the objects to the subject of anger and apply philosophical critique to the presuppositions making it possible, using philosophy as a means for the elimination of anger through the transformation of perspective. To this end, the final third of Śāntideva's tripartite patience, *dharmanidhyānakṣānti*, concerns how to understand reality. While Nussbaum agrees with Aristotle and Śāntideva that reactive emotions reflect metaphysical standpoints and criticizes metaphysical error both in her work on disgust and her rejection of cosmic retributivism, her critique is primarily normative. Śāntideva, by contrast, is concerned with exposing the faulty metaphysics anger presupposes.

According to Śāntideva, the optimally patient person experiences wrongdoing as the result of impersonal causal forces, therefore avoiding the anger that would arise from reifying a culpable wrongdoer, regardless of the presence or absence of retributive intent. Such patience arises from correctly perceiving and understanding that anger presupposes, generates, and reinforces a primal, atavistic metaphysical error—a ubiquitous reificationism built into our perceptual apparatus which is hyperactive in the (mis)attribution of autonomous culpability. As well as metaphysics, analysis of physical, biological, psychic, sociolinguistic, and geopolitical interdependence refutes this view. As opposed to anger's erroneous assumption of subjective moral autonomy, patience remains open to complex causal analysis. As Śāntideva asks, "Everything is dependent on something else, and even that on which something is dependent is not autonomous. Hence, why would one get angry?" (Śāntideva 1996 VI, v. 31). In truth, there is no good reason to. The commitment to supporting others and a willingness to suffer channeled through metaphysical study leads to an awareness of anger as both grounded in and generative of deception, and an obstacle to cultivating an inclusive and active compassion.

Indicating the centrality of this view in the lineage of Indo-Tibetan Buddhism, in *The Essential Jewel of Holy Practice* Dza Patrul Rinpoche defends Śāntideva's case for the elimination of anger and the generation of compassion as mutually entailing and requisite commitments for attaining moral objectivity: "As the two conceptual obscurations diminish, realization grows" (Rinpoche 2018, 57).[25] The first obscuration refers to reactive emotions including despondency, greed, and lust, but most of all anger. The second obscuration refers to the metaphysical views underpinning reactive emotions, most of all the reification of autonomy. Following Śāntideva, Patrul Rinpoche explains that anger is irredeemably dysfunctional, that it arises from a faulty conception of reality, and is unequivocal in the view that anger is never required. When angry, Patrul Rinpoche prescribes that we should attend to the angry mind, not the object of anger: "Subdue the enemy of anger with the sword of love. Protect the family of the denizens of the six realms [sentient beings] with skillful compassion" (Rinpoche 2017, 57).

CONCLUSION

Taking anger to have a unique power to acknowledge wrongdoing, to empower those disempowered by wrongdoing, and to motivate us to address it, Martha Nussbaum and Emily McRae defend the view that anger, if non-retributive, can be morally required. Through an analysis of the complex casual relations associated with wrongdoing Śāntideva debunks the metaphysics inherent to anger's intentional structure, taking as it does, an autonomous culpable object (be it singular plural, actual, abstract, or implied). As Śāntideva also makes clear, due to presupposing and reinforcing self-regard, anger risks forsaking moral objectivity for self-edification, obscuring the morally salient features of a situation by blinding us to people and truths marginalized by our local perspectives, and by inhibiting a more realistic and compassionate mode of interpersonal experience and interaction.

For these reasons, Śāntideva argues, anger should be eliminated. The primary means to do so is to move our attention from the object to the subject of anger and criticize anger's metaphysical presuppositions. This project presupposes and is reinforced by Śāntideva's cluster of cultivated attitudes combining the commitment to an analysis of the causes and conditions of suffering; the fear of other's pain, a driving moral enthusiasm, and a complex willingness to grieve. Free from grasping for a culpable party and the satisfying but illusory explanatory power it provides, ksānti and vīrya acknowledge wrongdoing without reification and subjective edification and with heightened inclusivity, equipped to comprehensively empower those disempowered by wrongdoings and motivate us to address it more effectively than anger. Unlike anger, grief enables us to accept vulnerability and interdependence rather than fantasize invulnerability to wrongdoing, allowing for a radically inclusive compassion born from an appreciation of collective interdependence and precariousness to arise.

Acknowledging wrongdoing appropriately requires that we understand it. To this end, patience is significantly more useful than anger. To address wrongdoing, we need the motivation that patience and moral enthusiasm provide. We also require the complex virtues comprising patience and moral enthusiasm for empowering those disempowered by wrongdoing. For these reasons, anger is not uniquely, or even particularly, well equipped to acknowledge wrongdoing, to empower those disempowered by wrongdoing, and to motivate us to address it. Therefore, anger is never morally required.

NOTES

1. Translation from Nussbaum (2016).
2. "On the right grounds and against the right persons, and in the right manner and at the right moment and for the right length of time" (*NE* II.5, 1105b27 and IV.5, 1125b).
3. For example, Strawson's famous work on reactive emotions, feminist theorists Frye (1983), Lorde (1984), Spelman (1989), Meyers (2004), and Tessman (2005) have all argued that anger can be morally required.
4. The rational critique, absent in Nussbaum's book, would focus on taking status as a good, and thereby removing the rationale for this justification of retributivism.
5. When we talk about anger in Śāntideva we are referring primarily to the word *krodha* meaning excessive mental turmoil on account of the obstacles in the gratification of some desire; its cognates are dark, negative, destructive, and an undesirable psychological state. Candrakīrti defines *krodha* as *sattvāsattvaviṣayaṃ cittaprakopamātram* and argues that anger arises from *pratigha*, which has the semantic range including hindrance, obstruction, resistance, opposition, struggle, wrath, enmity, combat, fighting, an enemy: *krodherṣye pratighasamutthe*. Candrakīrti defines *pratigha* "*vyāpādo*"—destruction, death, malice, "*dveṣaḥ*" aversion, dislike,

hostility, foe, enemy, betraying dislike or aversion, "*sattvaviṣaye*" existing in the area of "*āghātaḥ*" slaughter. Candrakīrti describes anger as a perpetual enemy: *vairānubandhanaṃ cittasya kopanīyavastubahulīkāra upanāhaḥ. Upanāhaḥ* is an *upakleśa* then; that out of which *pratigha* naturally flows: *tatraiṣāṃ māyāmadau rāgamalasya niṣyandaḥ* | *upanāhavihiṃse pratighasya* from the *Pañcaskandhaka* (as quoted in the *Munimatālaṁkāra*).

6. It may be argued, as it was kindly suggested to me by Gregory Bock, that Nussbaum's qualification of Transitional Anger with what she calls the "unconditional love and generosity" approach (2016, 12, 77) renders her argument compatible with the Buddhist tradition. However, insofar as Śāntideva is concerned, there is always a preferable alterative to anger, and despite the proximity, Nussbaum defends the view that anger can be morally required for reasons Śāntideva shows to be ill-conceived.

7. Although chapter IV of the BCA deals with the perfection of forbearance, *kṣānti-paramita* Śāntideva does not refer to kṣānti-paramita once. The word he uses most often is *kṣama*. Sanskritists have concluded that this is because of the traditional association of the term *kṣānti* with the verbal roots *khan* and *kṣam*. This in effect combines the term for patience *kṣam* with *khan* "to be pleased, to be willing to," with the result that one frequently finds *kṣānti* employed in contexts where connotations of willingness seem more appropriate than those of forbearance. I have followed this convention with the translation of *kṣānti*.

8. There is an immediate worry we should engage before detailing Śāntideva's antidote. A likely response to valorizing the willingness to suffer and refusal to blame is that it encourages exploitation and servility. This connects to concerns associated with familiar Buddhist views on the merits of enduring suffering, the idea that past karma for inflicting harm makes one deserving of harm in the present, and that therefore one should not be bothered by receiving harm (BCA 7.42). It is troubling to think about what this suggests for people in any number of contexts. What does this mean for a child born into an abusive family, for instance? Not only have they "earned" it, as the passage suggests, but it also seems to imply that the person should accept their lot in life and not try to change it. The objection then, to the valorization of forbearance, relates to the over-demandingness and immorality of the call to endure. This worry is not without ground. In *Śikṣāsamuccaya* Śāntideva references the *Meeting of Father and Son Sūtra* to argue the virtues of patient endurance "while being beaten . . . thrown in prison . . . set on fire . . . cut like a coin . . . impaled on stakes" (SS, 180). When able to forbear such violence, one "fully perfects all forms of renunciation [. . .] Therefore, you should always be joyful" (SS, 181). The worry is how someone experiencing intimate partner violence, being sexually assaulted by their boss, or being targeted by police for being black, for example, could accept their lot in life and allow themselves to be abused. A related objection comes into play when, in addition to the question of how the victim should respond, Śāntideva makes some suggestions about a bystander observing abuse: "Upon seeing a friend or an enemy committing a wrong deed, one should reflect, 'Such are his conditions,' and be at ease" (BCA 7.33). This seems to be saying that, even in the face of such situations described above, a person

should simply allow the actions to happen and do nothing. How can we justify a virtue that calls for allowing abuse to happen to others, and more generally, where is there room for fighting for social justice in the context of Śāntideva's argument for patient endurance? In reply, it is possible to respond and interrupt abuse from a place of compassion rather than from a place of anger. The advice is not to allow oneself to be the victim of injustice or abuse, only to attempt to disallow one's response to injustice or to abuse to be one of anger, which might make one less effective in combating it. A more general response to worries about the sociopolitical role for patience refers to Śāntideva's definition of kṣānti, which is juxtaposed with anger. In the *Śikṣāsamuccaya* Śāntideva writes that forbearance includes the acceptance of unhappiness, patience with regard to developing the Buddhist perspective, and patience in regard to "helping the injuries of others" (SS, IX, 179, p. 175). The idea that kṣānti prescribes passive self-care in the face of one's suffering and the suffering of others, then, is simply false. Given that these distinct parts are cultivated simultaneously - helping others and bearing suffering - it is impossible to reduce kṣānti to a submission that could motivate impassivity toward wrongs fit for resistance. Furthermore, the endurance of suffering due to lack of courage, care, or the result of abuse is not kṣānti. Indeed, seeing patience as accurate perspective and selfless devotion allows us to see why such cases do not count as patience. Concerning the traumatized individual who "patiently" endures abuse or is forced to deny their own rights, their perspective has been cruelly manipulated. Those who accept suffering because of ignorance are missing a sense of what is important. The bystander who allows proximate injustice to persist is, by Śāntideva's definition of patience, insufficiently compassionate.

9. Here, I follow Bendall and Rouse's translation of *kparāpakāramarṣanakṣānti*

10. Translation from Nussbaum (2016).

11. "It [anger] must always be attended by a certain pleasure—that which arises from the expectation of revenge" (*Rhetoric*, Book II, Chapter 2, 1378a 31–33) (Aristotle 2004).

12. Dr. Emily McRae, professor of philosophy at the University of New Mexico, suggested in generous and helpful correspondence that this line of argument could imply that, for Śāntideva, self-orientation is inherently ethically wrong. The position I defend here is not that self-orientation is necessarily ethically problematic, nor that Śāntideva would think so. When I suggest that reflection on Śāntideva concerning anger leads to the conclusion that is suspect because it is structurally self-oriented, that it clouds moral judgment, and that it presupposes and reinforces self-regard, it is not to claim that these elements are inherently immoral, but rather that these elements are not part of the ideal response to wrongdoing (understanding its causes and conditions, and working to change them). By contrast, grief, which can be less oriented toward personal amelioration than anger, may be better suited for understanding and addressing wrongdoing, at least enough to successfully problematize the view that anger can be morally required. That these views can be attributed to Śāntideva are laid out in my analyses of how the correct understanding of wrongdoing and the willingness to grieve are considered both superior alternatives and antidotes to anger, in both the *Bodhicaryāvatāra* and the *Śikṣāsamuccaya*.

13. By extension, we can see how agent-oriented moral anger targets opponents of its moral view, such that the anger removes the agent toward which it is directed from full moral consideration.

14. This is a form of love (*sneha*) that is not defiled by sexual attraction or by expecting something in return. (*Śikṣāsamuccaya*, 212)

15. It may be that a misunderstanding of *Karuṇā* born from its translation as compassion which has English words such as "passive," as its cognate, leads to the preference of anger. *Karuṇā*, by contrast to compassion, has as its root kṛ, "to do"—the same root from which *karma* comes, and thus while compassion might only be something we have, *Karuṇā* is something we do.

16. As well as prescribing antidotes to passivity in the face of wrongdoing, Śāntideva writes that we must reject "despondency," and "dejection" by casting away "weakness, and softness of the mind" (Śṣ, IX, 180, 176). For a recent study of the Buddhist theory of emotion see Padmasiri de Silva (2014). De Silva lays out how conative elements and affective states are built into the early Buddhist conception of emotions, including anger and grief.

17. Attempting to establish the germinal seeds of her defense of tantric anger in Śāntideva McRae cites where Śāntideva writes, "I shall never turn back from vanquishing mental afflictions. I shall be tenacious in this matter and fixed on revenge, I shall wage war, except against those mental afflictions that are related to the elimination of mental afflictions" (BCA VII. 54). There are other verses in the *Bodhicaryāvatāra* employed for tantric purposes in the Tibetan tradition along the lines of McRae's interpretations. For example, in verse 41 Śāntideva grants provisional value to hatred: "If, disregarding the principle cause, such as a stick or a weapon, I become angry with the person who impels it, he too is impelled by hatred. It is better that I hate the hatred" (BCA VII. 41). However, aside from the hatred of hatred, which is described as preferable only to other kinds of hatred, and only if one is already overcome by hatred, Śāntideva's occasional self-conscious appropriation of dangerous emotions is always housed within a specific simultaneously metaphysical and moral framework which calls for the elimination of any and all anger which takes an autonomous agent as its object. There is a complication if we look again at Bodhicaryāvatāra 4.43: "I shall be tenacious in this matter; and fixed on revenge, I shall wage war, except against those mental afflictions that are related to the elimination of mental afflictions." This seems to be an implicit reference to upanāha, or at least an echo of its definition (which brings us in the domain of dveṣa, as upanāha is its outflow, which in Candrakīrti's definition is a form of krodha; one of the closest Sanskrit words, in terms of semantic range, to the English word, anger). In this sense then, Śāntideva endorses anger. But what Śāntideva endorses here is not anger toward other sentient beings, but toward the *kleṣa*-s and specifically one's own *kleṣa*-s; and, possibly, toward oneself. The crucial difference, then, is that Śāntideva never endorses anger toward an autonomous moral agent. This point is subtle, and worth laboring if we are to speak on Śāntideva's behalf: Śāntideva does endorse anger against agents in the strict Sanskrit sense of agency. The worldview in which Śāntideva writes and operates is one where questions such as agency are analyzed primarily through the role of phenomena capable of performing an action as developed in language. Given that for *Mādhyamikas*,

collective reality is, in an important and complex sense, intersubjectively and linguistically realized, Sanskrit itself becomes the location for ontological analysis. This complicates the thesis defended here. Where I use agent in English, I am speaking primarily of persons but secondarily institutions, states of affairs, and the world in a sense which allows for a realism which is not found in the *Madhyamaka* Buddhism of Śāntideva. Furthermore, when I say anger takes a culpable autonomous agent, it is the autonomy that I take Śāntideva to categorically oppose, rather than agency per se. For example, Śāntideva talks about personal and impersonal moral agents as existing on the conventional level, which means they are casually efficacious aspects of the world as it appears to non-enlightened beings. For example, for Madhyamaka Buddhists persons exists on the conventional level, and they are agents whose moral responsibility is shaped by understanding and practice; that is, on the conventional level there are personal moral agents. Secondly, for *Madhyāmikas*, since they are sources of morally effective actions, the afflictions, or *kleṣa*-s, such as ignorance, hatred, and greed, are taken to be impersonal moral agents. This complicates things because Śāntideva does grant instrumental value to anger aimed toward oneself as a personal moral agent, and toward the *kleṣa*-s. That this complicates, rather than problematizes, my thesis can be seen in that Śāntideva does not take any of these moral agents as autonomous, while autonomy is a crucial part of non-retributive anger in McRae and Nussbaum. Furthermore, every application of anger is only instrumentally valuable, and only permissible when thoroughly non-egocentric, never towards moral persons *other than oneself*, and subservient to bodhicitta: the desire to achieve the highest degrees of well-being for all sentient beings. In this way, it remains correct that Śāntideva never endorses anger toward agents taken to be autonomous and culpable of wrongdoing. All of this is compatible with taking Śāntideva to be opposed to the view that anger can be morally required.

18. Dr. McRae reminded me that her position is not that grief is morally inferior to anger, but rather that it has a different scope such that grief won't substitute for anger in every case. McRae mentioned the recent murder of George Floyd, and suggested that it is anger rather than grief, which can point at not just the tragedy of his death, but to the injustice of systemic white supremacy implicit in the police brutality disproportionately targeting African Americans. First, I wrote this chapter before Floyd's murder, and would not have written this particular chapter at this particular time. Nevertheless, while preferable to indifference or fear, the mere possibility that anger may compel the lust for retribution, simplify causal analysis, overlook moral objectivity for self-edification, obscure morally salient features of truths and people marginalized by overly local perspectives, and inhibit a more realistic and compassionate mode of interpersonal experience and interaction is enough to question its requisite status. A philosophical paper is not written in the heat of the moment, but in the safe privileged space where critical thought can accompany and ideally clarify moral conviction. It is from, and to, this point of privilege where I make the very specific claim that there is not a good enough reason to conclude that anger is morally required. For me, the job of a philosopher is to imagine a better world and imagine how to get there, in such a way that the means can also be considered an end. It is

my conviction that claiming anger is morally required is not part of that aspiration. Secondly, and directed more squarely at McRae's view that anger is a more powerful tool to signal the recognition of injustice than grief, even if it is, signaling injustice is only one step toward removing it, and for that larger project, while anger can be morally valuable, it is, nevertheless, not required.

19. For example, where absolute exclusivity is encoded within naturalized categories of heterosexuality, sexual identity is achieved at the loss of instincts, desires, and impulses that fall outside the purview of that norm. In such cases, grieving such losses is prohibited. This failure to grieve manifests in anger toward the instability of sexual norms, toward alternative sexual norms, and toward those who acknowledge the instability of, or embody, alternative sexual norms. This anger involves a cognitive perception that a moral damage has occurred, that culpability is involved, and a desire satiating wish for payback, it heightens the perceptive power cornering wrongdoing, and empowers the angry, but we should not endorse it if we are invested in justice and collective well-being.

20. Contemporary philosopher Judith Butler traces identitarian anger and hatred's current renaissance to a refusal to grieve for challenges to invulnerability, superiority, autonomy, power, and independence. The solution is to cultivate a willingness to grieve precisely where anger emerges, and instead of it. For Butler, grief challenges the sense-of-self buttressed by anger and makes it possible to recognize and forgo the illusions of superiority, omnipotence, and invulnerability. According to Butler, this skillful reappropriation of vulnerability can ground "a new direction for ethics." Butler, Judith. *Precarious Life: The Powers of Mourning and Violence.* Verso, 2006.

21. Dr. McRae's view is that anger's ability to signal distress is itself an insight because it motivates us to look for its causes. This is true, but in this case the moral insight is a response *to* anger and need not itself *be* anger. Consider microaggressions, the anger at which can enable the micro-aggressor, and others, to see the ways in which racism and oppression are normalized. Because this kind of anger can contribute to the understanding of systemic oppression and racism, then, it is morally valuable in such cases. Since my argument is not that anger is without moral value, rather that it is not morally required, the response is "Can such moral insights be communicated successfully without anger?" My discussion with Dr. McRae was a great example of where moral insights were communicated without anger, and although they occurred in a safe and privileged context, they sufficed to say that the communication of moral insights does not require anger.

22. Dr. McRae also pointed out that for members of oppressed groups anger has often denied them because of taboo. One is not allowed by white supremacy or patriarchy or capitalism to be angry, especially about your own oppression. In these cases, experiencing anger, using anger, directing one's anger can be more empowering than sanctioned alternatives. In response, I would say again because anger is not the optimal option for empowerment (because of its compulsive power and tendency to cause harm to self and others it is not free in the morally optimal sense) even if it is the most morally valuable option available, it is still wrong to argue that anger is morally required. When asking what to do with anger that is already there, as it usually is, especially for people oppressed by white supremacy

and patriarchy, recognizing, using, and redeploying existing anger can be, of course, morally valuable. Indeed it was appealed to by King and the Mahāyāna Buddhist tradition. However, the skillful appropriation of anger is not only compatible with the view that anger is never morally required, or indeed that its presence is a sign of work needed. This is the view expressed by Martin Luther King Jnr. in "The Letter from a Birmingham Jail" and Śāntideva's *Bodhicaryāvatāra* and *Śikṣāsamuccaya.* Emphasizing this instrumental value is part of the vital work being done by Nussbaum and McRae. Indeed, McRae's more recent article "Anger and the Oppressed" is an excellent articulation both of the instrumental moral value of anger, tantric Buddhism's methods for its skillful appropriation, and why condemning the anger of the oppressed forces the violently marginalized into a double bind, exposed, as they are, to multiple and daily causes for moral anger, and condemning the occasions where moral restraint is breached, rather than focusing on how to contest their oppression.

23. This is why Martin Luther King called on his fellow activists to "undertake a process of self-purification" wherein moral agents asked themselves, "Are you able to accept blows without retaliating?" "Are you able to endure the ordeal of jail?" as means to ensure that they avoided "the superficial kind of social analysis that deals merely with effects and does not grapple with underlying causes." King, Martin Luther. 1981. *Loving Your Enemies; Letter from a Birmingham Jail; Declaration of Independence from the War in Vietnam.* A.J. Muste Memorial Institute.

24. It should be made clear that in valorizing grief, I am not suggesting that on the Buddhist analysis grief is ever morally required, or indeed of more than an expedient value in the Buddhist view. Indeed, as a form of suffering Early Buddhism regards grief as an obstacle to be overcome; consider the following examples: "Having killed anger you sleep in ease. Having killed anger you do not grieve. The noble ones praise the slaying of anger—with its honeyed crest & poison root—for having killed it you do not grieve" (*Saṃyutta Nikāya* 1.71), "Marvelous it is, most wonderful it is, bhikkhus, concerning the Perfect Ones [Buddhas], that when such a pair of disciples [the Buddha's two chief disciples] has passed away there is no grief, no lamentation on the part of the Perfect One. For of that which is born, come to being, put together, and so is subject to dissolution, how should it be said that it should not depart? That indeed, is not possible" (Saṃyutta Nikāya 47.14). On the Theravāda Pali Buddhist view, because grief presupposes a metaphysical reification of persons and their inherent value, it manifests an attachment that the Buddhist path is designed to help us remove. Nevertheless, the Bodhisattva and Śāntideva's *Mahāyāna* tradition that focuses on it regard attachment to the suffering of others as the most skillful illusion and the last illusion to be rescinded for the sake of *Nirvāṇa.* And this is why non-egocentric grief is considered to be a more sophisticated emotion than anger in the majority of the Indo-Tibetan *Mahāyāna* Buddhist traditions.

25. In the words of His Holiness the Dalai Lama, Dza Patrul Rinpoche "dedicated himself to practicing what is taught in Śāntideva's *Bodhicaryāvatāra.*" *The Essential Jewel of Holy Practice, Patrul Rinpoche*, translated by Jay Garfield and Emily McRae, foreword by His Holiness the Dalai Lama, ix.

REFERENCE LIST

Aristotle. 2004. *Rhetoric*. Translated by Rhys W. Roberts. New York: Dover Publications.

———. 2010. *Rhetoric*. Translated by Edward Meredith Cope and John Edwin Sandys. Cambridge: Cambridge University Press.

———. 2019. *Nicomachean Ethics*, 3rd ed. Translated with Introduction, Notes, and Glossary by Terrance Irwin. Indianapolis, IN: Hackett Publishing Co.

Butler, Judith. 2006. *Precarious Life: the Powers of Mourning and Violence*. London: Verso.

Candrakīrti. 2019. "Pañcaskandhaka." In *Munimatālaṁkāra*, translated by Miroj Shakya. Digital Sanskrit Buddhist Canon—Books, Nagarjuna Institute of Buddhist Studies/University of the West. www.dsbcproject.org/canon-text/content/846/2974.

Candrakīrti, and Mi-pham-rgya-mtsho. 2004. *Introduction to the Middle Way: Candrakīrti's Madhyamakāvatara*. Translated by Padmakara Translation Group. Shambhala: Boston & London.

De Silva, Padmasiri. 2014. *Introduction to Buddhist Psychology and Counselling: Pathways of Mindfulness-Based Therapies*. Basingstoke: Palgrave Macmillan.

Donner, Wendy. 2002. "Feminist Ethics and Anger: A Feminist Buddhist Reflection." In *APA Newsletter on Feminism and Philosophy*, edited by Joan Callahan. Newark, DE: The American Philosophical Association, University of Delaware 1, no. 2: 67–70.

Frye, Marilyn. 1983. *The Politics of Reality: Essays in Feminist Theory*. Berkeley: Crossing Press.

Geshe, Luncrup Sopa. 2001. *Peacock in the Poison Grove, Two Buddhist Texts on Training the Mind*. Translated by Michael Sweet and Leonard Zwilling. Somerville, MA: Wisdom Publications.

King, Martin Luther. 1981. *Loving Your Enemies; Letter from a Birmingham Jail; Declaration of Independence from the War in Vietnam*. A.J. Muste Memorial Institute.

Lorde, Audre. 1984. *Sister Outsider: Essays and Speeches*. Berkeley: Crossing Press.

McRae, Emily. 2015. "Metabolizing Anger: A Tantric Buddhist Solution to the Problem of Moral Anger." *Philosophy East and West* 65, no. 2: 466–484.

———. 2019. "Anger and the Oppressed: Indo-Tibetan Buddhist Perspectives." In *The Moral Psychology of Anger*, edited by Myisha Cherry and Owen Flanagan, 105–121. Lanham, MD: Rowman & Littlefield.

Meyers, Diana Tietjens. 2004. "Emotion and Heterodox Moral Perception: An Essay in Moral Social Psychology." In *Being Yourself: Essays on Identity Action, and Social Life*, edited by Diana Tietjens Meyers, 137–157. Lanham, MD: Rowman & Littlefield.

Nussbaum, Martha. 1994. *Therapy of Desire: Theory and Practice in Hellenistic Ethics*. Princeton, NJ: Princeton University Press.

———. 2016. *Anger and Forgiveness: Resentment, Generosity, Justice*. New York: Oxford University Press.

Nyoponika, Thera. 2013. "Cunda Sutta: At Ukkacela." *Saṃyutta Nikāya* 47, no. 14. Accessed May 31, 2020. http://www.accesstoinsight.org/tipitaka/sn/sn47/sn47.014.nypo.html.

Rinpoche, Patrul. 2017. *The Essential Jewel of Holy Practice*. Translated by Jay Garfield and Emily McRae. Somerville, MA: Wisdom Publications.

Śāntideva. 1990. *Śikṣāsamuccaya*. Translated by Cecil Bendall and W. H. D. Rouse. Delhi: Motilal Banarsidas Publications.

———. 1996. *Bodhicaryāvatāra*. Translated by Kate Crosby and Andrew Skilton. Oxford: Oxford University Press.

Spelman, Elizabeth. 1989. "Anger and Insubordination." In *Women, Knowledge and Reality*, edited by Marilyn Pearsall and Ann Garry, 263–273. Boston: Unwin Hyman.

Strawson, Peter Frederick. 2008. *Freedom and Resentment*. Abingdon: Routledge.

Tessman, Lisa. 2005. *Burdened Virtues: Virtue Ethics for Liberatory Struggles*. New York: Oxford University Press.

Thanissaro, Bhikku. 2010. "Ghatva Sutta: Having Killed." *Saṃyutta Nikāya* 1, no. 71. Accessed May 31, 2020. http://www.accesstoinsight.org/tipitaka/sn/sn01/sn01.071.than.html.

Part III

PRACTICAL RESPONSES

Chapter 8

Stoking Anger and Weaponizing Untruth

How Mind Viruses Undermine Social Justice

Paula Smithka

Everyone gets angry. It is an emotion that is deeply engrained in our biology, no doubt associated with the instincts associated with "fight" or "flight." Philosophers have long debated whether emotions should play a role in ethical decision-making. For cognitivists, emotions simply cloud moral judgment. So moral theories should rely on reason in order to ensure principles of impartiality and fairness. Examples are Immanuel Kant and W. D. Ross's deontological approaches or Jeremy Bentham and John Stuart Mill's Utilitarianism. Yet, as David Hume insisted, "reason is and ought only to be the slave of the passions" ([1739–40]/1978). However, making ethical decisions solely on the basis of emotions would be fraught with partiality that would undermine the principle of justice as fairness. In contrast to the more traditional cognitivist approaches, in an ethics of care approach, Virginia Held (among others) points out that ethical decisions are often influenced by emotions and so emotions should be valued rather than completely discounted; but that is not to say that reason is to be displaced by emotion (2006, 10–13). As Held and Martha Nussbaum (among others) have suggested, anger can be an emotion that is appropriate in response to wrongs done and injustices committed and, additionally, can serve to motivate one to act in ways to better society by attempting to correct social injustices (Held 2006; Nussbaum 2015). And in this context, one can ask whether anger is a moral emotion. I think it can be, so long as it meets certain criteria. This is my starting point in this chapter.

I then consider the notion of mind viruses, a biological model for understanding the importance of cultural diversity for a well-balanced and tolerant society, developed by Jeffrey Gold and Niall Shanks who build on the work of Richard Dawkins regarding memes (2002, 187–199). Mind viruses are the results of "dogmatism-inducing" meme-complexes, which foster "homogenized thinking" that undermines the host's ability to consider alternative views and counter-evidence. Dawkins and Gold and Shanks argue that memes and mind viruses are not mere metaphors, but are genuine biological phenomena. Neuroscientists have demonstrated that neurological pathways are changed by what we hear and read. So, Gold and Shanks argue that just as genetic heterogeneity is useful for organisms' immunological health against infection, so also cultural and ideological heterogeneity is important for the health of a society, to ward off racism, sexism, and so on. I then show that the transmission of mind viruses occurs, in part, by the weaponization of untruth, which stokes anger in the host. I argue that though anger may be a moral emotion, the anger associated with mind viruses is typically not morally justifiable, even in cases where one might consider it apt, because the focus of the anger is frequently based on untruths and the target of the anger is often inappropriate, since the host was not wronged by the target and, crucially, because the behavioral manifestations of the mind virus too often result in linguistic or physical violence.[1] Finally, I suggest a partial "vaccine" to boost immunity against mind viruses.[2]

ANGER: A MORAL EMOTION?

Because anger can be an emotion that is appropriate in response to wrongs done to oneself or others as well as to social injustices, and because it can serve to motivate one to act in ways to better society, that is, acting in ways to correct those social injustices, anger might be considered to be a moral emotion if that anger meets certain criteria. Aaron Ben-Ze'ev suggests two criteria for being a moral emotion: "(a) whether the core evaluative concern of the emotion is moral, and (b) whether the emotion tends to lead to beneficial moral consequences" (2002, 148). So, if the anger response is the result of an injustice done to oneself, someone else, or even a group of people, then it meets the first criterion. This would seem to be in contrast to the anger I might feel when I drop my full wine glass and it shatters on the floor, or when someone shakes a vending machine because it failed to dispense the candy bar one paid for. These latter cases are instances of being frustrated rather than as a result of some injustice done (Heyd 2018, 191; Nussbaum 2015, 43).[3] In the first case, I am frustrated with myself for having been careless, and in the second case, the vending machine patron is frustrated because the machine malfunctioned. These two cases would not meet the first criterion and would be considered to be, at least potentially, more irrational than anger resulting from an instance of racial discrimination, for example, and so they would not be cases of a moral emotion.

The consequences of anger seem to be the main focus for many philosophers concerning whether the emotion is moral, or perhaps we might say, morally justified or morally flawed. Aristotle's definition of emotions focuses on "affecting judgements"; he states:

> The emotions are all those feelings that so change men as to affect their judgements, and that are also attended by pain or pleasure. Such are anger, pity, fear and the like, with their opposites. (*Rhetoric*, book 2.1, 1378a21-23)

Emotions alter the way we make judgments, which is why emotions are avoided in traditional ethical theories. When we are angry, we tend to say or do things that we would not otherwise say or do if we were calm, some of which may be extreme or even violent. I will return to this notion in due course. Aristotle further characterizes anger in the following way, which entails the notion of revenge:

> Anger may be defined as a desire accompanied by pain, for a conspicuous revenge for a conspicuous slight at the hands of men who have no call to slight oneself or one's friends. If this is a proper definition of anger, it must always be felt towards some particular individual, e.g. Cleon, and not man in general. It must be felt because the other has done or intended to do something to him or one of his friends. It must always be attended by a certain pleasure—that which arises from the expectation of revenge. (*Rhetoric*, book 2.2, 1378a31-34,1378b1-4, 2195)

So, for Aristotle, when someone has wronged us or our friends, retaliation or "getting even" in some sense for that wrong is part of being angry. This is clearly a retributive notion of justice. The wrongdoer must be held accountable for the offense, and the "victim" deserves some sort of compensation for the injury sustained. The payback need not entail violence, though it might and sometimes does (e.g., revenge killings), but in a (an ideal) legal context, we say that the punishment must fit the crime; that is, it must be proportional to the wrong committed. We sometimes say things like "the victim finally got justice; the assailant got the maximum prison sentence." However, Martha Nussbaum thinks that the notion of retribution being associated with anger is misguided and irrational because "in reality, harsh punishment of the offender rarely repairs the damage" (2015, 47). She is right about this. While there is some comfort ("pleasure") in knowing that a murderer is serving a prison sentence for his crime and is off the streets so he cannot hurt anyone else, it does not restore the life of the victim. Furthermore, because of the consequences of anger, some philosophers have argued that being angry, particularly in political contexts, is "counterproductive"; that is, the consequences of becoming angry and acting on that anger could produce worse outcomes than what are already present in society. Amia Srinivasan discusses several instances of this "counterproductive critique" in her article "The Aptness of Anger" (2018, 123–144). One of the cases she discusses is *New York Times* columnist Nicholas Kristof's piece covering Israel's 2014 Operation Protective Edge where Israel killed approximately 1,500 civilians in the Gaza strip. She says the following:

> Kristof exhorted Palestinians to abandon the anger that "has accomplished nothing but increasing the misery of the Palestinian people"; if only Palestinians would adopt the model of Gandhi, Kristof argued, the result would "reverberate around the world and Palestinians would achieve statehood and freedom." (ibid., 125)

Srinivasan clarifies that she is not claiming that Kristof endorses such a "counterproductivity critique of anger," but the kind of claim that Kristof makes illustrates the counterproductivity critique. This is why the philosopher Glen Pettigrove defends a "meek" approach toward wrongs, rather than the "hostile affects and lashing out" associated with moral anger. He provides the Dalai Lama as an example of one without moral anger but who cares about the Tibetan people and recognizes that they have been unjustly treated by the Chinese government. Pettigrove's point is that one need not embrace moral anger in order to seek social change (2012). Yet, Srinivasan defends that anger is often apt because it is a response to a moral injustice and it is a recognition and "appreciation" for that injustice. Notice the aptness of anger is a focus on that first criterion given by Ben-Ze'ev. Srinivasan contends that to suggest to someone that they ought not to get angry because that will make things worse is to diminish the severity of the immoral action or unjust social situation and to put the burden on the victim to fix the problem rather than on the perpetrator(s) (2018, 132, 133). I think that she is correct in this regard. Being angry at social injustices is the beginning of recognizing that there is a problem that ought to be remedied and serves as a moral motivator for supporting efforts to correct the injustice. This is why Nussbaum makes an exception to her more general view that anger is normatively problematic for cases of discrimination. When the efforts are "forward-looking" toward improving the welfare of those enduring the social injustices and not focused on retribution, she calls this type of moral anger, "transitional anger" (Nussbaum 2015, 52–54). Her focus here tends to be more traditional, like that of Aristotle, in the sense that she focuses on the consequences of the anger, but unlike Aristotle, the consequences are not "pleasure in revenge," but rather effecting social justice. She characterizes it as a transition from "anger to compassionate hope" (ibid., 52). Martin Luther King, Jr.'s nonviolent, direct action approach toward addressing and correcting racial discrimination and inequality is a paradigm of "transitional anger" as well as the aptness of anger. So, while anger can be moral emotion that can lead to morally good or morally bad consequences, too often the focus of anger, even when morally apt, is on retaliation that is carried out in linguistically and physically violent ways. The anger emotion is stoked by the presence of mind viruses whose virulence is fueled by fear and the weaponization of untruth. The hosts infected by the mind viruses then sometimes manifest linguistically and physically violent behavior, which threatens social stability and justice. What, then, is a mind virus?

MIND VIRUSES

Mind viruses are parasitic conformity meme-complexes or "memeplexes" that shut down the host's ability to rationally consider other points of view, including additional evidence or counter-evidence to one's position.[4] They tend to foster dogmatism and intolerance. Richard Dawkins introduced the notion of memes as cultural information-bearing units in *The Selfish Gene*. Just as genes are bearers of genetic information that is transmitted via replication within populations of organisms, memes are, analogously, information-bearing units that are transmitted from one brain to another. Examples of memes are "tunes, ideas, catch phrases, clothes fashions, ways of making pots or building arches" (Dawkins 1989, 92). Memes move from brain to brain through various means of communication: in discourse, letters, books, radio, television, emails, social media, and so on. Recent studies in neuroscience have shown that the transmission of memes actually causes changes in the recipients' neurological patterns.[5] Neuroscientist Juan Delius characterizes the transfer of cultural traits (memes) as patterns of "activated/inactivated synapses." He says, "A given cultural trait borne by an individual is encoded informationally as a particular configuration of modified synapses in his or her brain" (1991, 82). And, Dawkins quotes his neuropsychologist colleague, N. K. Humphrey, that memes are not mere metaphors:

> Memes should be regarded as living structures, not just metaphorically but technically. When you plant a fertile meme in my mind you literally parasitize my brain, turning it into a vehicle for the meme's propagation in just the way that a virus may parasitize the genetic mechanism of a host cell. And this isn't just a way of talking. (1989, 192)

So, memes are cultural information-bearing units that, when transmitted from brain to brain, actually cause physiological changes in those brains.

Jeffrey Gold and Niall Shanks expand Dawkins's conception of memes and their transmission into the notion of "mind viruses" or "informational parasites"[6] in their "Mind Viruses and the Importance of Cultural Diversity" (Bailey and Smithka 2002, 187–199). They argue that "conformity memes" can generate "dogmatism-inducing viruses" that undermine cultural heterogeneity in favor of an ideological homogeneity. So, just as organisms are weakened immunologically by genetic homogeneity, they contend culture can be weakened in the form of censorship of ideas (Gold and Shanks 2002, 193).[7]

Conformity memes undermine cultural diversity and foster hostility to alternative or competing ways of viewing the world, and, like genes, typically work within "complexes." Examples of gene-complexes include those groups of genes working together to produce teeth, claws, digestive systems, and so on in organisms (ibid., 190). Some examples of meme-complexes or memeplexes are religious and political ideologies (ibid.). Cultural conformity memeplexes include the very potent example of the anti-Semitism present in 1920s and 1930s Germany, along with racist, sexist, and homophobic memeplexes (ibid.). Such memeplexes "work together in ways that are inhospitable to cultural heterogeneity" because they foster intolerance for difference (ibid.). Regarding the success of meme transmission, Dawkins states:

> The catchier [a tune is] the more likely it is to be copied. If it is a scientific idea, its chances of spreading through the world's scientific brains will be influenced by its compatibility with the already established corpus of ideas. If it is a political or religious idea, it may assist its own survival if one of its phenotypic effects is to make its bodies violently intolerant of new and unfamiliar ideas. (1992, 109)

Successful meme transmission is also fostered by repetition of catchy phrases replayed in the media. One might here think of Donald Trump's "Build the wall!" campaign slogan or his frequent ad hominem mantra regarding Hillary Clinton: "Crooked Hillary." The more brains that hear the phrases, the more neural pathways are altered, and the more times the phrases are heard, the more that neural pathway is habituated, so the meme spreads successfully. I want to stress that not all memes are deleterious. We might argue that memes that promote individual liberty, free speech, and tolerance are just the sort of memes that civil society should espouse and propagate because they provide the foundation for a peaceful, just society. But it is the intolerance for "new and unfamiliar ideas" that reinforces conformity and these conformity memeplexes have the potential to become mind viruses. And, just as viruses cause symptoms of illness and alter the host's behaviors, so also mind viruses cause symptoms and alter the behavior of their hosts.

Some symptoms of mind viruses include the shutting down of the host's ability to rationally consider other points of view. The host "clings to particular memes with unshakeable conviction," including additional evidence or counter-evidence to one's position, "[dogmatically refusing] to hear and consider evidence for opposition positions" (Gold and Shanks 2002, 192). Gold and Shanks contend that mind viruses are detrimental to their hosts because they "arrest aspects of cognitive development" leading to a kind of "cognitive paralysis" where the host assumes "infallibility" and fails to "utilize their own powers of judgment and discrimination" (ibid., 192–193). So, dogmatism-inducing mind viruses generate homogenized thinking which fosters intolerance in their hosts. And, like a virus that causes illness in a host, it alters the behavior of that infected host, for example, sneezing, taking cold medications, stashing Kleenex, staying home, or seeking medical attention, some behavioral manifestations of a mind virus include only interacting with like-minded people, immediate dismissal of differing viewpoints, only watching one news channel, or, more significantly, the anger induced by the mind virus as a result of intolerance for "the other" might lead to linguistic and physical violence toward that "other" (Gay 1999, 13–35). On a larger scale, homogenized thinking in society produces factions, or tribes, where allegiance to those tribes is more important than facts or truth and the intolerance for others is manifested in angry and sometimes violent encounters. The spread of deleterious memes and mind viruses is fueled by the weaponizing of untruth in lies and fake news, creating fear and stoking anger, parasitizing the brains of potential hosts.

SPREADING MIND VIRUSES: WEAPONIZING UNTRUTH, CREATING FEAR, AND STOKING ANGER

Media outlets and particularly social media platforms are primary vectors of transmission of mind viruses. One problem for consumers is that it is becoming increasingly difficult to be able to discern which sources are reliable, particularly because technology makes it possible to spread "news" at an exponential rate.[8] So, "fake news" travels fast. Adding to this are our own natural cognitive biases. We tend not to like information that conflicts with our beliefs, attitudes, and behaviors. This "cognitive dissonance" is unsettling, so we look for news and other media sources that are consistent with our own views; this is "confirmation bias." Even when the media outlets are respectable and reliable, they often contribute to the spread of deleterious memes and mind viruses by repeating those memes or memeplexes over and over. And, it is the endless repetition of phrases, claims, and lies that not only creates new neural pathways in first-time hearers but also reinforces the pathways in previous hearers, creating habitual use of those pathways. This endless repetition creates, what neuroscientist David Eagleman calls "the-illusion-of-truth effect." Essentially, people tend to believe things that they have heard before, whether the claims are true or not. Eagleman states:

> You are more likely to believe that a statement is true if you have heard it before—whether or not it is actually true . . . [Experimenters] found a clear result: if subjects had heard a sentence in previous weeks, they were more likely to now rate it as true, even if they swore they had never heard it before. This is the case even when the experimenter *tells* the subjects that the sentences they are about to hear are false: despite this, mere exposure to an idea is enough to boost its believability upon later contact. The illusion-of-truth effect highlights the potential danger for people who are repeatedly exposed to the same religious edicts or political slogans. (2011, 65)

Notice that even when the subjects were told that something was false, they were more likely to rate it as true. Thus, the endless repetition of memes, lies, and so on, along with the promulgation of fake news, is an effective means of spreading mind viruses that can create fear, stoke anger, and, in some virus hosts, lead to linguistic and physical violence.

TRANSMISSION VIA LIES AND AD HOMINEMS

Lee McIntyre contends that we are living in an era of post-truth. "Post" in the sense that "truth has been eclipsed—that it is irrelevant" (2018, 5). In an era of post-truth, truth and objective facts are less important in influencing public opinion than personal beliefs and emotions (Oxford Dictionary 2018). Donald Trump has clearly embraced post-truth tactics to influence public opinion and for his own political gain both as a presidential candidate and now as president. Trump understands what Aristotle called *pathos* in the *Rhetoric*, namely, that the art of persuasion requires being able to manipulate listeners' decision-making processes presenting your own view in a positive light while denigrating the view of another through the arousal of their emotions (Konstan 2015, 402, 405). If truth is less important than emotion and if lies will arouse emotions needed for persuasion, then lies and misleading claims become useful tools for persuasion. The *Washington Post*'s Fact Checker Blog (updated April 3, 2020) reports that President Trump has made 18,000 false or misleading claims in 1,170 days in office (Fact Checker Blog). *New York Times* columnist Charles M. Blow characterizes Trump's strategy this way: "Tell a lie bigger than people think a lie can be, thereby forcing their brains to seek truth in it, or vest some faith in it, even after no proof can be found" (2017). Blow's point is that Hitler understood this tactic well, and, though Trump isn't Hitler, he, like Hitler, uses lies and misleading statements in ways that garner him social and political gain. Blow calls this the "weaponizing untruth" (ibid.). Combining the "weaponizing of untruth" with the "illusion-of-truth effect" and "endless repetition" of memes is a recipe for effectively parasitizing brains and achieving social and political influence. Then-candidate, now-President Trump's words matter, and he knows it. Let us consider a few of the ways Trump has facilitated mind virus transmission that has stoked anger, sometimes leading to violence.

As a candidate, Trump's repeated use of ad hominems served him well, particularly as they were used against Hillary Clinton.[9] The endless repetition of the phrase "Crooked Hillary" and the "Lock her up!" chant criminalized her, and it was an effective tool. There were the Benghazi Hearings and then her irresponsible use of a private email server that was presented as a "national emergency" but for which no felony or misdemeanor charge was brought forth (Zeitz 2017). But Trump had help from Chris Christie who conducted a mock trial, the extreme polarization of the political parties, but also from journalists. Of this situation, *Politico* contributing editor Joshua Zeitz writes in his article "Why Do They Hate Her?":

> It created a toxic environment and false narrative that may have led especially gullible voters to believe that Clinton, if elected, would face imminent impeachment, removal and imprisonment. In its pursuit of this scorched-earth project, the GOP was aided by mainstream journalists who covered the email story far out of proportion to its legal consequence; bad actors who exploited today's fractured media environment; and the Russian government. And then, of course, there was James Comey. (ibid.)

The false narrative and Trump's deleterious memes became mind viruses infecting many future voters, fostering anger against, and hatred for, the "criminal" Hillary who should be "locked up" for her "crimes"—taking "pleasure in the expected revenge," as presented in Aristotle. Now, *had* Hillary Clinton *actually* been involved in criminal behavior, indeed that would constitute a real moral concern grounding the anger and that anger would have been apt. However, the anger felt against Clinton and that was manifested in Trump's rallies chanting "Lock her up!" was not morally justified because the focus of the anger is erroneous—as a matter of objective fact, there was no moral wrong inflicted by Hillary Clinton—and as the target of the anger, she did not inflict the moral wrong she was imputed to have done.

Another endlessly repeated Trump meme on the campaign trail was "Make America great again!". This gave populist candidate Trump purchase with those blue-collar workers who had not seen their lives improved with increased globalization, despite the recession having ended and unemployment was declining. Instead, blue-collar workers were losing, and are continuing to lose, their jobs because of shifts in manufacturing processes. And, many are dealing with stagnant salaries; they are worse off than their parents' generation (Luce 2017, 36). Furthermore, income mobility is declining; people are more likely to remain stuck in their economic class. Edward Luce, in his book, *The Retreat from Western Liberalism*, claims that America, which had traditionally had the "highest class mobility of any Western country, now has the lowest" (ibid., 43). There was, and continues to be, anger and frustration by the "'precariat'—those whose lives are dominated by economic insecurity" (ibid., 12). They felt that the Obama administration did not deliver on the promise of a better nation for them. Given these dire economic conditions and the bleak prospects for bettering their economic class, one might grant that the anger of the precariat is apt since it can be seen as a form of economic social injustice. Despite the irony of Trump's own wealth, he made blue-collar workers feel as though he understood their economic plight and he promised he would bring "hundreds of thousands of jobs." He presented himself as "one of them," saying for example, "I love the poorly educated" (ibid., 103). This is in contrast to Hillary Clinton's concession speech, where she acknowledged those who contributed to her coalition, including "people of all races and religions," "immigrants," "LGBT people," and "people with disabilities," but she made no mention of blue-collar workers or "the guy in the pickup truck" (ibid., 96). Clinton was seen as part of the cultural elitism of the Obama administration.[10] As part of the memeplex associated with "Make America great again!" Trump blamed China and unfair trade practices for the loss of American manufacturing jobs. In his 2016 opinion piece for CNN, Tom Rogan characterized Trump's strategy this way:

> Using the decline in US manufacturing jobs as a metaphor for all economic doubts, Trump blames China and free trade and ignores technological changes. Though disingenuous, this populism—delivered with anger and charisma—is Trump's Excalibur. And he wields it by weaponizing these doubts against his opponent. Trump claims he'll bring back hundreds of thousands of jobs. Then, in the next sentence, he attacks Clinton as a globalist beholden to global liberalism, rather than American workers. (2016)

So, Trump became the candidate of the alienated and disenchanted, stoking anger to create an increased divide between himself and the elitist, globalist, "status quo" candidate, Hillary Clinton. Furthermore, candidate Trump openly accepted and endorsed retaliatory violence against protestors at his rallies. At a rally in Cedar Rapids, Iowa, he encouraged supporters to beat up any would-be tomato-throwing protestor, and even offered to pay their legal fees, saying: "If you see somebody getting ready to throw a tomato, knock the crap out of them, would you? Seriously. Just knock the hell out of them. I promise you I will pay the legal fees. I promise" (Finnegan and Bierman 2016). So, while the focus of the anger of those whose lives are "dominated by economic insecurity" is apt—it is a form of social injustice and so should be of moral concern—Trump's rhetorical tactics of shifting the target of that anger to China, to Clinton, and to protesters at his rallies, and away from the real moral concern of economic insecurity, to unfair trade practices, global liberalism, elitism, and people who don't like him, while endorsing violence make *that* anger morally unjustified. Instead, it spreads mind viruses that have led to violent behavior in their hosts, such as John McGraw of Linden, NC, the seventy-eight-year-old white man who, at the Fayetteville, NC, Trump rally in 2016, hit a black protester (whom police were ejecting from the rally) in the face and who, according to Michael Finnegan and Noah Bierman, "told 'Inside Edition' on his way out of the rally: 'Next time we see him, we might have to kill him'" (ibid.). Mr. McGraw's anger was not based on a moral concern and so was not apt. Neither is his violent behavior morally justifiable but neither was candidate Trump's stoking of that anger and endorsing violence. As then-candidate Bernie Sanders rightly pointed out, "A candidate for president of the United States should condemn violence, not encourage violence" (ibid.). I turn now to some other cases of violent behavior resulting from anger stoked by mind viruses spread via fake news and social media.

TRANSMISSION VIA FAKE NEWS AND SOCIAL MEDIA

Mind viruses are effectively transmitted via fake news and social media outlets and can affect persons on both sides of the political spectrum, parasitizing the brains of their hosts stoking anger and fostering discrimination, sometimes leading to physical violence. Two cases that effectively illustrate that persons on both sides of the political spectrum can be infected with mind viruses are "Pizzagate" (the attack directed against Democrats) and the James Hodgkinson shooting incident (the attack directed against Republicans). Recently, in the wake of the coronavirus pandemic, mind viruses fostering racism against Asians have been spreading, which have led to open acts of discrimination and racist assaults on Asians. I address each of these in turn.

In the first case, what has been called "Pizzagate," in response to Internet rumors about Democrats harboring child sex slaves at the restaurant, which was allegedly the home-base of this child-abuse ring led by Hillary Clinton and her campaign manager John D. Podesta, Edgar Welch fired a weapon in the Comet Ping Pong pizza restaurant in Washington, DC, on December 4, 2016. Cecilia Kang reported in her *New York Times* article that the conjecture that there was a Democratic child-trafficking ring "was a theory long held by some conservative blogs" and that the connection between the Democratic party and the child-abuse ring "jumped to other social media services such as Twitter and Reddit, where it gained momentum on the page "The_Donald." A new Reddit discussion thread called "Pizzagate" quickly attracted 20,000 subscribers" (Kang 2016). Fake news travels fast. She also reported that the owner, James Alefantis, and his employees had received threatening texts and messages (ibid.). Edgar Welch became a threat and acted on his anger. This case demonstrates just how dangerous (genuine) fake news can be. These Internet rumors are clear instances of the "weaponizing of untruth." Welch believed the lies; they seemed true to his brain, due in part, to the illusion-of-truth effect and as a result of numerous and readily available stories on social media. Other contributing factors to Welch's anger and actions were probably the various memeplexes associated with criminalizing Clinton by Trump and Republicans and the partisan hyper-polarization reinforcing his confirmation biases. To his parasitized brain, he had no reason to seek additional information; he had ample sources. The problem, of course, is that the sources were not reliable, and it is increasingly more difficult for consumers to make this discrimination. He was angry and to him, the moral wrong had to be righted; retribution was required. If there *had* been a child sex slave operation at the pizza restaurant, then the focus of Welch's anger would have been morally justifiable; it would have been apt because child sexual abuse is certainly of moral concern. However, the violent means chosen by Welch to correct this alleged moral wrong would not have been considered to be morally right. Nonetheless, in this case, his anger is not morally justified because both the focus and the targets (Clinton, Podesta, and Democrats) of his anger were incorrect and based on a false narrative promulgated by fake news posted on numerous social media sites. There was no child-abuse ring and patrons of the pizza parlor were not those whom he considered to be the moral wrongdoers.

The second case is that of Bernie Sanders supporter James Hodgkinson of Belleville, Illinois, who shot Steve Scalise, House Majority Whip, on June 14, 2017 while Scalise and others were practicing for a congressional baseball game, which is an annual charity event at Eugene Simpson Stadium Park in Alexandria, VA. Hodgkinson was vehemently opposed to Trump. In their *New York Times* article, Michael D. Shear, Adam Goldman, and Emily Cochrane report that Hodgkinson "signed an online petition calling for the president to be impeached, posting it on Facebook with a chilling comment: 'It's time to destroy Trump & co.' and posted a picture of Bernie Sanders on a LinkedIn page with the words, 'The Dawn of a New Democracy'" (2017). In this case, unlike Welch's, the focus of Hodgkinson's anger is unclear. What is the moral concern that is involved here? Simply being a Republican? And, even though the target of Hodgkinson's anger is "Trump & co.," in order for his anger to have been morally justified in this particular case, Scalise would have had to have been the one who wronged Hodgkinson, since it was Scalise whom Hodgkinson shot. Since Scalise did not wrong Hodgkinson directly, the target of Hodgkinson's anger is inappropriate. Furthermore, morally justifiable anger requires a proportional retributive response to the moral wrong perpetrated. The attempted murder of Scalise does not meet that criterion, especially if the "moral concern" is simply being a Republican.

Gold and Shanks have pointed out that mind viruses are detrimental to their hosts. Welch is serving four years in prison and Hodgkinson is dead. The spread of such mind viruses with their manifestation in intolerant and linguistically and physically violent behavior by their hosts can be seen in the recent attacks against Asians during the coronavirus pandemic in the United States and elsewhere in the world.

The anger stoked by anti-Asian racist and xenophobic mind viruses has manifested itself in hate speech and violent attacks against Asians. Politicians, such as President Donald Trump and Secretary of State Mike Pompeo, have directly or indirectly contributed to the spread of these mind viruses by calling the coronavirus "the China virus" and the "Wuhan virus," respectively.[11] These are terms that suggest Chinese people are to blame for the virus, and the repeated use of these terms to refer to COVID-19 tends to promote discrimination against Chinese people, or anyone who is of Asian descent because of the "illusion-of-truth" effect. The virus came from China, so Chinese people must be the cause of the pandemic. One case of discrimination happened in Indiana, where Kao Lor and his uncle Lee Lor, who are of Hmong descent, were seeking lodging. They were turned away from a Motel 8 in Plymouth, IN, and then again from a Days Inn that was nearby. In the Motel 8 scenario, the men were asked if they were Chinese by the employee and were told that if they were, they needed "to be picked up" to be quarantined for two weeks, because that is what he was "told." This was an inaccurate statement. Instead, the two-week quarantine requirement pertained to U.S. citizens returning from Hubei Province in China. This misinformation led to the Lors being denied lodging. They then went on to another motel, a Days Inn, where when Kao Lor asked if Asians were permitted. The employee on video "appears to say no. Asians are not allowed" (Yan et al. 2020). Racial discrimination is a social injustice and warrants moral concern, and instances like this need to be avoided, in part by having correct and credible information. However, Asians are not only experiencing discrimination, they are experiencing racially motivated linguistic and physical assaults.

A Thai-American woman, Tanny Jiraprapasuke, experienced the ten-minute tirade from a man on a Los Angeles subway who, glaring at her and gesturing, claimed that the Chinese are responsible for all diseases and then said to another passenger, "Every disease has ever came from China, homie. Everything comes from China because they're f****** disgusting" (ibid.). In another incident, an Asian woman, who was wearing a face mask, was called a "diseased b****" and was assaulted by a man in a New York subway station on February 2, 2020. He hit the woman on the head (ibid.). Cases of linguistic and physical violence against Asians are not restricted to the United States. They are happening around the globe. Human Rights Watch posted on May 12, 2020, that there were fifty reports and accounts in the media of "assaults, verbal harassment, bullying and discrimination against people of Asian descent" in Italy since February. Asian people have "been punched in the face and taunted, accused of spreading coronavirus" in the UK. In Australia, two women attacked Chinese students yelling, "Go back to China," and "You fucking immigrants." A Chinese-American man who was in Spain was so badly beaten he was in a coma for two days (Human Rights Watch 2020). These are only a few of the examples cited by Human Rights Watch. These instances of linguistic and physical violence are behavioral manifestations of racist mind viruses and anger stoked, perhaps by fear of COVID-19, but also by misinformation and social media that increase the virulence of the mind viruses. Eoghan Macguire, for Al Jazeera, reports large-scale anti-Asian abuse on social media. He writes:

> An analysis by Al Jazeera found more than 10,000 posts on Twitter that included the term "kung-flu" during March alone—although the true total was likely much higher given a number of variations of the phrase were being used across the site. (2020)

Macguire further states that "Al Jazeera found 72,000 posts tagged #WuhanVirus and 10,000 tagged #KungFlu" on Instagram (ibid.). These numbers demonstrate just how effective social media is at spreading mind viruses. The transmission is successful because social media is easily accessible by large numbers of people and because of the sheer number of sites. Information is propagated and shared at exponential rates. The trouble with such exponential transmission is that the information shared largely remains unchecked for accuracy and racism, despite claims by platforms like Facebook, Twitter, and TikTok claiming to keep watch on these issues (ibid.). This is why so much misleading information and fake news, along with deleterious memes and mind viruses, travel so fast and infect so many. On the consumers' end of social media, they often do not have the time or sometimes the means, even if they are inclined to do some fact-checking to determine which sources and stories are more reliable and accurate. And, for those already infected with mind viruses, in this case racist mind viruses, those social media sites are the means by which linguistically violent abuse can take place. Even the United Nations Secretary-General, Antonio Guterres, characterized recent anti-Asian discrimination during the coronavirus pandemic and the verbal and physical attacks on Asians as "a virus of hate." He said on May 8, 2020, "The pandemic continues to unleash a tsunami of hate and xenophobia, scapegoating and scare-mongering" and added that governments need to "act now to strengthen the immunity of our societies against the virus of hate" (Human Rights Watch). This discrimination against Asians is social injustice and the morally unjustifiable anger of the perpetrators, stoked by some politicians' use of racist language and racist social media posts, needs to be counteracted. Just as we need a vaccine to boost immunity for the coronavirus, so we need a vaccine to boost the immunity against mind viruses. What sort of vaccine might this be?

FEAR, TRANSITIONAL ANGER, AND THE HOPE FOR A VACCINE

Fear is one of the main ways the mind viruses of sexism, racism, and ethnic hatred spread because it is propagated through myths about "the other" in conformity-memeplexes that undermine cultural heterogeneity. The weaponization of untruth and speedy transmission of that information via various media and social media outlets fosters and reinforces dogmatism and intolerance. The homogenized thinking in mind viruses hampers the ability of the host to consider other views or counter-evidence, playing into one's confirmation bias. When we lack understanding and tolerance, fear often turns into hatred and anger which is directed at "the other," oftentimes leading to violence. As Admiral Picard counseled Captain Rios in the episode "Broken Pieces": "Fear is the great destroyer" (Michael Chabon, *Star Trek: Picard*, 2020). We are seeing such fear manifested in anger and hatred with the rise of anti-Asian sentiment in the midst of the coronavirus pandemic and in the linguistically and physically violent attacks carried out against them. Gold and Shanks recommend a multicultural education committed to tolerance and respect to combat and dispel the myths of "the other," promoting cultural heterogeneity, which provides some immunity against those dogmatism-inducing mind viruses (2002, 198). I agree with this project; however, where there is discrimination and social injustice, anger toward these injustices seems to be morally justifiable and apt. That moral anger should be "transitional" in Martha Nussbaum's sense, where it is "forward-looking" and serves as a motivator to correct the social injustice (2015, 52). We should be angry at the weaponization of untruth in the form of fake news which spreads mind viruses that contribute to social injustices. In this regard, this puts the burden on news consumers to realize there are confirmation biases, work harder to check the accuracy of one's news sources and be cognizant of "the-illusion-of-truth" effect. Just because we hear something repeated frequently in the media does not make that claim accurate or true. It also puts a moral responsibility on journalists and reporters to do good reporting, call out the lies and fake news, and to depoliticize facts. In the fight against post-truth, Lee McIntyre contends the facts have a way of asserting themselves. He suggests that people listen when they are most affected. COVID-19 has come to everyone's doorstep, but there continues to be much misinformation and fake news being promulgated. Instead, the genuine facts need to be asserted over and over. We know that people tend to believe what they have heard repeated. It is just that the truth should be what is being repeated and not simply mere beliefs or opinions. Senator Daniel Moynihan reminded us, "You are entitled to your own opinion, but not your own facts."[12]

This "prescription" is certainly not enough. In this post-truth era, where, as Paul Krugman has said, "truth isn't truth" (Krugman 2018), there has to be a "transitional anger" approach toward those who spread mind viruses promoting fear and stoking anger leading to discrimination and linguistic and physical violence against others. In response to the wake of xenophobia, racism, and assaults against Asians during this COVID-19 pandemic, according to Human Rights Watch:

> The UN committee responsible for monitoring compliance with the International Convention on the Elimination of All Forms of Racial Discrimination, which 182 countries have ratified, has recommended that governments adopt "national action plans against racial discrimination." Plans should lay out specific approaches to combat racism and discrimination, from enhanced policing of hate crimes to public messaging and education programming encouraging tolerance. (2013)

Fighting post-truth by repeating the (genuine) facts, public messaging about tolerance and respect, as well as a multicultural education fostering tolerance and respect, together with governmental policies combating racism and discrimination, seems to be the means by which immunity can be boosted to combat mind viruses that undermine social justice.

NOTES

1. The notion of "apt anger" is defended by Amia Srinivasan (2018). Martha Nussbaum defines the "target" of anger as the one who has wrongly inflicted the damage and the "focus" as the wrongfully inflicted damage by the target (2015, 43). The phrase "linguistic violence" was coined by William C. Gay (1999, 13–35).

2. This chapter builds upon and employs ideas from two of my previous works: Paula Smithka, "How Mind Viruses and Rhinoceroses Promote Tyranny," in *Civility,*

Nonviolent Resistance, and the New Struggle for Social Justice (2020, 181–202), and Paula Smithka, "The Lies of the Land: Post-Truth, the Erosion of Democracy, and the Challenge for Positive Peace," in *Peaceful Approaches for a More Peaceful World* (forthcoming).

3. I grant that in a sense, the vending machine patron is wronged, in that he or she did not get what he or she paid for; however, the wrong was not an intentional harm but as a result of the failure of an inanimate object to perform the function it was designed to do. Depending upon the location of the vending machine, the patron may be able to be reimbursed for the monetary loss.

4. The term "memeplex" for meme-complexes is Hokky Situngkir's (2004, 20–32).

5. See for example, Juan Delius (1991).

6. These are phrases Gold and Shanks borrow from Michael Szpir (1995, 26–27).

7. Gold and Shanks, 193.

8. See for example Natalia Osipova and Aaron Byrd, "How Russian Bots and Trolls Invade our Lives—and Elections" (2017).

9. President Trump's continued use of ad hominems frequently repeated by him and in the media continues to serve him well in gaining purchase with the public for social and political gain.

10. See for example Peter Baker (2010).

11. See Allyson Chiu (2020) and Craig Graziosi (2020).

12. Quoted in McIntyre (2018, 163).

REFERENCE LIST

Aristotle. 1984. "Rhetoric." In *The Complete Works of Aristotle*, edited by Jonathan Barnes. Princeton, NJ: Princeton University Press.

Baker, Peter. 2020. "Elitism: The Charge that Obama Can't Shake." *New York Times*, October 30, 2010. Accessed May 23, 2020. https://www.nytimes.com/2010/10/31/weekinreview/31baker.html.

Ben-Ze'ev, Aaron. 2020. "Are Envy, Anger, and Resentment Moral Emotions?" *Philosophical Explorations* 5, no. 2: 148–154. Accessed May 18, 2020. https://doi.org/10.1080/10002002058538728.

Blow, Charles M. 2017. "Trump Isn't Hitler. But the Lying . . ." *New York Times*, October 19, 2017. Accessed October 24, 2017. https://www.nytimes.com/2017/10/19/opinion/trump-isnt-hitler-but-the-lying.html.

Chabon, Michael, Writer. 2020. *Star Trek: Picard*, season 1, episode 8, "Broken Pieces." Aired March 12, 2020 on CBS All Access.

Chiu, Allyson. 2020. "Trump Has No Qualms About Calling Corona Virus 'the Chinese Virus'. That's A Dangerous Attitude, Experts Say." *The Washington Post*, March 20, 2020. Accessed May 19, 2020. https://www.washingtonpost.com/nation/2020/03/20/coronavirus-trump-chinese-virus/.

Dawkins, Richard. 1989. *The Selfish Gene*. Oxford: Oxford University Press.

———. 1992. *The Extended Phenotype*. Oxford: Oxford University Press.

Delius, Juan D. 1991. "The Nature of Culture." First published in *The Tinbergen Legacy*, edited by M. S. Dawkins, T. R. Halliday, and R. Dawkins. London:

Chapman & Hall. Uploaded by the author to researchgate.net. Accessed July 11, 2017. https://www.researchgate.net/publication/233820866.

Eagleman, David. 2011. *Incognito: The Secret Lives of the Brain.* New York: Vintage Books.

Fact-Checker Blog. *The Washington Post.* Updated April 3, 2020. Accessed May 22, 2020. https://www.washingtonpost.com/graphics/politics/trump-claims-database/.

Finnegan, Michael, and Noah Bierman. 2016. "Trump's Endorsement of Violence Reaches New Level: He May Pay Legal Fees for Assault Suspect." *Los Angeles Times*, March 13, 2016. Accessed March 31, 2019. https://www.latimes.com/politics/la-na-trump-campaign-protests-20160313-story.html.

Gay, William C. 1999. "Linguistic Violence." In *Institutional Violence*, edited by Robert Litke and Deane Curtin, 13–35. Amsterdam: Rodopi.

Gold, Jeffrey, and Niall Shanks. 2002. "Mind Viruses and the Importance of Cultural Diversity." In *Community, Diversity, and Difference: Implications for Peace*, edited by Alison Bailey and Paula J. Smithka, 187–199. Amsterdam-New York: Rodopi.

Graziosi, Craig. 2020. "Coronavirus: Mike Pompeo Insists G7 Use 'Wuhan Virus'—But World Officials Refuse." *Independent*, March 25, 2020. Accessed May 20, 2020. https://www.independent.co.uk/news/coronavirus-g7-wuhan-virus-mike-pompeo-trump-a9426261.html.

Held, Virginia. 2006. *The Ethics of Care.* Oxford: Oxford University Press.

Heyd, David. 2018. "Keeping the Moral Score." Review essay of Martha Nussbaum's *Anger and Forgiveness: Resentment, Generosity, Justice. Criminal Justice Ethics*, 37, no. 2: 189–200. Accessed May 18, 2020. https://doi.org/10.1080/0731129X.2018.1499699.

Human Rights Watch. 2020. "COVID-19 Fueling Anti-Asian Racism and Xenophobia Worldwide: National Action Plans Needed to Counter Intolerance." May 12, 2020. Accessed May 20, 2020. https://www.hrw.org/news/2020/05/12/covid-19-fueling-anti-asian-racism-and-xenophobia-worldwide.

Hume, David. [1739–40] 1978. *Treatise on Human Nature.* Edited by L. A. Selby-Bigge and P. H. Nidditch, 2nd ed. Oxford: Oxford Clarendon Press.

Kang, Cecilia. 2016. "Fake News Onslaught Targets Pizzeria as Nest of Child-Trafficking." *New York Times*, November 21, 2016. Accessed July 12, 2017. https://www.nytimes.com/2016/11/21/technology/fact-check-this-pizzeria-is-not-a-child-trafficking-site.html?_r=0.

Konstan, David. 2015. "Emotions and Morality: The View from Classical Antiquity." *Topoi* 34: 401–407. Accessed May 18, 2020. https://doi.org/10.1007/s11245-013-9229-0.

Krugman, Paul. 2018. "The G.O.P's Climate of Paranoia." *New York Times*, August 20, 2018. Accessed August 21, 2018. https://www.nytimes.com/2018/08/20/opinion/trump-republican-truth-climate-change.html?action=click&pgtype=Homepage&clickSource=story-heading&module=opinion-c-col-left-region®ion=opinion-c-col-left-region&WT.nav=opinion-c-col-left-region.

Luce, Edward. 2017. *The Retreat from Western Liberalism.* London: Little, Brown.

Macguire, Eoghan. 2020. "Anti-Asian Hate Continues to Spread Online Amid COVID-19 Pandemic." *Al Jazeera*, April 5, 2020. Accessed May 18, 2020. https://www.aljazeera.com/news/2020/04/anti-asian-hate-continues-spread-online-covid-19-pandemic-200405063015286.html.

McIntyre, Lee. 2018. *Post-Truth*. Cambridge, MA: MIT Press.

Nussbaum, Martha. 2015. "Transitional Anger." *Journal of the American Philosophical Association*: 41–56. Accessed April 29, 2020. https://doi.org/10.1017/apa.2014.19.

Osipova, Natalia, and Aaron Byrd. 2017. "How Russian Bots and Trolls Invade Our Lives—And Elections." *New York Times*, video. November 10, 2017. Accessed December 9, 2017. https://www.nytimes.com/video/us/politics/100000005414346/how-russian-bots-and-trolls-invade-our-lives-and-elections.html.

Oxford Dictionaries. 2018. "Post-Truth." Accessed August 21, 2018. https://en.oxforddictionaries.com/definition/post-truth.

Pettigrove, Glen. 2012. "Meekness and 'Moral' Anger." *Ethics* 122, no. 2: 341–370. Accessed May 19, 2020. https://www.jstor.org/stable/10.1086/663230.

Rogan, Tom. 2016. "Why Do So Many Americans Hate Hillary Clinton?" *CNN*, November 4, 2016. Accessed May 23, 2020. https://www.cnn.com/2016/11/04/opinions/why-do-americans-hate-hillary-rogan-opinion/index.html.

Shear, Michael D., Adam Goldman, and Emily Cochrane. 2017. "Congressman Steve Scalise Gravely Wounded in Alexandria Baseball Field Ambush." *New York Times*, June 14, 2017. Accessed July 12, 2017. https://www.nytimes.com/2017/06/14/us/steve-scalise-congress-shot-alexandria-virginia.html.

Situngkir, Hokky. 2004. "On Selfish Memes: Culture as Complex Adaptive System." *Journal of Social Complexity* 2, no. 1: 20–32.

Smithka, Paula. 2020. "How Mind Viruses and Rhinoceroses Promote Tyranny." In *Civility, Nonviolent Resistance, and the New Struggle for Social Justice*, edited by Amin Asfari, 181–202. Leiden: Brill/Rodopi.

———. Forthcoming. "The Lies of the Land: Post-Truth, the Erosion of Democracy, and the Challenge for Positive Peace." In *Peaceful Approaches for a More Peaceful World*, edited by Sanjay Lal. Leiden: Brill/Rodopi.

Srinivasan, Amia. 2018. "The Aptness of Anger." *The Journal of Political Philosophy* 26, no. 2: 123–144. Accessed May 18, 2020. https://doi.org/10.1111/jopp.12130.

Szpir, Michael. 1995. "Mind Viruses." *American Scientist* 83, no. 1 (January–February): 26–27.

Yan, Holly, Natasha Chen, and Dushyant Naresh. 2020. "What's Spreading Faster than Coronavirus in the US? Racist Assaults and Ignorant Attacks Against Asians." *CNN*, February 20, 2020. Accessed May 18, 2020. https://www.cnn.com/2020/02/20/us/coronavirus-racist-attacks-against-asian-americans/index.html.

Zeitz, Joshua. 2017. "Why Do They Hate Her?" *Politico* (June). Accessed May 23, 2020. https://www.politico.com/magazine/story/2017/06/03/why-do-they-hate-her-215220.

Chapter 9

Rage against the Machine

The Virtues of Anger in Response to Oppression

Jennifer Kling

> ...The wise man will never cease to be angry, if once he begins, so full is every place of vices and crimes.
>
> —Seneca (1928, II.9)

> I have suckled the wolf's lip of anger
> and I have used it for illumination, laughter,
> protection, fire in places where there was no light,
> no food, no sisters, no quarter.
>
> —Audre Lorde (1997, 285)

Oppression makes me angry. So, I am angry almost all of the time, as oppression (of various kinds) is endemic to our sociopolitical world. However, there is a growing philosophical literature that argues against anger as a necessary, virtuous, or important response to wrongdoing. Martha Nussbaum, in particular, argues that "anger is always normatively problematic, whether in the personal or in the public realm" (2016, introduction). It is certainly true that anger can have bad or problematic effects, and it may well be true that Nussbaum, and others who hold similar views, are on the right track in the moral realm.[1] However, despite the serious moral worries surrounding anger (which I discuss in more detail below), I contend that maintaining an anti-anger position is mistaken in regard to the sociopolitical realm. In particular, I argue that anger is both an important, and a virtuous, response to the presence of oppression, that is, to the presence of widespread injustices that disproportionately negatively affect certain social groups, and their members, within and across societies. Anger, when in response to oppression, has the potential to be, not a vice, but a virtue.

The first section of the chapter is devoted to outlining my conception of oppression, and its operation, in our sociopolitical world. Oppression, I maintain, is importantly different than interpersonal wrongdoing; this is why the moral and sociopolitical projects regarding anger can, and do, come apart. The second section turns to a discussion of anger: What is it, and why is it a virtuous and important response to oppression? I here introduce the analogy of a vaccine to explain (a) why anger is important, and even potentially necessary, for fighting oppression, and (b) how anger can operate—assuming all goes well—in that fight. At this point, the argument might lead one to conclude that anger is instrumentally politically valuable; in response, the third section develops the idea of anger as a political virtue. Deployed properly, anger toward oppression can both galvanize political change and enable its wielder(s) to live a flourishing life in the midst of oppression. Of course, like any virtue, anger can go wrong. Deployed poorly, it can have many of the negative effects described by Nussbaum and others. But, in the ideal case, anger in response to oppression not only helps propel the fight for justice, but also promotes mental, emotional, and social flourishing for those who must live their lives in an oppressive society.[2]

OPPRESSION AND INTERPERSONAL WRONGDOING

There are many different ways of thinking and theorizing about oppression. In the most general sense, a person is oppressed when their life goes badly across many, if not all, of the various spheres that comprise personal, social, and political life *because of* their perceived membership in a particular group (Frye 1983, 10–11; Haslanger 2004; Crenshaw 1991). As Sally Haslanger puts it, "the notion of oppression . . . point[s] to the ways in which groups of individuals are systematically and unfairly disadvantaged within a particular social structure" (2004, 98). Oppression has to do not only with a particular individual's interpersonal, social, and political actions and consequences, but also with the meaning that the background structure of the society assigns to those actions and consequences, on the basis of the individual's salient social identity(ies).

For instance, microaggressions are such only because of the societal backdrop against which they occur. In a world where women's bodies are not policed in a variety of ways, one of my male students telling me (a woman) that I should smile more is not a micro-instance of misogyny. It may be an insufficiently professional comment in that possible world, but it is not oppressive. Contrast this with the actual world, where such an act by my student is (most likely inadvertently) misogynist. But the reason that it is misogynistic, notice, is not because of any intrinsic qualities of his action—assuming, of course, that he does not do it in a creepy or otherwise problematic way. Let us assume the best possible scenario, wherein it is said kindly, is obviously meant as genuinely helpful advice to his (admittedly somewhat socially awkward) professor, and is clearly done in complete or near-complete ignorance of the patriarchy. Even this best-case scenario misogyny is still misogyny, because our societal context is one wherein oppression on the basis of gender is alive and well. In such a sociopolitical context, his interpersonal comment cannot help but be misogynistic.

Oppression, then, because of the ways in which sociopolitical context determines meaning, is both an interpersonal and a structural-institutional phenomenon.[3] For this reason (among others), it can be difficult, both to see oppression in the world and to capture it as a concept. Many theorists have done excellent work to demonstrate the ways in which women, persons of color, poor people, and disabled people are oppressed (Frye 1983; Boxill 1972; Cudd 1994; Wasserstrom 1977; Beauvoir 2011; Kadi 2006; Nussbaum 2007; Kittay 1999). I will not repeat that work here. Instead, I focus on this general understanding of oppression to draw out the ways in which it is different from interpersonal wrongdoing. When a person is subject to oppression, whether in the form of interpersonal microaggressions, macroaggressions, social norms and policies, or political laws, policies, and procedures, they are not only wronged as an individual, they are wronged as a member of, and *because of their membership in*, a particular social group. Often, the oppressive act, norm, policy, law, or procedure is not aimed—either intentionally or inadvertently—at them personally, but at their group as a whole; they just happen to get caught in the crosshairs. If they were not a member of that group, they would not have been targeted or affected. (If I weren't a woman, my student's comment wouldn't be misogynistic.) Thus, oppression, unlike interpersonal wrongdoing, is neither random (as when one individual attacks another for no discernable reason), nor due to a perceived fault in an individual person's character or actions (as when one person attacks another for—justified or unjustified—reasons pertaining to the victim as an individual). Rather, it is both individualized, and the product of particular social structures and the meanings and identities that those structures assign and promote.[4]

Ultimately, this results in instances of oppression, unlike instances of interpersonal wrongdoing, always having multiple necessary perpetrators, so to speak. An individual cannot commit an instance of oppression (again, either intentionally or inadvertently), without the relevant systemic conditions being in place. And conversely, if the relevant systemic conditions are in place, then sometimes an individual cannot help but commit an instance of oppression. Because oppression is, by its nature, both interpersonal and sociopolitical, this means that the moral project and the political project regarding anger can come apart. Arguably, I ought not be angry with my student; in the best-case scenario that we are considering, he is certainly not *blameworthy* for his misogyny. Interpersonal anger in this situation would be, I think, misplaced, not least because he is not, as Iris Marion Young (2011) would put it, backward-looking responsible, but also because he is my student, and I am his professor.[5] More generally, I am sympathetic to Nussbaum's claim (2016, chapter 4), which echoes Nel Noddings's ethics of care (1998), that interpersonal anger is corrosive of caring relationships, and so anger may well be normatively problematic in the interpersonal realm.

And furthermore, even in situations where the instance of oppression is intentionally done, it is still not clear that anger is the appropriate interpersonal response. As Seneca argues,

> no one should be angry at the mistakes of men . . . The wise man will have no anger toward sinners. Do you ask why? Because he knows that no one is born wise but becomes so, knows that only the fewest in every age turn out wise, because he has fully grasped the conditions of human life, and no sensible man becomes angry with nature . . . And so the wise man is kindly and just toward errors, he is not the foe, but the reformer of sinners . . . He will view all these things in as kindly a way as a physician views the sick. (1928, II.9–11)

Of course, this is a Stoic sensibility that many of us find difficult to implement. However, the sentiment is somewhat compelling, in that it reminds us that intentional wrongdoing, at the interpersonal level, is often the result of error rather than true maliciousness, and so we should be kind and understanding, and seek to reform and repair, rather than be angry (and seek to punish or pay back). And this may be especially true for instances of oppression; as Seneca puts it, "If anyone follows in the footsteps of others who have taken the wrong road, should he not be excused because it was the public highway that led him astray?" (1928, II.10). Taking oppression to be the public highway here, we can conclude that perhaps we should not be angry at individuals who commit oppressive wrongdoings, in particular because they cannot help the sociopolitical context by which they have been and continue to be socially conditioned, and within which their actions take place.

However, to say that anger in response to oppressive actions may well be inappropriate in the moral, interpersonal realm, is not yet to say that it is inappropriate in the political realm. Perhaps I ought to reconcile with oppressive individuals, strive to avoid being angry at them, or work to convert my interpersonal anger into a caring, kindly understanding.[6] But this is all compatible with being (and remaining) angry at the public highway, that is, at the systems of oppression themselves! I can engage in interpersonal caring relationships with others while refusing to reconcile myself to—that is, refusing to tamp down, or dissipate, my anger at—the sociopolitical structures and institutions that make many of their actions oppressive. This separation is possible because of the nature of oppression; because it is both personal and political, anger in response to it can, in turn, be both personal and political (or one or the other, as appropriate). So, I do not get angry at my student; I instead remain angry at the society that taught him to say such things, and that makes his comment one more pinprick in the thousands of societal pokes and prods that seek to force women, and their bodies, to exist in exacting, submissive ways. We can thus separate political anger toward an oppressive society from interpersonal anger toward oppressive individuals. Then, we can ask the further question of whether such political anger is always, as Nussbaum concludes, normatively problematic (2016, chap. 6 and 7), or whether it can be virtuous.

One final note about oppression before moving on to my discussion of anger. Oppression, in addition to being both an interpersonal and a structural-institutional phenomenon, is like smoke; constantly shifting and moving, and thus almost impossible to eradicate. Its nature is to shift its form, rather than its essential elements, in response to challenge. For instance, the oppression of black and brown Americans was once accomplished by chattel slavery. Upon challenge and successful overthrow, this particular system of racial oppression was replaced by the infamous Jim Crow laws, which in turn were challenged and overthrown, only to be replaced by the racial oppression of the contemporary American criminal justice system (Alexander 2011). American racial oppression has not disappeared; it has just migrated. Similarly, second-wave feminism brought women out of the home (where they were mothers, wives, and domestic workers) and into the professional workforce. In response, the patriarchy did not break; it simply shifted into the forms of the wage gap, the glass ceiling, and the glass cliff, among other oppressive structures (Bruckmüller et al. 2014).

Fighting oppression can sometimes, for lack of a better term, feel like playing an endless game of whack-a-mole: no matter how many times you manage to hit the mole down, it simply pops back up in another place. It is easy to despair in the face of this seemingly endless and ever-evolving threat; as Court Lewis writes, "For those involved in fighting structural oppression, it can often feel like chasing Moby Dick, which if you are unfamiliar with its ending, almost everyone dies in a futile attempt to catch the giant whale" (2019, 41). This combination of exhaustion and seeming futility can lead those who fight oppression to fall prey to political cynicism and a general world-weariness. Lewis cautions that "the seeming inability to positively influence 'the leviathan' of social structures . . . can inhibit a person's flourishing and turn resentment into feelings of despair and vengeance, which then promote attitudes of anger and violence" (2019, 41). Here, Lewis seems to understand anger as a sentiment that arises in response to the despair that can often attend the fight against oppression. By contrast, I propose that, in the face of oppression, we should proactively *get angry*. Political anger at oppression, I maintain, can operate as a vaccine against political cynicism and despair, and, in so doing, can actually prevent the kinds of violence that concern Lewis, Nussbaum, and others. In addition, such anger, when virtuous, can help propel the fight for social change, for the attainment of some measure of justice, and can contribute to a flourishing life.

POLITICAL ANGER AS A VACCINE

However, "anger" is a broad category; before I can argue in its favor, I first need to say something about what it is. Importantly, the following is not a complete analysis of anger, as that would take me too far afield from my focus on the virtues of anger in response to oppression. The goal is simply to say enough here to get a grip on the concept, before discussing its importance and operation as a kind of vaccine. I think of anger as a general category of sentiment that contains within it a spectrum of particular sentiments. In many ways, this is why it is helpful to think of it as an Aristotelian virtue category. By sentiment, I just mean that anger contains both intellectual and emotional components; it is a moral emotion that is, as Agnes Callard puts it, "a way of concerning oneself with the (unchangeable) fact that some wrong was done," at least in the angry person's eyes (2018, 126). Anger is one way of showing that you care that something you value has been betrayed, injured, damaged, threatened, or otherwise disvalued (Callard 2018, 127). For instance, I am angry when black and brown Americans are prevented from voting, precisely because I value democratic equality (i.e., I take it to be good), and my anger at its suppression demonstrates (to both myself and others) the significance of that value to me.[7] Without the evaluation of something as good, I would not be angry at its dis-valuation by others; hence, anger includes a moral intellectual component. And, it is also emotional. Anger is not only a sign of our evaluations; it is a way of caring about that which we value. As Callard concludes, "The person's concern for the good thing in question—the object of value—manifests itself in the form of a concern for the injurious action or event . . . My anger at his or her failure to call is the only way in which my valuation of our friendship can, under these nonideal circumstances, manifest itself" (2018, 127).

Importantly, by calling anger a moral emotion, neither Callard nor I mean to say that anger is always *moral*; it certainly can be immoral in some cases, as when the angry person values something they ought not value, or when they misperceive another's actions as damaging or threatening what they value, when those actions are really non-damaging or non-threatening, or when they misevaluate who or what bears responsibility for the relevant injury or wrong done to what they value. Rather, it is to say that anger always includes the evaluation of something *as good*, and is one manifestation of a person's caring about, or being concerned about, the (perceived) wrongs that have happened to that thing (because they value that thing).[8] Of course, this categorical concern about wrongs done to that which we value can take many different forms; this is the sense in which anger is a spectrum of particular sentiments.

On the one extreme, there is a refusal to get righteously indignant, to purposely fail to recognize when wrongs have occurred that ought to be rectified. The most common form of this is the "excuser" figure, the person who always seeks to explain away wrongs as either not really wrong, once you understand the circumstances, or as wrong, but really no one's fault or responsibility, once you understand the circumstances. In the first case, we can think of victim-blaming (which is a variation of the just world hypothesis), and in the second, we can think of those who defend police brutality by pointing to police officers' fear or duress as excusing conditions. In both cases, the attempt (intentionally or inadvertently) is to suppress the recognition that a moral wrong—in the full and important sense of the term—has been done to something that the person values. These excuses work to cut off the development of anger at the pass; in practice, such strategies do not often succeed perfectly, but they mitigate the development of anger so that it becomes something like mild worry or sorrow instead. Slightly different, but still at this end of the spectrum, is the person who fully recognizes that a wrong has occurred, but strives to respond to that wrong only intellectually, and not emotionally. This kind of detachment can transmute potential anger into quietism or aloofness, which often in practice becomes a kind of remoteness, standoffishness, or, in some cases, bemusement. (Think of the "Oxford don"-type figure here who is curious about or bewildered by genocide, but who is not, at any point, angered and sickened by it.)

At the other end of the spectrum, there is a blind rage that strikes out without bothering to distinguish between apt and inapt targets. This is the person who is consumed by their anger, and fails to recognize it as a sentiment internal to them over which they have some influence, if not complete control. Everything is a wrong or a slight, and everything that happens is equally deserving of a wrathful or raging response. Those in a blind rage are often terrifying, because there is no sense that their rage is either controlled or limited to those responsible for the wrong to which their anger is a response. This is part of why a man getting angry and punching a wall is scary; his rage is blind in an important sense (assuming, I think fairly, that walls are not responsible for wrongs), and that means that anything could happen as a result of his wrath. The intellectual component of anger is all but gone for those who are in a blind rage—presumably this is why we talk of being "in the grip of" anger, rage, or wrath when discussing this end of the anger spectrum. Blind rage is all-consuming, and because of this, it "exposes one to dangers . . . being overwhelmed by rage" is exhausting, can have serious negative effects on one's health and peace of mind, and can lead both to one's harming others and to one's being demonized by others (McRae 2018, 107).

But in the middle, between these two extremes, is what bell hooks (1995) refers to as "constructive rage," which seeks to dismantle the systems of oppression by targeting those systems, and their upholders, in the right manner, at the right time, and in the right way, both strategically and in a way that avoids either extreme. hooks argues that constructive rage "is a necessary aspect of resistance struggle"; it moves beyond "fruitless scapegoating of any group" and instead "illuminates, heals, and makes redemptive struggle possible" by highlighting the ways in which our individual fates are tied to our collective fate under systems of oppression (1995, 3–4). This constructive rage is neither useless nor disruptive/destructive (as Audre Lorde writes, these are the two most common objections to anger), but rather is "loaded with information and energy" (1997, 280). Constructive rage identifies, in response to structural oppression and systemic and interpersonal oppressive acts, "who are our allies with whom we have grave differences, and who [and what] are our genuine enemies" (Lorde 1997, 280). This anger is not blind, but rather is responsive to essential information about the nature of the wrongs done to that which we value; thus, it is targeted toward structural-institutional oppression, rather than the interpersonal oppressive acts and actors that individuals face every day.[9]

This kind of anger can operate as a vaccine against political cynicism and despair. This is because anger in general, when fitting, forces the person who is angry to see the targets of their rage as subjects who are able to respond appropriately or inappropriately to that rage. As hooks puts it, rage is only apt within "the mutuality of a subject-to-subject encounter," because only in such an encounter can it "be heard" and so "be used constructively" (1995, 4). It is inapt to direct one's anger toward something, or someone, who is unable to or cannot respond—either well or poorly—to that anger. I might get frustrated with the wrench that doesn't work, but I should not get angry at it. The sentiment of anger, to use P. F. Strawson's term (1962, section 4), is a reactive attitude that is fitting only when it has the ability to bring about an intentional response of some kind from its target. The wrench cannot respond to my anger, either appropriately or inappropriately; thus, it is an inapt target of my anger. (Importantly, this aligns with the point made above, about anger being a response to a *wronging* of some sort. Part of what it is to be able to commit a wronging is the ability to—intentionally or inadvertently—act purposively; with this ability to act purposively comes the ability to respond purposively to another's subsequent anger at that initial action. The wrench did not do anything on purpose; it cannot. And linked to that, the wrench cannot respond to my anger. Thus, for both reasons, my anger toward the wrench is simply inapt.[10])

My student, on the other hand, has the capacity to respond well or poorly to my anger. Thus, my anger is an apt, or fitting, reactive attitude toward his sexist behavior. Here, I do not mean that it is appropriate to get angry *at him*; as I say above, I wish to remain neutral about the normative status of anger in the moral realm. Rather, I mean that anger toward the oppressive system of which he is a necessary component—and in this case, a purveyor—is apt, because he has the capacity to respond to my anger in an intentional, meaningful way. And furthermore, because oppressive systems are (at least partially) composed of individuals, his ability to respond to my anger can, if it is a good response, lead to changes in the relevant oppressive system. To see this, consider: if every single person who engages in sexist behavior stopped engaging in that behavior in response to the constructive rage of others, sexism would, by and large, cease to exist. Of course, some institutional sexism—based in laws, policies, and procedures—would remain, but insofar as those are also under the control of individuals, they would quickly be changed as well. A bit far-fetched, to be sure, but it makes the point. Constructive rage at structural oppression is an apt reactive attitude, because the main mediums through which oppression is created, sustained, and occurs—namely, individuals—are responsive to anger.[11]

Getting angry at oppression, then, enables and encourages us to see that political change is possible, because it helps us to recognize that oppression is a function of subjects, who could—although they often, of course, do not—respond well to our rage. As hooks writes, oppression "is real. And it is humanizing to be able to resist it with militant [constructive] rage" (1995, 4). Such rage not only humanizes those enraged, but also humanizes the oppressors at whom they (we) are enraged. And with such humanization comes the knowledge that they could change; in fact, this is part of what is so enraging about them, that they could, and yet do not, make different interpersonal, social, and political decisions. In this way, constructive rage, because it practically forces us to see our oppressors as subjects sustaining a system that is (more or less) under their control, leads us to realize that we *can* be heard by them, that we can use our rage to create real political change, to attain some measure of justice. In the face of this realization, neither political cynicism nor despair is appropriate.

Cynicism and despair are appropriate, I suggest, when there is absolute certainty that nothing can be done, that there is no possible action that will lead to the desired result. And, as I said earlier, these sentiments often attend the existence of oppression, with its propensity to shift its form and continually pop up again in what appeared to be cleared ground. Constructive rage can act as a vaccine against these sentiments, by foiling such cynical and despairing certainty with its constant demand that you see oppressors as subjects who could, and someday might, make different sociopolitical decisions. It is a shot in the arm that reminds you that things have changed in the past, and they could change again, if the right actions are taken, in the right way, at the right time. People create and sustain oppression; so, they can also dismantle it. Constructively rage, not at them, but at the systems they uphold, and they might. Of course, the analogy is not perfect. But insofar as vaccines block diseases (when all goes well) from gaining a stronghold in the body, so too can constructive rage block political cynicism and despair (when all goes well) from gaining a foothold in the mind. This is hooks's point that rage, when linked to a passion for freedom and justice and thus made constructive, makes redemptive struggle possible (1995, 3–4).

In a perhaps unexpected way, then, political anger can also promote hope; when it takes the form of constructive rage, it propels the fight for justice by keeping our eyes open to the possibility, as Lorde writes, of "a basic and radical alteration in all those [oppressive] assumptions underlining our lives" (1997, 280). She stresses that "when we turn from anger we turn from insight, saying we will accept only the designs already known, those deadly and safely familiar" (1997, 283). When we are afraid of our anger, and so abandon it as a creative and energetic force for profound change, we fall back into the familiar traps and trappings of oppression, and thus become powerless and hopeless. This, in turn, can lead to lashing out violently. But when we embrace constructive rage, we can "stand to those distortions" of oppression and violence, and see them as "ours to alter" in whatever way we deem best (Lorde 1997, 283). From this form of anger thus comes hope and empowerment for radical political transformation. So, constructive rage operates not only as a vaccine against political cynicism and despair, but also as a bedrock of hope, and a source of positive, rather than violent, energy; as Lorde concludes, the oppressed and their allies have "a well-stocked arsenal of anger potentially useful," so long as it is "focused with precision," for fighting oppression and attaining some measure of justice (1997, 280).

ANGER AS A POLITICAL VIRTUE

At this point, we might conclude that political anger, or more specifically, constructive rage, is instrumentally politically valuable. That is, it can be a useful political tool in the fight against oppression, but no more than that.

And as Emily McRae nicely notes, if anger is only instrumentally politically valuable, then its benefits must be weighed against its burdens before deciding whether to utilize it, either on a case-by-case basis or as a general rule (2018, 106–109). Nussbaum carefully conducts such a weighing and concludes that anger in the political realm is, for the most part, not worth it (2016, chapters 6 and 7).[12] In response, I contend that anger is not only instrumental in the fight against oppression, but also has the potential to be a political virtue. Following Aristotle, virtues are those character traits that, when instantiated in accordance with practical wisdom, partially constitute, and enable a person to live, a flourishing life (Annas 2011). To take a classic example (Aristotle 1999, III.6-9), a courageous person, first and foremost, has the settled disposition to act and feel courageously, that is, to be willing and able to face danger. However, to truly have the virtue of courage, she must be neither cowardly nor foolhardy in her actions—she must bring her courage to bear wisely, at the right time (when it is called for), in the right manner (such that it manifests effectively), and in the right way (so that it actually solves, or seeks to solve, the core of the problem that demands a courageous response). To be courageous, then, is to achieve a "golden mean" between the vices that surround it, in a way that is wholehearted and indicative of, we might say, who someone truly is as a person (Aristotle 1999, II.1). This virtue of courage is partially constitutive of, and thus helps enable its possessor to live, a flourishing life.

Of course, this quick sketch does not consider the many important debates within virtue ethics; however, it does help demonstrate what I mean when I say that constructive rage has the potential to be a political virtue. To begin, by describing this kind of anger as a political virtue, I simply mean to distinguish between the personal and political, much as I did above in the discussion of oppression. Some virtues are more appropriately described as pertaining to our personal lives (the moral virtues), while others pertain more clearly to our political lives (the political virtues) (LeBar 2013). Of course, the two are not wholly separate: "The personal is political," after all. But still, it is possible, and I think helpful, to make some rough distinctions here. Constructive rage is potentially a political virtue (when instantiated in accordance with practical wisdom, it *is* a political virtue) because it primarily applies to our political lives, as they are carried out at the socio-institutional level and, consequently, interpersonally. Furthermore, constructive rage falls between the two extremes of a refusal to get angry on the one hand, and blind rage on the other; it thus aims at a kind of golden mean between two vicious dispositions. In addition, it is the sort of disposition that needs to be wielded in the right way, at the right time, and in the right manner in order to be truly virtuous. As hooks and Lorde repeatedly emphasize, (although not in so many words), constructive rage is subject to practical wisdom. It must be aptly targeted, sensitive, and constructive, rather than destructive, to properly galvanize positive political change.

Finally, and perhaps most importantly, constructive rage is partially constitutive of, and can enable its possessor to live, a flourishing life in the midst of oppression. It does this by helping its possessor to avoid falling prey to any of the many false consciousnesses that oppressed persons are pressured, throughout their lives, to adopt. For instance, my anger at sexism can help me recognize, and fight off, the temptation to internalize the nagging societal whisper that says I must have somehow encouraged the unwanted attentions of an older man at a cocktail party. My constructive rage can pull me up short, as it were: it (metaphorically) shouts in my ear that that whisper is not me, it's the patriarchy! Fight it! Constructive rage reminds its possessor where the blame for oppression really lies, and thus helps to ward off the internalization of oppression. As hooks puts it, "Mainstream white culture offers the mantle of victimization . . . [the] internalization of victimization renders black folks powerless" (1995, 4). Rage is the antidote to this acceptance of victimization and powerlessness; it "burns in [the] psyche with an intensity that creates clarity. It is a constructive healing rage" (hooks 1995, 4). Constructive rage helps oppressed persons to see the truth, that they are not who or what the oppressive system says they are. It can thus promote mental and emotional flourishing by aiding the oppressed in both spotting, and fighting off, the insidious whispers of oppressive ideologies that would have them believe (both falsely and detrimentally) that they truly are lesser and to blame. Here again, constructive rage operates as a kind of vaccine.

In addition to mental and emotional flourishing, constructive rage can also promote social flourishing in the midst of oppression. To take another example, it can help young black American men fight off, both in their own minds and in their social circles, the labels "thug" or "boy." If enough black men draw on their constructive rage to reject, and thus refuse to use or acknowledge, such derogatory labels, such distortions of their identity, this encourages other black men in their social groups to do so as well. In this way, constructive rage (again like a vaccine) can confer a kind of herd immunity; by encouraging themselves and each other to reject such imposed oppressive group identities with an eye to flourishing, black men can create a social space wherein they are free to create and explore their own social, political, and personal identities. So, in an oppressive society that seeks to deny, through its use of such reductive labels, black men full and creative individual agency, such constructive rage can be—assuming all goes well, in accordance with practical wisdom—conducive to social flourishing.

Of course, like any virtue, political or otherwise, anger in response to oppression can go wrong; it can quickly become a vice if deployed poorly (either too much, or too little, or in the wrong manner, or at the wrong target). Vicious anger, unsurprisingly, can have many of the negative effects described by Nussbaum (2016, introduction) and others, including negative external effects such as wanton violence and lopsided retribution, and negative internal effects such as bitterness and an all-consuming vengefulness. (At the other end, of course, are negative external effects such as complicity in oppression and being, for lack of a better word, a pushover, and negative internal effects such as repression, disassociation, and apathy.) But we should not confuse the vicious extremes of anger for the whole of anger; rather, we should recognize that there is a sentiment in the middle, between the two extremes, that is both instrumentally valuable and politically virtuous. In the ideal case, constructive rage not only helps propel the fight for justice by acting as a vaccine against political cynicism and despair, but also promotes mental, emotional, and social flourishing for those who must live their lives in the midst of an oppressive society. Ultimately, I maintain that we should never cease to be angry, so long as oppression remains in the world. We should rage (constructively) against the machine.

NOTES

1. Nussbaum (2016, introduction, chapter 2) provides a comprehensive list of the players in this debate.

2. My thanks to Court Lewis, Kiran Bhardwaj, Colin Lewis, and the participants at the 2019 Concerned Philosophers for Peace conference for their insightful and very helpful comments. Any remaining mistakes or errors are my own.

3. For more on how sociopolitical context determines meaning, see Haslanger (2017, 1–22).

4. Of course, social meanings and group identities are constructed; but this is not to say either that they are not real or that they are under our control. They are constructed by historical-sociopolitical relations, and as such, are both real and not subject to direct control. As Catharine MacKinnon points out, the reality of one's social identity inevitably hits one like a bridge abutment at sixty miles per hour, regardless of what one does to try to avoid it (1989, 123).

5. Young distinguishes between backward-looking (liability) responsibility, which considers who or what is morally to blame for the wrong/injustice/oppression in question, and forward-looking (political) responsibility, which considers who or what bears responsibility for fixing or solving that wrong/injustice/oppression. As Young convincingly argues, sometimes these kinds of responsibility come apart (2011).

6. To be clear, I am not sure that interpersonal anger is always bad or normatively problematic. While I am sympathetic to Noddings' arguments especially, I do not have a firm stance on the anti-anger debate in the moral realm.

7. In fact, on occasion, anger can teach us that we value something: I discover someone is my friend when I grow angry at others teasing him, I learn that I care

about the oppression of war refugees, and thus value their lives and well-being, when the picture of a refugee child's body washed ashore fills me with fury.

8. It is an interesting question whether it is possible to evaluate something as good, and yet not care (emotionally speaking) what happens to it. I will not try to answer this question here. I take it as given that, in most ordinary cases, evaluating something as good either leads to, or includes, caring about what happens to it. Anger is the sentiment that arises when some wronging happens to it.

9. hooks (1995, 4) notes that oppressive interpersonal interactions can often be the catalyst for such constructive rage. As she points out, though, the initial spark or inferno of anger at an oppressive interaction "must be tempered" by a clear-eyed engagement with, and understanding of, the collective black struggle for self-determination. Thus, the initial flash of anger, when all goes well, is developed into constructive rage.

10. Of course, people do get angry at inanimate objects and phenomena all of the time—I certainly do not want to deny that! However, I do think such anger is nearer to the "blind rage" end of the spectrum, and so approaches being vicious rather than virtuous.

11. Incidentally, I think that institutions themselves can also respond purposively to anger, and so it is fitting to get angry at institutions directly, as well. However, I do not lean on this claim in this chapter, and so will not rehearse the argument here. For this argument, see Kling (2019, chapter 5).

12. The exception to this general rule is transition-anger, which Nussbaum admits may not really be a species of anger at all (2016, 30–31, 36, chapter 7).

REFERENCE LIST

Alexander, Michelle. 2011. *The New Jim Crow: Mass Incarceration in the Age of Colorblindness*. New York: The New Press.

Annas, Julia. 2011. *Intelligent Virtue*. New York: Oxford University Press.

Aristotle. 1999. *Nicomachean Ethics*. Translated with an introduction by Terence Irwin. Indianapolis: Hackett Publishing.

Beauvoir, Simone de. 2011. *The Second Sex*. Translated by Constance Borde and Sheila Malovany Chevallier. New York: Vintage Books.

Boxill, Bernard. 1972. "The Morality of Reparation." *Social Theory and Practice* 2 (1): 113–123.

Bruckmüller, Susanne, Michelle Ryan, Floor Rink, and S. Alexander Haslam. 2014. "Beyond the Glass Ceiling: The Glass Cliff and Its Lessons for Organizational Policy." *Social Issues and Policy Review* 8 (1): 202–232.

Callard, Agnes. 2018. "The Reason to Be Angry Forever." In *The Moral Psychology of Anger*, edited by Myisha Cherry and Owen Flanagan, 123–138. London: Rowman & Littlefield International.

Crenshaw, Kimberlé. 1991. "Mapping the Margins: Intersectionality, Identity Politics, and Violence Against Women of Color." *Stanford Law Review* 43 (6): 1241–1299.

Cudd, Ann E. 1994. "Oppression by Choice." *Journal of Social Philosophy* 25 (S1): 22–44.

Frye, Marilyn. 1983. "Oppression." *The Politics of Reality: Essays in Feminist Theory*. New York: Crossing Press.

Haslanger, Sally. 2004. "Oppressions: Racial and Other." In *Racism in Mind*, edited by Michael P. Levine and Tamas Pataki, 97–123. Ithaca: Cornell University Press.

Haslanger, Sally. 2017. "Racism, Ideology and Social Movements." *Res Philosophica* 94 (1): 1–22.

hooks, bell. 1995. "Killing Rage: Militant Resistance." In *Killing Rage: Ending Racism*. New York: Holt Paperbacks.

Kadi, Joanna. 2006. "Stupidity 'Deconstructed.'" In *Theorizing Feminisms: A Reader*, edited by Elizabeth Hackett and Sally Haslanger, 40–50. Oxford: Oxford University Press.

Kittay, Eva Feder. 1999. *Love's Labor: Essays on Women, Equality, and Dependency*. New York: Routledge.

Kling, Jennifer. 2019. "Who's Responsible for Refugee Justice?" In *War Refugees: Risk, Justice, and Moral Responsibility*. Lanham, MD: Lexington Books.

LeBar, Mark. 2013. "Virtue and Politics." In *The Cambridge Companion to Virtue Ethics*, edited by Daniel C. Russell, 265–289. Cambridge: Cambridge University Press.

Lewis, Court D. 2019. "Forgiveness as a Right? Author Meets Critics: Court D. Lewis, Author of *Repentance and the Right to Forgiveness*, Meets Critics Gregory L. Bock, David Boersema, and Jennifer Kling." *The Acorn: Philosophical Studies in Pacifism and Nonviolence* 19 (1): 19–41.

Lorde, Audre. 1997. "The Uses of Anger." *Women's Studies Quarterly* 25 (1/2): 278–285.

MacKinnon, Catharine. 1989. *Towards a Feminist Theory of the State*. Cambridge, MA: Harvard University Press.

McRae, Emily. 2018. "Anger and the Oppressed: Indo-Tibetan Buddhist Perspectives." In *The Moral Psychology of Anger*, edited by Myisha Cherry and Owen Flanagan, 105–122. London: Rowman & Littlefield International.

Noddings, Nel. 1998. "Thinking, Feeling, and Moral Imagination." *Midwest Studies in Philosophy* 22 (1): 135–145.

Nussbaum, Martha C. 2007. *Frontiers of Justice: Disability, Nationality, Species Membership*. Cambridge, MA: Harvard University Press.

Nussbaum, Martha C. 2016. *Anger and Forgiveness: Resentment, Generosity, Justice*. Oxford: Oxford University Press. Google Books.

Seneca. 1928. "De Ira." In *Moral Essays, Volume 1*. Translated by John W. Basore. Cambridge, MA: Harvard University Press.

Strawson, P. F. 1962. "Freedom and Resentment." *Proceedings of the British Academy* 48: 1–25.

Wasserstrom, Richard. 1977. "Racism, Sexism, and Preferential Treatment." *UCLA Law Review* 24 (3): 581–622.

Young, Iris Marion. 2011. *Responsibility for Justice*. Oxford: Oxford University Press.

Chapter 10

Feminism and Anger

Danielle Poe

In 1981, at the National Women's Studies Association's annual meeting, Audre Lorde gave the keynote address titled "The Uses of Anger." In this address, she listed the many ways in which white women cause and perpetuate the suffering and injustice against women of color, and she counsels women of color to use anger to begin the process of creating change:

> Anger is loaded with information and energy. When I speak of women of Color, I do not only mean Black women. We are also Asian American, Caribbean, Chicana, Latina, Hispanic, Native American, and we have a right to each of our names. The woman of Color who charges me with rendering her invisible by assuming that her struggles with racism are identical with my own has something to tell me that I had better learn from, lest we both waste ourselves fighting the truths between us . . . It wastes energy I need to join with her. And yes, it is very difficult to stand still and to listen to another woman's voice delineate an agony I do not share, or even one in which I may have participated . . . The angers between women will not kill us if we can articulate them with precision, if we listen to the content of what is said with at least as much intensity as defend ourselves from the manner of saying. (8–9)

Almost forty years later, feminists continue to struggle to understand our own anger, to harness that anger, to listen to others' anger, and to build solidarity with women who are angry at us. For this chapter, I will consider the anger and sources of anger that occur between white women and women of other races. While the tension between races is an important aspect of human identity to consider, I also recognize that this chapter is leaving aside other important relationships of privilege, including class, sexual orientation, gender-identity, religion, and disability. Nevertheless, I hope this chapter and the lessons that I draw are applicable since these other relationships of privilege and power may also be interrupted through the expressions of anger, listening to that anger, and building solidarity.

THE CALL TO ACKNOWLEDGE RACISM

Most of this chapter will rely on work by feminists and their analysis of anger. However, I want to begin with a piece that explores sexism and racism and in doing so invites a path forward for those of us who need to hear hard truths about the impact of our actions. So, I will begin with a letter written for *The New York Times, Opinionator Blog*. The letter is "Dear White America" by the philosopher George Yancy. In this letter, Yancy recognizes his own contributions to institutional sexism, and then pushes his white readers to recognize our racism. Yancy begins by confessing that he is sexist:

> As a sexist, I have failed women. I have failed to speak out when I should have. I have failed to engage critically and extensively their pain and suffering in my writing. I have failed to transcend the rigidity of gender roles in my own life. I have failed to challenge those poisonous assumptions that women are "inferior" to men or to speak out loudly in the company of male philosophers who believe that feminist philosophy is just a nonphilosophical fad. I have been complicit with, and have allowed myself to be seduced by, a country that makes billions of dollars from sexually objectifying women, from pornography, commercials, video games, to Hollywood movies. I am not innocent. (Yancy 2015)

Yancy's confession is significant because it calls on all of his readers to recognize that in U.S. society, those of us with privilege participate in sexism and racism by virtue of the structures in place from which we benefit and by virtue of standing aside or staying silent when we recognize the injustice. His confession is also important because it gives the reader a framework to analyze the many forms of injustice that are part of our lives not because we choose them but because we fail to think about and question our privilege. By leading with this self-critique, Yancy prepares the way for his readers to really listen to the pain and suffering that we cause by our thoughtlessness and inaction. And, once we have truly heard that suffering, we are called to find ways to resist inequity.

Yancy uses the letter to call white readers to engage in our own critique even as he anticipates our defensiveness: "Don't hide from your responsibility. Rather, begin, right now, to practice being vulnerable" (Yancy 2015). Notice that he links the ideas of shelter, responsibility, and vulnerability. First, we can think about the "shelter" that being white provides. That is, as a white person I have a choice to think about race and racism or to take cover and pretend that not-thinking about it, or being color blind, means that I am treating everyone equally. Next, we can think about "responsibility"; that is, as a white person I am responsible for confronting my racism or for perpetuating racism by ignoring it. Finally, Yancy asks his white readers to "practice being vulnerable." We are called to leave our shelter, recognize our privilege, critique our inaction, and to act in ways to create structural and personal change. The need to be vulnerable will be particularly important in the next section when we analyze the just expressions of anger from women of color who have been oppressed by white women.

Yancy's call to be vulnerable and to resist taking shelter is a theme that he repeats throughout his letter. He invites his readers to explore vulnerability by calling out our resistances and exposing them as a means of hiding and avoiding responsibility:

> Again, take a deep breath. Don't tell me about how many black friends you have. Don't tell me that you are married to someone of color. Don't tell me that you voted for Obama. Don't tell me that *I'm* the racist. Don't tell me that you don't see color. Don't tell me that I'm blaming whites for everything. To do so is to hide yet again. You may have never used the N-word in your life, you may hate the K.K.K., but that does not mean that you don't harbor racism and benefit from racism. (Yancy 2015)

Yancy anticipates his white readers' defensiveness and resistance to the idea that they could possibly be racist since they are not intentionally racist and are likely opposed to outright expressions of racism (e.g., Klan rallies, hate speech, racial slurs). No matter how vigorously white people object to the label of racism, the infrastructure in which we live perpetuates racism, and the failure to recognize those structures, to call them racist, and to dismantle them makes white people racist. While some white people may recognize that structural racism exists, many do not make the further connection of acknowledging that their own privilege is a result of those structures. In the next section, I will explain why anger is an important tool for uncovering racism and exposing the connection between white privilege and institutional injustice.

COST OF PRIVILEGE

One of the most important insights from Yancy's letter is that sexism and racism are not unfortunate circumstances that happen to people; sexism and racism are connected to acts and failures to act by those with privilege. This connection becomes clear in *Rage Becomes Her*, when Soraya Chemaly recounts a story about her preschool daughter's experience of anger when a male classmate continually destroyed a castle she was building. The daughter was understandably angry at her classmate for his acts, but what is most powerful in Chemaly's account is her description of the boy's parents and their failure to act:

> They sympathized with my daughter's frustration but only to the extent that they sincerely hoped she found a way to feel better. They didn't seem to "see" that she was angry, nor did they understand that her anger was a demand on their son in direct relation to their own inaction. (2018, 3)

While the boy was the primary cause of the anger, the parents had power to intercede and to correct the behavior. But, instead of doing so they encouraged the girl to react differently and became a secondary cause of anger. Chemaly also emphasizes that her daughter's anger was an appeal, or a demand for those with power to act. Her anger is a moral demand, not an emotional appeal.

This story is important because it illustrates the distinction between anger and displeasure that Marilyn Frye writes about in "A Note on Anger": "The frustrating situations which generate anger, as opposed to those which merely make you displeased or depressed, are those in which you see yourself not simply as obstructed or hindered, but as wronged" (1983, 85). Anger, then, is more than a feeling. It is a claim about one's dignity and humanity. She describes a very problematic response to anger in which a woman expresses anger at a man, and he reacts by "calling her a crazy bitch" (89). She explains that the man refuses to accept or challenge the claims implied by her anger. Instead his response is such that "the woman's anger is left as just a burst of expression of individual feeling. As a social act, an act of communication, it just doesn't happen" (89). Even worse, the dismissal of the woman's anger employs ableist privilege to dismiss the validity of her claim.

In both of these examples, anger is used to reveal an injustice and to make a claim on the observer to correct the wrong, to form an alliance with the wronged. But, in both cases the observer dismisses the claim and reduces the claimant to someone with an individual, emotional problem. Another way to think about this disconnect is that they are failures to connect the wrong to their actions and to examine the ways in which their behavior allows the wrong to persist. Instead, the anger is understood as a problem for the person experiencing it and for that person to correct. This feminist insight means that it is important for feminist philosophers to be clear about our particular identity and the privileges or oppressions implied by that particularity. For example, I am a cisgender, white, middle-class, American, straight woman. While I face institutional sexism, the other aspects of my identity lead to structural privilege, and those benefits come at a cost to others. When I am confronted with others' anger and frustration, I should work to understand how I contribute to the injustice instead of feeling sympathy for them and hoping that they can take actions to make themselves feel better.

While the above examples illustrate the ways in which white people respond to anger by ignoring their responsibility for it or by turning it back on the angry person, another common response from white women is to dissolve into tears. This particular response may seem annoying at worst and sympathetic at best, but in reality it may be even more damaging than the earlier responses. Shay Stewart Bouley posts about this in her blog, titled "Weapon of Lass Destruction: The Tears of a White Woman":

> Perhaps the only thing deadlier to a Black person's soul and well-being than actually being killed or incarcerated are the tears of a white woman—among other weaponized emotions. White women's emotions, particularly their tears, have taken countless lives over the generations. These tears and emotions are weapons of mass destruction and we rarely allows [*sic*] ourselves the chance to have an honest conversation about it. White women's tears kill the soul, they make you doubt yourself and your right to exist, they render you voiceless because an emotionally distraught white woman becomes the priority in whatever space she is in. It doesn't matter if you are right—once her tears are activated, you cease to exist. And few things bring other white people—especially men, and sometimes no matter how misogynist they are—to a white woman's defense than her declaring that she is feeling hurt, sad or discomfited by the words, arguments or actions (no matter how reasonable or nonviolent) of a Black person. (2018, 2)

Bouley's analysis is important because she draws out the impact of white women's tears within a conversation on race. If a white woman is challenged or confronted with the effects of racism on people, she may think that she's being empathetic to others' plight when she cries and demonstrates her profound distress. But, what in fact happens is that she centers her experience within the conversation; what's important is no longer the racism and its effects, but rather the emotional well-being of the white woman. Hence, her tears re-inscribe and reinforce her power and her privilege. Further, the person who has caused the tears becomes the harming party and can be stereotyped as the angry black woman instead of being heard. And, most disturbing of all is the rush to protect white women, which has resulted in violence and death for those who were thought to have upset a white woman.

In "White Women, Please Don't Expect Me to Wipe Away Your Tears," Stacy Patton also takes white women to task for shifting the focus of discussion about race and racism to their emotional response:

> It's stressful enough that Black people have to see endless posts [on Facebook] documenting racism, our fears, and stress related to the fact that a Black person is killed by the police every 28 hours. So when our White friends venture into our space to challenge our lived reality with their subjective responses, we're left stewing in frustration. Why do some White women feel the need to express their disappointment and emotional pushback, and contest the points Black people are making? It's as if they're trying to overpower our reality, our pain, and our anger with their own. (Patton 2014)

Patton's post brings out another important detail about white women's emotional pushback to black women's lived experience: energy that would otherwise be spent ministering to their own grief and fear and generating responses to racism shifts to educating and soothing white women. What both Patton and Shay are asking of their white readers (particularly white women readers) is to stay in the conversation and to truly listen. They are asking white women to set aside their own experiences and responses in order to allow those who are harmed to express that harm and to make a moral claim on the listener. Once white women hear that moral claim, they must then find ways to build solidarity and to resist their own racism.

In *Good and Mad: The Revolutionary Power of Women's Anger*, Rebecca Traister characterizes the needed response in this way:

> We can change [the system built to repress women's ire and power] by doing what the world does *not* do: by acknowledging, paying attention to, respecting, and not shying away from *other* women's anger. Seek it out, notice it, ask women what makes them angry and then listen to them when they tell you. If part of what they're angry at is you, take it in, acknowledge how their frustrations might mirror your own, even if they are refracted at you. (2018, 245)

Traister acknowledges in her work the difficulty involved in what she's asking of her reader: seeking out women's anger, particularly if that anger is directed at me, but the cost of not doing so is to allow divisions between women to continue and to allow current power structures and injustice to thrive.

ANZALDÚA AND ANGER

When white women take the time to really hear from others about their intersectional experiences, we begin to take the first steps toward solidarity and more just relationships. In this section, I'll focus on Gloria Anzaldúa's work from *Borderlands/La Frontera: The New Mestiza*, in which she conveys her frustration and anger with white U.S. society and the ways in which her identity is managed, stunted, and shamed.

Anzaldúa's work is especially powerful for describing the importance of language for identity and consequently the damage that happens when language is suppressed. She describes the many languages she speaks and the ways in which her Chicano experience, language, and identity are attacked when her language is denigrated, "Ethnic identity is twin skin to linguistic identity—I am my language" (Anzaldúa 1987, 59). And, in her description she draws out that identity for her is more than speaking Spanish or English, but rather it's the ability to move between the languages that form her identity:

> Until I am free to write bilingually and to switch codes without having always to translate, while I still have to speak English or Spanish when I would rather speak Spanglish, and as long as I have to accommodate the English speakers rather than having them accommodate me, my tongue will be illegitimate. (59)

To carve out space to be who she is in spite of cultural pressures to translate her thoughts for English speakers and to adapt to the expectations to be polite, Anzaldúa writes that blending Spanish and English disrupts the power of those who insist on English as the dominant language:

> We know what it is to live under the hammer blow of the dominant *notreamericano* culture. But more than we count the blows, we count the days the weeks the years the centuries the eons until the white laws and commerce and customs will rot in the deserts they've created, lie bleached. (63–64)

Amanda Espinosa-Aguilar's analysis of the anger in Anzaldúa's work reveals the connection between anger and transformation that is available to us if we are willing to hear and act when anger reveals our complicity with injustice: "By using angry rhetoric in her works, Anzaldúa intentionally disrupts readers' *desconocimientos* (avoidance/ignorance), thereby challenging their worldviews. Those readers who embrace and accept her anger are often persuaded of the moral obligation to join Anzaldúa, as agents, in building coalitions" (2005, 228).

Espinosa-Aguilar pays particular attention to Anzaldúa's critique of white women who force women of color into silence because "our white allies or colleagues get a hurt look in their eyes when we bring up their racism in their interactions with us and quickly change the subject" (quoting Anzaldúa, 231). In response to this passage from Anzaldúa, Espinosa-Aguilar writes: "Anzaldúa shatters white women's illusion of sisterhood, exposing the complacency on which it relies" (231). In conclusion, Espinosa-Aguilar writes:

> Angry rhetoric, then functions not to divide or evoke defense, which is the typical response and expectation of anger, but paradoxically to unite the actors experiencing it. By actively engaging or affecting readers with explicit expressions of strong emotion, by making readers struggle with the ideas on emotional as well as intellectual levels, Anzaldúa inspires praxis. (232)

The message for white women is clear: we must recognize that when we make being liked our highest priority, we are complicit in oppressing others, especially women of color. The desire to be likeable has led us to respond to just anger with tears and defensiveness, which in turn silences the very women with whom we think we are allied.

ALLIANCES

For white women who want to do the hard work of becoming an anti-racist, they must take deliberate action. The first step has been modeled well by Robin DiAngelo in *White Fragility* and Debby Irving in *Waking Up White*. In both of these books, the authors engage in a deep dive into their own formation as white racists, and they engage in significant work to understand the history of racism in the United States. These books are important because they place the burden of education about race and racism on white women instead of on women of color who are already doing the daily work of confronting racism. These books are also important because they define racism as present whenever the effects are racist, regardless of the intention. DiAngelo describes the work in which she engages in the following way:

> When I start from the premise that *of course* I have been thoroughly socialized into the racist culture in which I was born, I no longer need to expend energy denying that fact. I am eager—even excited—to identify my inevitable collusion so that I can figure out how to stop colluding! Denial and the defensiveness that is needed to maintain it is exhausting. (2018, 150)

While these books can play an important role for white women to begin to come to terms with our own racism, we must also guard against centering white experience in the fight against racism. Thus, I will return to the work of Stacey Patton, Vanessa Echols, and Audre Lord for guidance on what a true alliance would entail.

Patton's insights in the previous section were important for understanding the toll that white women's defensiveness and tears cause black women. And, in her refusal to provide comfort for those who perpetuate racism, she also provides guidance for white friends who may want to help:

> Stop asking us [Black people] to respond and navigate your digital attacks and meltdowns. We can't afford to use the energy we need to find solutions to save our own lives while arguing with or trying to educate you when you push back with resistance to even acknowledging what is real and true in our lives . . . We need you to listen, rather than trying to assert dominance or challenging us to prove our worth. We need you to stop deflecting the hard conversation and join us in trying to have it in an honest, authentic, and respectful way. (Patton 2014)

Patton's boundaries around what she's willing to tolerate include an invitation to conversation. But, this is not an invitation to a conversation that will be easy for either party. Instead the conversation will require vulnerability and trust on Patton's part because she will be sharing her anger and her grief. And, this conversation requires her listener to also be vulnerable and to hear how the impact of her privilege and actions lands regardless of intent.

The emphasis on conversations about race as a starting point for resisting racism is central to the work in which Vanessa Echols engages. Echols hosts a podcast, *Colorblind: Race across Generations*, in which she and guests explore issues around race. This podcast has engaged in conversations on everything from the ways in which young adults today experience race to the disproportionate mortality rates during childbirth when comparing outcomes for white and black mothers. In a recent podcast, Echols interviews Minister Valerie Parson, senior minister of Unity Church of Melbourne, and Jennifer Tomlinson, professor at Valencia College West Campus in Orlando, FL. They discuss what it means for someone to be a racial ally. Their insights can help us to map our actions and responses to the rampant racism in U.S. society.

In this episode, Tomlinson offers the following advice to white people who want to become a racial ally:

> The first step is to get educated and not to rely on people of color to do the education work for you. You have to take the courage to want to be informed, and that could be through formal education. Through school, maybe take a couple of courses that are different. Or, it could be informally finding people that you can have those crucial conversations with so that you can be more cognizant, more educated, hopefully more enlightenment. I always say when I talk to students: enlightenment comes when you're not just getting the knowledge but internally something has shifted, something has changed. And that internal work is so vital because once your frameworks have shifted now you're ready to do work or to teach others or to go back out. (8:40–9:40)

Tomlinson's comments are helpful in part because they are incredibly concrete and practical. Allies can become educated on their own through a variety of ways: taking classes, reading books and articles, listening to podcasts, attending public lectures, watching documentaries. But, she is also addressing a critical state of mind that takes place when one becomes educated on racial justice: a desire for change, a desire for justice. These desires are much more than wanting to be thought of as good and nice, wanting to avoid being called a racist. Instead, the desires she describes are about becoming someone who actively works to undo structures of injustice.

Tomlinson then addresses the importance of having racial allies: "Why is that important? People that are disenfranchised cannot do the work by themselves. They need people who have the access, or resources, or are in the right spaces to be advocates for them, to be allies for them, to be their voices" (16–16:20). And, she adds to this idea when she explains that "we're dismantling social systems that involve everyone so we have to work together in order to break those systems down" (18:40–18:50). Through the work of racial alliances, white women can seek out the sources of anger that other women have expressed, can recognize the role that their privilege plays in creating the injustice, and can then build systems in which privilege is dismantled.

In concluding this chapter, I want to return to Lorde's work to emphasize again the role that anger plays as a force for change:

> Every woman has a well-stocked arsenal of anger potentially useful against those oppressions, personal and institutional, which brought that anger into being. Focused with precision it can become a powerful source of energy serving progress and change. And when I speak of change, I do not mean a simple switch of positions or temporary lessening of tensions, nor the ability to smile or feel good. I am speaking of a basic and radical alteration in all those assumptions underlining our lives. (1981, 280)

Lorde's insight into anger as a force of change centers around the observation that anger supplies energy. We cannot overemphasize the energy needed to fight systemic racism. When we think about the ways in which racism permeates popular culture, the legal system, education, housing, and finances, we see how much work must be done to expose privilege and to create new models. When we think about the ways in which privilege is invisible to so many white people and the many micro-aggressions that ignorance breeds, we see how exhausting the work of unraveling racism can be. When that exhaustion can be overcome by anger, as a racial ally we should seek out that anger and let that anger alter every assumption of U.S. society.

In closing, Lorde reminds us that "the angers between women will not kill us if we can articulate them with precision, if we listen to the content of what is said with at least as much intensity as we defend ourselves from the manner of saying. Anger is a source of empowerment we must not fear to tap for energy rather than guilt" (283). The work in front of us is to work together as women, fueled by the energy of anger.

REFERENCE LIST

Anzaldúa, Gloria. 1987. *Borderlands/La Frontera: The New Mestiza*. San Francisco: Aunt Lute Books.

Bouley, Shay Stewart. 2018. "Weapon of Lass Destruction: The Tears of a White Woman." *Black Girl in Maine*. https://www.blackgirlinmaine.com/black-life-in-maine/.

Chemaly, Soraya. 2018. *Rage Becomes Her: The Power of Women's Anger*. New York: Atria Books.

DiAngelo, Robin. 2018. *White Fragility: Why It's So Hard for White People to Talk About Racism*. Boston: Beacon Press.

Echols, Vanessa. 2019. "Racial Allies." In *Colorblind: Race Across Generations*. Cox Media Group, August 6, 2019.

Espinosa-Aguilar, Amanda. 2005. "Radical Rhetoric: Anger, Activism and Change." In *EntreMundos/Among Worlds: New Perspectives on Gloria Anzaldúa*, edited by AnaLouise Keating, 228–232. New York: Palgrave MacMillan.

Frye, Marilyn. 1983. *The Politics of Reality: Essays in Feminist Theory*. Trumansburg, NY: The Crossing Press.

Irving, Debby. 2014. *Waking Up White: And Finding Myself in the Story of Race*. Cambridge, MA: Elephant Room Press.

Lorde, Audre. 1981. "The Uses of Anger." *National Women's Studies Quarterly* 9, no. 3: 7–10.

Patton, Stacey. 2014. "White Women, Please Don't Expect Me to Wipe Away Your Tears." *Dame*, December 15, 2014. https://www.damemagazine.com/2014/12/15/white-women-please-dont-expect-me-wipe-away-your-tears/.

Traister, Rebecca. 2018. *Good and Mad: The Revolutionary Power of Women's Anger*. New York: Simon & Schuster.

Yancy, George. 2015. "Dear White People." *New York Times*, December 24, 2015. https://opinionator.blogs.nytimes.com/2015/12/24/dear-white-america/.

Chapter 11

Anger and Punishment

Zachary Hoskins

In recent years, a critique of retributivist theories of punishment has gained prominence that focuses on retributivism's links to anger. Retributivism refers to a family of views united by the claim that punishment is an intrinsically appropriate, because deserved, response to wrongdoing. These views are typically contrasted with consequentialist accounts, according to which punishment is justified solely in virtue of its contribution to some valuable consequences. The anger-based critique of retributivism has been developed in somewhat different forms, most notably by Martha Nussbaum (2016) and Joshua Greene (2008). The gist is that retributivist theories are essentially rationalizations of retributive emotions, especially anger, and that anger is an unsavory basis for making decisions about whether and how to punish; thus retributivist theories are not well supported. Nussbaum and Greene each conclude that punishment should be grounded in consequentialist considerations instead.

This chapter first briefly surveys some ways in which anger may be relevant to a theory of punishment. Then, in the bulk of the chapter, I focus on anger as the basis of critiques of retributivism, and I consider two potential lines of defense open to retributivists: they might defend anger as a justifiable basis for a theory of punishment, or, alternatively, they might contend that retributivism need not be merely a rationalization of intuitions driven by anger. I contend that either of these lines of response has promise, and that anger-based critiques of retributivism are less damaging than what their proponents claim.

To lay my own cards on the table at the outset, I am not a retributivist. Rather, I endorse a hybrid, or mixed, account of punishment, according to which the compelling rationale for the practice is its contribution to public safety and security, but the practice should be constrained in part by retributivist considerations of desert (Hoskins 2011A). Thus in what follows my interest is not to provide an extended defense of some favored retributivist view against the anger-based critique. Rather, my aim is to sketch various lines of response that are open to retributivists in response to this critique. For although I do not endorse retributivism, I regard it as a formidable theory (or, more precisely, family of theories), one that cannot be dismissed as easily as the anger-based critique would suggest.

ANGER'S RELEVANCE TO A THEORY OF PUNISHMENT

Perhaps the most straightforward way we might associate anger with punishment is that anger can motivate punishment as a form of payback, or retribution. Aquinas wrote that an angry person desires to punish as a means of "just vengeance" (2014, I-II 46.6). More recently, a host of psychological studies have concluded that anger plays a motivational role in people's decisions to punish those who harm them[1] and also those who harm others.[2] It is this connection of anger to retributive punishment that informs the line of criticism to be examined in subsequent sections. First, though, in this section I want briefly to consider a range of other ways in which anger may have implications for punishment. My aim in this section is not to evaluate each argument discussed here, but rather to give a sense of the variety of respects in which considerations of anger might bear on normative theorizing about punishment.

The question of punishment's justification—what has been termed "the problem of punishment"[3]—is actually better understood as a cluster of questions. Arguably the central question, and the one that has received the most philosophical attention, is what we might call the question of punishment's in-principle permissibility: What makes it morally permissible to treat people who commit crimes in ways (e.g., locking them in cells for extended periods) that would normally be morally impermissible? The retributivist answer to this question is that offenders deserve punishment, and, as we will see later, critics charge that this appeal to desert is essentially a rationalization of anger or similar emotions. But anger might figure in a consequentialist answer, as well.

On a consequentialist account, punishment's justification depends on the consequences of the practice. Anger might be said to count among its positive or negative consequences. On one hand, people who are angered by the commission of an offense may therefore derive utility in knowing that the offender receives punishment. Victims or their friends and loved ones may be particularly angered by an offense and take satisfaction in its punishment.

But other members of the community may also gain utility from punishment of wrongdoing. Jeremy Bentham wrote that "a pleasure of the dissocial kind is produced almost of course, on the part of all persons in whose breasts the offence has excited the sentiment of ill-will," where anger was for Bentham a particular type of ill will (1996, 180, 111). Thus punishment may generate utility for those who are angry about an offense. If so, then at least on hedonistic utilitarian varieties of consequentialism, the fact that punishment helps to quench the anger of victims or other community members would count among its positive consequences. On the other hand, if punishment tends, as some studies have suggested, to foster anger in those punished, and as a result they are more likely to engage in violent behavior, then this would count against the practice in utilitarian calculations.[4]

In addition to the question of punishment's in-principle permissibility, another question involves what severity of sentence is appropriate in particular cases. Here again, anger might be relevant in different ways. In some jurisdictions, a person who kills while in a state of extreme anger motivated by an "adequate provocation" may have his sentence reduced from murder to voluntary manslaughter.[5] The rationale seems to be that a person provoked to extreme anger is less blameworthy for killing, and thus deserves a less severe punishment, than someone who is not provoked. This logic is essentially retributive in that it focuses on what degree of punishment the offender deserves.

From a utilitarian perspective, however, it might seem that a stiffer sentence would be warranted in cases of provoked anger. In particular, if punishment's utility derives chiefly from its role in helping to deter potential offenders, then it might seem that the person provoked to extreme anger would require the threat of a more severe punishment as a deterrent. As David Boonin writes:

> An angry person will be more likely to focus on the immediate satisfaction he will get from punching his provoker and less likely to focus on the long-term cost he will incur by being punished for it. If, on the other hand, a person under such provocation knew that people who punch others in the nose after being provoked receive a much greater sentence . . . he would be much more likely to be deterred. (2002, 964)

It seems counterintuitive, though, that a person who commits a crime when provoked to anger should receive a more severe sentence than a person who commits that crime in a calm, cool state. Boonin thus takes this to be one argument against utilitarian defenses of punishment (ibid., 59–60).[6]

Although punishment theorists tend to focus on severity when thinking about sentencing principles, another important question is what modes of punishment are appropriate. Here again, anger may be relevant. If certain modes of punishment tend to foster anger in those punished, and if this anger leads to violence or other negative outcomes, then at least on consequentialist accounts, this would be a strike against such forms of punishment. Studies have found, for example, that incarceration can generate anger, stress, and frustration among prisoners. Lorna Rhodes's research on prisoners in maximum-security units in Washington state found a common refrain that the confinement conditions fostered anger. As one prisoner told Rhodes:

> There's a big part of the day with nothing to do. Anger does build up. I don't know how to put it into words. Most of us have an anger problem, but we have no security to express it. We don't trust the guards, and if we go to psych we have to keep our guard up. Anger just boils up. (2004, 25)

In another study, prisoners in a medium-security prison in England similarly reported that lack of mental stimulation caused anger and frustration. As one prisoner said:

> Not letting me get to education, not giving me a chance to work, not giving me a chance to do anything . . . you build up anger, you know what I mean . . . It's going to release one day, it's just building up inside you and you got to hold it down, hold it down, hold it down. (Nurse et al. 2003, 2)

For consequentialist accounts, imprisonment's tendency to foster anger in those punished, and the potential of this anger to motivate further violence, will be relevant to assessment of this mode of punishment. It may also be relevant for retributivist accounts, at least those that characterize punishment as the deserved communication of censure. Antony Duff contends that part of what is involved in communicating deserved censure for wrongdoing is urging the offender to come to see that what he has done is wrong.[7] If imprisonment tends to foster anger and frustration in prisoners rather than reflection and repentance, then at least according to this version of communicative retributivism, imprisonment appears a poorly suited mode of punishment to convey the deserved message of censure.

Beyond questions of whether punishment is in principle permissible, and what severity or modes of punishment are appropriate, a further question that has received somewhat less attention from philosophers focuses on whether the state, in particular, is justified in punishing. That is, why is it the state's right, rather than the right of individual people, to inflict punishment?[8] For at least one proposed answer to this question, considerations of anger are central. Lisa Perkins offers a utilitarian account according to which state punishment plays a vital role by preventing acts of private vengeance motivated by anger. Perkins writes:

> It was observed [by legal historians] at an early date that whenever an injury was performed by one subject to another, the injured subject was likely to perform an injury to the injured, or, if he was unable to, his family or friends or community would perform one for him. Further, it was observed that, if unchecked by authorities, the retaliatory injury would be greater than the one originally dealt, and would be followed in turn by greater retaliatory injuries upon the retaliator. Thus the first breach of the peace called forth more and more violence, until both sides in the private war were exhausted and depleted. Under these conditions, any legal device which stops the bloodshed has an excellent Utilitarian justification. (1970, 56)[9]

Perkins's account doesn't specify what sort of sentencing principles are called for by this utilitarian justification. It may be that in order for state punishment to serve this utilitarian purpose of stopping the spiral of anger-driven vengeance, criminal sentences must themselves be perceived by community members to be meting out payback (albeit in a proportionate, nonarbitrary way). If so, then Perkins's utilitarian rationale for state punishment may require that sentencing be governed by retributivist principles. Alternatively, it may be that simply having a state institution of punishment is sufficient to satisfy angry individuals that they do not need to seek vengeance; in this case, either consequentialist or retributivist sentencing principles may adequately stop the cycle of vengeance and escalating violence.

Anger may be relevant, then, to a normative account of punishment in a variety of ways. Recent philosophical discussion of anger and punishment has centered, however, on a critique of retributivist theories as rationalizations of anger. In the remainder of this chapter, we will consider prominent versions of this critique followed by possible retributivist lines of response.

RETRIBUTIVISM AND ANGER

The anger-based critique of retributivism is essentially a two-step argument: first, critics contend that anger is an unsavory basis for moral judgments generally, and for decisions about how to respond to wrongdoing in particular. Second, they argue that retributivist theories are essentially rationalizations of anger-driven intuitions. In this section, I will examine each of these claims, as developed in distinct ways by Martha Nussbaum and Joshua Greene.

Nussbaum understands the concept of anger as a painful appraisal that someone has intentionally inflicted wrongful damage on oneself or those one cares about, accompanied by a desire to seek payback (2016, 17–18). In this respect, her account follows Aristotle, who defined anger as an impulse "to a conspicuous revenge for a conspicuous slight directed without justification toward what concerns oneself or one's friends" (1984B, II.2 1378a31–33). Nussbaum's central critiques of anger are based on its conceptual link to payback. She contends that the idea of payback is either irrational or morally flawed. It is irrational insofar as the payback, it is hoped, will assuage the victim's pain or repair the damage done. Nussbaum describes this as "magical thinking" (2016, 25). Inflicting damage on an offender cannot cancel or repair the damage the offender has already done.

The only case in which anger-fueled retaliation may not represent this sort of magical thinking, Nussbaum argues, is when the damage to which the retaliation responds is a humiliation or diminishment of relative status. People may "care a great deal about public standing," she writes, "and they can see quite clearly that to be pushed around has indeed diminished that" (ibid., 26). In these sorts of cases, she believes that retaliation can be an effective way to restore one's relative status; it humiliates or brings the offender low, which thereby cancels one's own humiliation and restores one's own relative standing. But although retaliation in this context is not magical thinking, it is morally flawed in that it commits a "narcissistic error": it is too focused on status rankings and thus makes "the world revolve around the desire of vulnerable selves for domination and control" (ibid., 29). Thus on Nussbaum's account, retaliation is driven either by irrational, magical thinking, or by a narcissistic concern about status rankings. And because the drive to retaliate is an essential feature of anger, she concludes that we should work to rid ourselves of anger, focusing instead on personal and social welfare, and on forward-looking attitudes such as unconditional love and generosity.

Regarding the second step in the argument—that retributivist theories of punishment are essentially rationalizations of anger-based intuitions—Nussbaum acknowledges that not all retributivist theories "endorse anger or build their proposals on a validation of anger's cognitive content" (ibid., 184). But she believes even those retributivist accounts that purport to be grounded in other considerations either fall back into anger-based intuitions about payback (the "magical thinking") or ultimately are not truly retributivist after all (ibid., 184–91). Thus anger is an unappealing basis for making decisions about how to respond to wrongdoing, and theories that are properly regarded as retributivist are ultimately grounded in anger-driven intuitions.

Greene's critique of anger takes a different form. Drawing on a range of neuroimaging studies, Greene argues that two types of neural activity can be involved in moral judgments: "emotional" processes, which he associates with deontological judgments (including retributivist judgments), and more "cognitive" processes, which he associates with consequentialist judgments (2008, 40–41). Emotional processes tend to be more automatic, triggering certain types of behaviors or dispositions; cognitive processes, by contrast, are more flexible, and less likely automatically to trigger certain behaviors or dispositions (ibid.). Importantly, Greene contends that anger is an emotional process.

Greene then cites various social psychology studies indicating that people's ordinary moral judgments about punishment are retributivist, as well as studies suggesting that these ordinary judgments are based on anger-fueled intuitions (ibid., 51–54). The problem with anger as a basis for moral judgments, Greene contends, is that anger and the associated desire to retaliate evolved "as an efficient mechanism for stabilizing cooperation, both between individuals and within larger groups" (ibid., 70). If this is so, then it seems that we feel an angry urge to retaliate against wrongdoing because of the evolutionary fitness of these feelings—that is, "because of the morally irrelevant constraints placed on natural selection in designing creatures that behave in fitness-enhancing ways" (ibid., 71). It would thus be merely a coincidence if our naturally selected angry reactions tracked moral truths.

Given these worries about anger as a basis for moral judgments, the other main step of the argument, as before, is to claim that retributivist theories of punishment are essentially post hoc rationalizations of anger-fueled judgments about how to respond to wrongdoing in particular cases. Here, Greene draws on an extensive literature about the human tendency to invent rational narratives to explain behavior that is in fact driven by unconscious perceptual or emotional processes. It is well documented, he writes, that people are "irrepressible explainers and justifiers of their own behavior. Psychologists have repeatedly found that when people don't know why they're doing what they're doing, they just make up a plausible sounding story" (ibid., 61). To mention just one often cited example, an experiment asked people to choose a pair of pantyhose from among several displayed in a row. When asked to explain their choices, people cited features of the hose, such as their elasticity or sheerness. But the pairs of pantyhose were in fact identical. In reality, people had consistently chosen the pair on the right-hand side of the display (Nisbett and Wilson 1977, 231–59). If we pair the fact that our intuitions about responding to wrongdoing are driven by anger with the fact that we are prone to invent rational stories to explain our emotionally based behavior, Greene believes we arrive at an explanation for the development of retributivist theories.

Like Nussbaum, then, Greene contends that anger is a poor foundation for making decisions about whether and how to punish, and that retributivist theories are essentially rationalizations of anger in the face of wrongdoing. Both Greene and Nussbaum conclude that punishment should be governed by consequentialist principles instead. How might retributivists respond? Two broad lines of response suggest themselves: First, retributivists might come to the defense of anger as a basis for moral judgments; second, they might articulate versions of retributivism that are not merely rationalizations of angry intuitions. In the next two sections, I consider each of these strategies in turn.

VIRTUOUS ANGER

Suppose Nussbaum and Greene are right that retributivist theories of punishment are best understood as grounded in anger-fueled intuitions about payback. Could anger, contrary to their claims, actually be a legitimate basis for moral judgments, and thus for retributivist theory? Anger has had its share of philosophical defenders. Aristotle held that anger can be a virtue if expressed in appropriate circumstances and in appropriate ways (1984A, IV.5 1125b7-1126b2). David Hume similarly believed anger could be warranted in some circumstances; failure to be angry when anger is called for "may even be a proof of weakness and imbecility" (1978, III 3.3). More recent defenders of anger include Jeffrie Murphy (1988, 3–14), Zac Cogley (2014), Audre Lorde (1997, 278–85), Lisa Tessman (2005), and Nicolas Bommarito (2017, 1–27). In this section, I consider whether there might be value in anger.

More specifically, I want to focus on cases in which anger is *fitting*, to use Justin D'Arms and Dan Jacobson's term. On D'Arms and Jacobson's account, an emotion is fitting when the object of the emotion has the features that the emotion presents it as having (2010, 65–90). Thus as Cogley puts it, drawing on D'Arms and Jacobson's account, "anger is fitting for you to feel when, for example, it is directed toward a person who has wronged you out of ill will," and when the degree of your anger is "roughly proportionate to the seriousness of the wrong" (2014, 202–3). To say that anger is often fitting is not yet to say that it is morally justified all things considered (to conflate these two claims is to commit what D'Arms and Jacobson call "the moralistic fallacy" [2010]), but presumably even anger's critics can acknowledge that our anger often meets the conditions of fittingness. Indeed, Nussbaum recognizes this sort of anger, which she calls "well-grounded" (2016, 35). At any rate, in what follows, the sort of anger I am interested in is fitting anger. I want to consider whether fitting anger can have value. I focus on three types of value: motivational value, epistemic value, and expressive value.

First, defenses of virtuous anger often point to its value in helping to focus our attention on wrongdoing and to motivate us to seek justice. For example, Lorde writes:

> The angers of women can transform difference through insight into power. Anger between peers births change, not destruction, and the discomfort and

> sense of loss it causes is not fatal, but a sign of growth. My response to racism is anger. (1997, 283)

Similarly, Cogley (2014) contrasts anger with sadness and fear and writes that anger "has more beneficial motivational effects in that it moves angry people to engage with perceived wrongdoers" (209). Anger's motivational power has been on display in spring 2020, as protests have erupted in cities across the world in response to the killing of George Floyd by Minneapolis police officers and other acts of police brutality.[10] Anger seems valuable, then, insofar as it motivates people to confront and seek to end injustice.

Interestingly, Nussbaum acknowledges the positive value of this sort of anger, which she calls "transition-anger." Transition-anger sees injustice and says, "How outrageous! Something must be done about this" (Nussbaum 2016, 35). Nussbaum contends, though, that transition-anger is at most a borderline case of anger (she characterizes it as "quasi-anger"), because it does not involve "garden variety" anger's characteristic desire for payback (ibid., 35–36). In my view, anger is no less anger when it manifests in a desire to fight against or change the wrongdoing that caused it. But I don't aim to argue for this point here; I'm less interested in whether this is genuine anger or quasi-anger than whether its motivational value offers a line of defense for retributivist theories grounded in anger.

Retributivism comes in various shapes and sizes, but, as mentioned before, what unites the different versions of retributivism is the claim that punishment is justified insofar as it is an intrinsically appropriate, because deserved, response to wrongdoing. If Nussbaum and Greene are right that retributivist theories are essentially grounded in our anger in the face of wrongdoing, then what is needed is some explanation of how this anger supports the central retributivist claim. But we cannot appeal to anger's instrumental value in motivating us to confront wrongdoing as a justificatory basis for the thesis that punishment is intrinsically appropriate. Thus, insofar as anger has value in virtue of the good consequences to which it contributes, this will be the wrong sort of value on which to base retributivist theories of punishment. We would need to look elsewhere for some value of anger that might support the retributivist idea that punishment is intrinsically appropriate because people who commit crimes deserve it.

It might be objected that part of anger's value is that it motivates us not only to confront or seek to stop wrongdoing, but also to give wrongdoers their just deserts. This value initially appears more suitable to retributivist theories, given that an essential feature of these theories is the claim that punishment is intrinsically appropriate because deserved. But again, the problem with this line of thinking is that, even if giving wrongdoers their just deserts is intrinsically appropriate, anger's value in this story is still instrumental: it motivates the meting out of just deserts. To justify retributivist punishment, we need to establish that giving people their just deserts is intrinsically appropriate; anger's motivational value would not itself contribute anything to this justificatory explanation.

Perhaps, however, the relevant value of anger is epistemic rather than motivational. That is, maybe when we appropriately feel anger (that is, when our anger is fitting), this can warrant the judgment that the person who is the object of our anger deserves punishment. Michael Moore develops a similar sort of argument, though Moore focuses on the emotion of guilt as a basis of epistemic justification regarding punishment. Moore asks us to imagine how we would feel if we had committed a heinous crime. His own response, he says, would be a deep sense of guilt, and he argues that this guilt can ground justified moral judgments about the permissibility of punishing such crimes. "We should trust the judgments such imagined guilt feelings spawn because non-neurotic guilt . . . comes with good epistemic credentials" (Moore 1997, 147). Perhaps anger similarly can provide epistemic justification of judgments that punishment is deserved in response to wrongdoing.

As discussed earlier, Greene argues against this notion that anger might provide insights into moral truths about desert. It would be quite a coincidence, he contends, if our angry reactions to wrongdoing, naturally selected for their biological fitness, happened to track moral truths about just deserts (2008, 71). But there are reasons to resist Greene's coincidence argument. First, as has been widely noted, the argument appears to threaten not only retributivism and deontological theories more generally, but consequentialist theories as well.[11] For consequentialism, no less than deontology, requires a theory of value. Without an account of what is valuable, there would be no basis for assessing which consequences are better or worse than others. Theories of value, in turn, are inevitably influenced by intuitions about what is valuable, intuitions that were naturally selected for their biological fitness. Thus Greene's argument, if it succeeds, appears to undermine not only retributivism, or deontological theories more generally, but consequentialism as well.[12]

Another reason to be skeptical about Greene's argument is that it appears to rely on the premise that retributivism takes its central claim (that punishment is justified in virtue of the fact that it is an intrinsically appropriate, because deserved, response to wrongdoing) to be morally true. It would be entirely coincidental, Greene argues, if our naturally selected, anger-driven intuitions corresponded with moral truth; thus anger should not be taken to have epistemic value. Admittedly, retributivist theories have tended to endorse the central desert claim as morally true. In recent years, however, a growing number of scholars have suggested that the challenge of punishment's justification should be seen as more a problem for political philosophy than for moral philosophy.[13] What this means, at least on one common characterization of the challenge, is that rather than debating whether the polity's reasons for punishment (be they consequentialist, retributivist, or something else) are morally true, we should instead begin by asking whether these reasons are publicly justified. John Rawls wrote that in modern liberal democratic societies, whose members hold a wide range of reasonable moral and religious views, "it is unreasonable or worse to want to use the sanctions of state power to correct, or to punish, those who disagree with us" (2005, 138). For state exercises of power to be legitimate, then, they must be based not on this or that contested moral view, but rather on shared public political values—values that any reasonable member of the polity could be expected to endorse. Although Rawls himself did not write much about the institution of punishment, others have drawn on his ideas about public justification to develop accounts of punishment.[14]

My aim here is not to defend Rawlsian political liberalism; other theorists have grounded their accounts of punishment in broadly republican political theories, but they have shared with Rawlsians the view that the justification of punishment is primarily a political, rather than a moral, challenge.[15] For our purposes, the salient point is that if we take the central question to be not whether anger-based retributivist judgments are morally true but whether such judgments constitute publicly justified reasons, then the prospect that our naturally selected, anger-based judgments correspond with the shared public political values on which public justification is based need not strike us as a particularly unlikely coincidence. These shared public values, after all, are not objective moral truths existing independently of our beliefs or attitudes; rather they are *our* values, and thus they will have developed from emotions, beliefs, or attitudes that have themselves been naturally selected.

If fitting anger in response to wrongdoing is among this set of emotions, beliefs, and attitudes from which our shared public political values have developed, and if retributivism (as Nussbaum and Greene allege) is essentially grounded in this anger, then perhaps anger can provide at least some prima facie epistemic justification for retributivist judgments—not that they are morally true, but that they are publicly justified. It is a matter for debate, of course, whether fitting anger is among the emotions, beliefs, or attitudes from which our shared public political values have developed. I do not attempt to settle this question here.[16] My aim has simply been to point out that Greene's coincidence argument fails to undercut anger's epistemic value if we focus on public justification rather than moral truth.

Rather than citing anger's motivational or epistemic value, defenders might instead highlight its expressive value. An expression of fitting anger might be appropriate for its own sake, as an affirmation of the victim's worth or as a condemnation of the perpetrator's wrongdoing. Expressing anger when we are wronged may be a way of affirming our worth—our status as moral persons meriting equal respect and concern—to ourselves, to those who have wronged us, and to our community generally. Jeffrie Murphy writes that a person who did not get angry as a result of moral injuries to himself "would almost necessarily be a person lacking in self-respect" (1988, 5). Expressing anger, then, may serve to manifest this self-respect.

This is not to turn anger's expressive value into instrumental value: an affirmation of worth, on this view, is not some further valuable consequence brought about by the expression of anger; rather, the angry expression itself constitutes this affirmation. Also note that fitting anger's expressive value need not be limited to cases of wrongs to ourselves. We may also be fittingly angry when confronted with wrongdoing to our loved ones, or perhaps to those with whom we concern ourselves more generally. In such cases, expressions of anger may serve to affirm the worth of those others who were wronged.

Anger as an affirmation of status need not be narcissistic, in Nussbaum's sense of it. Nussbaum contends that anger concerned with status "converts all injuries into problems of relative position" (2016, 29). But it does not seem narcissistic to express anger in the face of moral injury as a reaffirmation of one's status as a member of the community with equal moral standing as others. Neither is it narcissistic to express anger at wrongdoing inflicted on those we care about, as an affirmation of their worth.

Expressions of fitting anger may also serve to affirm the moral status of the perpetrator of the wrongdoing. P. F. Strawson, in his influential paper "Freedom and Resentment," contends that we respond with anger and other moral attitudes (resentment, gratitude, etc.) to what we perceive to be "the quality of others' wills towards us" (1993, 56). It matters deeply to us, Strawson, writes, "whether the actions of other people . . . reflect attitudes towards us of goodwill, affection, or esteem on the one hand or contempt, indifference, or malevolence on the other" (ibid., 49). Thus the reactive attitudes, such as anger, by which we respond to our perception of others' goodwill or ill will toward us, are essentially a way of affirming others' status as responsible moral agents. To withhold reactive attitudes in response to someone, Strawson believes, is to take up the "objective attitude" toward her. The objective attitude fails to regard her as "a morally responsible agent . . . as a member of the moral community" (ibid., 59). Rather, the objective attitude sees the other as "an object of social policy," a subject for treatment, or something "to be managed or handled or cured or trained" (ibid., 52). On a Strawsonian account, expressing fitting anger can be a way of respecting one who wrongs you or others as a responsible moral person. And respecting others as moral persons is appropriate for its own sake, not because of the consequences of doing so.

If we accept that expressions of fitting anger in response to wrongdoing can be intrinsically appropriate, then how does this support the retributivist? More specifically, how do we move from the appropriateness of expressing anger in response to wrongdoing to the thesis that state punishment is intrinsically justified? Two further claims are needed to bridge the gap: first, that at least in some cases the proper way to express anger is by subjecting the wrongdoer to intentionally burdensome treatment; and second, that it is the state's role to impose such burdens. To support the first claim, we can draw on a line of argument common to communicative retributivist accounts, which defend punishment as a deserved communication of censure, or condemnation. The argument is that to convey censure adequately, sometimes words are not enough; as Falls writes, "Calmly telling a friend she ought not to have lied to us communicates neither the pain she has caused nor our unqualified insistence that we not be so treated" (1987, 42). Similarly, perhaps expressing fitting anger sometimes requires more than just words; in some cases, it may require imposing some type of burdens on the wrongdoer.

Once we establish that expressing fitting anger can in some cases require the imposition of burdens on a wrongdoer, there are various routes we might take to establish the second claim, that it is properly the state's role to impose such burdens. For example, we might note that certain types of serious wrongdoing are the proper concern of the entire community, and thus it appropriately falls to the state to express anger at such wrongdoing on the community's behalf. We might instead contend that the state is better placed than individuals to ensure that punitive expressions of anger are not disproportionate, arbitrary, or misdirected. Or we might argue that all members of a polity transfer their natural right to punish to the state (by, for example, tacit consent). I do not aim to defend one of these lines of argument here. Rather, my point is just to show how one might go from a claim about the expressive value of anger to the central retributivist claim that punishment is an intrinsically appropriate response to wrongdoing.

In this section, I have considered three ways in which fitting anger may be valuable. It may motivate us to confront and stop wrongdoing, it may provide epistemic warrant for our judgments about how to respond to wrongdoing, and expressing anger may affirm the moral status of the victims as well as the wrongdoers. I have contended that retributivists cannot draw on anger's motivational value to ground their central thesis that punishment is an intrinsically appropriate, because deserved, response to wrongdoing. I have suggested, though, that fitting anger might provide epistemic support for a certain type of retributivist view, one which purports to be publicly justified rather than morally true. And I have sketched an account of anger's expressive value in affirming the status of people as moral persons, an account that could support the central retributivist claim. My aim has not been to provide anything like a full defense of anger's epistemic or expressive value as a basis for retributivism. Rather, my goal has been to demonstrate that, for those persuaded by Nussbaum's and Greene's claims that retributivism is ultimately grounded in anger, this need not count as a decisive point against retributivism. In the next section, I contend that retributivist theories need not be merely rationalizations of anger-driven intuitions.

FOUNDATIONS OF RETRIBUTIVISM

Nussbaum and Greene both insist that retributivist theories are ultimately grounded in anger-fueled reactions to perceived wrongful inflictions of harm against us or others with whom we concern ourselves. Nussbaum takes the desire for payback to be at the conceptual core of anger, and she believes properly retributivist accounts all ultimately rest on the "payback fantasy" (2016, 185). Greene cites a host of empirical experiments that purport to show that people's ordinary judgments about punishment are (a) retributive and (b) motivated by anger (2008, 51–5).[17] He then contends that, given the well-documented human tendency to create rational stories to explain emotion-driven behavior, the most reasonable conclusion is that retributivist theories are post hoc rationalizations of our anger-fueled intuitions.

We might interpret the charge that retributivist theories are rationalizations of anger-driven intuitions in different ways. On a strong interpretation, the claim is that retributivist theories are nothing more than stories created to make sense of, and lend normative theoretical support to, our anger-driven intuitions. If this is the charge, though, it rests on an oversimplified conception of retributivist theories. Retributivism, as mentioned earlier, describes a family of diverse theories that are united by the idea that punishment is justified insofar as it is an intrinsically appropriate, because deserved, response to wrongdoing. These theories are responsive to a much wider range of considerations than just angry, payback intuitions.

Perhaps most obviously, retributivist theories draw on deeply held intuitions about desert, but our desert intuitions need not be grounded in anger. We may judge that "a superior athlete deserved to win a contest he lost on a fluke" (Sher 2007, 5), or that women deserve equal pay as men for equal work, or that a virtuous person deserved the good fortune that befell her. None of these desert intuitions appears to derive from anger. Even in the context of punishment, it's important to bear in mind that retributivist theories take themselves to be offering not only an answer to the question of what positive reason we have to punish wrongdoing, but also constraints on the severity of sentences: namely, punishment should be no more severe than a person deserves, given the seriousness of her wrongdoing and her degree of culpability. It strikes most people as deeply unjust to treat offenders more harshly than they deserve. Indeed, one traditional retributivist argument against consequentialist theories of punishment is that they can only, at best, rule out disproportionately harsh punishment as a contingent matter, insofar as inflicting disproportionate punishment might not in practice promote the best consequences. For many people, though, disproportionate punishment intuitively seems unjust regardless of its consequences, because such punishment is harsher than is deserved. Again, this desert intuition does not seem fueled by anger, but it grounds a key retributivist principle.

In addition to intuitions about desert, retributivist theories have drawn on claims about the importance of respecting persons as autonomous moral agents, or as fellow members of a political community, and claims about individual rights or about fairness in cooperative social schemes.[18] These claims are undoubtedly responsive to various deeply held intuitions, but I doubt that any of them originate in anger. Thus the strong interpretation of the charge—that retributivist theories are nothing more than stories created to explain and justify anger-fueled intuitions—seems unsupported, insofar as it fails to account for the range of non-anger-based intuitions to which retributivist theories are responsive.

Nussbaum contends that despite various retributivist theories' appeals to these other considerations, it is really the anger-driven payback intuition that is doing the work in justifying punishment on such views. For example, Nussbaum critiques Herbert Morris's retributivist account on which punishment is deserved because it removes the unfair advantage an offender gained from the commission of the crime. She writes:

> Although Morris's idea of payback is far more subtle and symbolic than the standard one, it still gets its grip through a payback fantasy. For it is only the intuition that proportional payback makes sense that enables him to bypass the question of its value as a way of preserving the social contract and, more important, the human wellbeing that the contract is really about. . . . The fact that Morris does not feel the need to justify his choice of penal . . . suffering as a response to the problem of crime shows, I believe, that he is riding on the back of powerful intuitions about payback and proportionality that are a form of magical thinking and not a particularly good way of promoting the social goals that he actually has. (2016, 185)

Remember that for Nussbaum anger and the "payback fantasy" are conceptually linked. Here, she argues that it is only Morris's adherence to this payback fantasy that could explain his failure to articulate punishment's value in promoting social goals and human well-being. One problem with this critique is that it begs the question against retributivism. Retributivists such as Morris claim that punishment is an intrinsically appropriate response to crime; thus they would reject the implicit premise that punishment's justification must appeal to its contribution to human well-being or other social goals. Another problem with the critique is that it presents a false dichotomy: either a theory explains punishment's value in terms of social goals and well-being, or it is grounded in anger-driven payback intuitions. Morris's account, by contrast, is grounded in intuitions about fairness: he claims that a person who enjoys benefits made possible by general levels of compliance with a society's laws but then fails similarly to comply with the laws has gained an unfair advantage (1968, 478).

I don't actually believe Morris's account is successful.[19] For present purposes, though, my point is just that it's not clear that the intuitions about fairness on which his account is based originate in anger. There is a good bit of empirical literature linking appraisals of unfairness to anger, but typically the link is thought to be that the perception of unfairness sometimes, but not always, generates the anger.[20] Thus insofar as some retributivist theories are responsive to intuitions about fairness, this suggests that they are not merely rationalizations of anger, but rather are responsive to more fundamental intuitions about fairness that can in some cases motivate anger.

Greene might argue that these other intuitions—about fairness, desert, respect for moral persons, respect for fellow members of the polity, and so on—are not really doing any work in these cases, just as considerations of sheerness, elasticity, and so on were not doing any real work in people's choices in the pantyhose experiment described earlier. But how can we know if this is the case? In the pantyhose experiment, it was easy to determine that people's accounts of their choice behavior that cited features such as sheerness and elasticity were mistaken, because the pantyhose were in fact identical; thus sheerness and elasticity were irrelevant factors. But we cannot stipulate in advance that respect for persons, fairness, and so on are similarly irrelevant to the justification of punishment.

Greene might point to the various empirical studies indicating that anger motivates ordinary judgments about punishment and conclude that desert, respect, and fairness are irrelevant. Retributivist theorists, however, are not merely trying to develop explanations, or even justifications, of people's ordinary judgments in the sorts of scenarios created in the empirical studies, which typically place the subjects in the role of sentencer, asking them to decide whether and how much punishment is appropriate in response to harms to themselves or others. Retributivists aim to provide normative theories that answer a much broader range of questions—why punishment is permissible in principle, how severely we may punish in particular cases, what modes of punishment are appropriate, why it is the state's role to impose punishment. In answering these questions, retributivist theories aim to be responsive to, and make coherent, a host of beliefs, intuitions, and judgments—about respect for persons, fair play, desert, and so on—that people take to be important across a range of contexts.

The strong interpretation of the rationalization claim thus seems unsupported. On a weaker interpretation, the claim might acknowledge that retributivist theories are grounded in a range of intuitions—about fairness, desert, respecting people as autonomous moral agents or as fellow members of a polity, and so on—that do not derive from anger, but then insist that among these intuitions are anger-based intuitions about payback. On this interpretation of the claim, though, it seems to me no real objection to retributivist theories. There are no doubt various ways to engage in normative theorizing, but one common methodology is to seek what Rawls called "reflective equilibrium" (1951, 177–97). Seeking reflective equilibrium involves working back and forth among our moral judgments about particular cases and our preferred normative principles and theories, revising these various elements as needed until we reach an acceptable coherence among them. Among our ordinary moral judgements are those grounded in angry intuitions; but I have contended that other sorts of intuitions can inform our moral judgments in a range of cases—intuitions about desert, fairness, respecting people as autonomous agents, and so on—and it seems unlikely that all of these judgments derive from anger. Retributivist theories aim to accommodate these various intuitions and to integrate them into a coherent theory. This seems to me a sensible way to go about normative theorizing.

Perhaps, though, the charge that retributivist theories are rationalizations of anger is best interpreted as claiming that, although these theories do draw on, and seek coherence among, a range of intuitions, the anger-based payback intuitions are dominant. To evaluate this interpretation, we would need to consider each theory in turn, and such an undertaking is beyond the scope of this chapter. But I will briefly highlight one influential retributivist theory, developed by Antony Duff.

On Duff's account, punishment can be justified as a deserved communication of censure, or blame. He argues that this rationale of punishment as deserved censure is consistent, as consequentialist rationales are not, with respecting those who commit crimes as fellow members of a liberal political community (Duff 2001, 79–82). When we blame someone, he contends, we call on the person to reconsider her wrongdoing, to accept that it is wrong, and to commit not to do it again. Doing so just is part of what it is to blame someone. Thus on his view, punishment can be justified as a form of deserved public censure: "a burden imposed on an offender for his crime, through which, it is hoped, he will come to repent his crime, to begin to reform himself, and thus reconcile himself with those he has wronged" (ibid., 106).

Duff believes his account provides "a conception of punishment that is suitable for a liberal political community—a conception of punishment as a communicative and inclusionary response to the public wrongs committed by citizens of such a polity" (ibid.). The account is inclusionary in that it calls for a law that addresses members of the political community "in terms of the values it embodies—values to which they should, as members of the community, already be committed" (ibid., 78). Duff is concerned, commendably, that the law must engage with offenders as (still) members of the political community, rather than as a "they" against whom "we" must be protected. Consequentialist systems of punishment, he believes, fail to be properly inclusionary in this sense. Deterrent punishment, for example, "addresses those whom it seeks to deter, not in terms of the communal values that it aims to protect, but simply in the brute language of self-interest" (ibid., 79).

> It thus addresses them, not as members of the normative community of citizens, but as threatening outsiders against whom the community must protect itself. It implicitly excludes them from membership of the citizen community by no longer addressing them in terms of that community's values. (ibid.)

My aim here is not to defend Duff's view. Rather, my interest is in whether it seems plausible to believe that this account is primarily a rationalization of anger-fueled payback intuitions. Duff's account is subtle and multifaceted, drawing on ideas about desert and blame, and about what sorts of communication and treatment are appropriate among members of a liberal political community. It's possible, I suppose, that this is all just an elaborate story told by a clever philosopher (though not so clever as to recognize that his views about punishment are *actually* motivated by angry "payback fantasies"). Possible, but in my view highly unlikely.

CONCLUSION

In this chapter, I have aimed to highlight a range of respects in which considerations of anger can be relevant to theorizing about criminal punishment. I have focused, however, on a critique of retributivism raised notably by Nussbaum and Greene, which contends that retributivist theories are ultimately grounded in anger-fueled intuitions and therefore poorly supported. I have argued that retributivists have various resources available to meet this objection, either by defending the value of fitting anger as an element in our normative theorizing about punishment, or by endorsing retributivist theories that are not merely rationalizations of anger. This does not, of course, amount to a full defense of retributivism; as I endorse a hybrid theory of punishment,

I would be the wrong person to offer such a defense. But although I am not entirely persuaded by retributivist theories, I believe they are more formidable than what Nussbaum's and Greene's anger-based objections suggest.

NOTES

1. See, for example, Ben-Shakhar et al. (2007, 314–23), Bosman and van Winden (2002, 147–69); Gummerum et al. (2020, 126–42), Pillutla and Murninghan (1996, 208–24), Sanfey et al. (2003, 1755–58), and Seip et al. (2014, 578–88).

2. See, for example, Gummerum et al. (2016, 94–104; 2020) and Nelissen and Zeelenberg (2009, 543–53).

3. See, for example, David Boonin (2008).

4. See, for example, Cornell et al. (1999, 108–15) and Selby (1984, 531–44).

5. See, for example, American Law Institute (1980, commentaries to §210.3). The defense is controversial for a number of reasons, which I do not attempt to evaluate in this chapter.

6. See also Brandt (1959, 493).

7. See, for example, Duff (2001, 30).

8. See, for example, John Simmons (1991, 311–49), Christopher Heath Wellman (2009, 419–39), and Douglas Husak (2016, 97–112).

9. We find a similar sentiment in Locke, although Locke's political theory was not utilitarian. He wrote that that one of the chief inconveniences of the state of nature was that, if people are left to judge and punish supposed wrongdoing against them or their loved ones, "ill nature, passion, and revenge will carry them too far in punishing others, and hence nothing but confusion and disorder will follow" (Locke 1988, 275).

10. See, for example, Hernández and Mueller (2020).

11. See, for example, Katia Vavova (2014), Selim Berker (2009, 293–329), and Guy Kahane (2011, 103–25).

12. For a modified version of Greene's argument that attempts to avoid the implication that consequentialist theories would be undermined as well as retributivist ones, see Isaac Wiegman (2017, 193–217).

13. See, for example, Vincent Chiao (2016); Chad Flanders (2017, 61–77); and Mary Sigler (2011, 403–30).

14. See Chiao (2016), Flanders (2017, 61–77), and Sharon Dolovich (2004, 307–44).

15. See, for example, Duff (2001, 35–73), Ekow N. Yankah (2015, 457–75), and Richard Dagger (2011).

16. One might claim that social psychological and neuroimaging studies could yield insights about the polity's shared public political values. I am skeptical of this claim, but for those more sympathetic to it, the data cited by Greene, which indicate that "commonsense punitive judgment is almost entirely retributivist" (Green 2008, 55), might seem to lend support to the notion that retributivist judgments *are* part of the shared values that can constitute reasons for publicly justifiable state punishment.

17. One might challenge Greene's account by questioning whether the empirical literature really supports these two inferences. See, for example, Richard Dean (2010, 57–59). In this chapter, I focus instead on whether retributivist theories are merely rationalizations of anger-based intuitions.

18. See, respectively, Falls (1987), Jeffrie G. Murphy (1973, 217–43), and Herbert Morris (1968, 475–501).

19. See Zachary Hoskins (2011B, 55–58).

20. See, for example, Daniel Batson et al. (2007, 1272–85), Hoffman (2000), and Montada and Schneider (1989, 313–44).

REFERENCE LIST

American Law Institute. 1980. *Model Penal Code and Commentaries*. Philadelphia, PA: The Institute.

Aquinas, Thomas. 2014. *Summa Theologica.* New York: Catholic Way Publishing.

Aristotle. 1984A. "Nicomachean Ethics." In *The Complete Works of Aristotle*, vol. 2, edited by Jonathan Barnes, 1729–867. Princeton, NJ: Princeton University Press.

Aristotle. 1984B. "Rhetoric." In *The Complete Works of Aristotle*, vol. 2, edited by Jonathan Barnes, 2152–269. Princeton, NJ: Princeton University Press.

Batson, C. Daniel, Christopher L. Kennedy, Lesley-Anne Nord, E. L. Stocks, D'Yani A. Fleming, Christian M. Marzette, David A. Lishner, Robin E. Hayes, Leah M. Kolchinsky, and Tricia Zerger. 2007. "Anger at Unfairness: Is It Moral Outrage?" *European Journal of Social Psychology* 37: 1272–85.

Ben-Shakhar, G., G. Bornstein, A. Hopfensitz, and F. van Winden. 2007. "Reciprocity and Emotions in Bargaining Using Physiological and Self-Report Measures." *Journal of Economic Psychology* 28: 314–23.

Bentham, J. 1996. *An Introduction to the Principles of Morals and Legislation*. Edited by J. H. Burns and H. L. A. Hart. Oxford: Clarendon Press.

Berker, Selim. 2009. "The Normative Insignificance of Neuroscience." *Philosophy & Public Affairs* 37, no. 4: 293–329.

Boonin, David. 2008. *The Problem of Punishment.* Cambridge: Cambridge University Press.

Bosman, Ronald, and Frans van Winden. 2002. "Emotional Hazard in a Power to Take Experiment." *The Economic Journal* 112: 147–69.

Brandt, Richard B. 1959. *Ethical Theory: The Problems of Normative and Critical Ethics*. New York: Prentice Hall.

Chiao, Vincent. 2016. "Two Conceptions of the Criminal Law." In *The New Philosophy of Criminal Law*, edited by Chad Flanders and Zachary Hoskins, 19–36. London: Rowman & Littlefield International.

Cogley, Zac. 2014. "A Study of Virtuous and Vicious Anger." In *Virtues and Their Vices*, edited by Kevin Timpe and Craig Boyd, 199–224. New York: Oxford University Press.

Cornell, Dewey G., Catherine S. Peterson, and Herbert Richards. 1999. "Anger as a Predictor of Aggression Among Incarcerated Adolescents." *Journal of Consulting and Clinical Psychology* 67, no. 1: 108–15.

Dagger, Richard. 2011. "Republicanism and the Foundations of Criminal Law." In *Philosophical Foundations of Criminal Law*, edited by R. A. Duff and Stuart Green, 44–66. Oxford: Oxford University Press.

D'Arms, Justin, and Dan Jacobson. 2010. "The Moralistic Fallacy: On the 'Appropriateness' of Emotions." *Philosophy and Phenomenological Research* 61, no. 1: 65–90.

Dean, Richard. 2010. "Does Neuroscience Undermine Deontological Theory?" *Neuroethics* 3: 43–60.

Dolovich, Sharon. 2004. "Legitimate Punishment in a Liberal Democracy." *Buffalo Criminal Law Review* 7: 307–44.

Dressler, Joshua. 2002. "Why Keep the Provocation Defense: Some Reflections on a Difficult Subject." *Minnesota Law Review* 86: 959–1002.

Duff, R. A. 2001. *Punishment, Communication, and Community*. Oxford: Oxford University Press.

Falls, M. Margaret. 1987. "Retribution, Reciprocity, and Respect for Persons." *Law and Philosophy* 6, no. 1: 25–51.

Flanders, Chad. 2017. "Punishment, Liberalism, and Public Reason." *Criminal Justice Ethics* 36, no. 1: 61–77.

Greene, Joshua D. 2008. "The Secret Joke of Kant's Soul." In *Moral Psychology, Vol. 3. The Neuroscience of Morality: Emotion, Brain Disorders, and Development*, edited by W. Sinnott-Armstrong, 35–80. Cambridge, MA: MIT Press.

Gummerum, Michaela, Belén López-Pérez, Eric van Dijk, and Lotte F. van Dillen. 2020. "When Punishment is Emotion-Driven: Children's, Adolescents', and Adults' Costly Punishment of Unfair Allocations." *Social Development* 29: 126–42.

Gummerum, Michaela, Lotte F. van Dillen, Eric van Dijk, and Belén López-Pérez. 2016. "Costly Third-Party Interventions: The Role of Incidental Anger and Attention Focus in Punishment of the Perpetrator and Compensation of the Victim." *Journal of Experimental Social Psychology* 65: 94–104.

Hernández, Javier C., and Benjamin Mueller. 2020. "Global Anger Grows Over George Floyd Death, and Becomes an Anti-Trump Cudgel." *New York Times*, June 1, 2020. https://www.nytimes.com/2020/06/01/world/asia/george-floyd-protest-global.html.

Hoffman, M. L. 2000. *Empathy and Moral Development: Implications for Caring and Justice*. New York: Cambridge University Press.

Hoskins, Zachary. 2011A. "The Moral Permissibility of Punishment." PhD diss., Washington University in St. Louis.

Hoskins, Zachary. 2011B. "Fair Play, Political Obligation, and Punishment." *Criminal Law and Philosophy* 5: 53–71.

Hume, David. 1978. *A Treatise of Human Nature*. New York: Oxford University Press.

Husak, Douglas. 2016. "Does the State Have a Monopoly to Punish Crime?" In *The New Philosophy of Criminal Law*, edited by Chad Flanders and Zachary Hoskins, 97–113. London: Rowman & Littlefield International.

Kahane, Guy. 2011. "Evolutionary Debunking Arguments." *Noûs* 45, no. 1: 103–25.

Locke, John. 1988. *Two Treatises of Government*, student edition. Edited by P. Laslett. Cambridge: Cambridge University Press.

Lorde, Audra. 1997. "The Uses of Anger." *Women's Studies Quarterly* 25, no. 1/2: 278–85.

Montada, L., and A. Schneider. 1989. "Justice and Emotional Reactions to the Disadvantaged." *Social Justice Research* 3: 313–44.

Moore, Michael S. 1997. *Placing Blame*. Oxford: Oxford University Press.

Morris, Herbert. 1968. "Persons and Punishment." *The Monist* 52, no. 4: 475–501.

Murphy, Jeffrie G. 1973. "Marxism and Retribution." *Philosophy & Public Affairs* 2, no. 3: 271–43.

Murphy, Jeffrie G. 1988. "Forgiveness, Mercy, and the Retributive Emotions." *Criminal Justice Ethics* 7, no. 2: 3–14.

Nelissen, Rob M. A., and Marcel Zeelenberg. 2009. "Moral Emotions as Determinants of Third-Party Punishment: Anger, Guilt, and the Functions of Altruistic Sanctions." *Judgment and Decision-Making* 4, no. 7: 543–53.

Nisbett, Richard E., and Timothy D. Wilson. 1977. "Telling More than We Can Know: Verbal Reports on Mental Processes." *Psychological Review* 84: 231–59.

Nurse, Jo, Paul Woodcock, and Jim Ormsby. 2003. "Influence of Environmental Health Factors on Mental Health Within Prisons: Focus Group Study." *BMJ* 327: 1–5.

Nussbaum, Martha. 2016. *Anger and Forgiveness: Resentment, Generosity, Justice*. Oxford: Oxford University Press.

Perkins, Lisa H. 1970. "Suggestion for a Justification of Punishment." *Ethics* 81, no. 1: 55–61.

Pillutla, Madan M., and J. Keith Murninghan. 1996. "Unfairness, Anger, and Spite: Emotional Rejections of Ultimatum Offers." *Organizational Behavior and Human Decision Processes* 68: 208–24.

Rawls, John. 1951. "Outline of a Decision Procedure for Ethics." *Philosophical Review* 60, no. 2: 177–97.

Rawls, John. 2005. *Political Liberalism*, expanded edition. New York: Columbia University Press.

Rhodes, Lorna A. 2004. *Total Confinement: Madness and Reason in the Maximum Security Prison*. Berkeley, CA: University of California Press.

Sanfey, Alan G., James K. Rilling, Jessica A. Aronson, Leigh E. Nystrom, and Jonathan D. Cohen. 2003. "The Neural Basis of Economic Decision-Making in the Ultimatum Game." *Science* 300: 1755–58.

Seip, Elise C., Wilco W. van Dijk, and Mark Rotteveel. 2014. "Anger Motivates Costly Punishment of Unfair Behavior." *Motivation and Emotion* 38: 578–88.

Selby, Michael J. 1984. "Assessment of Violence Potential Using Measures of Anger, Hostility, and Social Desirability." *Journal of Personality Assessment* 48, no. 5: 531–44.

Sher, George. 1987. *Desert*. Princeton, NJ: Princeton University Press.

Sigler, Mary. 2011. "The Political Morality of the Eighth Amendment." *Ohio State a Journal of Criminal Law* 8: 403–30.

Simmons, A. John. 1991. "Locke and the Right to Punish." *Philosophy & Public Affairs* 20, no. 4: 311–49.

Strawson, P. F. 1993. "Freedom and Resentment." In *Perspectives on Moral Responsibility*, edited by John Martin Fischer and Mark Ravizza, 45–66. Ithaca, NY: Cornell University Press.

Tessman, Lisa. 2005. *Burdened Virtues: Virtue Ethics for Liberatory Struggles*. New York: Oxford University Press.

Vavova, Katia. 2014. "Debunking Evolutionary Debunking." In *Oxford Studies in Metaethics 9*, edited by Russ Shafer-Landau. Oxford: Oxford University Press.

Wellman, Christopher Heath. 2009. "Rights and State Punishment." *The Journal of Philosophy* 106, no. 8: 419–39.

Wiegman, Isaac. 2017. "The Evolution of Retribution: Intuitions Undermined." *Pacific Philosophical Quarterly* 98: 193–217.

Yankah, Ekow N. 2015. "Republican Responsibility in Criminal Law." *Criminal Law and Philosophy* 9: 457–75.

Chapter 12

Avoiding the Dark Side

Anger in Popular Culture

Court D. Lewis and Gregory L. Bock

In Plato's *Republic*, Socrates warns against letting young people hear stories that are not "fit to be told" (378b). He is concerned that certain stories, music, and poems will have a corrupting effect on the young, giving them a "strong inclination to do bad things" (392a), such as giving in to their anger (*thymos*, 606d and 375b-c). For this reason, Socrates argues for exiling artists from his utopian society or severely censoring them. Nowadays, young people still imitate the stories they hear and the celebrities they follow, so it is just as important today as it was then to critically examine popular works of art being produced for consumption. What messages do they send? What effect do they have on young people? Is Yoda correct, when he says, "Beware of the dark side: anger, fear, aggression. The dark side of the force are they . . . if once you start down the dark path . . . consume you it will." These are some of the questions we explore in this chapter. We start by examining *Star Wars*' Anakin Skywalker and his journey through the dark side of the Force. Next, we look at several other prominent characters from popular culture, including *Star Trek*'s Spock and Worf, and Marvel Comics' Logan/Wolverine and Bruce Banner/Hulk. Finally, we examine metal music as a counterargument to the ubiquitous presentation of anger as something dark and best to be avoided.

ANAKIN'S TURN TO THE DARK SIDE

Anakin Skywalker (Darth Vader) is an evil Sith lord and is one of the most famous villains in the history of film; however, as the story unfolds over the course of the first three *Star Wars* episodes (IV, V, and VI), we learn that he is not entirely evil. The later prequels (Episodes I, II, and III) tell the story of his childhood, his Jedi training, and his eventual turn to the dark side of the

Force. He is the chosen one who is destined to bring balance to the Force, but not without suffering greatly himself.

As a young Padawan, Anakin is full of anger because he is afraid of losing those closest to him. This anger is prominently on display when he slaughters a whole tribe of Tusken Raiders who kidnap and kill his mother in *Attack of the Clones*. As a Jedi master during the Clone Wars, he gives in to his anger several times, most significantly when he severely beats a man named Clovis for making moves on his wife Padmé (*The Clone Wars*, season 6, episode 6). His anger is on full display in *Revenge of the Sith* as his desire to save Padmé from her fate, which he sees in a vision, leads him to believe the lies of Emperor Palpatine (Darth Sidious). Palpatine says he can help Anakin find the secret of immortality so that Padmé will never die. His anger at the Jedi Council and Obi-Wan for standing in his way, as he sees it, finally turns him to the dark side of the Force.

Anakin's anger is understandable. Anyone would have strong feelings in situations in which one's loved ones were in danger. However, for this reason, the Jedi Order prohibits its members from having close relationships. Young Anakin is warned by Yoda to be mindful of his feelings:

> *Yoda:* How feel you?
> *Anakin:* Cold, sir.
> *Yoda:* Afraid are you?
> *Anakin:* No, sir.
> *Yoda:* See through you we can.
> *Mace Windu:* Be mindful of your feelings.
> *Ki-Adi-Mundi:* Your thoughts dwell on your mother.
> *Anakin:* I miss her.
> *Yoda:* Afraid to lose her, I think, hmm?
> *Anakin:* What has that got to do with anything?
> *Yoda:* Everything! Fear is the path to the dark side. Fear leads to anger. Anger leads to hate. Hate leads to suffering. I sense much fear in you (*The Phantom Menace*).

Anakin struggles with this aspect of his training and eventually violates the rules by marrying Padmé, an action he hides from both Obi-Wan and the Jedi Order. Choosing her over the Order is partly what allows Darth Sidious to manipulate him for his own purposes. Anakin is led to believe that he must choose between remaining a Jedi and saving Padmé. He chooses the latter and becomes a dark lord.

Yoda's point of view is like the ancient Greek philosophy of Stoicism, which teaches *apatheia*, which is "equanimity in the face of what the world throws at us" (Pigliucci). Stoicism is not opposed to having good emotions but is about controlling negative ones. This is also like the view of the

Buddhist monk Thich Nhat Hanh. He says, "Our anger is a field of energy," and "Thanks to our mindful observation and insight into its roots, we can change this energy into the energy of love and compassion – a constructive and healing energy" (Ellsberg 2001, 97). These ideas play an important role in Jedi philosophy, sending the message that "the good guys" eliminate or transform their anger and do not allow themselves to get too attached to others because of the fear they might have of losing the ones they love.

However, as beloved as Yoda is among *Star Wars* fans and as central as his philosophy is to the way of the Jedi, he is not the one who brings balance to the Force. After fighting Darth Sidious, Yoda admits, "Into exile I must go. Failed I have" (*Revenge of the Sith*). The balance is instead restored by Anakin, which makes him, not Yoda, the central hero of the story.[1] For one, the Skywalker lineage would not have existed if it were not for Anakin's deep attachment to Padmé. Second, his love for her carries over into his care for their children, Luke and Leia, and it is this which causes Anakin to get angry when Luke's life is threatened by Darth Sidious in *Return of the Jedi*. As one blogger notes, "Although Yoda continually discourages Anakin and Luke from personal love of family members, this type of love (and the intense desire it embodies), saves Luke, redeems Vader, and defeats the Emperor, saving the galaxy" (Andrew 2015). Anakin's success is possible only because of his feelings for his loved ones and the anger that is expressed when their lives are threatened. This means that the path of deep relational attachment is vindicated over against the Jedi way of emotional detachment.

This does not mean that Anakin's anger is never excessive. Certainly, he lacks the virtue of self-control and occasionally lets his anger get away from him, such as when he kills the Tusken women and children. However, as Padmé soothingly says: "To be angry is to be human" (*Attack of the Clones*). To be angry is also to be a caring son, a caring father, and a caring husband.[2] Anger can be appropriate, which squares with what Aristotle says about anger in the *Nicomachean Ethics*: "The person who is angry at the right things and toward the right people, and also in the right way, at the right time, and for the right length of time, is praised" (1125b32-36). To have virtuous anger, we must learn to control our feelings so that we do not end up hurting others and ourselves. The message about anger in *Star Wars* is an Aristotelian one, not a Buddhist one, and perhaps at the end of his life when it matters the most, Anakin perfectly exemplifies the virtue of anger.

CHARACTERS WHO STRUGGLE WITH THE DARK SIDE

Besides the example of Anakin's struggle with anger, popular culture is full of characters who endure their own struggle with the dark side of anger.

If there is one unifying theme between all of them, it is that the struggle to contain or control one's anger is difficult and that though we often fail at the task, there is often redemption for those who seek to be and do better. The next few pages will examine the unique features of some of popular culture's most enduring characters, so as to better understand how anger is portrayed.

Spock

Arguably, the most famous example of a character who struggles with controlling his emotions is Commander Spock, the Vulcan first officer from *Star Trek: The Original Series* (TOS). Of course, a common misconception is that Vulcans do not have emotions. Vulcans have emotions, but at some point in their distant past, called the "Time of Awakening," they determined unchecked emotions would lead to the destruction of their civilization. Thanks to visionaries, such as Surak, Vulcans developed techniques utilizing logic to control and subdue their emotions. As a human-Vulcan hybrid, Spock presents an exaggerated tension between logic and emotion. Like Socrates's allegory of the soul, found in Plato's *Phaedrus* (246B-249E), Spock's human nature is the dark horse of appetites that attempts to dominate thoughts and actions with human passions, while his Vulcan nature attempts to use logic and reason to allow the horse of spiritedness to focus on higher pursuits of understanding and true knowledge.

Spock's tragic internal flaw of being half-human makes him an enduring character because it makes him all-too-human. He lacks his other Vulcan half, the one thing needed to control his overwhelming emotions, while at the same time possessing a human nature that calls on him to embrace his emotions. Even though we are all thoroughly human, as viewers, we feel the same struggle. Our rational minds allow us to see the value of controlling our emotions in certain situations, yet those situations often cause us to lose our grip on reason and let our passions rule. We make plans for how to handle stressful situations, like difficult relationships and tasks, then all of the sudden emotions like jealously, frustration, and anger flare to life, and we become like Spock in "Amok Time" (TOS)—so full of rage and anger that we are capable of killing our friends. Spock's lesson about our journey to the dark side is a story of our internal, natural tendency to let anger dominate. We know how anger can destroy our character, relationships, and jobs, yet anger remains a constant threat. Spock teaches us that anger is part of who we are as humans, but shows how with practice and logic, we can subdue this anger; and when we are unable to subdue it, we must accept our "flaw" and utilize means to use anger in more constructive ways in the future. We will never be Vulcans with complete control of our anger, but we can use their techniques to help quench the fire of anger that rages inside.

Worf

Another *Star Trek* character who struggles with anger is Lieutenant Commander Worf, from *Star Trek: The Next Generation* (TNG). Like Spock and humans, Worf has an internal struggle to control his anger, but his main struggle is an external one, where he tries to live as an honorable Klingon within a human society that values calm and reason over bombastic emotional outbursts. Worf is fully Klingon, so he has all of the natural urges of your typical hyperaggressive Klingon warrior. He is angry, loyal, and is dedicated to living an honorable life. As a Klingon raised by humans in a human society, however, he has tried to assimilate to his new culture. He sees the value and honor in living as a human, but his appearance and emotional nature often make him an outsider, both physically and culturally. He was not always so focused on living a restrained human life, but after accidently killing a fellow player during a game of soccer (*Star Trek: Deep Space Nine* (DS9): "Let He Who Is Without Sin. . ."), he begins to fully appreciate the honor of restraint, and feels honor-bound to inhibit his emotions. Therefore, as a result of this tragedy, he developed methods of controlling his anger and aggression, which were further exemplified and bolstered by his Starfleet training.

Oddly enough, Worf's lesson is more human than Spock's. For Worf, like most humans, we often find ourselves in situations where our surroundings dictate how we control our emotions. We want to keep our job, so we remain quiet. We want to stay in our relationship, so we refrain from lashing out at our loved ones, no matter how irritating they can be ("Family," TNG). We realize that our children need love and compassion and not anger and wrath ("New Ground," TNG). There are plenty of people out there who fail to control their anger, so they lose their jobs, relationships, and/or harm their children; or they find the attempt to control their anger leads to the need to escape through sports, fandom, drugs, and other means of escapism. Some escapism is healthy, but Worf—and *Star Trek* as a whole—teaches viewers to confront weaknesses, mend and promote positive relationships, and find healthy means of escape. Worf is often frustrated and teeming with anger, but throughout the series, especially the episodes noted previously, Worf finds a balance and comes to terms with his struggle to deal with external events and relationships he cannot control. Instead of lashing out like a Klingon, he seeks a path of restrained wisdom. He is rarely perfect in this pursuit, but that is why he is one of the most "human" examples of the struggle between our internal emotions and the social expectations we must engage.

Wolverine

Of course, *Star Trek* tends to focus on humanity's goodness, presenting viewers with the ideals we should all strive to achieve. Marvel Comics, on the other hand, offers characters like Logan (i.e., Wolverine) and Bruce Banner (i.e., Hulk) who exemplify characters not only struggling with anger, but who often let their anger rule. Their lashing out at everything and everyone, sometimes even those they love, provide lessons on how even if anger rules our lives, we can find ways to be redeemed.

Like the adamantium that resides throughout his body, Logan is full of anger and rage. Who could blame him? Born James Howlett, the illegitimate son of Thomas Logan, he was raised by John and Elizabeth Howlett, until Thomas Logan killed John Howlett. In an act of rage, James Howlett discovers his mutant abilities when a set of bone claws emerge from his hands, which he then uses to kill his birth-father, Thomas. So, his adoptive father is killed by his birth father, who he then kills upon learning he is a mutant. That is enough to make anyone angry, but as he ages, he learns he has a seemingly endless ability to regenerate, is recruited by Team X, and has adamantium forcibly fused onto his bones. To top it off, everyone he seems to care for ends up dying, usually because others want to kill or use Wolverine for their own purposes.

There are too many stories to cover them all, but two of the most challenging storylines come from the 2017 movie *Logan* and the comic series *Old Man Logan*. In *Logan*, Wolverine is old and defunct. He drinks too much, is in constant pain, and struggles to regenerate. He drives a rental limo with hopes of buying a boat one day, and buys black market drugs to help care for his ailing friend (and father-figure) Charles Francis Xavier, known as Professor X. He is the epitome of growing old, caring for one's aging parents, and realizing that your dreams in life will never be achieved. Instead, you will probably live in pain and slowly die in pain, alone.

Logan is a fantastic movie because it so accurately depicts human life, especially twenty-first-century life. The only places in the movie not full of struggles and sufferings are entertainment cities, full of gambling, night life, and consumerism. Throughout the movie we see people avoiding the reality of suffering all around them, choosing to focus on the fleeting enjoyment of consuming pleasure. Of course, once you leave the centers of hedonism, you are forced to face the realities of poverty, crime, human trafficking, addiction, aging, death, and unethical experiments on children. Unless completely oblivious, it is hard to imagine viewers not feeling the same rage coursing inside Logan. The violence throughout the movie is extraordinary, yet viewers delight in seeing the villains be utterly obliterated. The catharsis of this violence is mitigated only by the deep emotional sadness that results from innocent families being murdered, Professor X slain by the Wolverine clone, and seeing children killing with the same anger and rage that plagues Wolverine—oh yeah (spoiler), he dies too. Is there any redemption in the story, or is it simply a tale of how greed and anger rule humanity and lead to death? Maybe, when we see the young boy cuddling his yellow-clad Wolverine doll at the end of the movie, but even that is a stretch.

As if *Logan* were not depressing enough, the comic series *Old Man Logan*, first written in 2008 by Mark Millar, with art by Steve McNiven, finds even more depressing depths of Logan's suffering. The 2016–2017 story arc from Jeff Lemire and Andrea Sorrentino is especially harsh. Set in the near future, where the Hulk's children run a gang, Wolverine scrapes by with his wife and two children on a small farm. When the Hulk children are not extorting money or throwing cows just to watch them explode when punched, they delight in torture, rape, and murder, which is what they do to Wolverine's family. Logan is unable to fight back, until he gets transported to the past. Once in the past, he sets out to kill everyone responsible for his future suffering. The only problem is that the past to which he is transported is different from the one that created his future. In other words, the people who caused his suffering in his future are different from those who exist in the past to which he now lives. Regardless, his anger leads him to hunt and kill innocent persons. Eventually, he secures a way to return to his original timeline, but instead of getting the revenge he craves, he is forced to relive the torture, rape, and murder of his family.

Like the movie *Logan*, reading *Old Man Logan* makes you angry. You feel the frustration of the character, and part of you wants to find anyone and everyone who seems to delight in human suffering and *snikt* (the sound of Wolverine's claws extending), show them the anger and wrath of Wolverine. This is where viewers and readers must be careful. It is too easy to interpret the lessons of Wolverine as lessons on why to become a terrorist. Terrorists are usually individuals who have suffered, or at least perceived some suffering, at the hand of those in power. With no political or social means to address this suffering, they turn to extrajudicial means of enacting change and "justice." They let their anger rule, and attack anyone they believe to be supporters of the power system, often through the targeted killing of innocents, in order to apply pressure on those in power. This is not the lesson we are to learn from *Logan* and *Old Man Logan*.

Wolverine teaches us that we cannot simply internalize our anger, like the examples of Spock and Worf sometimes suggest. If we do, then eventually our anger will explode out of us in fits of rage; and even though Logan strives to avoid harming innocents, they often suffer in the aftermath. We must find creative and beneficial ways to release our anger. Professor X always saw Wolverine's potential and sought ways to provide both safe spaces for Wolverine and for him to be a teacher of younger mutants. Professor X knew that Logan's anger was a direct result of Wolverine's traumatic life, and he wanted Wolverine to see how helping others avoid internalizing such anger provides an outlet to deal with one's own anger. Of course, since anger is an intrinsic part of Wolverine's character, it could not be erased, but it could be focused on helping those in need and used against those intent on harm and destruction. Wolverine's struggle, then, is a struggle to focus anger on targets that deserve anger (greedy humans who are willing to discriminate, torture, rape, kill, and harm children), while at the same time finding constructive ways of focusing and limiting anger.

At the end of Lemire's *Old Man Logan*, he seems to have learned this lesson. He uses an amulet to return to his family in the "original" timeline. Upon arriving, however, he realizes that the future where his family is brutalized is destined to happen and that there's nothing he can do to stop it. Instead of being filled with anger, which would have had him plotting and attempting to destroy the Hulk gang, he decides to delight in the precious time together as a family. He accepts that all we have is the present, and even knowledge of a terrible future cannot remove the joy of being together, now. It is only when we choose to let anger rule our lives that we miss out on the joy of living in the present. He sums this valuable lesson during the final scenes, saying:

> Spent the last year running around trying to find a way back home. And when I wasn't doing that, I was trying to forget who I was, what happened to me. I was trying to forget them [his family]. Because to remember them would mean feeling the pain all over again. That pain took over. It blocked everything else out. It made me forget the good stuff . . . The past will always be with me, but my life is here. My life is now. Maybe it's time I started living again.

Hulk

In Ang Lee's *Hulk* (2003), David Banner alters his own DNA by conducting experiments on himself, unintentionally passing along corrupted genes to his son Bruce when he is conceived. To fix this mistake, David intends to kill the four-year-old Bruce but accidentally kills Bruce's mother instead when she steps in the way. Bruce is traumatized by this experience but represses the memory of it, growing into an emotionally distant young man. He has emotions, but they are bottled up inside. When they do come out, they spill out in a violent rage, amplified by his altered genes and exposure to gamma radiation. For Bruce, his anger is a curse, something he wants to be rid of. He hates himself for it and wishes he would have died in place of his mother.

Ang Lee's *Hulk* focuses on the psychological struggle with anger and never quite resolves it. It is consuming and violent and caused by fear. Adam Barkman writes: "This is the perverse, subconscious Hulk event (known in the comics as the Devil Hulk). The hate, anger, or rage that drowns out the anxiety brought on by repressed memories is no long-term or healthy solution to the problem" (Barkman 2013, 172). However, there are signs that the Hulk event might be reined in and used for good. For example, as the Hulk, Bruce protects his girlfriend Betty from mutant dogs sent to kill her. Also, he seems careful not to injure the soldiers who come to kill him. He also directs his anger at criminals who attempt to steal medicine intended for needy people. However, Bruce is afraid of his alter ego. It comes to him in a vision and almost kills him. It grabs him by the neck and calls him a "puny human." It even causes him to grab Betty by the neck for a moment before he gets a hold of himself. In the end, he moves far away, apparently to hide from the military and to protect the ones he loves. Anger is a raging green monster that threatens to destroy everything around it.

The Incredible Hulk (2008) puts a different spin on the story. Although for half the movie Bruce is set on curing his greenness, once the new villain named Abomination emerges, he realizes that he might have a responsibility to use the Hulk for good. Betty says, "You think you can control it?" He replies, "No but maybe I can aim it." He then jumps out of the back of a helicopter to fight Abomination. He has turned from fighting his alter ego to fighting evil with it. He has turned from fighting the military to fighting on their side. Nevertheless, by the end he flees into exile once again still not at peace with the Hulk.

In *The Avengers* (2012), Bruce is pulled out of exile by Nick Fury and S.H.I.E.L.D. to join a team of superheroes to defend the planet from the threat of Loki and his alien army. In a tense conversation with the others, Bruce shares his opinion about being on the team and describes the depths of his journey and the moral progress he made on his own. He says, "I got low. I didn't see an end, so I put a bullet in my mouth, and the other guy spit it out! So, I moved on. I focused on helping other people. I was good, until you dragged me back into this freak show and put everyone here at risk!" Tony Stark tries to help him see his potential:

> *Tony:* But you can control it.
> *Bruce:* So you're saying the Hulk, the other guy, saved my life? That's nice. That's a nice sentiment. Saved it for what?
> *Tony:* Guess we'll find out.
> *Bruce:* You may not enjoy that.

These early lines from *The Avengers* seem to show that Bruce is still not at peace with his angry side and has been focused mostly on suppressing it. However, a surprise occurs once the alien invasion commences—he has learned to control it:

Captain America: Dr. Banner, now might be a really good time for you to get angry.
Bruce: That's my secret, Cap—I'm always angry.

And with that powerful line, Bruce turns green (with apparent ease) and helps the team save New York City.

Bruce reveals many more surprises in the Avengers Infinity Saga, especially when he melds the "brains and the brawn" together in *Avengers: Endgame* (2019), but from the point Bruce joins the Avengers team, the Hulk is established as a superhero, meaning he controls his anger and directs it against evil in the universe. This sends the message that anger can be good when it is controlled and directed at the right things. This supports Aristotle's view that anger can be a virtue. He says, "The intermediate state is praiseworthy, and in accord with it we are angry toward the right people, about the right things, in the right way, and so on" (1126b5-7). Barkman writes, "If fifty years of the incredible Hulk has taught us one thing, it's that the solution isn't to label all anger as bad, but rather to recognize that anger is good in and of itself, and must be naturally or properly manifested, which is to say manifested in the service of rational deliberation aimed at truth" (Barkman 2013, 172).

THE DARK SIDE OF MUSIC

Music contains many messages. Pop has an easy-to-consume, bubble-gum-like style that is popular with children, pre-teens, and the general public. Country is known for its twang, stories of breakups, carousing, farms, beer, dogs, church, and often patriotism. Rock-n-roll is known for its raucous, good-time-rebellious attitude, which harkens back to the origin of the word "rock-n-roll" as a euphemism for sex. For the most part, the messages of pop, country, and rock are tame, though they sometime include songs of anger. Alanis Morissette's anthem "You Oughta Know," Carrie Underwood's "Before He Cheats," Taylor Swift's "Picture to Burn," Toby Keith's "Courtesy of the Red, White and Blue," and Ugly Kid Joe's "Everything about You" all have a message of anger. So does the gangsta rap of the 1980s, such as N.W.A.'s "Fuck the Police" and Public Enemy's "Fight the Power," and hip-hop of the past several decades, exemplified by feuds and one-upmanship, such as those between Tupac Shakur and The Notorious B.I.G.—eventually resulting in the tragic death of both in separate assassinations. All of these pale in comparison to heavy metal. With its emphasis on speed, destruction, anti-authoritarianism, and the occult, metal (and all its corollary sub-genres) takes pride in savagery, from sound and lyrics to mosh pits, where fans brutalize each other during concerts. Due to its nature, most research on violence and anger in music focuses on metal, and though other forms of music highlight anger, any truths gained from examining metal music, by implication, will be true for all other genres of music.

Researchers Yanan Sun, Xuejing Lu, Mark Williams, and William Forde Thompson examined thirty-two fans and forty-eight non-fans, providing each participant with a series of violent and neutral pictures, simultaneously presenting one to each eye, while having them listening to either happy music or violent music (2019). While listening to such music, participants were to tell whether they perceived the violent picture, the neutral picture, or a mixture of the two. Sun, Lu, Williams, and Thompson "found both fans and non-fans of violent music exhibited a general negativity bias for violent imagery over neutral imagery regardless of the music genres" (2019). For the researchers, the results show "both fans and non-fans of violent music exhibit a reliable bias for processing violent imagery over neutral imagery regardless of what genres of music they were listening to" (ibid.). In other words, violent music does not desensitize fans to violence, therefore, becoming more prone to engage in violent acts, and "fans and non-fans of death metal music exhibit similar empathic capability, which raises doubts about the grave concerns that have been voiced about the dangers of exposure to violent music" (ibid.).

In "Bang Your Head: Using Heavy Metal Music to Promote Scientific Thinking in the Classroom," Rodney M. Schmaltz supports such a conclusion by discussing the corollary relationship between music preference and problematic behavior. Schmaltz explains, "People who engage in problematic or criminal behaviors are more likely to listen to problem music [. . .] however, the style of music a person prefers does not allow us to predict any problematic behavior" (2019). A violent person might listen to metal and then perform violent acts; but the music did not promote or inspire the violent act. In other words, there is a correlation between violent music and violent acts, but there is no causal relationship. A violent person already has violent tendencies, so they are apt to behave violently. They are just as likely to be violent listening to Barry Manilow, or, as in *American Psycho*, Huey Lewis and the News. As Schmaltz points out, however, the correlation between metal and violence occurs in our ability to gauge the type of music a violent person is likely to enjoy. As he says, "If we know though, that a person has burned down a church, we are able to predict which type of music they most likely prefer" (ibid.). In these cases, other variables are at play, such as psychoticism, sensation-seeking, or negative family relationships. So, it is not the music, but the person, that determines one's path to the dark side.

These two studies show there is no causal relationship between metal and violence, but they do not discuss anger specifically. Leah Sharman and Genevieve A. Dingle's research in "Extreme Metal Music and Anger Processing" provides the bridge between violence, anger, and music. Their research shows "extreme music [defined as music 'characterized by chaotic, loud, heavy, and powerful sounds, with emotional vocals, often containing lyrical themes of anxiety, depression, social isolation, and loneliness'] did not make angry participants angrier; rather, it appeared to match their physiological arousal and result in an increase in positive emotions" (2015). Building off the impressive research into the effects of extreme music, which shows how music influences attitudes and manipulates emotions, listeners are drawn to music that reflects or improves their emotional state. In regard to how extreme music supposedly leads to anger and expressions of anger such as aggression, delinquency, drug use, and suicidal acts, Sharman and Dingle show that instead of music causing anger, extreme music is listened to as a response to being angry. In other words, extreme music is used as a way of exploring and processing the emotional state of anger.

Sharman and Dingle had experimental subjects listen to ten minutes of extreme music after becoming angry, while control subjects experienced ten minutes of silence. As to be expected, heart rate and hostility, irritability, and stress decreased for the control group who listened to silence. If extreme music promotes anger, then we would expect the same measures to increase, but instead of increasing, they remained the same. The experiment also showed that those listening to extreme music had an increase in active and inspired ratings, which was not seen in the control group.

So, what can we make of the study? First, claims that listening to extreme music leads to anger, aggression, and delinquency are unsubstantiated. By implication, messages of anger found in pop, country, rock, hip-hop, and rap will be unsubstantiated. Second, the self-reporting from Sharman and Dingle's study suggests that listening to messages of anger in music is both therapeutic and motivational. Seventy-nine percent of subjects claimed they listened to extreme music to "fully experience anger," while 69 percent claimed it calmed them down. Seventy-four percent claimed that extreme music improved negative moods like sadness, with 33 percent saying it helped with anxiety. Most interestingly, 87 percent said that extreme music enhanced their happiness, with 100 percent saying it enhanced their well-being (ibid.). Combined, these results offer strong evidence that not only does "angry" music *not* cause or promote anger, but it actually serves as a coping mechanism for listeners. As a coping mechanism, anger in music actually helps listeners avoid the dark side. It serves as a release, an outlet, and as a means of self-reflection and self-understanding.

CONCLUDING REMARKS

Could the citizens of Plato's republic have used a little death metal in their day? Perhaps the mythical stories that Socrates warns about are not as dangerous for children as he thinks. At any rate, what we have shown here is that in the case of contemporary storytelling and music, we have reasons to be optimistic. In some of the most popular films in which anger is a theme, the dangers of anger are clearly on display and the message is clear that it ought to be controlled. In the *Star Wars* saga, Yoda warns that anger can lead to the dark side of the Force, but Anakin balances the force by exemplifying anger as a virtue. We also showed how a couple of *Star Trek* characters dealt with their anger and how a couple of Marvel superheroes can teach us how to direct our anger at good ends. We also examined the claim that listening to some forms of music might make listeners angrier and discovered that research actually shows that listening to such music can help some people feel better.

As our book comes to an end, we hope that the chapters contained within, as well as these examples from popular culture, will inspire your own examination into the appropriateness/inappropriateness of anger, both on a personal moral level and a broader theoretical level. As the characters and research in the previous pages illustrate, anger is complex, but the more we study both its theoretical and practical aspects, the more likely we will act wisely in the face of our own personal embrace and/or struggle with anger.

NOTES

1. For an in-depth discussion for why anger might have been required to bring balance to the force, see chapter 6 of this book, "Moral Anger in Classical Confucianism," by Colin Lewis. Specifically, note how Kings Wen and Wu use anger to effectively rule.
2. Padmé's advice is sound moral advice except that Jedi Knights are supposed to avoid relational attachments as part of their service to the Order and hence are supposed to remain celibate, but Anakin is a husband and father. As such, he appropriately gets angry when his family is threatened. One might argue both that the celibacy requirement is a prudent part of the Jedi Code and that it is not a universal moral obligation. Compare this to the Ten Precepts in Buddhism. The first five are moral commands that apply universally. The last five apply only to monks. So, Anakin's anger may make him an imperfect Jedi Knight, while at the same time making him a perfectly acceptable husband and father.

REFERENCE LIST

Andrew. 2015. "Yoda Was Wrong." Accessed May 11, 2020. https://asyourpoetshavesaid.com/yoda-was-wrong/.

Barkman, Adam. 2013. "The Power to Go Beyond God's Boundaries? *Hulk*, Human Nature, and Some Ethical Concerns Thereof." In *The Philosophy of Ang Lee*, edited by Robert Arp, Adam Barkman, and James McRae, 165–176. Lexington, KY: The University Press of Kentucky.

Ellsberg, Robert. 2001. *Thich Nhat Hanh: Essential Writings*. Maryknoll, New York: Orbis Books.

Pigliucci, Massimo. n.d. "Stoicism." Accessed May 11, 2020. https://www.iep.utm.edu/stoicism/.

Sharman, Leah, and Genevieve A. Dingle. 2015. "Extreme Metal Music and Anger Processing." *Frontiers in Human Neuroscience*. Accessed January 10, 2020. https://doi.org/10.3389/fnhum.2015.00272.

Sun, Yanan, Xuejing Lu, Mark Williams, and William Forde Thompson. 2019. "Implicit Violent Imagery Processing Among Fans and Non-Fans of Music with Violent Themes." *Royal Society Open Science* 6, no. 3. Accessed January 10, 2020. https://royalsocietypublishing.org/doi/10.1098/rsos.181580.

Index

About the Contributors

Will Barnes, Curry College
Will Barnes works with transformative philosophy from ancient through to contemporary cross-cultural settings, currently focusing on twentieth-century continental social and political philosophy and non-Western philosophy, particularly Indo-Tibetan Buddhist philosophy. Barnes' current research develops the ethical implications of Judith Butler's fusion of psychoanalysis with Foucauldianism alongside Indo-Tibetan metaphysics and epistemology. Will's publications include, as editor, *Politics, Polarity, and Peace* Part of Brill Rodopi's Philosophy of Peace series in conjunction with Concerned Philosophers for Peace (Brill forthcoming), as well as multiple book chapters, articles, and reviews drawing on non-Western, American, and European religion, philosophy, art, and film. Barnes has taught at five universities across three continents. He currently teaches at Curry College in Milton, and Bentley University in Waltham, both in Massachusetts.

Gregory L. Bock, The University of Texas at Tyler
Gregory L. Bock is assistant professor of Philosophy and Religion and program director of the Philosophy, Religion and Asian Studies Programs at UT Tyler. He is also Director of UT Tyler's Center for Ethics. His areas of research include bioethics, the ethics of forgiveness, and the philosophy of religion. He is the editor of volumes III and IV of *The Philosophy of Forgiveness* (Vernon, 2018, 2019).

Charles L. Griswold, Boston University
Charles L. Griswold is Borden Parker Bowne professor of Philosophy at Boston University. His work addresses various themes, figures, and historical periods. They include ancient philosophy, eighteenth-century philosophy (Adam Smith and Rousseau in particular), and moral and political philosophy (in particular, the theme of forgiveness). In addition, Griswold has written on subjects such as the American Enlightenment and Jefferson and the problem of slavery. His work has been translated into French, German, and Italian. For more information, please see http://blogs.bu.edu/griswold/.

Zachary Hoskins, University of Nottingham
Zachary Hoskins is associate professor of Philosophy at the University of Nottingham. His research focuses on normative criminal law theory, especially on criminal punishment and the collateral consequences of a conviction. He is the author of *Beyond Punishment? A Normative Account of the Collateral Legal Consequences of Conviction* (Oxford University Press, 2019).

Jennifer Kling, University of Colorado, Colorado Springs
Jennifer Kling is assistant professor of Philosophy and director of the Center for Legal Studies at the University of Colorado, Colorado Springs. Her research focuses on moral and political philosophy, particularly issues in war and peace, self- and other-defense, international relations, protest, and feminism. She is the author of *War Refugees: Risk, Justice, and Moral Responsibility* (Lexington, 2019), as well as articles in *Res Philosophica*, *Radical Philosophy Review*, *Journal of Global Ethics*, and *The Routledge Handbook of Pacifism and Nonviolence*; and is the editor of *Pacifism, Politics, and Feminism: Intersections and Innovations* (Brill, 2019). She is also the executive director of Concerned Philosophers for Peace (CPP), the largest, most active organization of professional philosophers in North America involved in the analysis of the causes of war and prospects for peace.

Colin J. Lewis, University of Colorado, Colorado Springs
Dr. Colin J. Lewis received his BA from Duke University (2009), MPhil from the University of Hong Kong (2012), and PhD from the University of Utah (2017). His areas of specialization include Chinese and comparative philosophy, ethics with a focus on moral psychology, and philosophy of education. He also maintains interests in the philosophies of cognitive and biological sciences. His work focuses on potential applications of pre-Qin Chinese thought to modern and empirically informed accounts of moral education, human flourishing, and sociopolitical harmony. Some of his most recent projects look at why rituals are useful for moral education, a distinctly Confucian

notion of desire, and a Mohist argument for the political importance of narrative control.

Court D. Lewis, Pellissippi State Community College
Court Lewis is associate professor of Philosophy at Pellissippi State Community College. Specializing in ethics, forgiveness, and justice, Lewis is the author of *Repentance and the Right to Forgiveness* (2018), the series editor of Vernon Press's series *The Philosophy of Forgiveness*, a member of the Concerned Philosophers for Peace, and a proud father, volunteer, and musician.

Danielle Poe, University of Dayton
Danielle Poe is professor of Philosophy and associate dean of Curriculum and Academic Outcomes for the College of Arts and Sciences at the University of Dayton in Dayton, Ohio. Her research expertise is in contemporary French philosophy, peace practice, and feminism. Her work frequently includes telling the stories of feminist, peace activists. Their work can inspire others to act on behalf of social justice in our daily practices instead of waiting for someone else to lead our efforts.

Paula Smithka, University of Southern Mississippi
Paula Smithka is associate professor of Philosophy and program coordinator for Philosophy and Religion at the University of Southern Mississippi. She received her PhD from Tulane University. Among her publications, Smithka has co-edited three books, two with Courtland Lewis—*Doctor Who and Philosophy: Bigger on the Inside* and *More Doctor Who and Philosophy: Regeneration Time*—and one with Alison Bailey, *Community, Diversity and Difference: Implications for Peace*. Her more recent publications focus on mind viruses, post-truth, and violence. Her general research interests include philosophy of science, in particular philosophy of biology, addressing the nature of biological species and homeostasis, namely, as homeostatic property cluster kinds; social/political philosophy, particularly issues in peace and just-war theory; and the intersections between popular culture and philosophy.

Krista K. Thomason, Swarthmore College
Krista K. Thomason is associate professor of Philosophy at Swarthmore College. She received her PhD from the University of Illinois, Urbana-Champaign, in 2009. Her areas of expertise include moral philosophy with an emphasis on moral emotions, Kant's moral and political theory, and human rights. Some of her publications appear in *Philosophy and Phenomenological Research*, *Kantian Review*, *European Journal of Philosophy*, and *The Monist*.

She is the author of the book *Naked: The Dark Side of Shame and Moral Life*, which was published with Oxford University Press in 2018. She recently provided an introduction and scholarly commentary for a new translation of Kant's *Groundwork for the Metaphysics of Morals*, which is forthcoming with Rowman & Littlefield.

Everett L. Worthington, Jr., Virginia Commonwealth University
Everett L. Worthington, Jr. is Commonwealth Professor Emeritus with Virginia Commonwealth University. He studies forgiveness and the way it intersects with other virtues. He has published over 400 psychological articles and scholarly chapters and 38 books, most of which are on forgiveness, humility, religion and spirituality, and couple relationships. His intervention REACH Forgiveness (see www.EvWorthington-forgiveness.com for no-cost resources) has been used throughout the world. He contributed chapters to volumes III and IV of *The Philosophy of Forgiveness* (Vernon, 2018, 2019).